PROJECT MANAGEMENT

THIS BOOK INCLUDES:
LEAN GUIDE & AGILE PROJECT MANAGEMENT.
PRACTICAL GUIDE FOR MANAGING PROJECTS, PRODUCTIVITY, PROFITS OF ENTERPRISES OR STARTUPS WITH LEAN, SCRUM, AGILE.

JACK LEAD

TABLE OF CONTENTS
LEAN GUIDE

TABLE OF CONTENTS
AGILE PROJECT MANGEMENT

Lean Guide

How successful Entrepreneurs improve Productivity, Quality and Profits applying 3 lean methods: Six Sigma, Startup, Enterprise to get Competitive Advantages and Continuous Innovations

Jack Lead

Section 1: Lean Startup

The Lean Startup vision presents a strategy for building a tech product. Simply speaking, a little Startup is really a low-burn technology venture that unites the customer advancement plan along with an agile software development program.

Eric Ries and his site 'Lessons Learned' offer insights about how best to construct a Lean Startup. A recent demonstration in Eric Ries' on Lean start-ups at the Stanford University's Entrepreneurship Corner explains his way to creating a tech product. In his pragmatic perspective about just how best to incorporate customer development with agile software development, " he recommends a method using two teams. The cross-functional problem team always validates the situation theory and upgrades the item theory, whereas the clear answer team utilizes an agile software development methodology to construct the item from the product or service idea.

The Pivot

A key facet to almost any startup is defining exactly the situation it attempts to address. Customer growth urges a cross-functional problem team which invisibly functions together with clients and always defines and adjusts the situation theory.

The systematic method of consumer development produces a string of invalidated problem hypotheses. At every iteration, the team adapts one particular part of this hypothesis which comprises, among others, customer segments, feature group and placement. Each switch builds up on the lessons learned in supporting the prior problem hypotheses. The pivot indicates the change of strategy of a startup in relation for example to the positioning of its product or service on the market or changes to the product itself to make it more interesting to customers. The vision of this start-up guarantees a coherent management despite lots of incremental alterations to this item idea. From the lack of a solid vision, incremental changes can direct the product theory to some random direction.

A pivot is really a structured path correction built to try a fresh basic concept about this item, strategy, and engine of growth. A prominent illustration of a business utilizing the pivot is Group on; once the business started, it had been an online activism stage known as the Point. After receiving nearly no grasp, the founders started a WordPress site and started their own very first voucher promotion to get a pizzeria situated inside their construction lobby. Even though they just received 20 redemptions, the creators realized that their idea had been significant, and had empowered visitors to organize team actions. Three decades later, Group on would grow to a billion-dollar enterprise.

Steve Blank defines pivot as "changing (and sometimes even shooting) the master plan rather than the executive (the earnings exec, promotion or maybe the CEO).

The Minimum Viable Product

Deciding when and what to send to clients is an integral part of a venture. As a result of very limited funds, startups are made to discover the minimum feature set needed to participate.

Eric asserts that startup teams regularly violate the minimum feature determined by a significant margin and also that the ideal strategy is to split that initial pair down a few times. Shipping the minimum group of features can create unexpected results from the buyer base.

Despite a restricted feature set, customer could actually be contented with the sent features. Visionary clients are extremely forgiving since they do not just buy in to the present product but also the vision of this startup. What's more, the opinion of the team on required features might not be exactly matched with the consumer's needs. While in the worst instance, clients provide their feedback regarding which features are overlooking to supply a value proposition for them.

By focusing to the minimal workable solution, start-ups avoid the error to build something that no one wants. By engaging with the aim area in early stages, the Client Growth methodology offers more information on building an item for some engaged clients rather than attempting to create an item from the beginning for everybody.

A Minimum viable product (MVP) is the "variant of a brand new product that permits a team to amass the most level of confirmed learning about clients together with minimum attempt" (like a pilot experimentation). The objective of an MVP will be always to examine fundamental business enterprise hypotheses (or even Leap-of-faith assumptions) also to help entrepreneurs begin the educational process as swiftly as achievable.

As for instance, Ries noticed that Zappos creator Nick Swinmurn desired to examine the hypothesis that clients were willing and ready to purchase shoes on line. Rather than building a site and also a massive database of apparel, Swinmurn approached local shoe stores, shot images of their inventory, published the images on the web, bought the shoes out of the stores at top dollar after he had made them available online, then shipped them directly to the costumers.

Swinmurn warned that customer demand was present and continuos, and that's how Zappos grew to become a billion dollar industry even thanks to online shoe sales.

Split Testing

A Split or A/B evaluation is a test by which different variants of something are provided to clients at precisely the exact same moment. The objective of a split up test is always to detect differences in behavior between the two classes and also to assess the effects of each variation in an incremental metric. A/B testing is occasionally erroneously achieved in consecutive mode, in which a set of user's week can see 1 variation of this product whilst the in a few days users view still another. (a set of users can see variation A and then some time later another set can see variation B). This undermines the statistical validity of their results, since external events can influence user behavior. For example, a split evaluation of 2 flavors of ice cream performed consecutively during the hot and cold seasons could observe a marked reduction in popularity (mainly due to the season and not to the taste).

Actionable metrics

All these have been compared to dressing table metrics—dimensions that offer the rosiest picture possible but don't accurately reflect the essential drivers of a business enterprise. Vanity metrics for a single company could be actionable metrics to get the next. By way of instance, an organization focusing on creating online dashboards for financial markets could view the amount of internet page views per person for a vanity as their revenue isn't predicated on amount of page views. But, an internet magazine with advertisements will view webpage viewpoints because site perspectives are directly linked to earnings.

A Normal instance of a vanity is that the amount of users that are new gained each day. While a large amount of users gained daily looks favorable for almost any organization, in the event the price of acquiring each user through costly advertising campaigns is somewhat higher compared to the revenue gained each user (generated by each new user), subsequently gaining more users can quickly cause bankruptcy.

Build-Measure-Learn

The Build-Measure-Learn loop highlights rate as a crucial element to merchandise development. A team or company's potency is dependent on its capacity to ideate, fast build a minimal workable product of this idea, quantify its own efficacy on the current market, and also study out of this experimentation. To put it differently, it's really a learning practice of turning ideas into products, measuring clients' responses and behaviors contrary to assembled services and products, and deciding whether to persevere or throw the idea; this technique repeats as often as required. The stages of this loop are: Suggestions → Construct → Merchandise → Quantify → Data → Learn.

This rapid iteration makes it possible for teams to detect a viable path towards product/market fit, and also to keep on maximizing and optimizing the company version after attaining product/market fit.

Lean Canvas

The Lean Canvas can be really a version of this Company Model Canvas accommodated by Ash Maurya in 2010 designed for startups. The Lean Canvas is targeted on fixing broad customer issues and solutions and bringing them into customer sections through an exceptional value proposition. "Problem" and "solution" cubes replace the "key partners" and also "key tasks" cubes in the Company Model Canvas, whereas "key metrics" and "unfair advantage" cubes replace the "key tools" and "customer relationships" cubes, respectively.

The Lean Concept

Lean startup principle are employed to certain competencies within average startups and larger businesses:

- Lean Analytics
- Lean Brand Management
- Lean Hardware
- Lean Events
- Lean Manufacturing
- Lean Marketing
- Lean Product Management
- Lean Sales
- Lean Software Development
- Lean UX
- Lean Information

Chapter 1.
What Is Lean Start Up?

While the idea of the Lean Startup has been around since 2011, many companies are still coming to grips with everything the system has to offer. This is despite the fact that most of the ideas presented in this system were hardly new. This is largely due to the fact that the system actually offers more value to established organizations than it does to startups. However, startups can still be able to build a Lean system from the ground up if they choose to.

Lean Startup Methodology

Build, measure, and learn: Perhaps more than anything else in recent history, the application of the scientific method to demolish uncertainty, where innovation is concerned, has transformed the way breakthroughs happen. Broken down, this includes the process of defining a hypothesis, creating a prototype to test the hypothesis, testing the prototype (and thus the hypothesis) and then adjusting as needed. While this may seem simple, it has the potential to generate massive results by enabling companies to take risks on smaller ideas without breaking the bank in the process.

It can be used to test things like customer service ideas, the process of managerial review, or even a new feature for an existing product or service. As long as you can perform a test that clearly validates or disproves the initial hypothesis, then you will be good to go because you must be able to gather enough data to justify approving or vetoing the idea.

The goal, then, is to do everything possible in order to ensure that build, measure, and learn process proceeds from start to finish as quickly as possible. This will make it feasible to run the process multiple times if needed, while also making it clear when such additional runs are needed. As such, it is important to have a very specific idea for each test because as more variables are added, the more difficult it will be to determine results with any real degree of accuracy. When it comes to products and services, this means determining if they are either wanted or needed by the target audience.

Minimal viable product: Generally speaking, most product development involves an extreme amount of work up front. The process involves working through the full specifications of the product, as well as a significant initial investment when it comes to capital in order to build and test multiple iterations of the product. The Lean Startup process thus encourages building only enough of the product in question to make it through a single round of the build, measure, and learn process at a time. This is what is known as the minimal variable product.

The minimal variation of the product is what enables a full cycle of the build, measure, and learn loop to be completed with the least amount of required time and effort on the part of the team. This may not be something as simple as writing a new line of code, it could be an elaborate process that outlines the customer journey, or a complete set of mockups made out of a cheaper substitute. As long as it is enough to test the hypothesis, then it is good to go.

Validated Learning: An important part of the Lean Startup process is ensuring that you are testing your hypothesis with an eye towards the right metrics. Failing to do so can make it easy to focus on vanity metrics instead. Focusing on vanity metrics may make you feel as though you are making progress while not actually telling you all that much about the value of the product. For example, for Facebook, the vanity metrics are the things like the total number of "Likes" that have been received or the number of total accounts created. The real meat and potatoes are in metrics such as the amount of time the average user spends on the service per week. Early on, the metric that validated the company's initial hypothesis was the fact that more than half its user base came back to the service every single day.

Innovation accounting: Innovation accounting is what makes it possible for startups of all sizes to prove, in an objective way, that they are creating a sustainable business. The process includes three steps, starting with determining the baseline. This involves taking the minimum viable product and doing what you can to determine relevant datapoints that can be referred back to the fact. This could involve things like a pure marketing test to determine if there is actually interest from customers. This, in turn, will make it possible for you to determine a baseline with which to compare the initial cycle of the build, measure, and learn process, too. While better numbers are always desired, poor numbers at this stage aren't terribly important, it only means that the team will have more work to do in the build, measure, and learn cycle.

After the baseline has been determined, the next step is going to be to make the first change to determine what can actually be improved upon. While this certainly makes the entire process take longer than it usually does, making too many changes at once makes it difficult to determine which one of the changes led to the biggest improvement. However, if you have a lot of potential changes to test, you can then test them in groups so when something pops, you will only have to retest a specific range in order to see what caused the inspiration to strike.

Once several build, measure, and learn cycles have been completed, the product should be well on its way from moving from the initial starting point to the final, ideal phase. At some point, however, if things don't seem to be proceeding according to plan, then the question becomes whether it is better to pivot to something new or to stick with the current baseline a while longer to see what improves. The choice between the two should be relatively obvious at this point based on the data provided up to this point.

If the decision is ultimately made to pivot at this point, then it can be quite demoralizing for the team because this means going back to square one, albeit with additional data to draw on in the future. Nevertheless, issues such as vanity metrics or a flawed hypothesis can lead teams down a path that is ultimately not viable. This scenario leaves them no choice but to tear it all down and start again with an alternate hypothesis and a clean slate. It is important to try and reframe the idea of a pivot from a failure to a success because it saved the startup from potentially taking a flawed product to market and paying in a big way further down the line.

There are a few additional types of pivots as well. A Pivot that zooms in is one that takes a signal successful feature of a failed prototype and turns it into its entirely own product. A zoom out pivot, on the other hand, is when a failed prototype is useful enough to become a feature on something larger and more complicated.

The customer segment pivot occurs when the prototype proves solid, but the target audience proves to be different than anticipated. A customer need pivot occurs when it becomes clear that a more pressing problem for the customer exists, so a new product needs to be created to handle it.

A platform pivot occurs when a single application becomes so successful that it spawns an entire related ecosystem. A business architecture pivot occurs when a business switches from having low volume and high margins to high volume and low margins. A value capture pivot is one of the most extreme as it involves restructuring the entire business to generate value in a new way. The engine of growth pivot occurs when the profit structure of the startup changes to keep pace with demand.

Small batches: When given the option to fill a large number of envelopes with newsletters before sending them out, the common approach is to do each step in batches, fold the newsletters, place them in the envelopes, etc. However, this is actually less efficient than doing each piece by itself first, thanks to a concept known as single piece flow, a tenant of Lean manufacturing. In this instance, individual performance is not as important as the overall performance of the system. Time is said to be wasted between each step because things need to be reorganized. If the entire process is looking at a single batch, then efficiency is improved.

Yet another benefit to smaller batches is that it is easier to spot an error in the midst of them. For example, if an error was found in the way the envelopes were folded once all the newsletters had been folded, then that entire step would need to be repeated, adding even more time to the process. On the contrary, a small batch approach would determine this error the first time all the steps were completed.

Andon cord: The Andon Cord was used by Toyota to allow any employee on the production line to halt the entire system if a defect was discovered at any point. While this is a lot of power to give to every team member on the floor, it makes sense as the longer a defect continues through the process, the more difficult and costlier it will eventually be to remove. As such, spotting and calling attention to the problem as quickly as possible is the more efficient choice, even if it means stopping the entire production line until the issue is fixed.

Continuous deployment: Continuous deployment is one of the most difficult Lean Startup processes for many companies to deal with as it means constantly updating live production systems each and every day until they reach an ideal state. The ability to learn directly from customers is essential in this scenario as it is one of the primary competitive advantages that startups possess.

Kanban: This is another part of the process that is taken directly from Lean manufacturing. Kanban has four different states. The first of which is the backlog which includes the items that are ready to be worked on but have not yet been actively started on. Next is in progress, which is all of the items that were currently under development. From there, things move to build after development has finished and all the major work has been done so that it is essentially ready for the customer. Finally, the item is validated by a positive review from the customer.

A good rule of thumb is that each of the four stages, also known as buckets, should contain more than three different projects at a time. If a project has been built, for example, it cannot then move into the validation stage until there is room for it. Likewise, work cannot start on items in the backlog until the progress bucket has been cleaned out enough to free up the space. One outcome that many Lean Startups don't anticipate is that this method also makes it easier for teams to measure their productivity based on the validated learning from the customer as opposed to the number of new features being produced.

Five whys: Many technical issues still have a root at a human cause at some point in the process. The five whys technique makes it possible to get close to that root cause from the beginning. It is a deceptively simple plan, but one that is extremely powerful when used by the right hands. The Lean Startup system posits that most problems that are discovered tend to be the result of a lack of personal training, which on the surface can either look like a simple technical issue or even one person's mistake.

For example, with a software company, they may see a negative response from their customers regarding their most recent update. Looking more closely at the issue, it was discovered that this was due to the fact that the update accidentally disabled a popular feature. Looking closer still, this was discovered to be due to a faulty service which failed because a subsystem was used incorrectly due to an engineer that wasn't trained correctly. Looking closer still, you will find that this is due to a fact that a specific manager doesn't believe in giving new engineers the full breadth of training they need because his team is overworked and everybody is needed in one capacity or another.

This type of technique can be especially useful for startups as it gives them the opportunity to determine the true optimum speed needed to make quality improvements. You could invest a huge amount in training, for example, but that doesn't mean this is always going to be the right choice at the given stage of development. However, by looking closely at the root causes of the problems in question, you can more easily determine where there are core areas that require immediate attention as opposed to solely focusing on surface issues.

Another related issue is connected to the fact that many team members are likely prone to overreacting to things at the moment, which is why the 5 Whys are useful when it comes to taking a closer look at what's really happening. There can be a tendency to use the Five Whys to point blame, at first, but the real goal of the Five Whys is to find any chronic problems caused by bad process, not bad people. This is also important to ensure that everyone is in the room together when the analysis takes place because it involves all of the people impacted by the issue, including both customer service and management. If blame has to be taken, it is important that management falls on the sword for not having a team-wide system in place to prevent the issue in the first place.

When it comes to getting started with the Five Whys, the first thing that should be focused on is instilling a feeling of trust and empowerment in the team as a whole. This means being tolerant of all mistakes the first time they happen, while at the same time making it clear that the same mistake should not happen twice. Next, it is important to focus on the system level as most mistakes are made due to a flaw in the system which means it is important to put the focus on this level when it comes to solving problems.

From there, it is important to face the truth, no matter how pleasant or unpleasant it might be. This method may bring up some unpleasantness about the company as a whole but the goal is to fix these issues, after all, and you can't fix what hasn't been brought to light. This is why it is easy to turn it into the Five Blames if you aren't careful which is why the blame should flow up in this instance. Start small and be specific. You want to get the process embedded, so start with small issues with small solutions.

Finally, it is important to designate one person on the team as the Five Whys Master. This person will be the one who is primarily in charge of seeing that change actually comes to the team. This, in turn, means they will need a fair amount of authority in order to ensure things get finished. This person will then be the one accountable for any related follow-up, determining if the system is ultimately paying off, or if it is better to cut your losses now and move on.

While it can ultimately be a great way to create a more adaptive startup, it can also be harder to get into the groove of than it first appears, so it is important to look at it as a long-term investment rather than something that will be completed in the short-term.

Chapter 2. Lean Startup Models

The lean startup model was introduced in the year 2011, and its impact on the economy has been enormous. The book written by Eric Ries gained immense publicity, and many companies use the information in the book to develop their startups.

However, the ideas in the book are not new; these ideas have been forgotten by most entrepreneurs since success is always measured in numbers in the business world. The methods and ideas in the book are valuable to startups as well as well-established organizations.

In his book, Eric Ries has defined a startup as a human institution whose goal is to create a new service or product under uncertain conditions.

Build-Measure-Learn

The way different companies pursue innovation in today's market has been affected by the idea of using certain scientific or statistical methods to handle or calculate uncertainty.

This means that the company must define a hypothesis, build a product or service to test that hypothesis, use that product or service and learn what happens and finally adjust the attributes of the product or service to increase the value for customers.

The Build-Measure-Learn methodology can be applied to almost anything. You do not have to use this methodology to test new products alone. You can also test a management review process, customer service idea, new features to existing products or website offers and tests. You have to carry out a test and validate the initial hypothesis to ensure that you have enough data to assess the value of the product to the customer.

The aim of every company should be to move through this methodology quickly. You have to identify if the product or service developed is worth going through another cycle or if you should come up with a new idea. This means that you must define a specific idea that you want to test with minimum criteria that can be used for measurement.

Minimal Viable Product (MVP)

A traditional company will first have to define the specifications of every product it wants to produce or manufacture and then assess the significant cost and time that will be invested to produce that product. The lean startup methodology encourages every startup to build the required amount of product through one loop of the Build-Measure-Learn Loop.

If the company can identify such a product, it becomes the minimal viable product. This product is manufactured or developed using minimal effort and less development time.

Every startup does not necessarily have to write a code to automate processes to create an MVP. An MVP could be as simple as a slide deck or design mockups. You have to ensure that you run these products by your customers to get enough validation to pass this product through the next cycle.

Validated Learning

Every startup must test or validate a hypothesis with the right idea in mind – learn from what is observed. There are times when startups have focused on vanity metrics that made them believe that they were indeed making progress. This is not the right approach since you must always look at metrics that will give you some insight on the product and how it can be changed to increase its value to the customers.

For example, the number of accounts opened on Instagram is a vanity metric for that platform. The actual metric would be the number of hours spent scrolling through Instagram by each account holder. This will give the developers the true value of the product.

In the book Lean Startup, Eric Ries has provided an example of his own. A company called IMVU always showed a chart that painted a good picture to its management and investors. Many registrations were being made every single day.

However, this graph did not show if the customers or users value the service. The graph did not show the costs that went into marketing to acquire new users. This chart only looked at vanity metrics and was not designed to test a hypothesis.

Innovation Accounting

Through innovation accounting, a startup can prove that it is learning to grow and sustain as a business. A company can do this in the following ways.

Establish a baseline

The startup can run an MVP test and collect data that will enable it to set some benchmark points. You can use a smoke test where you can market the product or service you want to offer and assess your customers' interests.

This includes a sign-up form to understand if the customers want to purchase the product or service. Using that information, you can set the baseline for the first iteration of the Build-Measure-Learn Cycle. It is alright to make mistakes or have low numbers since that will help you improve.

Tuning the Product

Once the baseline has been established, you should identify one change that must be made to the product and test that improvement. Do not make all the changes at once, as it can lead to chaos.

You can try to see how a change in the design of the form attracts more customers when compared to the earlier design. This step must be carried out slowly to ensure that every hypothesis is tested out carefully.

Persevere or Pivot

When you have made several iterations through the cycle, you have to move up from the initial baseline towards the goal that was set out in the business plan. If you are unable to reach that goal, you must learn why using the data collected at every step.

Pivot

A successful entrepreneur is one who has the foresight, the tools and the ability to identify which parts of the business plan are indeed working for the company. They also learn to adapt to changes in the market and their strategies according to the data collected during the iterations.

One of the hardest aspects of the lean startup method is to make the decision to pivot since every entrepreneur and founder is emotionally attached to the product they have created. They spend a lot of money and energy to get to where they are. If a team uses vanity metrics to test its products and hypothesis, it can go down the wrong path.

If the hypothesis selected is not defined clearly, then it is possible that the company may fail since the management does not know that the endeavor is not working. If you, as the management, decide to launch the product fully in the market and then assess the outcome, you will see what happens, and there is a higher probability that you may fail.

If you choose to pivot, it does not mean that you have failed. It means that you will change the hypothesis that you started out with. The following variations are often used when a startup chooses to pivot.

- Zoom-in Pivot: A single feature in the product that sets it apart from other products becomes the actual product.
- Zoom-out pivot: This is the opposite of the above definition where an entire product is used as a new feature in a larger product.
- Customer segment pivot: The product designed was correct. However, the customers that were selected

were wrong for the product. The startup can change the customer segment and sell the same product.

- Customer need pivot: When the startup follows the principles of validated learning, it will identify the problem that needs to be solved for the customer who was initially selected.
- Platform pivot: most platforms start off as applications. When the platform becomes a success, it transforms into a platform ecosystem.
- Business Architecture Pivot: Based on Geoffrey Moore's idea, the startup can choose to switch to low margin and high-volume products from high margin and low-value products.
- Value Capture Pivot: When you decide to measure the value differently, you will be able to change everything about the business right from the cost structure to the final product.
- The engine of Growth Pivot: According to Ries, most startups follow a paid, viral or sticky growth model. It would be more prudent for the company to switch from one model to the other to grow faster.
- Channel Pivot: In today's world, advertising channels and complex sales have reduced since the Internet provides a huge platform for a company to advertise its products.
- Technology Pivot: Technological advancements are being made every day, and any new technology can help to reduce the cost and increase performance and efficiency.

Small Batches

There is a story where a father had asked his daughters to help him stuff newsletters into a document. The children suggested that they fold every newsletter, put a stamp on the envelope and write the address on the envelope. They wanted to do every task one step at a time.

The father wanted to do it differently – he suggested that they finish every envelope fully before they moved on to the next envelope. The father and daughters competed with each other to see which the better method was.

The father's method won since he used an approach called "single-piece flow" which is common in lean manufacturing. It is better to repeat a task over and over again to ensure that you master that task. You will also learn to do the task faster and better.

You have to remember that an individual's performance is not as important as the performance of the system. You lose time when you should go back to the first task and restack the envelopes. If you consider the process as a unit, you will be able to improve your efficiency.

Another benefit of using small batches is that you will be able to spot the error immediately. If you fold all the newsletters and then find out that that newsletter does not fit into the envelope, you will need to fold all the newsletters again. This approach will help you identify the error at the beginning and improve your process.

The advantage of working with small batches is that you will be able to identify the problems soon.

Andon Cord

The Andon Cord is a method that was used by Taiichi Ohno in Toyota, which allowed an employee to stop the process if he or she identified a defect in the process. If the defect continues longer in the process, it is harder to remove that defect, and there is a higher cost involved.

It is highly efficient to spot the defect at an early stage even if it means that the process will need to stop to address the defect. This method has helped Toyota maintain high quality.

Eric Ries mentioned in his book that the company IMVU used a set of checks that ran every day to check if the site worked accurately. This meant that they were able to identify and address any production error quickly and automatically.

There were no changes made to the production until the defect was addressed. This was an automated Andon Cord.

Continuous Deployment

Continuous deployment is a scenario that is unimaginable and scary for most startups. The idea of this method is that the startup must update the production systems regularly.

IMVU was regularly updating its production system by running close to fifty updates. This was made possible since they made an investment in test scripts.

Over 14000 test scripts would run at least 60 times a day and simulate everything from a click on the browser to running the code in the database.

Eric Ries also talks about Wealthfront, which is a company that operates in an environment regulated by the SEC. However, this company practices continuous deployment and has more than ten production releases a day.

Kanban

Kanban is a technique that was borrowed from the world of lean manufacturing. It was developed by Taiichi Ohno in the late 1980s to improve the manufacturing unit of Toyota automobiles. Eric Ries mentions the company Grockit, which is an online tool that helps one build skills for standardized tests.

This tool creates a story in the development process, which is then used to develop a feature. They also mention to the user what the outcome or benefit of the tool is. These stories are validated to see how they work for different users. A test is conducted to see how this tool benefits the customer. There are four states:

- Backlog: The tasks that can be worked on but have not yet been started
- In Progress: The tasks that are currently being developed
- Built: The tasks that have been completed and are ready for the customer

- Validated: Products that have been released and have been validated by the customers.

If the story fails the validation test, then it will be removed from the product and produced again. A good practice would be to ensure that none of the buckets mentioned above have more than two projects at a given time. If there is a project or task that is in the built bucket, it cannot move to the validated stage until there is enough room for it. The same goes for the processes that are in the backlog bucket. These tasks cannot move to the "In Progress" bucket until it is free.

A valuable outcome of this method is that the team can start measuring its productivity based on the validated learning and feedback from the customer. The team will then stop measuring its productivity based on the number of new features developed.

The Five Whys

Every technical defect or issue has a human cause at its root. The five whys technique will allow the startup to get closer to the root cause. This is a deceptively simple technique but is powerful. Eric Ries has mentioned in his book that most problems or issues that are identified in a process are caused due to lack of training. These problems may look like an individual's mistake or a technical issue. Ries uses IMVU as an example to explain this technique.

- A new product feature or release was disabled for customers. Why? The feature tanked because of a failed server.
- Why did this server fail? There was a subsystem that was used incorrectly.
- Why was that server used incorrectly? The engineer using the server was not trained to use it properly.
- Why did he not know how to use the server? He was never trained.
- Why was he not trained? His manager did not believe that new engineers needed to be trained since he believed that he and his team were too busy.

This technique is extremely useful for startups since it helps them make improvements within a short period. A huge amount can be invested in training, but this may not be the optimal thing to do when the startup is still at its development stage.

If the startup takes a look at the root cause of every problem, it can identify the core areas that need to be worked on and not focus only on the issues at the surface.

Most people tend to overreact to issues that happen at the moment, and the Five Whys help them understand what they need to look at to understand what is happening.

There is a possibility that the Five Whys can be used as a way to blame people in the team to see whose fault it was. The goal of this method is to identify problems that are caused not by bad people but by bad processes. It is essential that every member of the team be in the same room when this analysis is made.

When blame needs to be taken, it is important that the management should take the hit for not having a solution at system-level. Good practices to follow to get started with this methodology are:

- Mutual empowerment and trust. If a mistake is made for the first time, you should be tolerant of them. Ensure that you do not make the same mistake twice.
- Maintain focus on the system since most mistakes happen due to a flaw in the system and ensure that people always solve problems at the system level.
- The company should always face some unpleasant truths. This method will bring out some unpleasant truths to the surface, and the management should ensure that these issues are taken care of at the initial stage. If this method is not conducted in the right manner, it will change into the Five Blames.
- Always start small and be specific. You have to look at the process in detail and always start with small issues. When you understand the issues, you must identify the solutions. Always run the process regularly and involve as many people from the team as you can.

- Appoint someone who is a master at Five Whys. This person must be the primary change agent and should have a good degree of authority to ensure that things get done. This person will be accountable for judging whether the costs were made to prevent or work on those problems are paying off or not.

The Five Whys methodology is used to transform the startup into a more organized and adaptive organization, which can be hard.

Chapter 3.
The 5 Principles of Lean Startup Method

Believe it or not, the lean startup methodology has had its fair share of criticisms, both constructive and destructive. For instance, some people said it's already an easy enough process; thus, oversimplifying it seemed redundant. So many blogs have been written about the subject claiming the lean startup is already simple - all of its basic elements are there to explore - so why make it simpler?

Well, dissatisfaction is, perhaps, human nature. It's impossible to please everybody. Here's the thing, though: inasmuch as the lean startup may seem simple, it's one heck of a complex system. You think you know what to do with it, but once you're actually doing it, you'll realize its intricacy.

Moreover, just as it is with any other system, you can't just window-shop for the parts you "like", choose those, and leave the rest behind. No. It's impossible to make a system work without tapping on all its parts to work seamlessly together. And that's what makes the lean startup multifaceted.

Like I have said earlier, it's a research-intensive process. You can't downplay the importance of research since it will gauge whether or not you're up for the challenge. If, during the course of research, you realize you're not cut out for the lean startup method, you're free to consider a different approach. At least, you haven't expended much time, effort, energy, and money yet since you're still on the research phase. On the other hand, if you think you can take on the challenge, by all means, go!

Perhaps understanding the five principles on which the lean startup is hinged will help you see if it's something you can work with. That's what I did, and that's why I can freely talk about the methodology in this book. I'm not saying I'm an expert at this method, but I try to apply what I learn (after all, it's a continuous process). And that's what I want you to do, too.

The Lean Startup Principles

Principle is defined as a fundamental truth serving as the cornerstone of a particular system of belief or reasoning. With that said, it's only right to assume that the lean startup methodology is founded on a set of fundamental truths that govern how it works. In this part of the book, I will try to expound on those five principles that are behind the lean startup methodology (The Lean Startup, n.d.).

Entrepreneurs are everywhere. Unlike regular employees who are cooped up in their offices from nine to five, entrepreneurs (self-made people, if you will) are found just about everywhere. You can create a startup from your garage or your bedroom (or dorm room like Mark Zuckerberg). That's the beauty of entrepreneurship: it, in itself, is a human institution from which innovative products and services can be created regardless if conditions are uncertain. With entrepreneurs being everywhere, it goes without saying that the lean startup method will work anywhere, regardless of the size of a business or which sector of the industry it belongs to.

Entrepreneurship is management. Just because it's a self-made business doesn't mean management practices can't be applied. Like I have discussed in the early goings of this book, there is such a thing as entrepreneurial management. It's a type of management specifically geared towards entrepreneurship. Keep in mind that entrepreneurship is a human institution, not a product or service, and an institution cannot function fully unless capable hands are managing it.

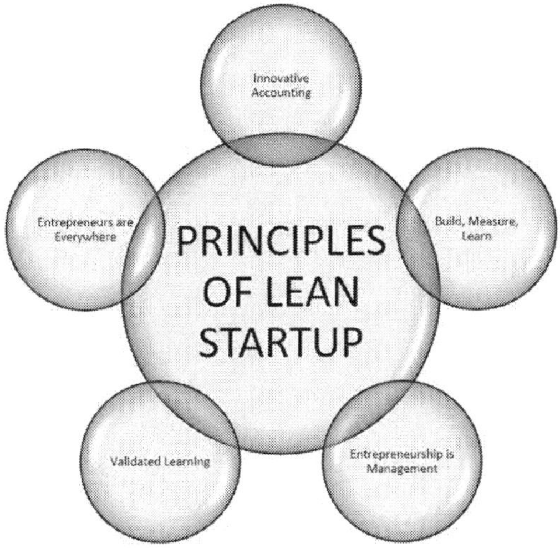

Validated learning. You don't create a business with the sole purpose of making money or being at your customers' beck and call. Heck, you don't even create it, so you'll have an excuse to make products or formulate services. You start a business with the aim of learning how to make it sustainable. Remember how I said the six parts of the scientific method applies to the lean startup method? Well, the experiment part applies when you need to validate your learnings scientifically to see whether these work. It's a continuous process.

Build-Measure-Learn. Ah, if it isn't our favorite concept. Seriously, though, this three-step concept is basically what makes the lean startup methodology tick. Overall, the primary activity of a startup business, is to formulate ideas, turn these ideas into viable products (build), see how customers react to the products (measure), and use customers' feedbacl to see whether you need to go to a new direction or continue until the product becomes marketable (learn). It's an on-going loop intended to accelerate the growth of a business.

Innovation accounting. In the lean startup method, it's important to measure certain metrics like how much progress you're making, how milestones should be set up, and which task should be prioritized. Implementing entrepreneurial management whole making sure these metrics are met can be difficult. Hence, innovation accounting is necessary. This novel type of accounting is specifically designed for startup businesses. Its use is the only way you can figure out if you are, indeed, making progress or if your efforts are for naught. This particular principle of the lean startup focuses on numbers that are pivotal for the growth of your business like engagement and customer acquisition cost.

Are you now fully convinced that you should try the lean startup methodology for your business? If you're still having second thoughts, then perhaps this next segment will tickle your fancy even more.

Is Adapting the Lean Startup Methodology Necessary?

I have been giving you the 411 about the lean startup methodology almost from the get-go, but I am quite sure you're still adamant about giving it a try. After all, it's the fate of your business at stake here. One wrong move and everything you have worked and been working hard for can go down the drain.

Of course, I can always convince you that it did work for me. However, what works for one will not always work for another, right? That's why I still want to share some reasons why I think you should adapt the lean startup in your business. In fact, these reasons will work whether yours is a new business or already an established organization.

Regardless if you're a startup or an existing business, you are bound to create new products or services. Hence, you will potentially be reaching new markets. Adapting the lean startup methodology will help your business decrease cycle time, gather customer feedback faster, and reduce waste.

There will be new processes you will want to employ in your business, processes that will certainly have a bearing on your customer base. So you want to ensure the best results by deploying a customer-validated process. Through the lean startup, you will get continuous feedback and validation.

You may already have a five-year projection in place. In a volatile environment, that five-year plan may not succeed. Nevertheless, adapting the lean startup will bring in the agility and speed you need so you can adapt in an ever-changing environment. It will certainly help you go a long way.

Adapting the lean startup methodology will help you foster innovation in your business minus the wasted money.

With the lean startup backing you up every step of the way, you will not be overly concerned about the success and adaption rates of the new digitized system you are planning to deploy.

Keep in mind that two of the main purposes of this methodology are: to make your business competitive in such a cutthroat environment and drive growth. In a nutshell, here are some benefits of adapting the method:

Throughout the course of adapting the process, you stay focused on your goals and you get clear visibility of which direction you plan on going.

The process gives you a heads up when it's time to make necessary changes to the strategies you are currently using. As a result, you spend less time, effort, and money.

By the time your product or service is deemed marketable, you will have already established a customer base. This includes the test customers you reached out to during the build-measure-learn phase.

The process/es you will create using the lean startup will already have been tried and tested.

The lean startup method is focused on five key points:

- Speed
- Flexibility
- Innovation
- Customer focus

Elimination of uncertainties

Chapter 4.
Why Do Most Startups Fail?

Marketing is considered by many as one of the most important investments for any small business. Without it, your target customers may never know about you, your products or services offered, or why buying from you is a better decision than buying from your competition. As a result, your products or services go unnoticed. Marketing is a broad discipline and entrepreneurs must be able to overcome the pitfalls of small business marketing in order for your business to succeed. Consider this a bonus section that will outline and discuss some of the most common pitfalls of small business marketing. This particular section will definitely provide you with useful insights that can help improve your marketing strategies and methods. That way, whether you're starting a small business or you're more likely to brave your way into a startup, you will know what you should and shouldn't do if you want a successful business that follows the lean startup methodology.

Defining Target Markets

Who do you plan to target? Where can you find them? This thing may seem like a very basic matter, but the groundwork of your marketing efforts actually starts here. If you want to achieve marketing success, you need to have a clear concept of who your target market will be. Create a brief narrative or profile of your target customer. Jot it down and polish it; collaborate with your team; figure out what your target client uses as its buying criteria. Defining who your ideal customer is will help you put everything in order and customize your marketing efforts based on their needs and wants.

Creating a Marketing Plan

Every small-scale entrepreneur must have a marketing plan to support their business goals. If developing a marketing plan is a challenge, there are plenty of resources on the

Internet that can provide you with marketing plan templates. Download some of these templates and use them as a guide. Be sure to keep it short and limit it to three pages if you can. If you can afford it, get a marketing specialist who can help you develop the plan.

Finding Resources for Marketing

One of the most common pitfalls of small business marketing is the cost of advertising, but small businesses cannot afford not to invest the time and money into this thing. Buying a full-page Saturday newspaper ad or NBA TV commercials is usually not a financial dilemma for large-scale businesses. However, such costs are obviously a predicament for many small businesses. To overcome this, spend some time studying and exploring what you can achieve with the low-cost marketing methods that are now available to small businesses.

Getting Referrals

Most small business entrepreneurs will probably agree that referrals are an important asset to their business. Even so, many remain cautious when openly asking for referrals. If you want to grow your business, be sure to let your existing customers, as well as your network of contacts, come to the realization that their referrals are a great help to your business. Try to make referrals an integral part of your marketing strategies so you can expand your reach and widen your customer base.

Increasing Sales Conversions

If you are faced with this common pitfall of small business marketing, try to look again at your marketing message. Deal with this challenge by making sure that you make a relevant and attractive offer to your intended customers. Before running a marketing campaign, test it first and then refine it. Small businesses cannot afford to only invest on advertisements that build image or brand. You can develop and promote your company image while causing increased sales by providing an offer to motivate your target customers to take action within a specific period of time. In general, your promotional campaign should focus on eliciting a response from your target customers that translates into sales while building your brand at the same time.

Whatever industry you are in, it is very likely that you would encounter one or more of the common pitfalls of small business marketing. Fortunately, there are ways to overcome this dilemma. All you have to do is explore your options and be creative in your marketing methods.

Now that you know the difference between the two, as well as the common pitfalls associated with marketing a small business, let's go back to the discussion on hand - the lean startup methodology. As the name of this innovative method implies, it was founded with startup entrepreneurs at the forefront of Ries' mind. Why do I say so?

We've mentioned earlier that a startup is riskier to create than a small business. Risk is the epitome of a startup because you are practically venturing into the unknown. Some of you have probably done it. I have done it. I have left a stable job just so I can start my own business without even considering what will become of me in case things don't go according to plan.

The risk factor of startup businesses is what prompted the idea of the lean startup. Its founder wanted to lend companies of all sizes a hand, so to speak, to help them navigate through rough waters and lower the risk factors through three things - minimum viable products or MVPs, painstaking experimentation, and full commitment to learning (McGowan, 2017). In a nutshell, the lean startup methodology centers on the creation of a sustainable business where minimal time and money is wasted.

Think of it this way: you spend an obscene amount of money trying to come up with products that you think the consuming public will love, "you think" being the operative words. Did you even stop to think if the products you're creating can solve a particular problem or address a pressing situation? You probably didn't, and guess what? You're more than likely to fail. Scratch that. YOU WILL FAIL.

Harsh words, right? However, I'm speaking the truth, and that is something that Ries' realized as well.

Earlier, I said that Ries' concept of the lean startup method was developed because of two Japanese men who worked for Toyota - Taiichi Ohno and Shigeo Shingo. Observing how these two worked, Ries' saw how the entire process of building Japanese cars worked - waste is reduced and eliminated, if at all, in order to release the cars at the lowest cost and without sacrificing the high value of the cars. Through his observation, Ries' was able to visualize a system that can likewise be applied by entrepreneurs.

Chapter 5.
Create a Useful Lean Startup Experiment

Qualitative or Quantitative: While many people assume that their startup experiment needs to be either quantitative or qualitative, the fact of the matter is that one is not inherently superior to the other. Instead, it is better to think of the two as if one was a hammer and the other was a screwdriver. While a hammer is better at putting nails in wood, that doesn't mean it is inherently superior on all fronts. Any tool can be used for good or evil, which is why it is important to focus more on validating the right metrics than it is to worry about which of these two processes is superior. In fact, using qualitative research and then validating it with quantitative research is likely going to do the most good anyway.

Generative or Evaluative: A generative research technique is one that doesn't start with a hypothesis per se but can still result in a wide variety of different ideas. Things like Customer Discovery Interviews fall under this type of technique. Evaluative, on the other hand, is all about testing a very specific hypothesis in order to determine a very specific result. The popular smoke test falls under this type of testing. It is perhaps this distinction, more than any other, that explains why some people end up with poor results from their experiments.

For example, a smoke test could be run to test the hypothesis that some percentage of the market will be interested in shoes that are compostable. To test this hypothesis, you would then put up a fake coming soon landing page explaining that compostable shoes are totally going to be a thing and see who signs up for the newsletter. After the work was done and the results were in, it turns out that there was about a 1 percent conversion rate when it comes to the shoes. The good news is that the hypothesis was confirmed, the bad news is that it wasn't particularly useful.

What's more, the results are unclear because it still isn't clear if the interest isn't there, if the advertising was poor, or if there is a third variable that you aren't yet aware of. This can be broadly defined as the difference between people not being interested in the value proposition and people not understanding it. The truth of the matter is that there are hundreds of reasons out there why someone might get a false negative result from a given test, just as there are a number of reasons why a false positive might be generated.

To get started, you will need to determine if the hypothesis is flawed or simply vague and, in this case, it is both. Some people are too vague when it comes to a target audience, some are a poor qualifier. As such, first, you would need to focus on a more specific demographic, and second, you would need to do research to determine how big the audience for compostable shoes would ultimately be. Only once the hypothesis is falsifiable and specific can it benefit from an evaluative experiment like the smoke test. If you can't clear up your hypothesis then you will want to start with Generative Research and work back from there.

Market or product: When it comes to the distinction between methods and tools, the biggest is perhaps the distinction between Product and Market. Some methods are useful when it comes to helping startups learn about their customers, their problems, and their best lines of communication. As an example, startups can listen to their potential customers to make it easier for them to understand their specific situations and what their day to day problems are like.

Other methods make it possible to learn about the product or a potential solution that will help to solve a specific problem. One good place to start is with a set of wireframes as a means of determining if the interface is as usable as it seems at face value. Unfortunately, this still won't make it clear if anyone is going to buy anything in the first place.

As these methods don't typically overlap all that well, it is important to choose one and stick with it throughout its cycle. If you combine evaluative research and generative research with Product and Market, you will end up with four different means of determining the best path forward.

Generative Market research asks questions like:

- Who is our customer?
- What are their pains?
- Is our customer segment too broad?
- What job needs to be done?
- How do we find them?

If you can't answer these questions clearly and easily, then your startup is in what is known as the Customer Discovery phase. During this phase, it is important to get to the basis of the problem prior to testing out any potential solutions to ensure that you are actually solving the right problem in the end. If you don't have a clear hypothesis to start, then you will need to generate ideas.

To do so, you may want to talk to customers to see what is bothering them or you could use a data mining approach to determine the problem, assuming you have access to enough data. You may even want to use a survey with open-ended questions if you are really fishing for ideas. Some of these methods will be qualitative and some will be quantitative, but this distinction is ultimately irrelevant in the long run. Data mining is a quantitative approach, but it helps identify problems, most famously the existence of food deserts which would have been difficult to determine in virtually any other way.

Generative Market Research Methods include:

- Surveys
- Focus groups
- Data mining
- Contextual inquiry / ethnography
- Customer Discovery Interviews

Evaluative Market experiment questions include things like:

- How much will they pay?
- How do we convince them to buy?

- How much will it cost to sell?
- Can we use scale marketing?

In order to properly evaluate a specific hypothesis, you may want to start with a landing page to determine if there is likely to be a demand. You may want to put together a basic sales pitch if you are working on a B2B enterprise type product. You could even go so far as to run a conjoint analysis as a means of further understanding the relative positioning of a few value propositions.

Evaluative market experiments that are useful if you have a clear hypothesis include:

- High bar
- Fake door
- Event
- Pocket test
- Flyers
- Pre-sales
- Sales pitch
- Landing page
- Video
- Smoke tests
- Surveys
- Data mining/market research
- Conjoint Analysis
- Comprehension – link to the tool
- 5-second tests

While this sort of research can provide lots of interesting data, it is important to keep in mind that much of it still has the potential to be wrong as signing up for a landing page is very different than actually putting money down on a product. In any situation where the customer doesn't have to commit anything more than an email address, then they don't signify an actual customer demand.

It is important to keep in mind that the value proposition and the product are not the same things. The value proposition is the benefit that your product will deliver to your target audience. As such, you cannot have a validated value proposition if you don't have a validated customer segment.

Chapter 6. Introducing The Lean Startup Method Foreword

When you build a startup, you have to know where to start which means that you will need to create a team that oversees the management of the startup.

You will also need to learn to define your product and startup to help customers understand why your product is different from the other products in the market.

Ensure that your learning is incorporated into the product and experiment with different ideas before you launch your product in the market.

How to Start

When you build a startup, you build an institution, which needs to be managed.

This may come as a surprise to some entrepreneurs since they believe that there is no correlation between management and startup. It is good that most entrepreneurs are wary of setting up a traditional management system since it can stifle creativity and invite bureaucracy.

Entrepreneurs in different industries have been trying to look for solutions to their problems in traditional management for quite some time which leads to the "just do it" attitude. These entrepreneurs avoid all forms of discipline, management and process.

What they forget is that this attitude leads to failure more often than it does success. It must be remembered that the principles of general management are not well suited to handle failure or chaos that every startup must face.

Every startup must have some level of managerial discipline to ensure that the company can harness all the opportunities it has been given. There are many entrepreneurs today when compared to any other time in history, which has been made possible due to globalization.

For example, most news channels and radio stations have commented about how people are losing jobs in the manufacturing industry. However, the manufacturing output of every company has increased over the last decade, which means that modern technology and management have helped to improve productivity.

If you wish to build a lean startup, you should consider entrepreneurial management since it encourages employees to expand their horizons and knowledge. Consider the following situation - there is an established company with a team that has not made any sales in over a year. This department has not roped in new customers either.

However, the employees in that department have identified a new industry or line of business the company can diversify its assets into. In an established organization, the department would be dissolved since the company is always looking for ways to make a profit.

However, in entrepreneurial management, these employees are considered entrepreneurs since they are looking for ways to improve the business.

Define

If you ever go for an entrepreneur meet, you will notice that many people have no idea what is expected of them. You will find a group of traditional entrepreneurs and managers from well-established companies who are expected to create product innovations or ventures.

These managers are good at organizational politics and know how the company can be divided into groups and how the profit and loss for each department can be separated.

The surprising thing is that these individuals are visionaries since they can see the future of their company and are prepared to take risks to find innovative and new solutions to any problem the company faces.

Entrepreneurs who work in an organization are called intrapreneurs since they work on products or build a startup within the organization. Intrapreneurs have a lot in common with entrepreneurs.

The lean startup method is a set of principles and practices that every entrepreneur can use to build a successful startup.

It was mentioned earlier that Eric Ries defined a startup as a human institution that is designed to develop a new product or service under uncertain conditions. This definition omits the industry, sector of the economy and the size of the business.

Most people lose sight of the fact that a startup is a brilliant idea, product or a breakthrough apart from being a human institution. Additionally, it is a product or service defined as an innovation.

It is important that the word innovation is understood in a broad sense. Every startup uses a different kind of innovation to increase value to its customer.

It is also important for the startup to understand the conditions under which innovation happens. Startups enter an industry where there is an established organization that already sells the same product.

They must find a new attribute to the product that has not been sold to the customers before developing it. The development stage is uncertain since the product could either be accepted or rejected by the customer.

Learn

Every entrepreneur must make an effort to learn and understand whether the company was indeed making progress. Many entrepreneurs develop a product using their creativity, and they launch that product in the market. If the product fails at the market, they believe they have learned why and they go ahead and develop a better product. Unfortunately, this is the oldest excuse for failure.

These entrepreneurs become wildly creative about what they have learned from their failure. However, this is not comforting for employees or investors since the former are giving the startup their time while the latter have allotted their money to the startup.

An entrepreneur cannot go to a bank and tell them that he or she has learned what needs to be done to sell the product in the market. It is no wonder the word learning has a bad name in the market.

It is important that every startup learns how a product can be improved and also understands what needs to be done better to succeed.

Experiment

When an entrepreneur has an idea in mind, he or she will want to find a way to execute that idea. Every startup is built in the hopes that the entrepreneur has identified a product or service that does not exist in the market and will increase value to its customers.

A mistake that most entrepreneurs make is that they launch the product on the market before they test it. There is a high probability that this product or service may not appeal to the customers.

Therefore, it becomes important that the startup launches the product to a smaller audience and gathers feedback before launching the product in the market. This gives the entrepreneur the chance to tweak the product to increase value to the customer.

How To Steer

When you have identified your product and developed it, you will launch it in the market and ask your customers to use it. You must remember that there is a possibility of a failure. But, do not worry too much since you can learn from that failure and develop a better product.

Leap

Every entrepreneur must have the ability to take a leap of faith and make a risky decision about his or her idea. There are two types of assumptions that can be made - Value Hypothesis and Growth Hypothesis.

Value Hypothesis

How can you as an entrepreneur validate every assumption you have made about your product's value? It depends on how quickly you can develop a prototype and give your customers the chance to use that prototype and give you feedback. You do not necessarily have to give the main product to the customers.

You can do what Zomato did. Deepinder Goyal saw that people had trouble waiting in a queue for food. Instead, they launched a website that had scanned copies of menus which enabled people to decide their order before they stepped into the line.

When this became a success, they developed Zomato and roped in more restaurants and cafes.

Growth Hypothesis

You must focus on the growth of your company only when you have an established product. You have to ask yourself how customers will use your product constantly.

The best way to do this would be to ask the customers for feedback. Facebook and WhatsApp are great examples.

Test

When you use the minimum viable product (MVP) approach, you will learn more about how the product can be improved. An MVP is not a small product, and it is simply a faster way to complete one iteration of the build-measure-learn cycle.

You have to remember that your first product does not have to be perfect. It should be a rough idea of what you had in mind and then test that idea with your customers and gather feedback. You must ensure that through this test, you can validate your initial hypothesis.

There are different tests that can be conducted to understand how the customers received the product.

Quantitative versus qualitative

There is a constant debate to understand which is superior. It is a good approach to first use qualitative research and assesses the feedback before validating a hypothesis using the quantitative approach.

Generative versus Evaluative

The former can be used to test the product if there is no hypothesis in place. The latter is where a hypothesis is tested to understand whether or not the product is a success or failure. If you do not have a clear hypothesis, you should use the generative approach to either obtain new ideas or to develop a particular hypothesis.

Market versus Product

There are some situations where the market will give you an idea of what the customers want. All you need to do is listen to the customers and understand what problems they face. There are other situations where a product or service must be developed to solve a problem.

Measure

Every startup is a more than just a piece of paper. The initial business plan will list out the number of customers the company expects to have, the cost it will incur and the revenue or profit it will make.

This plan is usually far from where the startup is in the early days. Therefore, it is important that a startup works on the following:

- It must identify where the startup is right now by accepting the truth that is revealed through constant assessment.

- Devise new experiments to understand how the startup can move towards the numbers mentioned in the business plan.

Most products, including the ones that fail, have some growth, positive results and customers. As an entrepreneur, you will be optimistic and will trust the ideas that you have. This does not mean that you can bumble around and be happy with the little traction that you have. You should ensure that you do not persevere when things do not go your way.

Persevere or Pivot

When one says pivot, it does not mean that they should give up on their ideas.

There are different ways that an entrepreneur can still make his or her product work. Try the methods mentioned above to help you when you reach the pivot stage.

If every test and experiment conducted gives you the best results, you should develop the product fully and launch it in the market. Ensure that you do not trick yourself by using vanity measures to test your hypothesis.

Always use criteria that will affect your company to assess the products that you are developing. You must also ensure that you listen to your customers and understand their wants and needs better.

You have to remember that a startup's productivity is not measured by adding more features to a product.

It is about how the startup aligns its efforts with a product or business to drive growth and create value. If you learn how to pivot successfully, you can reach the path of sustainable business growth.

How to Accelerate

Most decisions that need to be made by a startup are not clear or straightforward. They have to constantly question their product and assess when it can be launched in the market. They have to also look at how the product should be released and the cost that they will incur.

Batch

The issues mentioned in that example are found in every process in an organization, and they are of greater consequence in the work of small or large companies.

Some companies use a large-batch approach where they develop and deliver all the products at the end of the process and at once. Other companies use a small-batch approach where it produces and delivers a finished product every few minutes. A big advantage of working in small batches is that problems in the product can be identified faster. Lean manufacturing discovered small-batch processing a few decades ago when Taiichi Ohno and Shigeo Shingo worked to enhance the productivity of Toyota Automobiles. They started to manufacture products one at a time and stopped any activity if there was a defect in the process. Once the defect was removed, the product was manufactured in small batches. This gave Toyota the ability to produce diverse products. They gathered that every product can be different and does not have to be produced in bulk. This allowed them to serve smaller customer segments and give the customers products that they needed.

Grow

There are times when a startup can have customers at early stages and good revenue at that stage. However, the company may stop growing in the sense that it continues to make the same revenue and has the same number of customers now that it had at its start. So, where does growth stem from? A company can only grow if new customers are brought into it, which can only be done by the action of all its past customers. There are four ways to obtain new customers:

- A startup can use the Internet to advertise its products and services. Most businesses do this to encourage new customers to buy their products. If you want this to be a successful venture, you should pay for advertising through your revenue and not out of the initial capital.

- New customers can be brought through the use of products. For example, if a customer sees someone wearing new clothes, he or she may want to purchase similar clothing. The same can be said about cars and bikes. This is also true for products like PayPal and Instagram.
- If a customer is satisfied with the product or service provided by the company, he or she will spread the word and encourage more people to purchase that product.
- There are some products that need to be repeatedly purchased. If you develop such a product, you can create a subscription plan that ensures that customers keep coming back to you.

Adapt

It is important for a startup to adapt for change. Every employee in the startup should constantly be trained. Some people working in traditional organizations may tell you that you should not spend too much money on training when you are a startup. This is bad advice since it is important to train every employee in the organization to help them develop new ideas. It has become evident that technology is going to take over many jobs in the near future. This does not mean that someone should sit tight and continue with their work and not develop their skills. It is important that they learn new skills or programming languages that will give them an edge. New jobs can be created to cater to these new skills. The same can be said for a startup. It must constantly evolve its products and develop new products or services that will appeal to the customers. As an entrepreneur, you should be strong and deal with negative comments or feedback. You must learn from that feedback and develop products that will add value to the customers.

Use the Five Whys technique to help you understand what your customers want and why the initial prototype of your product failed in the market. You also have to learn to start small. Do not begin with four or five hypotheses. Start off with one hypothesis and test that with the data collected from the customers.

You must ensure that you do not blame an individual or a team for failure since that brings the morale of the employees down. Accept that mistakes do happen and learn from them.

Innovate

Innovation is the key to a bright future for any company. It is believed that when companies become large, they lose the ability to innovate. However, this is a myth that has been bringing many companies and employees down.

When a startup is growing, it will test its products in the market and find ways to make the product better to appeal to its customers. It will also need to find new attributes to add to the existing product to generate new customers. This is innovation since the company is looking for ways to enhance the existing product. If a well-established organization is willing to change its management, it can also start innovating. Innovation teams must be built to ensure that a company succeeds. This is what keeps Apple apart from all other companies. Apple is one company that has always developed new versions of its devices to meet customer demands. The developers include new features into the code every few months to generate a new product. Apple has also ensured that its products are user-friendly and can sustain bad handling. Most customers have confirmed that an Apple laptop has a firewall that makes it difficult for any virus to penetrate. This is the kind of product that you should develop. Ensure that you constantly innovate and make your products better to meet your customers' demands.

Remember to listen to the customers and make informed decisions about what the customers need. Customers are not sure of what they want or need on most occasions.

They believe that they know what they want, but in reality, they use the products that have great reviews. It is important that you pay attention to what your customers want before you develop a product or make changes to an existing product.

Chapter 7. Difference Between Lean Startup and Traditional Startup

Are you aware that business-plans arrive rather than just one, but 2 categories? More frequently than not, once we think about a business plan we think about a conventional format. This usually means a hefty record, roughly 30 to 40 pages in total, written three to four years outside which summarizes every detail which may result in the results of the small business.

A Lean start-up program, alternatively, requires less detail and time to put together, however should have the ability to convey the ongoing future of the company within an understated fashion. Which sort of business program if you draft for the own startup? If you are uncertain whether one format is more preferable on the other, then keep reading.

Traditional Business-plan

A traditional plan skewers towards becoming more extended and detailed than people at thin start-up arrangement; it's essentially a blue print that provides you a glimpse in to the near future of your own startup. In each Conventional company plan, You Will Need to pay for these regions:

Executive Overview—Here you ought to have the ability to explain, no longer than two pages, that you and your organization really are, what exactly your company does, exactly what industry it's in, where you are located (or are located), once you'll start conducting business when you have not begun already, the way the enterprise will earn money, and also consumers will probably require items and/or services provided by the company.

Business Description, strategy, and concept—This section contains extra info about your services and products, for example what they're doing, making them distinctive and unique, where in fact the concept of the organization originated out, where you are in the evolution stages, and also over all objectives and plans to your business, together with its projected deadline.

Industry Analysis—Who's the competition? Here you will examine competitions of your own brand and touch in their own offerings, company background, and also exactly why consumers may choose your services within theirs.

Marketplace Analysis—given you know that your rivals, that can be the target market? This section defines your marketplace, their requirements, and the way your company should have the ability to draw, capture, and maintain that particular audience.

Organization and Management—when you have staff or management engaged, this section enables you to share with you their biographies, wallpapers, and heart responsibilities.

Financial Projections—this provides readers a glimpse into the income of your business enterprise. It's really a table-heavy region which features projected profit and loss, a 12-month revenue announcement, expenses funding, sales prediction, and also a breakeven investigation with the revenue necessary for the primary investment. And talking about investment...

Financial Request—In case you're trying to get financing from investors, then this really is the place to summarize the sum of money asked, how it's going to be spent, and also the way it has been spent.

Appendix—Your appendix will incorporate business research, letters of incorporation, trade mark registrations, and venture arrangements, simply to list a couple records.

Lean Startup Plan

In case you have to compose a business plan fast or if your company is rather straightforward and straightforward to spell out, your arrangement of choice will be probable a lean startup program. This is not as much a rigorous layout and more of a fast overview—some times no further than 1 page!

However sweet and short that your arrangement is, a more lean start-up Program must include the following components:

Value Proposition—the worth your small business brings to its market, summed up at a transparent statement.

Key Partnerships, activities, and resources—extra info about the spouses working together alongside your small business, plans for gaining a competitive advantage, and tools, such as intellectual property or funding, used to make value for the intended audience.

Customer segments, channels, as well as relationships. Who's the audience? Where are you able to accomplish them? How are you going to build an enduring relationship together? Define your intended audience, options for having the ability to keep in touch with them, and tips to establishing the client experience.

Revenue streams—Explain and list the sales flows your organization gets for earning profits. Be certain that you include a fast section that defines your own cost structure plan too.

which format does your business need?

The good news about writing a business plan? There is room for editing. If you are displeased with the structure or will need to make adjustments, then you always have the option to update the file. Additionally, there is the choice to modify formats if you start with a slender plan, however, wish to shift to a more conventional plan, and vice versa.

No matter the arrangement, the main issue is always to be both succinct and critical regarding your business from the start. Your small business plan works to align with your team towards a frequent vision to your own organization and evaluate its feasibility as quickly and seriously as you possibly can. With this type of document leads to the results of the company and places you as being a certain CEO.

Startup Approach

A lean Startup approach is actually a style of business development which appreciates a small business's ability to improve quickly with very little waste of funds. The purpose is to use a set management arrangement (i.e. eliminating of central management) and tools in a manner that is flexible in order for the company runs economically. This means the evolution cycle of a startup gets briefer and much more predicated on iteration (repetition and revision) using three stages: build, quantify, learn.

The thought of the lean startup technique is that should start-ups invest their time in construction services or products to fit the requirements of premature clients (through iteration) they are able to cut the demand to get considerable quantities of initial financing and pricey product launches/tests. By way of instance, a technology startup utilizing the lean startup procedure will assemble a prototype fast (build platform) and launch it in the current market and measure the achievements of this item through data investigation in ancient market testing (step stage), then utilize this data to iterate and further develop the procedure to your next construction of this goods (learn period). This method will not only simply connect with technology startups and may be utilized across all kinds of start ups.

Solving Challenges at Your Site Using a Lean Approach

Adopting Lean techniques to address issues in medical settings is burdensome for just about any company. The transformation in to a small organization demands significant cultural modifications. I believe that the change could be like moving to some other country and never have to learn about new habits and a new vocabulary. You've got to learn how to behave in fresh ways and also think otherwise. The changes involve the adoption of fresh tactics to finding answers to issues, implementing the solutions, and sustaining the services. Lots of you could know such while the Plan, Do, Study, Act (PDSA) cycle.

One attitude that must be embraced could be the "continuous excellent improvement" mindset. If you embrace this mentality, then you definitely feel that procedures and outcomes on your website can always be improved. It's like the notion you could do more to increase your own personal wellbeing. Too frequently managers and physicians feel that just how things work is just nice and their website is quite efficient. Then there are people that think outcomes might possibly be better but merely pay attention to clinical impacts and those associated with clinical procedures. Practitioners of Lean recognize that all procedures in a site are interconnected-clinical and administrative staff also there is always room for advancement.

Still another switch for the majority of sites is how one discovers solutions to issues. Too frequently it's 1 person or even a small set of individuals who show up with methods to issues. Often times a physician or boss in a clinic determines how things will be carried out. One other health practitioners do not want to get bothered; they only desire to operate with patients and also become paid. If you would like to earn substantial improvements afterward you definitely want to feel that teams may solve problems better compared to 1 individual and everyone on the team could subscribe to answers to issues. I am not saying that for every prospect for advancement that the whole team needs to be engaged.

Rather, a wide representation of this team should help solve issues; a representative from each area afflicted with means of a procedure needs to really be involved. You may desire to involve some that do not appear to get involved in an activity you're improving. They may get a notion which features their participation also that boosts the approach. The vital attitude with this preparation area is that almost all issues might be solved by tapping on the ability, invention and understanding of their employees.

A compliment to the adoption of teams to address problems is really a big change in direction style. In the place of one individual dictating changes, the pioneer in Lean should be in a position to effortlessly direct classes. A pioneer of a problem-solving group has to have the ability to have answers from all of the team members, so get set members to work together effortlessly, and bring close at the right moment. The best choice of work groups shouldn't be exactly the exact same person every and every time; but an organization formerly formed should last to own exactly the exact same leader before an answer to a marked advancement problem can be available. If the other class is formed to get another problem, then it's okay to own a fresh pioneer.

Only as the practice of creating methods to process or quality issues will call for substantial changes for most health websites, the execution will probably necessitate changes too. Suppose you've produced a policy for a brand new process that you imagine will significantly enhance a few consequences and eradicate some waste in your website. Perhaps, for example, you've created a fresh means to handoff patients in 1 shift to another at a hospital ward. What exactly are several of the situations you want to accomplish in order to really make the roster from this master plan effective? You need to be certain all who'll participate from the master plan know the new procedure and are familiar with it. The participants at the new process must not just know their role but additionally the job to be played by other people. Once participants are correctly informed the various tools required for the newest process should maintain place. As an example, a brand new checkoff sheet for off patient hand may possibly have to get distributed and printed. Once the supplies and training are all in position, a startup period has to become designated.

Only as a brand fresh type of leadership is essential for team leadership and also the growth of methods to healthcare process issues, a brand new method of direction is needed for the execution of this answer. The first choice for the roster out must take note that the roster and execution is greatly influenced by people engaging; all too often at sites at which leaders do not count on teams, execution failures turned into a blame game.

A Leader that works well with teams may observe a nurse at off our hand problem may possibly have one concept of the appropriate approach to make use of the test off sheet developed to the method where as your doctor who additionally uses the sheet may possibly possess a slightly different perspective. The purpose is that the best choice of this roster outside should be conscious that since various folks may take place the onset of the clear answer could occur otherwise than intended. A fantastic leader will closely monitor the problem and also solve the bugs. A pioneer may even watch out to people that might desire to interrupt the newest process as a result of an awareness of loss in power or influence.

To ensure a powerful installation of a fresh process lasts and more buy to its own effectiveness, somebody will have to get data demonstrating favorable outcomes-improved clinical effects, positive perspectives of the involved from the procedure and the removal of waste (increased income). As an example, I know of a single hospital which used data to demonstrate they had paid down the time of Set for payables by more than 50%. This enhanced income because less attempt Was required for set to get a single thing as well as the cashflow improved.

The documentation of these outcome insured the continuation of this brand new strategy and additionally pointed into help paths for advancement. Thus, it's very important that you specify measures to track the outcomes of a brand new procedure and also to figure out strategies to finetune it. The demo of favorable outcomes may even contradict the commitment of these involved and also convert individuals who could have already been reluctant to connect. Obviously, it might be the data illustrates that the new process is not worse. Rarely are the situation.

At This stage you may possibly believe continuous excellent improvement (PDSA for a) is extremely tough and perhaps not worth every penny. New methods for working in teams, fresh styles of direction, complications in implementing new procedures and keeping up the fluctuations simply do not look worth every penny. The inertia you need to overcome to triumph is similar to obtaining an individual with newly diagnosed hypertension to adjust their life. Some will change instantly; a few may change gradually; plus a few may not change at all and certainly will build up more complications. Exactly like individuals who triumph in managing their hyper tension, you are going to realize this new method of problem-solving at the medical environment is worth. The data will probably establish it.

Funding A Startup

Funding a Startup is among the most challenging facets of establishing a brand new small business. If it boils down to it, you need to navigate investment capital firms, angel investors, angel investors, and consider what the funding will be worth in lack in control of one's own firm. Most start ups fail because while in early stages of the firm that they were underfunded from the evolution stages. Other folks neglect right after launching despite the fact that they've got an remarkable solution, however they ran out of capital to mark the business and gain the critical mass required to sustain operations. This is just a painful situation to know about as you will find simple ways to have Startup Funding and Business Credit to turn your Startup to a grown up. We've three questions which we'd suggest any Startup inquire before seeking financing from outside sources.

1. The amount of money would you NEED to receive your startup from the bottom? There's not any doubt you're shaking your head at the close absurdity with this question nevertheless you'd be amazed what you should figure out about your organization if you glance at just how thin you can conduct the business at first. Thus many businesses believe they want an enormous store front, higher end furnishings, and the complete staff the afternoon that they start their doors for the business. For this is an excellent 5-year-old goal however in the start you could well be in a position to complete so Apple failed and start having a notion and also a couple of talented employees. For those who haven't read re work it'd not be advisable to test it out since there are lots of fundamentals which may save your self-start-ups a significant little bit of hassle in the future.

2. Are you prepared to become a member of staff in your company? This too can seem as an unusual question but should you opt to assist a VC business in lots of instances you'll be in charge of the shareholders in ways you might not have initially hoped. There are reports out of Silicon Valley into Dubai that begin with a keen entrepreneur and also ending with a burnt out "employee-owner" who is made to simply take their startup at a fresh leadership due to the effect of their own investors. Entrepreneurs beware.
3. What's going to happen over the first ninety days to getting the financing you require. There are businesses available which have minimum $50,000 financing warranty which ensures qualified organizations can obtain access to this financing they desire; nonetheless it's remarkably important you get a very clear vision of exactly what your priorities will probably soon be later becoming financed. It sounds really straightforward but lots of times organizations get financed with no contingency collection of essentials; and after becoming ample funds they end up without essentials they should've procured from one.

Lean Startup - Startup Incubator

There are zillions of smart ideas that occur to people. Several of those individuals are extremely courageous to carry it forwards and put in an entrepreneurial journey. Because nearly all of these have previously read and comprehended that the characteristics clarified by 37Signals inside their publication Getting Real - entrepreneurs begin to create the very first minimal version in these product focusing only on the crux of the undertaking.

As a web consulting firm, we assembled those minimal versions quite inexpensively. This original variant is known as the Minimal Viable Product. And we found the wonder of the beasts, simply to appreciate it isn't bringing some clients and even though they perform, that the churn rate is high. Clients decide to try it rather than return. This fizzles off the driveway and we build greater enhancement to the goods and finally after losing time and money, we provide up departing the entrepreneurs disheartened.

Realization: It will take more than MVP to build a sustainable business enterprise.

Complementing the teachings of 37 signs could be the Startup moment. It discusses early adopters, supported learning, linking to this development engine and construction sustainable business enterprise. Entrepreneurship is all about going into the anonymous and although you fully grasp that the Lean startup approaches it becomes difficult to map those on you to your enterprise version. It's really a tough beginning, but undoubtedly a one. Returning into the failed startups, it's more surprising to observe that a day or two after, somebody managed to get by means of a comparable idea. What exactly did the MVP shortage could be that the question we frequently needed a thousand replies but none who have been funny.

Additionally, it boils down to how the majority of entrepreneurs possess certain expertise. They may be designers, programmers, marketer, business programmers or real visionaries. But before you started building the MVP, then you failed to answer the vital question - Which are the clients? Assembling an MVP is insufficient. The target ought to be to generate an MVC - Minimal Viable firm. To accomplish that you'll need pros in the branding, promotion, fund raising, web development, business construction and a lot more things. Solopreneurs could have one or even at the three of the aforementioned skills. Deficiency of mathematical abilities could be the key source of failure for the majority of startups. Seeing that, a fresh strain of incubators is forming which offers a more" Startup in a box" services with expertise in each of the elements required to make success. They truly are construction pros in each one of the four principal areas from business construction, promotion, financing and web development. Each one these services are extended in a structure that could permit cover while you grow version that's the vital requirement of almost any startup.

Chapter 8.
The Lean Startup Technology in Action

One specific area I will talk about in relation to lean startup is how you can efficiently manage your employees using the methodology (Sheth, 2019). It's a vital approach that ensures continuous progress for your business. Nevertheless, you need to anticipate that trials and errors will be part of the process since you will need to continue experimenting, testing, and investigating whatever it is your offering, whether products or services, repeatedly as these develop.

You will notice the stark difference between a business that follows the lean startup methodology and a traditional startup. A traditional startup follows a methodological process that is built on long-term vision, strategy, and plans. On the other hand, a business following the lean startup will expedite the processes by going through the steps. Another difference is that information about the products or services will be kept to a minimum few - employees, investors, and test customers - until such time that the offerings are deemed marketable, keeping in mind that the entire process is done in stealth mode.

By now you're probably wondering, "What do all these have to do with effective employee management?" The answer is quite simple, actually. The more streamlined process offers managers a chance to discern whether or not there are some inefficiencies with the current processes. Thus, they can correct or change whatever needs correction and only deliver to customers what they deserve - value for money.

Bonds Strengthened Because of Lean

Another example of the lean startup technology in action is the development of a strong A-team. Because the build-measure-learn process is put in effect, the right people are hired and put in the right place. As a result, each one is given tasks based on the skills they possess, as well as their adaptability to the lean startup methodology. As your business grows, you can transition your first batch of employees, you're A-team, as brand marketers. This time, their job will be to talk about your business to others. This will result in a chain reaction of sorts in which brand awareness is raised without you having to invest money. In turn, this awareness will start raking in revenue and improve the confidence of your employees. Once their confidence level is improved, they can go ahead and train a fresh group of employees with the same vision they had when they started with you. This unified faith in the vision and mission of your business is crucial because as much as possible, you want to have people working collectively for you to help you reach your main goal.

How to Get Started with an Effective Lean Startup A-Team

Here's the thing: a business' A-team doesn't just fall automatically down from the sky. In fact, one of the key elements in forming an A-team for your business using the lean startup approach is to hire people based only on the open positions. If there are no open positions in the business, then don't hire people. That is the best way to keep the business efficient. Moreover, because the lean startup methodology is somewhat of an unorthodox approach to starting a business, another vital element to forming your A-team is to choose people who will fit ideally to the lean startup culture you are trying to cultivate. Then, you will want to entice these employees comprising your A-team to stay with your company by offering them something tangible. Knowing what an employee can bring to the table to add a unique value to your business can help you determine what sort of "incentive" you'll offer them.

Some businesses that follow the lean startup methodology offer employee stock ownership plan (ESOP) to their employees. An ESOP is a benefit plan, an equity, in which employees are given ownership interest in a business (Ganti, 2019). The ESOP, will be based on a distinctive skill that an employee can offer to make the business better.

Why should you, the business owner, go through such great lengths to keep your current roster of employees that comprise your business' A-team? Well, most of those employees left the security that corporate jobs offer just to join a new business. It is such a huge leap of faith, one that requires you to make them see that the big risk they took was not for nothing. They will have something to gain out of their big move. On the flipside, you need to make sure the incentives you will offer the employees will not, in any way, impede with business activities. You need to ensure the company stays protected and that every business activity is always carried out in a professional manner. If you decide to give your employees ESOP, you need to ensure you're doing it properly. There needs to be a structure you will follow to make sure the process flows smoothly. Perhaps a good way to decide how much an employee will get is to have a pre-determined range of equity stake. This percentage will be paid over and above the salary that an employee receives. Here's a model you can follow:

- Rank-and-File Employees and Junior Managers - 0.2 to 0.33%
- Managers and Senior Lead Managers - 0.33 to 0.66%
- Directors - 0.4 to 1.25%
- Product Development Leads and Engineers - 0.5 to 1%
- Independent Board Members - 1%
- Vice Presidents - 1 to 2%
- Chief Operating Officer (COO) - 2 to 5%
- Chief Executive Officer (CEO) - 5 to 10%

As you can see, the bracket range above includes everyone, from the rank-and-file employees to the business founder(s). Keep in mind that the above is just a model you can use in your own business. There is no hard and fast rule as far as range brackets go. You will decide on the best compensation; thus, it's vital that you fully understand the types of ESOPs you can offer to employees. A flexible schedule is yet another thing you can offer employees. Believe it or not, there are people who work best during daytime and there are those who work best after the sun has set. If that is the case with your current roster of employees, then by all means, yield to the schedule that allows them to function in their fullest potential and efficiency. Really now, if you want to keep your top employees happy, you need to learn how to be flexible especially when it comes to their work hours. Applying the lean startup methodology in your business will allow your employees to either work together in teams following a rotational schedule or anytime that is convenient to them. If you will opt for the flexible schedule, then you may want to consider allowing some of your employees to work from home, too. Another way to allow for flexibility in a lean startup "environment" is to veer away from setting hours for team members. Try giving project-based work that follows a specific timeline. This means there is only a set number of hours they have to get the job done. Indeed, the lean startup methodology can do wonders to improve the efficiency of employees. Nevertheless, it will all depend on how "understanding" of their circumstances you are as an employer. If you're unyielding, then the growth of the business will be stunted no matter how hard you try to implement the lean startup approach. The whole idea of adopting a lean startup culture in abusiness is to help it improve continuously. If you will not be open to changes, continuous improvements in your business, no matter if these are big or small, will be impossible. Remember, a business that applies the lean startup approach revolves around change. Just make sure everyone of your employees, from the lowest to highest rung of the ladder, is aware when changes are implemented. It doesn't matter what the changes are about. The changes are meant to benefit not only the business as a whole but also each and every one of your employees. Hence, you need to make them aware of the changes if you want them to be on the same page as you are during the implementation period. Every one of the people comprising a "lean startup team" must be moving in the same direction. That is the key to the successful implementation of the lean startup methodology. Employee's commitment, whether you're the CEO or a rank-and-filer, is necessary since the whole idea of the lean startup is everyone having a shared purpose to foster a culture of improvement in a business.

Chapter 9.
What Is Lean Analytics?

Lean Analytics is part of Lean Startup methodology that is made up of 3 elements—Construction, Assessing and Learning. These three elements sort a lean analytics cycle of product creation. This highlights that fast assembles an MVP (Minimum Viable Product). You may create more intelligent decisions with accurate dimensions of lean Analytics.

The main aim of these lean analytics businesses needs to make the most of the educational at a quick time period. The end result of using lean analytics will probably be much more successful and nimble firm.

Lean Analytics that's a sub category of Lean Startup methodology insures the step and also learn section of this cycle. What this means is without proper dimensions you can't take any choice. Before employing this methodology that the businesses should definitely understand what ought to be monitored, for why it needs to be monitored and which would be the ways for use for tracking. The lean stats cycle is displayed at the picture underneath.

Recognizing An Excellent Metric

As we know more about the lean analytics cycle may be that the dimension of movement towards your specified aims. Thus as soon as you've defined your small business aims then you want to be aware of the dimensions to get progress towards your aims. There aren't many faculties of metrics that are good. It's recorded below

1. Comparable—A fantastic metric ought to have the ability to compare. You Can answer these questions together with your metric

- How was the metric the last season or even the preceding month?

- Is your conversion speed rising?
- The conversion rates could be monitored most useful with Cohort Analysis.

2. Understandable—Metrics ought to perhaps not be complicated or complex. It ought to be readily understandable by everybody else in order they are able to be aware of exactly what the metric measures.
3. A rate or ratio—Total numbers must not be utilized in Metrics. If whatever is expressed concerning percent it'll be far superior to compare and make conclusions based on this.

- Adaptability—Great metrics should alter the way your business varies. In case the metric is proceeding and you also don't understand for that which then it is perhaps not really a fantastic metric. It will always proceed alongside you personally.

Correlation and Causation in Lead Analytics

To get any company, it's extremely crucial to differentiate between your co-relational and also causational romance.

To get example, consumption of ice-cream can be associated with fever. The more folks eat up ice-cream you will find greater odds to obtaining a fever. We can't even arrive at the end that ice cream induces distress. That is only because fever may also occur as a result of times of year, that correlates with ice-cream ingestion. Fever mostly does occur through the summertime that's the growing season where folks eat more ice cream. This really is a spot in which significance and casualty match.

When we state two things are connected, then this usually means two factors affect just as ice-cream and congestion at the above mentioned example. An informal variable here's that the summer weeks since they directly impact both dependent factors, ice-cream, as well as congestion. The reason being the summertime are somewhat more vulnerable to ice cream consumption and congestion.

Correlation helps to forecast the near future and it's going to let you know what goes to happen

Casualty is a super power that will allow one change the upcoming

The process goes like this

- Locate the significance on your data
- Evaluation for casualty
- After locating the casualty factor optimize it

Lean Analytics Framework

The Lean analytics framework can allow one find out the business enterprise you're in and also the stages of one's small business. Your enterprise design should think about the clients and their buying procedure. You need to ask yourself a few questions before forming a company model such as

- How clients purchase your product or service?
- The reason why they purchase from you?
- At what point of one's company they're in?

What is the budget of your own customers?

Do not replicate the others business version. Frame your own personal company version. Your enterprise version needs to perform best for your own customers. Listed below is your picture symbolizing the company version.

Lean Analytics Stages

In Lean Analytics stages, you will find gates that the company have to maneuver to make it into the next point.

In the very first lean analytics phases, you want to discover a challenge where the folks are looking for an answer. This phase is more essential for B2B enterprise. For those who are finding this kind of issue then you are able to move ahead into this next point.

In the 2nd lean analytics phases stickiness, you should produce an MVP product to early adopter clients. Within this phase, you ought to target for user participation and preservation. It is possible to figure out that when folks begin to use your goods. It is possible to even be conscious of user participation and retention out of the moment that they stick to your own website. In the event the users remain quite a while then it demonstrates you have given what they wanted. Next, you could spread into this future stage Virality.

In 3rd lean analytics phases, you want to secure more clients in a cost-efficient way. Once you receive the clients it is possible to move ahead into the following stage Revenue.

In this 4th lean analytics phases, you're able to concentrate on the calculation of one's earnings and also do the economics work. You're able to pay attention to optimizing the revenue. LTV means that the revenue expected from an individual and CAC usually means that the fee required to find the client. The ratio is also seen out by dividing the LTV from CAC. You are able to assume your gross profits are good if the LTV is just three times in your CAC. After calculating your revenue you're able to go on into the previous point, Scale.

In this lean analytics phases, you could take crucial actions to cultivate your company. You're able to create plans at which to concentrate longer as a way to grow the development of the small business and enlarge it.

Chapter 10. Lean Analytics to Succeed

Implementing the Lean Analytics envisages the use of change in the thinking at the workplace. The first step to achieve this is to make a pivotal point in the hierarchy. When we use this, the clarity in the workplace remains enhanced. In most normal cases, this occurs by implementing the agent for change. This person remains responsible for all changes brought into force through Lean.

By choosing one leader, it becomes possible to revert any changes that do not work. This happens by streamlining the work through this central point. Also, we make the responsible person take action for all the work-related activity. So, if there is no action from the responsible person, the downstream activity ceases. Only when the leader agrees and approves of the changes, the rest of the work undergoes implementation.

The work then proceeds forward and the same condition gets applied to further activity. The change remains regulated by streamlining it through the central point of activity. And when any change gets detected that is not normal or expected, all the further downstream activity ceases. Once this flow path has come into force, it is easy to govern the natural evolutionary process for downstream activity.

Use the Services of a Lean Consultant

Learning the Lean Path is essential. It is easy to govern the workers once the process has begun. But, only the people who are conversant with the method of Lean will know when to make the needed changes. The knowledge is needed for the parallel working types in Lean that control each other. All the decisions and management principles remain data-driven and systemized through actual use.

For instance, you have two or three HR situations, which do not yield, direct answers in a normal analysis. One is the case where the turnover is low and the number of employees leaving the firm is rising. Next, the budget for training is big, but there is no clear-cut region where employee deployment will be profitable. And third, the hiring expense rises all the time due to attrition among the employees at the workplace.

To arrive at the solution, get a snapshot of the metrics. This will give a view of the nature of the problem. Check the metrics in related areas and see if there is any correlation. Use of KPI gives you the answers needed to make the changes. You can make use of pre-designed KPI software to do the analysis. It helps you to centralize the data related to the business and simplify real-time reporting. Actionable work gets broken into smaller pieces and removed until only those relevant to the work remain.

Use a Lever to Begin the Transformation

Most of the hardships one faces are situations begging for alternatives. And, every business undergoes these situations often. Rather than wait for a crisis to begin to make the change, begin the movement towards Lean by initiating the change yourself.

When you face a troublesome situation, one must change. The Lean philosophy anticipates changes and makes provisions for each. By preparing for the change, it is possible to overcome the negativity and create the positivity that will take the business to a profitable end. This situation applies to the client, the business owner, and the suppliers involved in transacting business.

The other alternative is to change the focus so that the problem does not seem as large. The Lean expert waits until the crisis has passed before he seeks the solution. In doing so, he gets a solution with ease.

Do Not Aim for Grand Solutions

The idea is avoidance of the key issues that precipitate the issue and look for solutions away from the hotspot. Many business problems solve themselves if you give it enough time. With this in mind, the Lean expert tries to figure out how to keep the mechanism of the business moving without overlapping in the key problem areas.

The first thing to do is to stop thinking of grand solutions. You will not get anything that will heal the situation instantly. And if you continue to think along those lines, you will only become disillusioned. It is better to think of small actionable solutions that have a better chance of working.

If you consider applying growth metrics in the workplace, you need to apply the Lean Analytics related to this metric. This includes the acquisition to growth employee life cycle and the lifecycle during retention. You must then consider the cycle after attrition to reacquisition.

One may improve the bottom line impact in the HR department by using better resource application. Also, use cross-training across all departments. Using Lean, you can improve the sensitivity of the training program by a huge amount.

Make a Map with the Implementation Timetable

The scientific approach to the problem of making the map involves the use of the positivist perspective on one hand. And, you use the hermeneutic perspective on the other. In the first, the user remains distanced from the aim and the research problem.

The problem gets divided into smaller pieces so that there is the possibility of refining the process and cutting out the waste. In the second method, the researcher remains central to the problem. All the flow processes get importance relative to him and those processes that lose their importance get eliminated.

The creation of the timetable helps to improve the flow value and the perspective. Each work function becomes more important or less important because they have to meet the time check. When the tasks fail to meet the time check, we check for alternative solutions that have a better possibility of meeting the timetable.

Take the First Step Immediately

It is important for progress in any business to begin activity immediately. This means that one uses any one of the scientific approaches existing between theory and reality to come through with an action plan. In the most normal case, one uses the induction-deduction method. These are opposing methods of analysis and find applicability to any kind of work situation.

If you have the reality worked out, then there is no need for any deep analysis. One may put into action the plan in a step by step approach. Inductive reasoning finds a use for most of the cases where there are no real results and the opinion remains needed to take the next step.

In the deductive or scientific method, there is an existing theory. This means that the reality is apparent. So, you can use it to proceed to the next step. The main focus is to show visible activity. This will set off the process and the chain reaction will continue until there is no more productivity. To see the result, one must begin the first step immediately.

Check for the Results Immediately

It is important to check the results fast and see the amount of progress one has made. Changes to the amount of working capital show in a clear way to all. But, the deeper metrics such as the Return on Equity and Vendor Expenses may not come to light as fast. Yet, these will impact the business in a big way.

You need to set the benchmarks and targets for the vendors in the first place. By checking the results immediately, you will know if you made the right decision and if so, how much profit is accruing from this.

You make use of Lean thinking and methods to improve profitability through timely action. You also cut the redundant processes. By concentrating on the processes that have more value, you improve the efficiency and lower the labor overheads.

Use Progressive Results into Value Stream Building

One side of the Lean method is where one cuts the unneeded processes. The other side is where one builds the processes that show positive results. When implementing qualitative processes, there is a lesser amount of control. You can improve the formalization and grade of control by the use of quantitative structures.

Use of real-time targets will cut the amount of uncertainty and bring more cohesiveness into play. For the practical values, one must use tests and questions. Then, one must study documents and information registers before using the suggested values. But, once you do this, you have a viable working system that you can depend on.

Tips for Using Lean Analytics to the Fullest

They're simple and to the point, so you can get down to brass tacks and generate movement within your company!

- If you're considering A/B testing, you need a large user base to give you an accurate picture.
- Make big changes so your A and B look different enough to matter.
- Take great pains to ensure you're measuring test results properly.
- Cut out the tools that don't work and hold onto the best one like your company's life depends on it because it does.

- Always be willing to reevaluate where your business stands in the present moment and make changes accordingly.
- Make sure you fully understand your metrics before doing anything with them.
- Focus on the main problem before the minutia.
- Cut back on waste wherever you find it. It is toxic to your business.

Chapter 11.
Benefits and Criticisms

It portrays another methodology for new businesses and endorses practices they ought to adjust to improve the probability that they will succeed. While the idea is most appropriate in an innovation or Internet setting, it has a more extensive application for all startups.

So what are the key precepts of the approach?

In numerous regards, the idea begins with a redefinition of what a startup is. For Steve Blank – a startup is basically 'an association shaped to scan for a repeatable and adaptable plan of action.'

I have reverberated this subject that depicts how a startup needs to concentrate on finding a feasible plan of action while working in a climate of 'extreme vulnerability.' Framing a startup along these lines causes move the concentration to a progressively logical methodology where activities attempted are seen as tests that rapidly assist you with approving presumptions (or something else).

Scanning for a suitable business model

Given that you are in examine mode, it is imperative to grasp some straightforward procedures to guarantee the quest for an adaptable business model is a productive one. From numerous points of view, these are lessons in hyper - proficiency, where time and money are valuable, and the reason for basic educated leadership is essentially on the rear of building what they call a Minimum Viable Product (MVP). An MVP is an essential rendition of the product that can be sent to certain clients (in a perfect world early adopters) who will give you input, which will enable you to choose what to do straightaway.

The accompanying example perfectly delineates the concept: As opposed to building the service and giving it a shot on clients, make a sign-up page that vows to convey this weighty ability. At that point, present it to some forthcoming customers. Contrast their enlistment rate and that of a benchmark group given the standard indication-up page. The outcomes will give the group the certainty either to continue or toss the thought into the round record. Nobody would get the new element yet, obviously, because it hasn't been manufactured.

As a result it has been proposed that you search for 'proof of interest' before building the total product, and a simple method to test for this is to watch genuine client conduct on the state, a web page. Each snap-on a catch signals plan, paying little heed to whether the product in the back end is there or not, and this information causes you to survey likely request.

Additional Lean Startup Concepts

The accompanying speaks to a short portrayal of a portion of the fundamental ideas related to the L.S. approach.

Test Frequently and Learn Quickly

As the above case of the MVP approach illustrated, they prompt that you don't assemble a detailed product before you have embraced various tests along the way (They are large supporters of A/B testing).

Watch and Measure Real Customer Behavior

Eschew focus group and watch how genuine clients carry on. Getting the MVP under the control of genuine clients right off the bat and rapidly gaining from what they do supports their entire methodology.

Concentrate Exclusively on Capturing Actionable Metrics

Maintain a strategic distance from metrics, for example, measurements that make an ideal impression about execution when they are fanciful. For instance: what great is

1 million page impressions if none of them convert? Rather business people need to concentrate on noteworthy measurements, for example, genuine measurements that can advise choices.

Be Comfortable Pivoting dependent on Key Learnings

The suggested you turn or stop what you are doing if the underlying arrangement isn't working (and your discoveries support the view that changing tack is bound to be effective than proceeding with the first arrangement). This view is especially steady with the perspectives on business arranging Guru John Mullins as portrayed in his book, getting to Plan B.

Grasp New Accounting Methods

Generally Accepted Accounting Principles (GAAP) have supported financial representing numerous years. In any case, it is contended that L.S needs to grasp 'innovation accounting' before they arrive at where traditional accounting kicks in. With this technique, he recommends that progress is best followed by watching things like client movement, commitment, maintenance, and virality. As it were, if client numbers are expanding, and they are being held with the end goal that Life Time Value (LTV) is developing fundamentally, this is a superior pointer of 'progress' than traditional accounting strategies.

Stay Lean

The word 'lean' alludes to speed and agility and not 'cost savings' as certain per-users confound (although that stated, they are against misuse 'all things considered'). Again it is prescribed that new businesses exploit the disclosure mode to rapidly realize what isn't working so they can make changes right away.

Some Criticism

Like every single 'new concept,' the methodology has a lot of critics too. A few people refer to the absence of fruitful examples as problematic, and others center on author's generally disappointing profession before composing the book. Others center on the risks of putting up a substandard product to market (MVP). In the meantime, Ben Horowitz has contended the case for the fat-startup:

"Quite a bit of what has been composed and said about lean beginning up's bodies well. In any case, that exhortation is regularly inadequate, and a portion of the things left inferred the least instinctive. There are just two needs for a beginning up: Winning the market and not coming up short on money. Running lean isn't an end. So far as that is concerned, nor is running fat. Both are strategies that you use to win the market and not come up short on money before you do as such. By making "running lean" an end, you may lose your chance to win the market, either because you neglect to support the R&D important to discover item/advertise fit or you let a contender out-execute you in taking the market. Some of the time, running fat is the correct activity. Thin is in, yet once in a while, you gotta eat."

For me, It feels that paying little mind to the idea; individuals will consistently discover defects and have solid counter contentions to specific components of the methodology. The consciousness of these contentions assists business visionaries with settling on progressively educated decisions in regards to whether they grasp elective methodologies. They are simply assessments of all things considered.

Chapter 12. The Lean Analytics Stages

There are several different stages that you will need to follow in order to have success when using Lean Analytics. You will find that you will not be able to proceed with a later stage until one is completed.

The stages are:

Stage 1

This is the finding and fixing stage. This is the stage at which you identify or find the problem that is causing difficulty on the lines of production or in your business. If your business specializes in Business to Business (B2B) selling, you will find this stage to be one with a great deal of impact for your business and your operations. Once the problem is found, you will need to decide on and carry out the steps to get is resolved. Get the problems you found completely remedied with whatever methodology (consider Six Sigma) works best for you and your business), then proceed to the next stage.

Stage 2

In this stage, you're going to create a Minimal Viable Product (MVP) that can be used by early adopter customers. This stage is the point at which you're aiming to retain the users or customers that you acquire. This stage may take some time, as you'll want to nail down your product, nail down the methods of retention, and to learn about the current habits of the customers or users that you do have. You may find that you need to cycle through a few different products before hitting the one that will get you the results that you need.

Stage 3

Once you have an idea of how the early adopter customers will respond to a product or a service that you offer, it's time to find the most cost-effective way to reach more customers that will want your product. Once you have a plan ready to obtain those customers, you can start to draw in more of them, get them purchasing your product, and move onto stage 4. You don't want to get a product that your customers love, but which you can't sell at a decent profit. Such products can make growth dodgy and difficult and should be avoided.

Stage 4

This stage involves a bit of an exercise in economics. You will want to optimize your revenue, which will mean calculating the ratio of Lifetime Value (LTV) to Customer Acquisition Cost (CAC). LTV is the revenue that you anticipate getting from each customer you've acquired for your business. CAC is the cost you've put into acquiring those customers. By simply dividing the LTV by the CAC, you will have an accurate picture of how viable the ratio is. If the result is three or higher, you're in great shape. LeadCrunch advises that you get $2.50 back for every $1 you spend on lead acquisition. You want a 250% return on your investment into those leads on potential customers. If you find that your LTV: CAC ratio is lower than 3:1, then you need to reevaluate the leads that you've chosen and find some with demographics or specifics that fit your target market more appropriately.

Stage 5

The final stage will require you to take the actions necessary to grow your business. You are welcome, to begin with, your current plan if that is making enough from the efforts of the previous steps to satisfy your margins or you might find that you need to make some changes in order to keep your business growing and thriving. It is also at this stage that you can make plans for later execution that will help your business to grow if you're content to continue using a certain plan for now, but you would like to work on another one in the future! The main goal is to keep your business moving and growing at all times. The speed at which this happens is completely up to you and what your team can reasonably handle. Laying out plans for this and carrying them out over a reasonable and digestible timeline is a valid approach to that end.

Chapter 13.
Types of Metrics

Learning to use Lean resources and principles is half the battle. Also, you will come across questions such as, "Is Lean better than Six Sigma?" Or, "Is it better to use the Theory of Constraints?" When you use more than one method, you will get lost. One may get over the arguments over philosophical or even technical differences with ease. You only have to stick to the basic Lean principle of avoiding excess and getting rid of waste.

Overview of Over-Production

The production cycle has in-built questions to start the next cycle. The first one is to please only the customer and stop when you reach the target. Have I achieved today's quota? If the answer is yes, then stop production. Until the customer places a new order, do not make anything.

This principle applies to all departments in the organization. The idea is to achieve the perfect value stream. Other than this, there is nothing you need to worry about. In Lean, we reduce the steps we use to help cut waste, while the Six Sigma principle checks for variation. The more variations there are in the process, the more chances there are for waste to accumulate. You need to follow only Lean principles of keeping the number of steps down.

Use of Lean Principle at Work

To separate technicality from the working, it is important the workers understand and use Lean principles. Often, there are problems that seem technical in nature but involve real people. You begin to use Lean principle at the core, the place where the problem arises with only one man. Then, expand the core team to as many as you need, until the problem gets resolved.

It takes some time for the principles to go into operation because there is a learning curve involved. If you do not have the Lean thinking, then there will not be much progress. Also, the team must know if the circumstances are right. If they are not, they must identify the cause and size of the problem. It may be due to one or more of the following:

Lack of commitment: The worker does not feel there is a need for Lean methods. He uses traditional principles but gets foxed when others seem to feel something is extraneous. Shift the focus and reexamine the problem.

Performance not aligned with commitment: This is more serious because work is ongoing and the value is not reaching the expected level. We need a change in the attitude because the worker wants to get measured according to the performance parameter. He is not worried about the process parameter.

Lack of training: The workers get deployed before they have got trained. So, they keep looking at the others when the work proceeds. Change the worker to another place and keep the work going. Wait until the person addresses the problem by confronting it.

We see that the Lean working method is not a toolbox we can pick from to achieve our ends. It is a total perspective that involves the entirety of the work process. When you see a segmentation of the workforce, say the people on the shop floor working at a different pace from the rest of the workers, you face a problem. Here the plant manager has to hit the stop button. Slow down the process, check where overproduction occurs.

He has a target to meet and must keep the workforce occupied. But, he can do other work and still meet the target. This is the Lean principle. Any extraneous work gets eliminated first. By moving the focus of the work to a new place, any kind of waste, in material or labor, is got rid of. The people need to have a Lean eye to develop the perspective they can depend on. This helps them understand how the factory works with each component getting linked to the next. They learn to recognize the elements that are important and work with these first.

Choose to Operate the Pull

You have many aspects affecting how to operate the Pull. The Pull is important because there will be instances where the workflow gets interrupted. One of the ways to use it is to address the question or problem from two or more perspectives. Pull exists at the nodes or joints of the structure in the organization.

The workflow question is, "Have you finished this work?" The problem question is, "Where is the box of material I am supposed to deliver?" And the Pull question becomes, "Who is the driver delivering the box to the work spot?" You can change the Pull in many ways until you have got rid of the externality existing in the structure.

So, you see the work proceeding, but there is a lag due to the lack of the box. The Lean principle tells you to cut the waste. Here you are wasting time. To cut this, you must address the issue by finding out who is bringing the box. The truck needed to deliver the box must undergo preparation. And then the box must get loaded onto the truck. But, since there is a problem, you shift the focus of the problem by diverting the loaders to a new place to do new work.

The problem is now resolved at two or three levels. One is the basic worker level where you give new work to the worker. The second is at the management level where you identify what caused the lack of the box. The third is at the deployment level where you keep alternatives ready to prevent any further occurrence of this event. Lean, thus, operates at many levels.

Make Comparison of the Steps

As the value stream progresses, the number of options keep on adding up. Many businesses keep these options open in the hope that some good will come of it. But, it ends up as a waste of space and effort. So, it is wise to get rid of all but one working option. When you have more than one option, it will end up in confusion.

If you have to make a choice, list out the options. Then, compare the merits and demerits of each one. Try reducing the steps in each and see, which one gets done first. This will prove to be the best choice.

Chapter 14.
How to Recognize a Good Metric

One of the first conclusions that will help you to learn what your business really needs is that most businesses are using the wrong data or doing the wrong things with the data that they've gathered. When you don't make appropriate use of your data, you will be getting just about the same results that you would be getting if you had no data at all.

The Biggest False Metrics to Watch Out For

Any business that is working on eliminating waste and on delivering the best and most effective customer service will find that false metrics are a big risk. Many people don't understand how data works, what it means, and what to do with it. When one doesn't quite know what to do with the data in front of them, it can be easy to think you know what you're looking at, and it can be easy to be enticed by the incorrect metrics for your business. Some of the most common false metrics are:

The number of hits. I blame the movies for this one. This metric tells you next to nothing about who is looking at your site or why. This metric doesn't tell you where those people heard about your site, why they're there, what they want, and how you can get them to come back in the future. This might initially feel great and get you excited about the number of people seeing what you've put online, but you ultimately need more focused data than this.

Page views. This metric refers to how many pages on your site are clicked on during a given time period. This is a slightly better metric than hits, as it does give you a bit more information than the previous metric. You typically will find that this metric won't bring about a lot of impact. In many cases, you will find that your business won't benefit very much from page views unless your business is in advertising.

You want to count people visiting your site and this is typically measured over the course of a month so you know how many people you're getting on your page.

Number of visitors. This metric is better, but since there aren't any specifics about the people who are visiting the page, it's often too broad for the average company to use unless your business is in something like advertising. This metric doesn't separate out people who are visiting multiple times, so this metric could also be called "Number of visits."

Number of unique visitors. Given what was just said about the number of visitors, you might think that this is the proper metric for you. That is where you see the demonstration of what was said earlier. These metrics can be very deceiving in some ways. You may think by their names that they will tell you what you need to know. This metric tells you how many individuals visited your page in a given timeframe, but it won't tell you anything about what they did once they got to your page, how long they were there, what brought them there, what they wanted if they got what they needed, or how to convert that visitor into a customer.

Number of likes, followers, or friends. With the vast rise in social media popularity and the traction of social media marketing, people will think that a vast number of likes, followers, or friends means that they hold a lot of influence, that they can sell things to all of those people, or that they've cultivated potential customers within those numbers. The fact is that those are very different things and they aren't necessarily synonymous. You can be a follower on a popular Instagram page without ever buying anything advertised on it, right? Having those likes, followers, and friends is a good thing if you know what to do with them, but they're not a good metric by which you can measure success of your company or the programs you're using.

Email addresses. Having a big list of valid email addresses is a great thing, and I won't tell you it's not. What it isn't, however, is a metric of success. It's a marketing tool that you can use to get the word out about your business, your plans, your products, and more. It's something that you can use to help you to bring more people in through your doors, as well as bring back past customers. Email addresses can and should be used for marketing, but they should not be used as a metric of the success of your company.

The number of downloads. If you have downloadable products for the public, you will find that it's easy to get excited over the quantity of people who have simply downloaded your materials. Those are your products in the hands of consumers, and that's what you want for your business. The things you miss out on when you count this include but are not limited to:

- How many people downloaded this multiple times?
- Who liked it?
- What did they use it for?
- Was this item helpful?
- Would they pay for it?
- Did they pay for it?

Time spent by customers on a page or website. Businesses that are directly tied to behavior or engaged time will find this metric helpful. Otherwise, you'll be tempted to make changes to your website to fill this metric, which won't do your business any long-term favors.

By avoiding these common false metrics and by understanding what these are really for, you will have a better shot at picking the metrics that will help you to expand and improve your business.

Chapter 15. Automatize the Company Thanks to the Analytics

Lean Analytics help you track the metrics vital to the growth and profitability of your business. The first step involves identifying those that are good. So, what is a good metric? A good metric is one that satisfies the following criteria:

1. **You Can Understand A Good Metric**

This is important because unless people understand the metric and discuss it, they will not try to get involved. Only when people are involved in the change, the metric has a real impact on the growth of the company.

2. **It Is Comparable**

The users and people in your company can relate to the change of the metric over time. They remember the time when the metric was not growing so fast or when the growth slowed almost to a standstill. They discuss this aspect with the metric of a different company or competitor. It makes them involved in the growth process.

3. **Ratios And Rates Are Good Metrics**

The nature of ratios and rates make them good metrics. This is because they already relate to something and so you get the growth aspect straight by reading the number given. If you have this kind of metrics, use them as they will help you develop the true picture of the company and its growth.

4. **Metrics Are Adaptable**

The changes you have in the business remain reflected by the metric. First, you must be able to read the metric. Then, you must be able to use the metric. An adaptable metric is more useful than one that is not.

Find the stage your business is in

You know what business you deal with and so you can arrive at the metrics involved in the process. To find the stage you are at, check the gating metrics.

- Empathy
- Stickiness
- Virality
- Revenue
- Scale

Starting from the lowest one, you can pass onto the next gate by checking your present position. For instance, if you have found a need in the market that did not have enough suppliers, then you pass through the Empathy Gate.

At the second stage, you find the MVP (Minimum Viable Product) that satisfies the customers in the market now. The MVP has only the bare minimum features but takes care of the need of the customers. This is the Stickiness stage and the early users will find your solution easy to use.

The third analytic stage is Virality. It means that you have the product with all the features that the customer looks for and they like it. You need to make your product more cost efficient and attainable. Once you do this, you can pass on to the next stage. This stage is the Revenue stage where you get involved in the economics of the product.

Find means to optimize the revenue. The calculation involves determining how much of money you expect from the customer and how much money you spend to get the customer. If the first amount is at least three times the second, you have good margins. This brings you to your last stage. This we call Scale.

The Scale is the stage where you grow your business. You can make plans to allow the business to grow. More than getting the metrics and working with it, you should make the wise choice of metrics at all times.

This means that you should work with one metric that matters to you most. This may be Churn. If the Churn is less than 3%, it means your business is stable and growing. But, if the Churn is more than 3%, then it means that your business is in trouble and that you have to take action.

Use Metrics for Your Automation

Automation means letting the machines, here computers, do the work. This will involve three big steps other than the calculation and the setting up of metrics. They are as described below:

Put a Global Strategy based on Lean into Place

To be a global player, the businessman must have the access to the foreign markets. It is easy to build the market through the supply chain network or the sub-network if you invest enough money. This step is crucial and once this is in place, you have the means to merge your gains through Lean.

Every market has its risks and international exposure brings its own share with it. Use Lean methods of testing and placing new footholds in the market. Eliminating wasteful methods and time-consuming processes will be the starting point in the process.

Many companies used low-risk and low-cost strategies for making the market entry. One example of this is export. This proved fruitful for those companies that did not face much competition. Using the Lean strategy of labor reduction and cost optimization proved beneficial to the businessmen.

- Use of mobile app monetization
- Applicability of media sites
- Balance the inventory
- Create website content

You can hire the local delivery services to take care of making deliveries in foreign lands. This is the first basis for expansion. The second is to establish an online presence that helps you become a household name. You need to use mobile-friendly content and ads. This will get you to most of the people in the world because they all use mobile phones.

Completing the Transformation

Create an SEO friendly website that has links to heritage sites. Only this helps you establish your product on the internet. Facebook, Twitter, Tumblr, Instagram, WhatsApp, and the others provide more exposure for your product. Provide the links for all these on your website. Conduct contests that give rewards to the users that link your website to the most number of sites. The publicity is cheap but effective.

Get your customers and suppliers into the Lean chain

Integrating the supply chain and the delivery network through the market and finding the best point of entry and delivery for your product is the first step. Value stream management has lots of interest among Lean users because of the way it gives the best solution. To maintain market viability, you need to have a good delivery system.

The supply chain will succeed if your end users remain satisfied. Value-adding activities for your product will depend on the choice and deployment of the decoupling points. While agile systems are best applied to the downstream side of the decoupling point, the Lean system gets applied to the upstream side.

Use good bookkeeping software to keep track of the inventory and bill management. Also, add good content to your website to attract more visitors. Use well-written content by a professional to add real value to the website.

Chapter 16. Case Studies of the Lean Startup Method

L.S. has numerous points of interest. As indicated by a survey from HBR, the best five advantages of the L.S. approach referenced most much of the time by their corporate respondents were:

- Settling on choices dependent on proof and information instead of executives' instincts;
- A quicker process duration for creating thoughts;
- Better-quality criticism from clients and partners, frequently because you're asking them to purchase something instead of gush sentiments in a center group;
- "Escaping the structure": addressing and watching genuine clients and partners;
- Greater adaptability about gaining changes to thoughts as they ground from idea to least practical product (MVP) to a completed product.

Inspiring Lean Startup Examples

The confirmation is in the pudding. To exhibit the plausibility of the L.S. approach, It will portray three motivating contextual analyses. Note how unique these associations are, while regardless, they profit by a similar technique.

- **Votizen**

In 2007, David Binetti propelled Votizen, a platform that composes US voters online, as an MVP. The L.S., Binetti's first MVP, was not a major achievement. In the underlying client accomplices, just 5% pursued the service, and just 17% checked their enrolled voter status.

"David went through the following two months and another $5,000 split-testing new product highlights, informing, and improving the product's plan to make it simpler to utilize. Those tests demonstrated sensational upgrades, going from a

5% enrollment rate to 17%, and from a 17% actuation rate to over 90%. Such is the intensity of split testing. This enhancement gave David a minimum amount of clients."

This entire procedure of building, emphasizing, and estimating is the center of L.S. It was the start of an example of overcoming adversity. In September 2010, Votizen reported it had brought $1.5 million up in subsidizing. After three years, Votizen was gained by Causes, an online civic-engagement established via Sean Parker.

- **General Electric**

As a 125-year-old organization, General Electric is by definition about as far away from being a startup as you could get. Notwithstanding, they are regularly referred to as a fruitful cause of an enormous association utilizing L.S.

L.S principles and other problematic methodologies over its environment to consolidate the speed and agility of a startup with the scale and resources of an enormous endeavor.

In this program, client-centricity is significant. GE starts by asking clients questions about what result they are attempting to accomplish. Hence, the group taking a shot at an issue concocts a theory for an answer, after which the hidden suppositions are tried.

FastWorks has been a triumph for GE. The procedure has brought about shorter item cycles, speedier IT implementation, and quicker client reactions.

- **RevelX**

At RevelX, we attempt to turn into somewhat better in what we do each day. The L.S. approach is one of our managing lights, explicitly the fabricate measure-learn feedback loop. We have instated our development group, working in 3 weeks sprints, continuously testing.

For example, we explore ceaselessly with our website to acquire further initiation and new acquisitions. The site normally experiences little upgrades dependent on what seems to work.

Another model is that we dispatch huge numbers of our thoughts as a feasible base product. Take, for example, our growth. Directory. A spot where you can locate the best and most recent curated tools for running your growth tests.

- **Dropbox**

Dropbox is outstanding amongst other known instances of a business that has developed utilizing L.S. principles.

The file transfer service presently has more than 500 million clients worldwide; however, it began life as an insignificant practical product as a 3-minute screencast indicating shoppers what Dropbox could do.

Reaction to the video-enabled Dropbox to test if there was interest for the product and, simultaneously, catch an underlying crowd through a holding up list.

But, above all, remarks on the video gave an approach to Dropbox to increase high--quality feedback from target clients, which the group in this way used to shape item advancement following customer needs.

- **Zappos**

Another incredible case of the L.S. in real-life originates from Zappos, one of the first online shoe retailers, which currently sells everything from boots to packs.

When Zappos began in 1999, founder Nick Swinmurn didn't have the foggiest idea of whether clients were prepared to purchase shoes online. Presently Swinmurn could have left, purchased stock, developed inventory systems, constructed a system of dissemination focuses, and checked whether the plan of action took off. However, rather Swinmurn needed to test his hypotheses that customers would purchase shoes online. What's more, he did this through a minimum viable product.

Swinmurn moved toward nearby shoe stores, took photos of their stock, and posted the photos online on a basic website. If he got a request, he'd purchase the shoes from the stores at the maximum and afterward sent them straightforwardly to clients. Swinmurn before long demonstrated that client request was available, and Zappos would, in the end, develop into a billion-dollar business dependent on the model of selling shoes online.

Chapter 17. Lean Startup Advantages

As a startup, you have the huge natural advantage of having more straightforward access to enter from your clients, and being able to actualize changes dependent on that info significantly more rapidly and productively. That is something most huge organizations would slaughter for and painfully miss. Here are a couple of ways you can take advantage of the nearer closeness to your clients.

The most effective method to Fully Exploit this Advantage:

- Uncover the entirety of your workers to your clients
- Build up input circles between deals and the remainder of your groups
- Concentrate your client service interactions
- Screen social interactions
- Jump on the telephone with your clients (or even better, meet they face to face)
- Mine your web analytics
- Consolidate data assembling straight into your product
- Make client feedback and information profoundly unmistakable over the association

You Can Turn on a Dime

Deftness and agility aren't two things enormous organizations are known for. Normally, the bigger an association gets, the more reliant it becomes on built-up structures and procedures. There's more bureaucracy to manage, lines of communication become less and less immediate, and to top it all off, there are a greater amount of the greatest efficiency enemies of all — groups. Accordingly, arranging skylines will, in general, be in years instead of days, weeks, or months. On the other hand, you can turn and respond to opportunities in the time it takes them to sort out a phone call.

The most effective method to Fully Exploit this Advantage:

- Pick a product to advertise that is quickly advancing or has dynamic needs or tastes
- Pick a product market that has huge long term advancement potential
- Fabricate your market before huge organizations comprehend what hit them
- Utilize new and creative innovations and plan of model segments
- Quickly advance all parts of your business
- Ensure senior management is getting out in the field however much as could be expected

You Can Develop an Intense Focus on a Target Niche Market

Huge organizations make some troublesome memories with focus. They, for the most part, need to expand their degree to support their development, creating products focused on various client sections utilizing numerous circulations draws near. Even they have more assets, and they need to spread those resources over an assortment of item showcases. Interestingly, you can commit all that you need to build up a laser center around one quite certain objective section. That gives you a ground-breaking advantage. Not exclusively would you be able to build up a rich and inside and out comprehension of your clients — their agony focuses, needs, needs, and purchasing forms (also how they utilize and acknowledge an incentive from your product) — you can likewise get staggeringly clear and compact with your informing.

Instructions to Fully Exploit this Advantage:

- Pursue a niche
- Get everybody in the organization concentrated on that niche
- Strengthen that concentrate each opportunity you get starting from the top
- Keep your groups as little as could reasonably be expected

You Can Go After Smaller Opportunities

Huge organizations need to follow enormous market openings. They regularly can't legitimize following what they see as little markets (especially if those business sectors have unique needs). That leaves a noteworthy number of chances of getting lost in an outright flood that you can jump on. The key for startup business people is to recognize and assault markets/socioeconomics that might be little presently yet are in an upward direction and have the potential for development. While this may paint you into a little corner in the first place, the upside is that you ought to have the option to build up yourself and become moderately undisturbed, after which you can hope to extend.

The most effective method to Fully Exploit this Advantage:

- Search for business sectors that are unreasonably little for huge organizations, or basically off their radar
- Search for client portions with extraordinary needs that aren't by and large completely tended to by enormous organizations
- Pinpoint a little or inert market that different new businesses are just starting to attack

You Can Innovate Much More Quickly and Effectively

Change is something any enormous association with built-up frameworks and procedures inalienably battles with. The equivalent goes for grasping risk. Not exclusively would it be able to be incredibly hard to arrange changes and new activities basically from a calculated perspective, there can likewise frequently be critical protection from it from workers and the executives the same. To finish it off, there's likewise the propensity that Gladwell featured in his keynote at HubSpot's inbound conference. For officeholders, inventive reasoning and critical thinking are frequently limited to making little changes and cycles to existing procedures and structures. They stall out in a "that is how we've constantly done it" attitude.

As a startup, you don't need to be controlled by those kinds of restrictions. In reality, the more imaginative and problematic you can make your business/arrangement, the harder it will be for greater organizations to duplicate, get up to speed, or compete with what you're doing.

Step by step instructions to Fully Exploit this Advantage:

- Be strong and take risks
- Fabricate innovation that contenders would experience issues incorporating with their present stage
- Execute a methodology that would be troublesome for a bigger organization to reproduce
- Enable individual groups and workers to test, repeat, and receive inventive methodologies

You Can Run on Next to Zero Sales and Marketing Costs

Perhaps the ideal way you can fight your Goliath-sized challenge is to make it your main goal to work as a high productivity benefit machine. The fundamental thought is to make all that you do — your item, evaluating, client support, and so forth — so convincing that you can change over your objective clients with next to zero deals and advertising costs on your part. Note: The stunt isn't to remove deals and to showcase, by and large, yet to continue pushing for effectiveness by keeping costs as low as conceivable comparative with the gross benefit created.

The most effective method to Fully Exploit this Advantage:

- Concentrate on UX
- Construct social sharing highlights legitimately into your product
- Make your sign up and buy process as straightforward and erosion free as would be prudent
- Always improve your item and join client input with fast advancement cycles
- Influence free beta and preliminary variants of your product, at that point value it intensely
- Keep deals and showcasing costs as low as could reasonably be expected, and put your assets to the past five things.

Chapter 18. Whom The Lean Method Is Not Made For

After the distribution of The L.S. in 2011, the underlying method immediately spread among entrepreneurs, enterprise instructors, incubators, quickening agents, and enormous organizations. The L.S. (L.S.) method has since gotten one of the foundations of enterprise education in business colleges around the globe.

During their investigations, business students overall are probably going to have gotten guidance in probably a few parts of the L.S. method - it's regularly depicted as an important aptitude to be a director in the 21st century. Rather than the more static nature of business arranging, L.S. is more involved, as business people look to approve the suppositions hidden their plan of action utilizing "live" testing.

At the core of the L.S., techniques are the plan of the falsifiable plan of action hypotheses and their resulting tests with potential clients utilizing a minimum viable product (MVP). Generally, entrepreneurs are informed about structuring an arrangement regarding investigations to test and refine their plan of action through direct cooperation with clients from the start of their endeavors.

Until this point in time, L.S.'s ubiquity has generally been unchallenged by any basic bits of knowledge about potential constraints of the technique. In any case, ongoing academic investigations alarm to significant limitations in three areas.

The L.S. Isn't Free

To start with, Contigiani and Levinthal (2019) point to the potential expenses and risks related to utilizing the L.S. method. A portion of these expenses and risks are industry-specific, while others are increasingly conventional. Testing in the market with an MVP requires some serious energy and resources, which can generally be high in industry parts, for example, biotech.

Rather than IT-related sectors, fixed expenses in biotech are considerable, making back to back cycles of testing the item unfeasible. Moreover, business visionaries need to understand that testing items with clients may include the revelation of significant strategic information. Particularly in businesses where IP security is feeble, the potential dangers of data exposure might be huge. Concerning the last mentioned, making changes to at least one part of the plan of action dependent on the criticism got from clients includes costs. Moreover, these expenses can go past unadulterated money related expenses as more than once changing the plan of action conceivably disintegrates the entrepreneurs' motivation.

Utilizing the L.S. technique may likewise include reputational risks. By definition, the L.S. method expects entrepreneurs to show a beginning period, inadequate product to potential clients. It puts the business people in danger of contrary input that may spread to the more extensive objective market.

A Lot Of Testing Can Kill You

Second, Ladd (2016) finds that more approval isn't better. While enterprising groups that detail and test speculations perform superior to anything those that don't, there seems, by all accounts, to be a reducing and negative connection between the number of approved theories and the group's prosperity. As it were, business visionaries need to realize when to quit utilizing the L.S. method since, at one point, the extra time, consideration, and assets of leading an extra investigation may exceed its latent capacity benefits. Business people need to quit testing, lock the key components of the plan of action, and begin to scale the endeavor.

Preparation Is As Yet Significant

Third, De Cock, Bruneel, and Bobelyn (2019) show that the experience of entrepreneurs has obtained likewise assumes a significant job in the degree to which they can get an incentive from applying the L.S. technique. It isn't the involvement in L.S. strategy that confines its latent capacity benefits, yet rather the degree to which the business visionaries have earlier market information. Business visionaries that need earlier market information are less ready to understand the feedback obtained from testing in the market. Accordingly, earlier market information empowers business visionaries to make significant emphases of the plan of action utilizing the L.S. method.

Bearing on the mind these three focuses, maybe it might, in this manner, be progressively helpful to show the L.S. method as a probability instead of a sweeping arrangement. As set forward by Ladd (2016):

"As is valid for any business procedure, the method must be tailored and utilized with reflection and imperatives, not visually impaired devotion."

Acolytes are quick to shun understood methodology devices, for example, SWOT analysis (investigation of inner Strengths and Weaknesses joined with an assessment of Opportunities and Threats that can be found remotely) and conventional market investigation, at the same time, as a general rule, such instruments are as yet applicable.

L.S. bad-to-the-bone clients ensure that flexibility is vital to finding that item showcase fit. We concur with this, by and large, yet, significantly, the enterprising administrator should be versatile to realize when to utilize L.S. and when to utilize other management tools.

Chapter 19. Managing The Threat of Competition

How do you feel about competition? Are you hoping that there isn't anyone else doing what you do, and therefore you will be able to get the whole market to yourself? Give it a minute and think about it.

Now, as you've been thinking for a while, what is your answer? If your answer is "yes", you are most likely wrong. Not having any competitors usually means that there is no market, or maybe just a small market. There is some market for almost anything that you can think of, right? But you aren't going to build a big company for a small market. And investors aren't going to invest in a startup that is targeting only a small market. Of course, investors usually don't want to see that you are entering a crowded market with a lot of competitors, either. So, what do you need to do?

First, you need to do your homework, identify your competitors and show them to the investors. There is nothing worse than saying that you don't have competitors (or only one or two), and the investor immediately names a couple of them that you didn't find. Once you've identified the competitors, you need to understand and show why you are different, and most importantly, why you are better.

Don't try to reinvent the wheel here. You need to show something that investors are used to seeing, because you want them to understand quickly. There are few ways to do that.

The most common is to show the four quadrants describing two benefits. One on the x axis and another on the y axis. Of course, the top right corner is reserved for your startup and no other is supposed to be anywhere close.

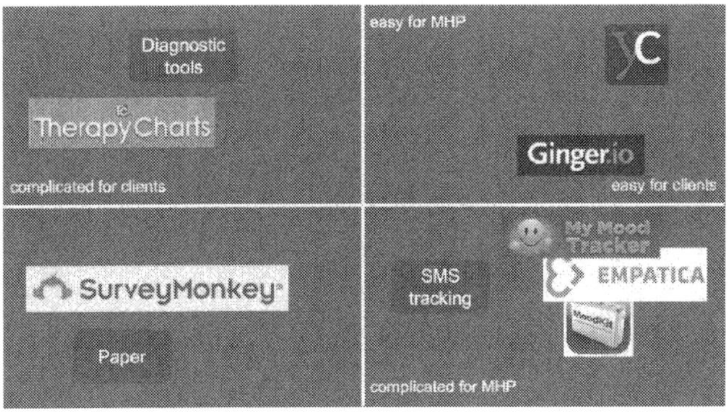

When we were raising the first seed round (we rebranded from Youcognize - or yc - to Mentegram after that), we were pretty confident that our niche wasn't very crowded. As we were growing, we learned that Mentegram overlaps with some other companies we hadn't considered before, as well as some new companies that had emerged in the meantime.

Healthcare is a huge industry, and there may be the cases when it's not easy to differentiate you from your competitors. When we were raising the second seed round, we had to be much more specific with our competitors and be able to show the clear difference. However, the same approach as above would put quite a lot of companies close to Mentegram. That, obviously, leads to a very important question from the investors - "How are you different and better?". You need to have a very clear and sharp answer on that.

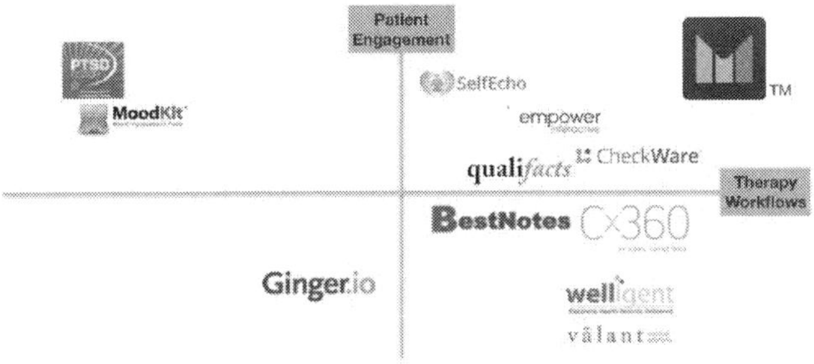

If you can't describe your competitive advantage in a few sentences, how do you expect investors to believe that you have the competitive advantage and are better than the competitors? In such a situation, you may want to consider a bit of a different way to show the competitors, listing them in a table with their benefits and features. Set it up just like you see prices being compared in a table on the websites that sell something. Can you imagine how pricing plans are compared? Think of something like that. However, a few minor features that competitors don't have aren't going to get you an investment. What investors like to say, you need to show that you are 10-times better than the existing competition. Clearly, a few minor

	Mentegram™	qualifacts	empower	SelfEcho
Patient/Consumer App	✓	✓	✓	✓
Clinical App/Dashboard	✓	✓	✓	✓
Custom Questionnaires	✓	-	-	✓
HIPAA Compliant	✓	✓	✓	✓
Software Integration	✓	-	-	-
Treatment Plan Integration	✓	-	-	-

features won't make it.

Another challenge waiting for you on the big market, especially when there are old and existing solutions, as well as young startups that haven't succeeded yet, is that you can find many overlapping products. The table will not be the best solution, either. That was also our case, so we ended up using the third approach. We listened very carefully to investors' questions about our competitors and used those as a hint to differentiate us. In general, there are three types of software that they knew, and they wanted to see how we were different. So, we took those and showed that we combined the best from all of them and that's what was making us unique.

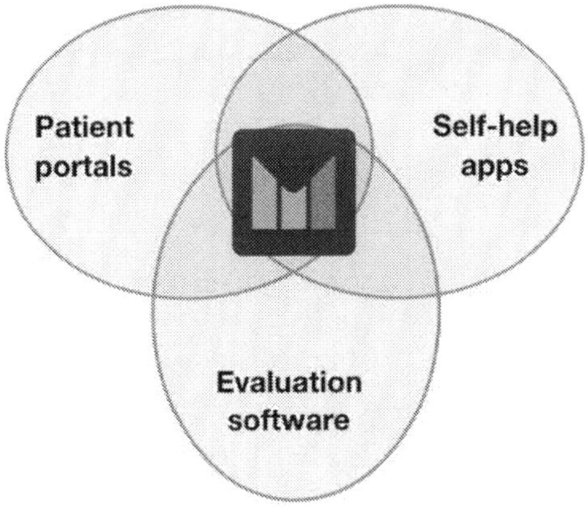

If the market doesn't have clear leaders that everyone knows, it might be better not to list the particular companies/products, but rather to describe the group. You are risking the fact that the one that investors know will be missing there. On the other hand, if there are some strong players, you should definitely show them and be pretty specific about how you are going to be better.

Questions for you

- Who are your competitors?
- Why are you better than your competitors?
- What are the barriers to entry for a new competitor?
- Is any intellectual property required?

Conclusions

The main key for achievement at lean is to know it is actually a journey. There's certainly no "silver bullet" in almost any service or manufacturing industry. When there have been, it will be sold along with every firm might contain it. Lean starts with the best management of this venture. Best management should have the vision to comprehend both requirements and expected outcome, and devote the funds to achieving these. In the event the expected requirements and tools do not fit, any platform such as lean manufacturing will likely neglect. The prerequisites depend on the business. If the business enterprise has 5000 employees spread across 1-5 centers in 20 distinct nations, certain requirements will probably be large. A tiny centre with 100 employees will demand less. Management needs to comprehend that Lean manufacturing is actually a journey. It's something of employed maxims which contributes the organization to a country of "lean". When direction is hoping to reach "head count loss", they have been going for the wrong process. Any head count reduction should happen before applying lean production.

Lean systems demand everybody in the Enterprise to operate faithfully to eliminate all muda (waste) from the computer system. There are just eight common kinds of waste found in lean manufacturing. These wastes are therefore pervasive in associations which everyone else needs to pursue and expel them. People simply aren't likely to work themselves out of work, and so everybody else has to be supportive of their travel.

Lean additionally entails constant advancement through "kaizen". Kaizen in Japanese means "small incremental progress". Kaizens involve employees from all possible purposes to interact to eradicate waste, improve productivity, and enhance the company in every facets. Again, direction should have employees permitted to boost the performance. 1 part flow is just another system employed in lean manufacturing. Hence SMED (single minute exchange of die) approaches to decrease changeover times needs to be employed.

Other lean concepts used include "pull systems", "cell production", "kanban", OEE (overall equipment effectiveness), TPM (total productive maintenance), mistake proofing, real cause removal, and lots of more. Each one these systems need the attempt of a huge mass of employees to become more prosperous. For that reason, employees should not be scared of losing a project or lean manufacturing won't succeed. Once employees believe that they are able to expect direction, the lean journey will begin. The journey begins with lean manufacturing training plus it never ceases.

Lean manufacturing isn't a method which can be managed or employed by some individuals. It could be directed by A couple of individuals, however, the execution will demand everybody else. Every Individual From the company needs to understand the provider is implementing Lean production. Can it be to possess a competitive edge? Can it be to remain in business?

Many company procedures exist in Various forms of organizations from the recovery of garbage into sending the products that are completed towards the waiting customer. Saving time makes everyone else happy by eliminating the requirement to hire workers to fulfill tasks which must not be accomplished. By finding work arounds to your activities which do not have any means to better the creation of goods, each one these goals might be gained. One method is ensuring proper positioning of products whenever they're off loaded. What this means is nothing is setting idle, and distance isn't bought out also it's simpler to obtain what exactly is necessary at time minus needing for those searching for goods as when they're wanted.

Employing technology and machines too helps. This, together with smart programming, lets computers to see when matters aren't moving according to plan. By doing this, no body has to determine where online the error occurred saving the requirement to hunt every part. The opportunity of injuries occurring is lessened when everybody else is given a particular job to maintain . Broadly speaking, these threats are generated when one person isn't fully capable in what they're doing.

Measure Learn loop highlights rate as a crucial element to merchandise development. A team or company's potency is dependent on its capacity to ideate, fast build a minimal workable product of this idea, quantify its own efficacy on the current market, and also study out of this experimentation. To put it differently, it's really a learning practice of turning ideas into products, measuring clients' responses and behaviors contrary to assembled services and products, and deciding whether to persevere or throw the thought; this technique repeats as often as required. The stages of this loop are: Suggestions → Construct → Merchandise → Quantify → Data → Learn.

This rapid iteration makes it possible for teams to detect a viable path towards product/market fit, and also to keep on maximizing and optimizing the company version after attaining product/market fit.

Section 2: Lean Enterprise

The core principle of lean is to minimize waste and maximize customer value. In other words, lean is to provide customers with products and services of greater value while using fewer resources.

Every lean business understands what the customers want and focuses on improving fundamental processes to meet those demands. The goal is to provide the customer with products and services of exceptional value through a process that has minimal or zero waste.

Lean thinking will change the areas that are focused on by management to accomplish this. Instead of focusing on separate technology, vertical departments and assets, the management will focus on how the flow of products and services can be optimized horizontally across assets, technology and departments to its customers.

The management will also need to look at how waste processes can be eliminated along the value stream. It will need to look at how processes can be optimized to reduce human time, human effort, space and capital, which help to reduce the cost incurred to finish the product or service.

Such companies can respond to the changing needs of their customers with high quality, high variety, speed and low cost. Information management will also become more accurate and more straightforward.

Lean Management for Production and Services

Most people believe that lean management works best in manufacturing. This is not true. Lean management can be applied to different businesses and processes and is not a cost reduction program or a tactic. It is a way of acting and thinking for the whole organization.

Businesses in all sectors and industries, including government and healthcare have started to use the lean principle to change the way they work and think. Many organizations choose not to call this type of management lean, but state that it is their system.

You may wonder why organizations do this. It is done to drive home the fact that lean management is not a short or long-term cost reduction program but is the way the company operates.

The term lean transformation is used to define a company that is moving away from old thinking towards a new way or lean way of thinking. This means that the company has started to change the way business is conducted which takes perseverance.

The term lean was coined in the late 1980s by a James Womack, Ph.D., who was leading a research team at an International Motor Vehicle Program at MIT, to describe Toyota's business.

Lean Business Principles

Lean business principles entered the American business market in the early 1990s through the book "Lean Thinking." Lean thinking originated in the manufacturing models in Toyota automotive in the late 1980s after the introduction of Kanban.

Lean models are now used in different industries to reduce time spent on delivering high-quality products and reducing the number of resources used to achieve that goal. Let us take a look at some lean model principles.

Value Identification

It is important to remember that value to a company begins and ends only with the stakeholders or customers. If a customer requires a specific product or service from your company, you must use all the resources you need to deliver the product within the stipulated time. It is essential for every business to identify the products or services that will add value to its customers.

Value Stream Mapping

When a business identifies the products and services that provide value to its customers, it should map every process and procedure that the company must follow to manufacture or produce that product or service. It is during the mapping process that the business can identify the steps that contribute to waste or add no value to the goal. For instance, if the business discovers the process to place orders by employees is complicated, it must either eliminate that process since it is a waste contributor.

Flow

When the business creates the process map, it will identify the steps that are unnecessary or waste contributors. The business must then remove those processes or steps to create a flow. This flow will ensure that there are no obstacles that will hinder the delivery of products or services to customers. For instance, if a gardening service must visit an off-site location to stock up on supplies, it will take a longer time to deliver its services. The business must look at whether it can increase on-site storage space to enhance the flow of the process.

Pull

Lean processes always produce based on the demand from customers, which makes the processes "pull processes." Pull processes are those that call for the production of products and services on an as-wanted or as-needed basis. In service businesses, the delivery is always dependent on the workforce. For example, a pizza delivery service can choose to hire delivery executives based on the demand for pizza. If it is football season, there are bound to be more orders from customers. It is prudent for the business to hire more delivery executives during that period.

Perfection

It is important for a business to continually refine the first four principles to ensure that processes have minimal or no waste in them. The idea behind this principle is that any waste that goes unnoticed in the first four stages is always exposed over time.

It is important to eliminate that waste to help a business adapt to the changing needs of its customers.

Peter Hines has argued that the five principles of lean thinking may be insufficient for some or most contemporary business situations. He stated that businesses need to apply lean thinking only to some processes like order fulfillment without giving any regard to communication, leadership or quality management.

Therefore, it is essential to understand how lean thinking can be applied to help a business develop a holistic approach to the delivery of products and services.

Charter 20
What is Lean Enterprise?

What sets apart the companies that have stood the test of time from those that failed to take off? Well, aside from learning how to polish their branding, they continuously work on improving their human capital and management systems — changing accordingly with the times, and adjusting their strategies as they seem fit.

In contrast, brands that were never heard of again weren't able to plant a firm footing in the industry. It's mainly because each step in their workflow had issues that they weren't able to solve. It most likely didn't occur all at once, though. More often than not, a failed business' downfall started with a seemingly harmless misstep — until the rest of their system followed.

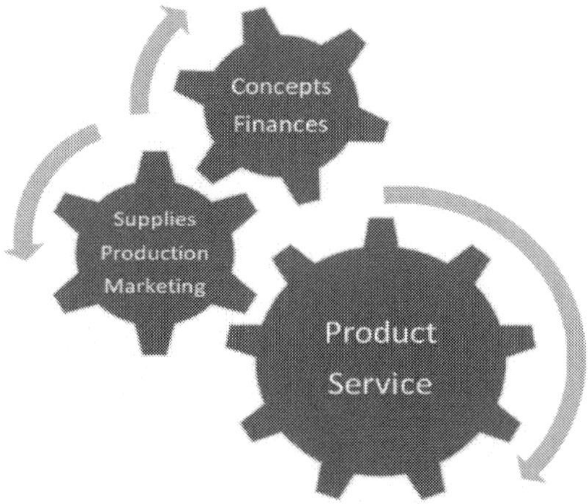

No matter how seemingly good a product or a service may be, it will only remain relevant to the market that it's supposed to serve if the whole work process is meticulously addressed. This is especially necessary during the beginning phases of building a business. The key is to lay down everything such that they will move in sync, so that when one part starts working, the rest will simply go with the right flow

The supposed workflow of any organization can be compared to a group of gears working in unison to move an entire machine. The picture is just an ultra-simplified version of how products and services — or more generally, outputs — are related to all the steps that come before it. So long as the gears are constantly well-oiled and nothing gets caught in them, the machine will move and operate as it should.

However, when faulty components start slowing down the movement of the smaller cogwheels, every part of the process becomes inefficient. Ultimately, the biggest cogwheel will be affected, and no output will be delivered according to the company's set standards — if any had been set at all.

This is why all parts of a process must be constantly assessed and measured. Otherwise, improvement will almost always be impossible, and moving towards the next goals will just remain a pipedream.

Thus, if you don't get your act together within the company, you're bound to offer people a bunch of products that aren't serving any real purpose for them. This may also damage your relationships with investors and suppliers. All it takes is another careless mistake and your reputation will now be forever tainted.

Successful businesses are going to have none of that. They know exactly how to get things done by using the most effective processes that they have applied through the years. Otherwise, they wouldn't be able to keep their gears rolling at the speed they want to. The question is, are they going through their workflow in the most cost-efficient and most resourceful way possible?

Lean Company, Lean Manufacturing, and Lean Enterprise

It's one thing to know how to get the job done. It's another thing to know how to get it done outstandingly. But it's a whole other level to know how to deliver high-quality outputs using the least amount of wastes and resources. Given the complexity of planning and production, it's normal to wonder whether it's possible that simple waste elimination can lead to the best products and services.

This is where the concept of lean thinking comes in. At its core, lean thinking focuses on how to come up with better methods of utilizing financial and human capital. Its ultimate goal is to provide maximum benefits not just to loyal and potential customers, but also to society as a whole.

This system attempts to operate on the idea that if each individual or group in the entire system can identify and eliminate the biggest wastes in their tasks, then all of them — as a whole — will be able to produce more valuable outputs using far less expenses. Not only will this drive an organization to its golden age, but it will also develop its employees' overall competence and confidence in themselves.

Lean thinking is the basis for all efficiency-driven mechanisms that are practiced in companies, manufacturing or productions, and even enterprises. But what does it really mean when every aspect of an organization is "lean"?

The following items illustrate the general idea of how lean enterprises are built:

1. **Building a Lean Company**

This is a company that follows lean thinking methodologies when it comes to production. Each step of the process has been aligned with the rest of the workflow to give way to a smooth and continuous cycle. Goals are typically addressed by creating a team that is composed of experts from various departments (cross-functional team).

2. **Employing Lean Manufacturing**

Also called "lean production", this involves a series of systematic methods for eliminating wastes and hurdles within production processes. It carefully assesses the wastes caused by uneven workloads, evens them out, and minimizes the chances of overburdening staff to improve output value and overall costs. A lean company abides by a number of lean manufacturing principles to enhance the workflow — beginning from the conceptualization phase, distribution, and even beyond.

3. **Establishing a Lean Enterprise**

This can be regarded as the ultimate product of all the offshoots of lean thinking. The lean enterprise is a grand collaboration among a number of companies — all of which are working to perfect a product or service that all of them will benefit from. The caveat, however, is that it can be tough for a lean company to reach its full potential if it's working with companies that aren't following lean methodologies.

Lean Thinking and Lean Behaviors

For lean thinking to make it to the enterprise level, it needs to be perfected on a personal level first. If individuals can make their tasks more efficient, these seemingly minute improvements are bound to translate to enterprise-wide successes.

However, members must also learn how to trade extreme individualism for team effort. It is inevitable that certain members or teams may have legitimate needs that are in conflict with other components of the system. A strong sense of cooperation then becomes necessary, which can only be achieved when all individuals agree to expand their roles in the name of a company or an enterprise's ultimate goal.

Members of cross-functional teams are usually trained to become more well-rounded. For example, full allegiance to their original function (e.g. marketing, financing, engineering, design, production) isn't encouraged in a lean environment. Team-oriented thinking and behaviors are needed to ensure that no phase in the workflow will ever end up being stuck.

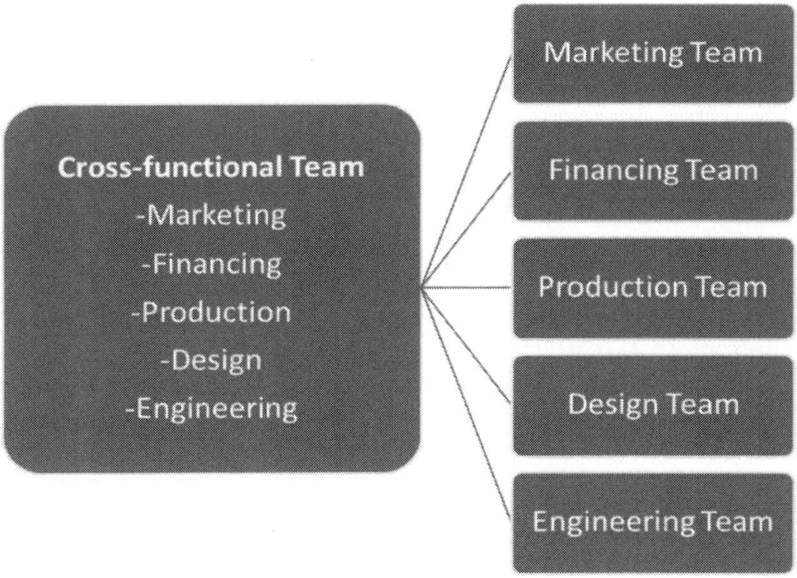

This is why it's necessary for members of cross-functional teams to accept, right from the beginning, that they will need to pursue an offshoot of their original career path to succeed as an employee of a lean company. Instead of performing their original function, they now work together with other experts to establish new value-adding processes or best practices for the roles that people like them play in an organization.

The picture illustrates how the members of a cross-functional team work with each other to develop a grand system that will sync team roles for maximum efficiency. They will look into the various roadblocks that get caught up between tasks performed by different teams. Once they come up with a viable solution, they will then meet with the respective teams so they can start implementing the new and improved system.

Now, when these roles are translated to the lean enterprise, member companies will need to establish new behavioral standards that will help regulate behaviors and activities involved in the enterprise workflow. What's important is that companies focus on what they're really good at to become a reliable member of the enterprise.

Lean as the Key to Productivity

In order for a lean enterprise to succeed, member companies need to refine their existing models to become more adept at doing more tasks using less resources. The problem is, while companies work towards eliminating wastes in their processes, this may cause stress in their employees, who fear that they might eventually be laid off from their jobs due to redundancy. Hence, companies need to explore and exhaust all of their options when it comes to job preservation as they work towards becoming lean.

Becoming a lean company may take years before you notice the fruits of all your efforts. Of course, when you have more wastes to eliminate, you also need more time to straighten out your workflow. This book will give you an overview of what you need to go through, plus the tools that can help you accomplish this huge task.

The lean models of business may be the key to building a company — and eventually an enterprise — that will generate the workflow efficiency that you've always wanted. If you're looking for ways to improve how business is done within your company, gradually shifting to lean thinking will not only help you increase your overall productivity, but also provide your employees with their much-needed career growth.

Chapter 21
What are the Advantages?

Becoming lean as an individual can make a big difference in your tasks as an employee. When you apply its concepts consistently enough, they're bound to affect your life's other aspects positively. Over time, you'll find that you're able to process decisions in a more systematic way. If lean concepts can have such a profound effect on a personal level, you can just imagine the possibilities if you scale the leanness all the way to an enterprise.

Shifting To Lean: What's In It For You?

Lean thinking encourages people to apply doable changes in small increments. The ultimate goal is to speed up all the workflows within a system without compromising product or service quality. Lean is certainly not a quick fix for eliminating company wastes. It involves being in a long-term commitment with continuous growth and improvement.

Even if a particular lean technique has been proven effective by many companies, changes certainly didn't happen within a few months of applying the methods. It usually takes far longer than that for anything significant to be noticeable. Of course, it's also understandable how people may feel discouraged to stick with the new methods if the benefits aren't that obvious. To help you stay lean when you're tempted to think that it doesn't work, here's a list of its short-term to long-term benefits:

Short-term Benefits

- Improved Management: Even though problems will still come up every now and then, lean makes the work environment more convenient to deal with if you're a manager. With better task standards in place, it will be easier for you to pinpoint anything that's disrupting the flow of the value stream. Most of the time, you will be able to figure out that something isn't quite right just by looking at an area's set-up or layout.

- Improved Efficiency and Productivity: As a result of standardizing every piece of the workflow, it becomes automatic for employees to know what exactly they need to do — and when they need to do it. It reduces a lot of redundancy and overlaps that stem from task confusion. It also ensures that they are doing their work correctly every single time. They no longer have to constantly ask whether a particular task is under their responsibility. They can just focus on their own task list without worrying about anything else.
- Safer and More Convenient Layouts: Since literal wastes will be decluttered, turning lean gives your company more space to move around. This will instantly make task movements a lot more convenient. Additionally, it will provide your staff with a safer space for working when the layout is reorganized to eliminate hazards.
- Involvement from the Whole Company: Lean is something that isn't applied only to one team or department. When a company decides to go lean, every level of the hierarchy is involved — from those on the top all the way to the ones on the bottom. After all, lean systems depend on the cooperation of everyone involved.

Medium and Long-term Benefits

- Improved Cash Flow: Once you get rid of DOWNTIME, you can now focus your energy on ensuring that the value-adding steps of your value stream flow as smoothly as possible. In the absence of roadblocks, workflow bottlenecks, and delays, not only will you be able to deliver products in a just-in-time manner, but you'll also improve the cash flow within your company.
- Customer Satisfaction and Loyalty: Customer satisfaction is one of the most immediate results of applying lean, so they become more likely to trust your brand again in the future. If you keep on doing

what works, you're bound to gain their loyalty in the long run.

- Employee Satisfaction and Loyalty: While lean systems are mainly focused on the desires of the customer, it also promotes better mood and morale among employees. The changes may be met with resistance at first, but once they see that it takes them far less time to complete tasks compared to before, they'll become more open to the overall idea of lean. Additionally, since lean is all about constant improvement and collaborations, they tend to feel better about themselves because they're part of a team that actually cares about others. Lean systems give them a safe space to voice out their concerns and provide suggestions for further improvement.
- Marketability for Collaboration: What makes something marketable? In terms of companies, marketable companies are usually unproblematic ones. You need to be that company if you wish to be a part of a lean enterprise. After all, lean is all about efficiency, and you need to be an efficient team player to ensure that you don't disrupt the flow of the entire system.
- Lean is not merely an exercise in cost-cutting. It is more of a long-term opportunity for consistent growth. Once you have smoothed out your lean processes within the company, you will eventually become the preferred suppliers of particular products and services.
- That's because your consistency and standards translate well to your products — something that lets both customers and collaborators know that you're a company that they can trust.

Challenges?

Lean thinking all sounds good in theory, and it can be exciting to continue applying it once you've seen how great it can be in practice. However, as Figure 8 shows, the tasks between teams or entities cannot always be as conveniently executed as getting from Point A to Point B in a clean, straight line. Their involvement with each other goes back and forth, which emphasizes how every component must be free of wastes to ensure a smooth flow.

Of course, shifting to lean has its own set of issues and challenges. Like any other form of change, you should resist hoping that it would do its "magic" in just a few weeks or months.

Technically speaking, when every factor is ironed out right from the beginning, it can be possible to have everything sorted out in just a short time. But that only applies when the scenario is ideal. Experience will tell you that situations are rarely ever ideal, especially when transitions are concerned.

Here are some issues that you might have to deal with on your way to lean:

Cultural Resistance

This may be the biggest hurdle that you have to get through when transitioning from wasteful to lean. When a status quo has already been set, most people are resistant to any change in the company culture. That's usually a result of staying in their comfort zones for long enough. They feel that change is unnecessary since they already like the current workflow.

To gradually ease the workforce into the lean system, training (or retraining) people must be prioritized. Here's what you need to clarify with them:

- What are the changes that you'll be implementing?
- Why are you implementing them?
- How are they going to benefit from these changes?
- How will it benefit the whole company?

Although all four of these are important considerations, they're likely going to be most concerned about the third point, as this involves their role in the company. However, if you can clearly explain the good things about these changes, then people will be more inclined to accept it.

Costs and Upkeep

On a personal level, there are cases in which you'll need to spend money today to be able to profit or save more money in the future.

Going lean requires the same thing. Eliminating wastes will need money because going for the long-term fix requires money. Eventually, however, the money you spent will eventually go back to you in the form of increased profits from minimized defects.

And, just like your home needs yearly maintenance, lean also requires upkeep. Proper planning and execution will ensure that you won't have to worry about running out of certain parts or having outdated systems.

Talent Gaps

Since lean processes may now require updated technologies, companies that are going lean must bridge the talent gap. This means that they may have to let go of general-labor employees in favor of those who have licenses and certifications to operate lean system equipment. These employees are adept not only at handling these systems, but they are also capable of performing maintenance, inspections, repairs, and designs.

Lean principles were first discussed by a MIT student named John Krafcik in his master's thesis. Before joining MIT, Krafcik had already spent time as an engineer at both Toyota and GM, and he used what he had learned from the Japanese manufacturing sector to set a set of standards that he believed companies of all sizes to be more efficient could work.

The basic idea is that, regardless of the type of business in which a business operates, it is still only a group of interconnected processes. These interconnected processes can be categorized such as primary processes and secondary processes. The primary processes are processes that directly create value for the company. In the meantime, secondary processes are needed to ensure that the primary processes run smoothly. Regardless of the type of process you are viewing, you will find that they are all made up of a number of steps that can be performed in a way that ensures that they work as effectively as possible and that they must be viewed as a whole in order to be effective complete the analysis.

As a whole, you can consider the Lean process as a group of useful tools that can be used to identify waste in the current paradigm, either for the company as a whole or for its upcoming projects. Specific attention is also paid to reducing costs and, where possible, improving production. This can be achieved by identifying individual steps and then considering how to complete them more effectively. Some tools that are often used in the process are:

- 5s value flow allocation
- Error resistant
- Elimination of time batching
- Restructuring of working cells
- Control cards
- Rank clustering
- Multi-process handling
- Total productive maintenance
- Mixed model processing
- Planning of one point
- Exchange of a minute of dice or smed
- Pulling systems

In addition to these tools, Lean also consists of a number of principles that are loosely linked around the dual ideas of eliminating waste and reducing costs as much as possible. Among which:

- Flexibility
- Automation
- Visual control
- Production flow
- Continuous improvement
- Load distribution
- Waste minimization
- Reliable quality and pull processing

- Build relationships with suppliers

If used correctly, these principles will ultimately lead to a dramatic increase in profitability. Whenever the opportunity is offered, the Lean process strives to ensure that the required items reach the required space within the required period. More importantly, it also works to ensure that the ideal amount of items are moved as needed to achieve a stable workflow that can be changed as needed without creating excess waste.

This is usually achieved through the tools mentioned above, but still requires extreme buy-in at all levels of your organization if you ever hope it will be effective in both the short and the long term. Ultimately, the Lean system will only be as strong as the tools that your company uses to implement it, and these tools will only be effective in situations where its values are expressed and understood.

Important principles

Although it was originally developed with a focus on production and production, Lean proved to be so effective that it has since been adapted for use in almost any type of business. Before taking over the Lean process, companies have only two primary tenants. The first focuses on the importance of incremental improvement, while the other is respecting both external and internal people.

Incremental improvement: the idea behind the importance of continuous improvement is based on three principles. The first is known as the Genchi Genbutsu and is discussed in detail below. Finally, to be truly effective, it is important to understand that you must lead your business with a clear understanding of the challenges that you are likely to face, as it is the only way to determine how you can effectively can handle.

In addition, it is important to approach every challenge with the right mindset, an approach that supports the idea that each challenge leads to growth, which in turn leads to positive progress. Finally, you also want to ensure that you take the time to regularly challenge your prejudices because you never know when your company could work with an assumption that is no longer true. This is ultimately the best way to find unexpected waste that will really start to improve, not only in the short term, but also in the long term.

Respect for people: this tenant is both internal and external, because it applies to both your own people and your customers. Respecting customers means taking an extra step when it comes to considering their problems and listening to what they have to say. When it comes to respecting your team, a strong internal culture that is committed to the idea of teamwork is a must. This should further express itself in an implicit commitment to improve the team as a means to improve the company as a whole.

Get a head start

Prior to the digital age, companies were able to determine their sales margin by starting with all relevant costs, adding a reasonable profit margin and calling it a day. Unfortunately, the prevalence of screens in today's society means that everyone is a bargain shop, simply because it takes so little effort. This in turn means that you are not only competing with other companies in your city, province or state, you are now also competing with companies around the world. As such, there are only a few options when it comes to overcoming any profit margin. Companies can add extra real or perceived value, or they can reduce the amount of waste they pay as much as possible.

Most companies think it is better to determine their margins by looking at what customers are likely to be willing to pay for specific goods or services and then working backwards. Ideally, you can lower that price by five percent to ensure that you are truly competitive in a cost-conscious world. Although it may not seem like much, this extra five percent is extremely important because customers are constantly looking for the next sale, regardless of how much is actually saved. The mental benefits that together with five percent are better than those around them will be more than enough to remain committed to your product or service.

Add value: no matter what your company does, you will find that there are Lean principles that can be implemented to improve the total amount of value that you offer your customers, while also showing that you value their company and them as individuals respects. In addition, you will be able to address the potential for wastage in your organization, while also maintaining the power and work to achieve perfection. Often you can manage this by doing something simple, such as listening to the specific wishes and needs of your customers, making it easier for you to determine what they really value most when it comes to the niche of your business habits. Value is usually generated by adding something tangible that improves or alters the most common aspects of the good or service being offered. The goal is that this improvement is something the customer wants to pay for, so if they receive it for free, they see this as a viable reason for your service to cost more out of the door. It is also very important that the added value for the customer is very easy to claim, because otherwise they will feel that you have misled them. Cost saving: since the Lean system is already quite large in reducing waste in all its forms, it is no surprise that it has some ideas when it comes to cost-saving measures. To begin with, it is important to understand that when it comes to Lean, all different types of waste can be divided into three types.

Muri is the name for the waste that arises when there is too much variation within common processes. Muda is the name given to seven different types of waste, including:

- Transport waste is created when parts, materials, or information for a specific task are not available because the process for allocating resources for active products is not where it should be.
- Waiting waste occurs when a part of the production chain has the ideal time when they are not actively working on a task.
- Waste overproduction is common when demand exceeds supply, and there is no plan to use this

situation to the advantage of the company. The Lean systems are designed to ensure that this number reaches zero, so that supply and demand are always in balance.

- Defective waste is known to occur when part of the standard business process generates a problem that must be sorted at a certain point later.
- It is known that inventory waste appears if the production chain remains inactive between runs because it does not have the physical materials required to run constantly.
- Motion wastage is generated when required parts, materials, or information must be successfully moved to complete a specific step in the process.
- Additional processing wastage is generated when work is completed that does not generate value or adds value to the company.
- An often added eighth muda is the waste that is caused by the under-utilization of your team. This can happen when a member of the team is placed in a position that does not fully use them. It can also refer to the waste that occurs when team members have to perform tasks for which they have not been properly trained.

Muda also comes in three categories, the first being muda that does not directly add value, but also cannot be easily removed if the system continues to function properly. When faced with this muda, the goal must be to minimize it slowly as a precursor to remove it completely. The second type of muda is that which has no real value, and you should work to remove it immediately once you become aware of it. Finally, the third type of muda does not directly add value, but it is required for legal purposes of one or the other type. Although it can be annoying, this type of muda is inevitable in most cases, and the best thing to do is make sure you are always aware of relevant policies.

Chapter 22
Why Lean Matters

As a whole, you are able to think about this process of Lean as a group of tools that are useful and can be called up in order to identify if there is any waste in the current system, either for the business overall or for an upcoming project. Lean is all about reducing waste. There are some businesses that will take a look at the Lean process because they want to fix the waste and issues within the whole business. They may see that they have too much time between processes, they see that there are a lot of customer complaints, or they run into other issues along the way. Other businesses may just want to work with just fixing and reducing the waste in just one process within them.

With Lean, there is going to be more focus given to reducing costs, while also improving how the production goes any time that is possible. This can be accomplished by identifying the small steps that are needed and then considering the ways that they can be completed in a manner that is more effective. There are a lot of different steps that will show up in the Lean methodology, and we will talk about some of them. Some that you may want to utilize with Lean includes:

- Pull systems
- Single minute exchange of die, or the SMED.
- Single point of scheduling
- Mixed model processing
- Total productive maintenance
- Multi-process handling
- Rank order clustering
- Control charts
- A restructuring process with the working cells
- The elimination of a process called time batching
- Error proofing
- 5S value stream mapping.

Beyond the tools above, Lean is going to be made up of a few principles that are all loosely connected thanks to the idea of reduction of costs and eliminating wastes as much as possible. These would include load leveling, continuous improvement, production flow, visual control, automation, flexibility, waste minimization, building up good relationships with the suppliers, pull processing, reliable quality and more.

If these principles are used in the proper manner, it will result in a small increase in the amount of profitability. If it is used in the proper way and it is given the opportunity, this kind of process is going to strive in order to ensure that all necessary items get the space they need and at the right periods of time. Most importantly, it is going to work to make sure that the ideal amount of items will move as needed so that your workflow remains stable while still allowing for any alterations that are needed without all the waste.

The Lean method is one that many different businesses are going to try to implement into them. They want to be able to meet a bunch of different goals, and Lean can help them to get there. First, they want to make sure that they are able to provide a high-quality product to their customers. In order to retain these customers, reduce customer complaints, and other things that can waste time and resources in order to solve any problems.

Along with this, the company wants to figure out how to reduce any waste, reduce their costs, and earn more profits in the long run. Many times the waste that the company is able to get rid of with the Lean process will result in the customer receiving more value as well. It may take some time, and you may need to work through the process of Lean for a while, but when Lean is done properly, it can help your business out with all of those issues and can help it to grow more than ever before.

Important Principles to Remember

While the Lean process was originally developed to help with the industry of manufacturing and production, Lean has been so effective that many other businesses and industries have found ways to adapt it to their own needs. Every business wants to increase profits, reduce waste, enhance the customer experience, and just become overall more efficient. The Lean Process can work to make this happen.

Before you adopt any of the Lean processes, you must understand the two primary tenants. The first one is to focus on the importance of incremental improvement. The second is that the company needs to have a high level of respect for people, both those who purchase the product, and for their own employees.

With regard to the businesses' focus on its incremental improvements, the improvements do not have to be done overnight. However, the business needs to strive in order to steadily and effectively improve their processes so that there is less waste present. You must take a good look at the processes that you currently use and see where things can be improved. Is there to much waiting time in one area? Are the suppliers not getting things in on time? Is there a lot of movement for one part, such as a paper needing approval from three different areas before starting? Are some of the departments that should be working together on different sides of the business?

All of these can lead to more waste in your business, and it is important to avoid them as much as possible. When you take a step back and look objectively at the system you have in place, you are likely to see several spots where you are able to make improvements. Even if these are small, or incremental changes, you will be amazed at what they can do to eliminate waste, speed up your process, and even help customers enjoy a better experience.

But when working on the Lean methodology, we can't forget that there needs to be a high level of respect for people. This tenant is meant to be applied not only to your customers but also to your own people, the employees. When we show respect to the customers, it means that we go the extra mile any time there is a problem. We listen to them and then work to make the experience better. We help to fix the problem, and maybe even throw in something extra to help it get solved.

This same idea needs to be applied to your employees when you are working in the Lean process. When a company wants to respect their team, they will work on creating a strong internal culture that is dedicated to teamwork and treating the employees fairly. Employees will learn that they are valued, and that their opinion means something and that they aren't just another number that brings in the money. Any business that wants to implement the Lean process will need to improve employee morale, teamwork and more because they realize that by improving the team, they are able to effectively improve the company as well.

Getting an Edge

Before the digital age we live in now, businesses were able to determine what margin they had with sales by starting with all of the costs that were relevant, and then adding on a reasonable amount for the profit margin, and call it a day. However, the prevalence of screens in our day, either on the phone or a computer screen, means that everyone is a bargain shopper and can look around to find the best deal.

What this means is that companies are not only competing against the other similar companies in their area but also with those that are all around the world. Since customers can get online, they can compare and then pick out products to be sent to them for better prices, the competition for many smaller companies is steep. As a result, there are only going to be a few options available for a company when it comes to squeaking by with any profit margin at all. Most companies need to either find a way to add perceived or real value to the product, or they can reduce how much waste is in the process to make and distribute that process, and then save money as well.

Many times a business is going to find that it is better to figure out their margins by looking at what the customers are most likely to pay for the goods and services, and then work their way back from there. Ideally, you would like to be able to reduce that first price by at least five percent to make you more competitive, while still providing good customer service. It may not be a huge amount, but in a world where the customer is always looking for a discount, it can be a difference.

No matter what your business does or produces, you will find that there are several principles of Lean that you are able to implement. This can help you to improve how much value you can provide to your customers, and in the process, you can still show them that you appreciate the business that they send your way and that you respect them as individuals. This may seem like a lot of things to bring together, but the Lean methodology makes it happen.

Often, you will be able to manage this simply by listening to your customers and figuring out their specific wants and needs. Value is often going to be generated when you are able to add in something tangible, something that can either modify or improve the most common aspects of the service or the good being provided. The goal is that this improvement must be something that the customer will actually pay for, so when they get that benefit for free, they see it as a viable reason for your service to cost more in the beginning.

You will find that it is also important that the added value is as easy for the customer to claim as possible. Otherwise, they are going to feel like you have deceived them along the way. By making the added value something easy to see, easy to show off, and something of value can make a big difference.

The next thing we need to focus on is cost reduction. Every business wants to reduce costs as much as possible. This allows them to stay competitive in the market, helps them to provide a better price point for their products, and can help them make more money.

To help your company reduce the cost, you need to focus on reducing the amount of waste that you have. There are three types of wastes - Muri, which is waste that is going to come when there is too much variation in your most-used processes. Muda, the name given to the seven types of waste, and Mura, which is any waste that happens due to fluctuations in demand.

Muda is often the one that is the easiest to control and eliminate out of all of them, and the seven wastes that are included in it include:

Transportation waste: This is going to form when information, materials, and parts for a task aren't available because the processes for allocating these resources aren't working the way that they should.

Waiting waste can be created when there is some part of the production chain that has time periods where they aren't working on a task. This could happen because they don't have the right parts or they are waiting for another group to finish first.

Overproduction waste can occur when the demand is exceeding the supply, and the business doesn't have a good plan in place to help deal with this. The Lean system is designed to make sure that this ends up at zero to help the supply and demand for a product to be in balance.

Defective waste is another part to watch out for. This type of waste is going to appear when a part of your operating process starts to generate some issues that must be sorted out later on, often when the product is in the hands of the customer.

Inventory waste is often going to appear if the production chain ends up being idle in between runs. This can happen because that part of the chain doesn't have all of the physical materials that are needed to run all the time. Movement waste can occur when information, materials, and parts must be moved around in order to complete that part of the process. Additional processing waste can be generated if the work completed doesn't end up adding any kind of value for the company. Sometimes there is an eight form of waste that needs to be considered. This is any waste that occurs because of the underutilization of the team. This can occur anytime that a member of the team is placed into a position that doesn't let them use their full potential. It could also refer to any waste that occurs when members of your team are working on tasks that they have not been trained to do.

Chapter 23
Creating A Lean System

Lean leadership

With so much emphasis placed on improving efficiency, the Lean process naturally puts a lot of emphasis on team leaders who should be working hard to directly inspire their teams to adopt the Lean mindset. In the end, many Lean systems live and die by the leadership involved, which means it is important that those who are put in charge of leading the Lean transition are able to not only explain what's going on but are truly committed to the work that is being done as well. Some of the things that Lean leaders should strive to emphasize include:

Customer retention: When it comes to customer retention, Lean leaders need to take the time to consider not only what their customers want at the moment, but what they are likely to want in the future as well. Additionally, it is important to understand what a customer will accept, what they will enjoy, and what they will stop at nothing to obtain. The Lean leader should also work to truly understand the many ways the specific wants and needs of their target audience throughout the customer base.

Team improvement: In order to help their team members be their best, Lean leaders should always be available to help the team throughout the problem-solving process. At the same time, they are going to need to show restraint and refrain from going so far as to take control and just do things on their own. Their role in the process should be to focus on locating the required resources that allow the team to solve their own problems. Open-ended questions are a big part of this process as they will make it possible for the team to seek out a much wider variety of solutions.

Incremental improvement: One of the major duties of the Lean leader is to constantly evaluate different aspects of the team in order to ensure that it is operating at peak efficiency. The leader will also need to keep up to date on customer requirements, as this is something that is going to be constantly changing as well. Doing so is one of the only truly reliable ways of staying ahead of the curve by making it possible to streamline the overall direction of the company towards the processes that will achieve the best results.

In order to ensure that this is the case, the Lean leader will want to make time in their schedule to look at the results and then compare them to the costs as a means of discovering the best ways to use all the resources available to them at the given time. This will include things like evaluating the organization as a whole in hopes of making it more efficient and reliable. It will also involve evaluating the value stream to ensure that it satisfies the customer on both the macro and micro levels.

Focus on sustained improvement: It is also the task of the Lean leader to ensure that improvements that are undertaken are seen through to the end as well. This will often include teaching the team members the correct Lean behaviors to use in a given situation and also approaching instances of failure as opportunities for improvement and innovation.

Three actuals

Lean leaders typically use a different leadership style than many of their peers, largely because being a Lean leader requires an understanding that the best way to analyze a situation is to physically be in the space where the situation occurred. Once there, the Lean leader needs to consider what is known as the three actuals, the broadest of which is known as Genchi and is the issue that led the leader to come to the place in question. Genbutsu is the idea that it is important to view what is being created or provided in action before making any moves. Finally, Genjitsu says it is always best to gather as much information as possible before making a decision one way or the other.

Creating a Lean system

In order to create a Lean system that lasts, the first thing you will need to do is consider the absolute simplest means of getting your product or service out to the public and put that system into effect. From there, you will need to continuously monitor the processes you have put in place to support your business in order to ensure that improvement breakthroughs happen from time to time. The last step is to then implement any improvements as you come across. While there are plenty of theories and tools that can help you do go on from there, the fact of the matter is that creating a Lean system really is that simple.

There's more to business than profits: When using the Lean system, the end goal is to determine the many ways that it might be possible to improve the efficiency of your business. While an increase in profits is often a natural result of this process, this should not be the primary motivating factor behind undertaking a Lean transformation. Instead, it is important to focus on streamlining as much as possible, regardless of what the upfront cost is going to be since you can confidentially expect every dollar you spend to come back to you in savings.

There are limits to this, of course, and at a certain point, the gains won't be worth the costs. To determine where this line is, you can use a simple value curve to determine how the changes will likely affect your bottom line. A value curve is often used to compare various products or services based on many relevant factors as well as the data on hand at the moment. In this instance, creating one to show the difference between a pre- and post-Lean state should make such decisions far easier to make.

Treat tools as what they are: When many new companies switch to a Lean style of doing things, they find it easy to slip into the trap of taking tools to the extreme, to the point that they follow them with near-religious fervor. It is important to keep in mind that the Lean principles are ultimately just guidelines and any Lean tools you use are just that, tools which are there to help your company work more effectively. This means that if they need to be tweaked to better serve your team and your customers, then there is nothing stopping you from doing just that. Your team should understand from the very beginning the limits and purpose of the Lean tools they are being provided and, most importantly, understand that they are not laws.

Prepare to follow through: Even if you bring in a trained professional to help your team over the initial Lean learning curve, it will still ultimately fall to you, as the team leader, to ensure that the learned practices don't fall by the wayside as time goes on. It takes time to take new ways of doing things and turn them into habits, and it will be your job to keep everyone on until everything clicks and they start operating via the new system without thinking about it. Likewise, it is important that you make it clear just why the Lean process is good for the team as a whole and for the individual team member as if they are personally invested in it, then it is far more likely that they will stick with it, even if the going gets tough.

Chapter 24
The 5 Principles of Lean Manufacturing

Many businesses are beginning to switch to lean thinking and lean manufacturing to develop the kinds of products that have a good chance of penetrating the global market. Aside from consistently meeting customer demands, it also enables them to earn more profits and enhance product quality with less cost.

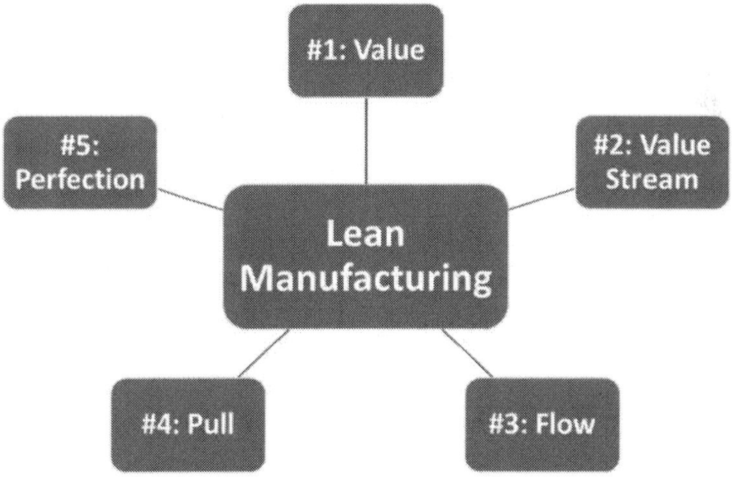

Lean thinking gave way to the five lean manufacturing principles that have greatly improved the workflow of many successful companies today. These are often considered as key factors in improving overall efficiency in the workplace.

Defining Value

The first step of lean manufacturing begins with learning what exactly the customer values in a particular product or service. This will help a business determine how much a customer is willing to pay for what, which then allows them to set a reasonable target price.

After which, the cost of manufacturing the product will then be defined.

To properly establish value in a lean system, it is vital to learn about the market's recognized and latent needs.

While some customers may already know what they want exactly, others may not be aware that there might be a product or service out there that they actually want or need. Or perhaps, they know they need a particular something, but cannot express what it's supposed to be.

That's where market research comes in. This is typically done through interviews, demographic assessment, web analytics, user testing, surveys, etc.

By defining what your customers really want, you get to create something of great value — not just a product that seems innovative in theory. This also helps you understand your customers' purchasing power, as well as the way in which they want this product to be delivered to them.

Determining and Planning the Value Stream

The value stream consists of all the activities that allow you to conceptualize and create the most useful yet most profitable product that matches the customer values that have been defined in the first step.

This is the product's journey from the raw materials stage all the way to the customer usage stage. The stream even includes the customer's eventual disposal of the product, which paves the way for considerable upgrades in the next release.

Naturally, activities that do not provide value at the end of the value stream (customer) are regarded as wastes. These wastes can be subdivided into two types: necessary waste (e.g. quality control) and pure waste (e.g. supplier delays).

The latter should be completely eliminated, while the former should be continuously perfected so they don't get in the way of the value stream. Otherwise, they'd only delay the rest of the process.

Creating Flow

A river will always make its way to the ocean eventually, provided that nothing stops the water in its tracks. However, a significant amount of debris in one part of the river system may cause the water to be trapped and unable to follow its natural path.

This is exactly what waste does in a value stream. It interrupts the natural flow of the production process, causing delays that might start out small. Eventually, however, it might end up becoming a massive setback that prevents everything from moving further forward.

That said, a company must take their time to fully understand their flow systems to eliminate wastes effectively and completely. The concept of flow in lean manufacturing is all about creating a series of steps that are in sync with each other — one that hardly ever gets interrupted.

Setting Pull

One of the most significant wastes involved in manufacturing is inventory. To solve this, a pull-based system must be established. This system aims to minimize inventories and works in progress as much as possible. Relevant materials should always be available to maintain the company's flow.

Instead of creating products way ahead of schedule based only on market forecasts, a pull-based system encourages you to begin working on something only when a customer expresses the need for it. Thus, you'll only begin production at the moment of need, and only in the quantities requested.

This allows you to develop the most efficient way to assemble a product, as you need to deliver your promise within a reasonable timeframe.

Pursuing Perfection

The first four principles of lean manufacturing are all about identifying and reducing wastes as much as possible. This last principle is the crucial point that holds all lean thinking concepts together. Perfection based on company standards helps deliver products in the best state possible to the end user.

Although a perfect product can never technically exist, pursuing perfection is what inspires companies to continue serving their customers to the best of their abilities.

This is what ultimately sets them apart from the competition. After all, if small mistakes can be removed from the value stream every single day, there will come a time when errors will be close to non-existent.

The shift towards lean thinking may not exactly be an easy task, especially if you've just realized that you have major roadblocks in all the steps of your value stream. But when you've identified what exactly your problem areas are, you've already taken the first step in creating a more efficient business. Applying the principles of lean thinking and lean manufacturing gives you a more competitive edge, simply because you've addressed all of your wastes.

Chapter 25
The Types of Waste

Manufacturing wastes come in various forms. We already know in theory that the lean manufacturing framework is all about keeping your value stream and final products aligned by minimizing wastes. But what are wastes, exactly? How do they play out in the real world?

Defects

A defect refers to any mistake that needs additional effort, money, resources, or time to rectify. In non-lean productions, defects typically halt the flow of the value stream because of a component that needs to be completely remade. The truth is, all wastes can never be fully eliminated. However, if you can work on eliminating defects, the rest of the lean wastes will follow suit. This can usually be accomplished by standardizing all aspects of the production process and applying stricter quality controls at every point of the value stream.

Overproduction

This is often the result of not following the pull-based or JIT-jidoka systems. As we have learned, lean systems try to minimize wastes by producing and assembling parts only when they are needed. Overproduction can get the value stream stuck when the flow ends up in a bottleneck. This is generally caused by:

- Just-in-case production as opposed to just-in-time production
- Producing based on uninformed forecasts
- Changes in product design and engineering
- Long production and assembly times
- Unassessed customer needs
- Ineffective automation processes

To solve issues with overproduction, it's important to focus on what the customer really cares about and then develop the most straightforward value stream. This ensures that none of the company's efforts will ever be put to waste.

Waiting

This happens when there's been a hold-up somewhere in the value stream. For instance, everything may have to be stopped because of machine breakdowns, lack of complete supplies, lack of approval from higher-ups, or overwhelmed staff. All of these may happen due to:

- Insufficient or unreliable staff (and managers)
- Staff absences
- Uneven workloads
- Unexpected downtimes
- Poor communication and processing

Just like overproduction, this waste is typically due to process bottlenecks. One way of solving this is by having enough staff so that the workload is evenly distributed at these points. Although you may think that having a smaller staff can help you save money from salaries, it may actually incur even more expenses. This is because waiting and delays cost more money than simply paying a few more people to do the job well.

Non-utilized Talent

This wasn't part of the TPS' original list of lean wastes, but this has become quite a common occurrence in many modern businesses. This happens when a company fails to utilize its staff in the best way possible. This is often seen through:

- Poor communication among departments
- Poor management
- Insufficient staff training
- Lack of cooperation
- Inefficient workflow at the admin level
- Mismatch between an employee's skills and their given tasks

Improper utilization of staff's skills and talents may not seem like a big deal, but its bad effects over the long-term are usually made apparent when the whole company fails to reach its goals within their scheduled timeframes. It's also one of the main reasons why there is a resounding lack of employee engagement within a company. On the other hand, businesses usually thrive once they begin to give employees the recognition that they deserve.

Transportation

This doesn't only refer to actual transportation by a vehicle from one place to the next. Transportation is a general term that covers any process that involves getting something from Point A to Point B — even if the task is purely digital in nature. For instance, sending memos via e-mail can already be considered as "transport". Oftentimes, transportation wastes are results of:

- Wasteful steps in the value stream
- Workflow that is out of sync
- Poorly-designed processes and systems
- Bad office layouts and/or poor planning of office locations

The longer it takes for a product to get where it's supposed to, the higher the transportation costs will be. Not only does this waste time, but it also makes the product more prone to deterioration and damage. Transportation wastes can be eliminated by simplifying workflows, improving layouts, or simply shortening the physical distances between steps.

Inventory

More often than not, inventories are necessities for a business — especially for one that is highly in demand. Production lines will need raw materials and manufactured parts that are value-adding to the final product. The retrieval processes for these materials need to be well-documented in order to spot any errors more conveniently. Additionally, having enough stock will allow you to be more adaptable when it comes to following through with the customer's needs.

The thing is, inventory can sometimes be the source of problems in lean systems. This is usually illustrated using the ship metaphor. However, what you don't know is that there are problems lurking beneath the surface — as represented by the rocks. Just because you're able to move, as usual, it doesn't mean that problems aren't there. In fact, it may only take a slight shift in water level before your ship finally hits one of those rocks. Examples of issues that are hidden by inventory are:

- Poor documentation and management
- Incompetent monitoring systems
- Unclear communication
- Lack of foresight
- Defective deliveries
- Unreliable suppliers
- Inconsistent manufacturing speeds
- Untrained or mismatched staff

Still going by the metaphor, this means that you need to dive deep into your inventories to figure out whether rocks are just waiting for their turn to bust through your ship. Once these issues have been detected, you must do whatever it takes to eliminate those rocks so you can steer your ship in any direction — without worrying about the water level.

Motion

Wastes relating to motion are quite similar to transportation wastes. This involves non-value adding steps that are covered by machines or employees. In contrast with transportation wastes, motion wastes are found in any unnecessary movement within the value stream. Generally, motion is affected by:

- Bad workstation or shop layouts
- Badly designed processes
- Bottleneck in workstations caused by shared tools
- Poor staff training

Eliminating motion wastes can be as simple as making the movement between workstations more convenient. More often than not, the reason why people aren't driven to do what they have to do is that the layout and circumstances make doing the task utterly inconvenient and difficult.

Excess Processing

While lean systems are all about providing quality, sometimes even quality controls can be over the top. Customers will only need a few key things, and constantly checking for something that goes beyond that only adds to waste. That's because you're investing time and resources in certain things when the customers have zero interest in what you're trying to offer.

Chapter 26
What Are the 5S's and How They Work

The next topic that we need to look at is known as the 5s's. When it comes to determining what processes your company has that are considered wasteful, it is important to ensure that the work environment is in optimum shape for the best results. The 5S organizational methodology is one commonly used system based around a number of Japanese words that, when they are taken together, are the first rate when it comes to improving efficiency and effectiveness by clearly identifying and storing items in the right space each time.Now, the goal that comes with this kind of system is to allow for more standardization in your company across more than one process. When you are able to do this, you will notice that there is a significant amount of savings that show up in the long term. The reason that this method can be so effective is that when you have the human eye work to track across a messy workspace, it can take a bit of time, even if that time period is short, for the person to locate what they want and then process everything that is in the room. While this amount of time may seem small at a glance, if it happens constantly, and the whole team is doing it, then it results in a ton of time that is lost, and finding ways to reduce this and keep your employees at the job can help save you time and money in the process.So, how do we work with the 5S organizational method? There are five parts that come with this and they include:

Sorting

The first part of this method is going to be sorting. Sorting is all about doing what you can in order to make sure that the workspace is as clean as possible, and that nothing that isn't required to complete the work is kept out. When sorting, you need to make sure that the space is organized in such a manner where you can remove anything and everything that could potentially create an obstacle when it comes to your team completing the task that they need to do. You will want to ensure that the items that are critical to the process have their own unique space, one that is labeled and easy for everyone on the team to find. You don't want to make your workspace a mess. If things get easily lost, if there are items there that aren't necessary to the production phase, and if you run into issues with items always being somewhere else, even in other parts of the building, then this can slow things down. Taking some time to organize things and putting them in the locations that are the most convenient to find later on can make a big difference in how well you will be able to find them, and how well the team can get the work done.After you organize the area, it becomes so much easier to keep the space free of any new distraction. Your leader should encourage the team members to prune their personal workspace on a regular basis to ensure that no new obstacles, and extra stuff, end up getting in the way.

Set in Order

When you are trying to organize the items in your workplace, it is important to ensure that all of the items are organized in the manner in which they are going to be used the most. While doing so, it is so important that you and your team take care to make sure that all of the items and tools that you need for the most common steps are nearby and easy to get. Your goal here is to reduce the amount of movement waste for getting items as much as possible.You will find that over time, keeping the items that you need in the same space each time is going to help you get faster and faster at completing the project each time. Muscle memory can take over, and the team members are able to reach for and grab things without even needing to think about or look at the item that they need.You need to have an open mind when you are working on this step because you may find that promoting the ease of workflow can be more than just organizing the area. It could even require some serious reworking of the facilities and how they are laid out at this point. In addition, you must make sure that all the items are arranged in the correct manner to make it easier for you to create steps for every part of the process. You want it to not only be easy for the people who are already on the team, but also for those who are new to the team so they can catch on and not slow down the process.

Shine

The next thing that we are going to take a look at is known as Shine. Keeping the workspace as clean as you can, and making sure that there isn't a lot of a mess around so that you maintain the most effective workspace possible. You want to talk to your team and emphasize how important it is to have some kind of daily cleaning to ensure that the overall efficiency of the team is boosted and to ensure that everything stays where it needs to be. This is also a good time for you to set up a schedule for regular maintenance, if any is very needed, which is going to serve to ensure that the whole office stays as safe as possible for everyone. The end goal here is that any member of the team should be able to walk into the workspace and understand, within five minutes or less, where the key items in the process are located.

Standardized

The standardized step in this methodology is going to be all about ensuring that the processes in the organization itself stay in line in such a way that you can take these same ideas and apply them throughout all the areas, the departments, and everywhere else throughout the whole business. The reason that you want to do this is to make sure that order is maintained, even when things get hectic. It makes it so that everyone is going to be held to the same standards of quality and reliability.

Sustain

Finally, we are going to look at the idea of sustain. Sustaining the process is going to be vital because it could take a week or more to set up this process. If you spend that much time learning about the process and getting it set up, you don't want to have it fall apart in just a few months. This makes all that hard work a waste of time, and it can be discouraging overall.

It is important to make sure that this new organizational method becomes a vital part of the business starting from day one and moving into the future. If things are truly sustainable in this kind of regard, then the team is going to successfully move through the process, without the management or the leader expressly having to ask them to do it. Of course, while sustainability is something that you should strive for with this method, it isn't something that you can expect overnight. It requires lots of training and adoption of the ideas of Lean and more, to become a part of the culture for your business. This does take time as everyone gets on board with the ideas and as they start to learn more about the process. But once it happens, you will really start to see all of the benefits that come with this method.

It's a Great Starter Tool

If you have some big plans for your business and these include transitioning yourself to more advanced concepts of Lean over time, then working with the 5S method is going to be a great way to help move employees in the right direction to make this happen. This method can be really effective with any employees who seem to be stuck in their ways. Once these individuals get on board, they will find that it is hard to deny all of the benefits of the Lean system and these organizational versions, and they will jump on even more. When they see these benefits, they are more likely to jump on board with some of the additional changes that you want to add in the future. One thing to remember when you are rolling out a new system like this one, you may find that the team members are only going to care about two main things. These include the way that this kind of new system is going to affect them specifically and whether the Lean process is actually going to provide some results. These concerns are also what make the 5S system a great place to start. It comes with some answers that are easily understandable for anyone who has a question and who wants to see if Lean and the other methods we have discussed in this guidebook will actually provide some results.

Is the 5S System Actually a good choice for my business?

While the 5S system is going to be a good choice for many businesses, no matter what kind of industry they are in, it isn't a solution that fits everyone. This is why it is so important for you as a business owner to have a good idea of both the strengths and weaknesses when you get started. One of the biggest strengths with this system is that when it gets implemented properly, it is going to help your team define their processes easier while helping them to claim some ownership on the processes that come. Remember that with Lean the goal is to not have one manager or one leader calling all of the shots. The point is to bring in all of the team members and hear their opinions and get everyone on board. When the team gets their voice heard and can have a say in what happens, it is going to add some more accountability in the process. And when everything goes according to plan in this manner, it is going to lead to performance that is improved even more, which then leads to better conditions of work for everyone on the team. In addition, implementing this process has the potential to make long-term employee contributions thanks to an internalized sense of improvement. In an ideal world, this is something that will continue on until the main ideas of continuous improvement start to become the order of the day. When the company and the team are able to use the 5S system in the proper way, it can provide them with some bigger insights into the worlds of work standardization, equipment reliability, and value analysis. However, while there may be a lot of things to love about the 5S system, there are also some drawbacks that businesses need to be prepared for. One of the biggest weaknesses that occur with this is that if the system and its purpose are not communicated to the team in the proper manner, then members of the team can sometimes make some mistakes. This is because they may see the system as more of an end goal, rather than as a means to an end. The 5S system needs to be the flagbearer of any kind of success that is going to come in the future, rather than the sum total of the journey the company made with the processes of Lean. Specifically, businesses whose movement is constrained quite a bit by some external factors (which they are not able to control), may find that it is hard to use the 5S system, and companies who run into lots of storage problems right now may need to solve these issues before they try to transition into the method. In addition, just because this method is a good fit for many different kinds of companies doesn't mean that it is automatically going to fit in with your business and your team. This can be seen when we are talking about some of the smaller teams, or for any team that has all of their members take on many roles at the same time. Just because the 5S system is seen as a very popular way to implement the Lean principles doesn't mean that it is going to fit for everyone. Choosing to ignore this information and moving ahead anyway and enforcing organization just because you think you need to, or just because another business has done it, won't do much of anything when you take a look at the results that it generates. In fact, if you try to implement this system into a process where it doesn't belong, you are just going to generate more waste in the long run. This is going to be even more true for any kind of business that works with a large variety of interactions with humans, various styles of management, and other management tools. However, when the different aspects work together in the proper manner, they may be able to generate some extra value to their customer, which of course is seen as a very vital part of a business that is able to see success in the market. While the 5S system can be a great way to help your business, if you blindly press forward with it, you are going to find that it is easy to lose sight of the proper outcome for your customer because you are trying to pursue the perfect outcome or a perfect implementation of the 5S principles. If this method isn't going to help you to serve the customer properly, and it wastes more time than it is worth, then don't worry about implementing it into your business. Finally, when you are trying to implement this system, you must take the time to stress to all the members of your team that 5S is something that needs to be a part of their natural routine and the best practices that are standard for the business. It should never be seen as any kind of additional task that they need to do outside of their daily work. The goal of the 5S system is to enhance how effective the workflow for your business is at every step of the process. If you try to separate out this system into a new layer that is in addition to the work, rather than going along with the work, then you are doing the complete opposite of what the process stands for.

Chapter 27
Applying The Lean Method

With so much emphasis on improving efficiency, the Lean process naturally places a lot of emphasis on team leaders who have to work hard to immediately inspire their teams to adopt the Lean mentality. In the end, many Lean systems live and die because of the leadership involved, which means that it is important that those in charge of leading the Lean transition can not only explain what is going on, but are really committed to it. work that is being done too. Some things Lean leaders should try to emphasize include:

Customer loyalty: when it comes to customer loyalty, Lean leaders must take the time to consider not only what their customers want right now, but also what they probably want in the future. Moreover, it is important to understand what a customer accepts, what they will like and what they will stop at nothing to have. The Lean leader must also work to understand the many ways in which the specific wishes and needs of their target audience are present throughout the customer base.

Team improvement: To help their team members be their best, Lean leaders must always be available to help the team during the problem-solving process. At the same time, they must be cautious and refrain from taking control and just doing it themselves. Their role in the process must be to focus on finding the resources that the team can use to solve their own problems. Open questions are a big part of this process because they make it possible for the team to find a much wider variety of solutions.

Incremental improvement: one of the most important tasks of the Lean leader is to constantly evaluate different aspects of the team to ensure that it performs optimally. The leader must also keep abreast of customer requirements, as this is something that will constantly change. This is one of the only truly reliable ways to stay ahead by allowing the overall direction of the company to be streamlined to the processes that will achieve the best results.

To ensure that this is the case, the Lean leader will want to make time in his schedule to view the results and then compare them with the costs to find the best ways to use all available resources at the given time. . This includes things like evaluating the organization as a whole in the hope of making it more efficient and reliable. It also includes evaluating the value flow to ensure that it satisfies the customer at both macro and micro levels.

Focus on sustainable improvement: it is also the task of the Lean leader to ensure that improvements that are made are implemented until the end. This often includes teaching team members the correct Lean behavior to use in a given situation and also approaching failure cases as opportunities for improvement and innovation.

Three Actuals

Lean leaders usually use a different leadership style than many of their peers, mainly because Lean leaders require an understanding that the best way to analyze a situation is to be physically in the room where the situation has occurred. Once there, the Lean leader must think about what is known as the three actuals, the widest of which is known as Genchi, and the issue that led the leader to the place in question. Genbutsu believes it is important to see what is created or put into action before you make a move. Finally, Genjitsu says it is always best to collect as much information as possible before you make a decision in any way.

Create A Lean System

To create a long-lasting Lean system, the first thing you need to do is to consider the simplest way to bring your product or service to the public's attention and operate that system. From there, you must continuously monitor the processes that you have set up to support your business to ensure that breakthroughs in improvement occur from time to time. The final step is to implement improvements that you come across. Although there are many theories and tools that can help you move on, the fact that creating a Lean system is really that simple.

Business is more than just profit: when using the Lean system, the ultimate goal is to determine in which ways it is possible to improve the efficiency of your company. Although an increase in profit is often a natural result of this process, this should not be the main motivating factor for a Lean transformation. Instead, it is important to focus as much as possible on streamlining, regardless of what the costs are beforehand, since you can confidentially expect that every dollar you spend will come back.

There are, of course, limits to this and at a certain point in time the revenues are not worth the costs. To determine where this line is, you can use a simple value curve to determine how the changes are likely to affect your bottom line. A value curve is often used to compare different products or services based on many relevant factors and the data currently available. In this case, making one to show the difference between a pre- and post-Lean state should make such decisions much easier.

Treat tools the way they are: when many new companies switch to a Lean style to do things, they find it easy to fall into the trap of taking tools to the limit, to the point that they follow them with almost religious zeal. It is important to remember that the Lean principles are ultimately guidelines only and all the Lean tools that you use are precisely the tools that will make your business work more effectively. This means that if they need to be adjusted to better serve your team and your customers, there is nothing to stop you from doing exactly that. From the start, your team must understand the limits and purpose of the Lean tools they receive and, above all, understand that they are not laws.

Prepare to continue: even if you hire a trained professional to help your team with the initial Lean learning curve, it will ultimately be up to you, as a team leader, to ensure that the learned practices do not fall out of the boat while time passes. It takes time to find new ways of doing things and making habits out of it, and it's your job to keep everyone on until everything clicks and they start working through the new system without thinking about it. Similarly, it is important to clarify why the Lean process is good for the team as a whole and for the individual team member as if they were invested in it personally, then it is much more likely that they will stick to it, even if it becomes difficult.

Setting Lean Goals

In order to ultimately make the right changes to your company, you must first ensure that you set the right goals. To ensure that your goals put you on the right track, you must ensure that they are SMART, which means that they are specific, measurable, achievable, realistic and current.

Specific: Charities are specific, which means that you want to be sure that the goal you choose is extremely clear, especially when you first start, because goals that are less well defined are much easier to avoid in favor of activities that provide more positive stimulation in a shorter period. Keeping specific goals in mind makes it much easier for you to continue with the tasks that you are currently performing.

If you are not entirely sure whether the goal you have chosen is specific enough to actually improve your chance to change for the better, you might find out by looking through who, why, where, when and how of the goal . In particular, do you want to consider who will be involved with you when it comes to achieving the goal? What exactly will be achieved? Where will it take place, why is it important that you ensure that it is completed as quickly as possible and how exactly you can expect you to do it. If you can answer all five major questions, you know that you have a goal that is specific enough to generate the kind of results you are looking for.

Measurable: SMART goals are goals that can be divided into small, easy-to-handle chunks that can be tackled piece by piece. A measurable goal should make it easy to determine when exactly you are on course, so that you can correct yourself as quickly as possible. Measuring your progress will make it easier for you to continue the good work.

Reachable: Perhaps more important than anything else, if a goal you set is unreachable, especially the first goal you set with this system, then you unknowingly waste valuable time and energy while creating negative patterns that end with failure. What's more, you will eventually strengthen fixed mindsets, making this a bad choice no matter how you look at it. This means that when it comes to setting goals, you want to have a clear understanding of the current situation and everything that is going on in the company, making it less likely for that purpose.

Realistic: a good goal is a realistic goal, besides being achievable, which means that you can expect success without something that is highly unlikely to push reality to your advantage. An ideal goal is one that requires a lot of work to achieve, while still not being too difficult to become unrealistic. Moreover, you will want to avoid goals that you can achieve without really going to much trouble, because too easy goals can be demotivating, because then it becomes easy to postpone them until they eventually fall into oblivion.

Timely: Studies show that the human mind is more active in problem-solving behavior when there is a time limit for successfully completing the task in question. What this means for the goals you set is that if you have a fixed end date in mind for when you want to reach your goal, you will work harder in the period prior to that date. This means that you want to choose completion dates that are strict enough to really motivate you to do what you have in mind while at the same time not being so strict that there is no realistic way to complete the task on time. The goal here is to put a little extra effort into your step and not force you to keep a tiring schedule, so make sure you can always follow the schedule that you have set for the best results.

Implementation Of Policy

Also known as Hoshin Kanri, policy implementation is a way to ensure that SMART goals that are set at management level are ultimately measurably filtered to the rest of the team. By making good use of policy implementation, you essentially ensure that everything you intend to implement does not accidentally cause more problems than has ultimately resolved. It will also help to ensure that as little waste as possible is generated as a result of issues such as inconsistent messages from management or poor communication. The goal in this case should not be to force different team members to act in a specific way. It is about generating the kind of vision for the company that everyone can appreciate and understand how it relates to both the team and the customers.

Implementation of the plan: After all relevant SMART goals have been completed, the next thing you want to do is to group them based on which team members are ultimately charged with solving them. Keep in mind that the fewer goals there are, the more likely it is that they will be executed within a reasonable time. If your goals cannot be generalized in such a way, it is important to start with the goals that definitely make the biggest difference and then work out the list from there.

Regardless of which goals you ultimately choose, it is important that you make sure that there are no goals to which no one has assigned specific instructions to track overall progress and at the same time provide status reports when needed. This person must also be someone who can be counted on to make clear to other team members how important the goal is for the company as a whole and how it will make things easier in the long run.

Consider your tactics: those responsible for achieving the goal must in turn be the ones who decide how the goal can best be achieved by the team as a whole. However, this process must still include interaction between all levels of the team, only to ensure that the tactics and the goal are well aligned. Tactics are likely to change if the goal is on its way to success, which means that it needs to be studied from time to time to ensure that it remains fit for the goal in question.

Progress: Once the tactics have been agreed by all parties, it is time to actually put them into practice. This will be the phase where the team can really take over, although quality goals still require a buy-in from relevant parties. During this period, it is important to ensure that all communications from management are up to date, to ensure that actions and wider goals continue to align.

Check from time to time: it is important to remember that once the action is implemented, the team leader must change the action if necessary. This means that they will also follow things while hopefully going according to plan. Remember that Lean systems are always being improved, which means that your goals and their implementation cannot be different.

Simplify Lean As Much As Possible

All products and services generated by your company have a combination of three different value streams that can ultimately be used productively if you take the time to fully understand them. These include the concept to launch stream, creating customer stream and the order to customer stream. To ensure that you get the greatest overall value from all the processes that your company completes, it is important to look at a value flow chart, as it is an excellent way to ensure that you maximize efficiency at every turn.

The average value flow card contains everything that ultimately comes together to generate value for the customer, including activities, people, materials and information. To properly visualize a value stream, you want to follow the Plan / Do / Study / Act process, also known as the Lean cycle. To begin with, you want to plan the task ahead by focusing on one goal at a time. From there you want to make a list of everything that needs to be done to ensure that the task is successfully completed. This is then followed by the step of following, where the results are studied and where necessary monitored.

Make Your Own Value Flow Card

A well-constructed value flow chart is an essential part of the process, as it allows you to see the big picture by mapping the full flow of resources from their different starting points all the way when they come together and ultimately in the hands of the customer. As such, it makes it much more of a manageable task to determine the points in the process that hamper the overall efficiency of your company's process and thus take the first steps to take over Lean processes.

Although one person can certainly go through the following steps, the value flow cards that prove to be the most effective are often the cards made by the entire team, so those with the most knowledge of each step can give them two cents. Your initial value flow card should be seen as a very rough sketch and must be constructed as such, which means that you must plan it in pencil and expect a lot of rewriting as you proceed.

Consider the process: the first step in this process is to consider what exactly you want to map. For companies that first start with the Lean system, you first want to consider the different processes that ultimately prove to be of the utmost importance to the team as a whole and then complete the list from there. If you still can't decide where to start, you want to turn to your customers, consider what they have to say, and start with the areas where you regularly receive the most complaints.

What is known as a pareto analysis is currently an effective tool because it can make it easier for you to find the right starting place if you are not sure where your efforts can best be used. It is a statistical analysis technique that can be especially useful if you are looking for a few different tasks that will certainly produce serious results if you can only decide which one to use first. The goal in this case is to focus on the 20 percent of your business that, if cherished, could eventually generate 80 percent of your total results. Your initial value stream card can be focused on just one service or product or on multiples that share a significant part of the process.

Choose your shorthand: the symbols that you use to indicate different phases of the process that you are mapping do not have really hard and fixed guidelines, because they will be unique for every project and every company. Regardless of what you and your team ultimately choose, it is important to make a list of all the symbols that you use and what they mean, so that anyone coming in after the fact can be easily entangled. From there, it's important to stick to the designated symbols and not to invent anything on the spot. If the company is working on more than one value stream card at the same time, it is important that the symbols match between the two. Otherwise things can quickly turn into illegibility.

Set limits: If these are used wide enough, almost any value flow card for your company can be connected to other value flow cards or go into more detail. At some point, however, this will be counterproductive and you have to set limits on what the value flow card will explain if you ever hope to continue successfully. Similarly, if you let this part of the process get out of hand, the map may lose focus and therefore become less useful.

Start with clearly defined steps: After you have a clear start and end for the mapping process, the next thing to do is make a list of all the logical steps to be taken from start to finish. This should not be an in-depth look at every link in the chain, but instead should be an overview of the most important phases that need to be considered as the process approaches.

Consider the information flow: An important step in the value flow allocation process that distinguishes it from other similar allocation processes is that each value flow card also takes into account the way information flows through the entire process from start to finish. It also shows the way in which information is passed on between team members. You must also ensure that the ways in which the customer interacts with your company and how often such interactions occur are taken into account. You must also ensure that the communication chain includes suppliers or other third parties with whom the company deals.

Further details: when it comes to splitting the process to the most detailed level, you may also want to include a flow chart with your value flow chart. A flow chart is a great way to chart the deepest details of how a certain process is completed. This is also an excellent way to determine which types of muda you are dealing with, so you can consider whether they can be removed from the process.

If you are interested in the ways in which your team physically moves through your space, a string diagram can also be effective. To generate these types of charts, map the workspace of your company by drawing what each team member should do and where they should go to fully complete the process. You want to draw different team members or different teams in different colors to prevent things from becoming too confusing. From there, mapping the flow of information with regard to this data can lead to surprising conclusions about errors that would otherwise go unnoticed for years.

Collecting data: when it comes to mapping your original map of a value stream, you may find that certain aspects of the process require additional data before something can be determined with a certain degree of certainty. The data that you may need to find include:

- Cycle time
- Total stock at hand
- Availability of the service
- Transition time
- Uptime
- Number of teams required to complete the process
- Total available working time

When it comes to collecting this data, it is important to always remember to go directly to the source and find the details that you are looking for instead of making assumptions. Furthermore, it is important to get the most recent figures instead of looking at older, better available figures or hypothetical benchmarks. This can mean something as practical as physically monitoring every part of the process so that you can make relevant notes.

View the inventory: even if you are relatively certain of the inventory requirements for the process in question, it is vital that you check this again before you commit to the value stream card. Minor miscalculations at this point can dramatically skew your overall results and essentially destroy all your hard work if you are not careful. This means that you absolutely have to take two measures to see the best results. After all, inventory is susceptible to construction for various reasons and there is a good chance that you will only know if you look closer and take a look at what is really at hand. You can also use this step as an excuse to take stock of exactly what the team is working with and to determine to what extent it will stretch effectively.

Use the data: once you have finished visualizing the steps you have found in your main process, you can now use it to determine where any issues are located. You will want to pay particular attention to processes that re-perform previously completed work, anything that requires a longer period of resetting before work can begin again, or long holes where parts of the team cannot do anything except wait for someone else, in the Finally, keep an eye on those who take more resources than your research indicates that you should, or even those who for no reason seem to last longer than they should.

Generate the ideal version of the value stream: after you have determined where the bottlenecks occur, you want to create an updated value stream map that indicates how you want the process to continue after you have sorted everything properly. This gives you an A to C scenario, where figuring out the pain points represents B. Ideally, it also gives an idea of how you can remove the waste from the process to create an idea that you can really strive for in both the short and the long term.

After you have determined the ideal state for the process, you can work out a future value flow chart that will serve as a plan to take the team from where you are currently to where you need to be. This type of plan is often subdivided into sections that last a few months depending on what needs to be done. In addition, most future value flow cards will contain multiple iterations, as they will have to be changed several times as the project is almost completed.

When you go through different variations of the value flow card, it is important to pay close attention to the lead time available for different processes. The lead time is the amount of time required to complete a certain task in the process and, if not used as efficiently as possible, it can easily lead to a wealth of bottlenecks. Remember that when it comes to creating the best possible flow chart, no part of the process is further investigated.

Chapter 28
Lean Thinking

Lean businesses always identify ways to maximize the value for their customers, which is the core objective of lean thinking. Most people are under the notion that lean thinking can only be implemented in sales and marketing departments since those departments work directly with customers.

This is not true since lean thinking is now being used to deliver value products to stakeholders of all departments.

Most people view lean as a tool that can be used to eliminate waste from processes and internal mechanisms thereby maximizing the value for the customer. But lean is a business process and kaizen is its cultural center. This is an important aspect to consider when a business wants to identify the value of long-term processes. Most businesses still believe that lean thinking is a way for the demand side since they are not looking at the value stream. These businesses can make better profits since the demand for their products exceeds their supply. However, most businesses are in a market where supply exceeds demand. Take mobile phones for instance. Numerous companies have been set up in different parts of the world that develop new phone models every day. However, most people choose to purchase Apple products, because the business has catered to the demands of the product and has always tried to identify ways to maximize the value of the customer. Therefore, businesses must remember that lean is not only about removing waste from the process, but also about identifying ways to enhance the value stream to maximize the value of the product. There is no company in today's economy that rejects more prospects or refuses orders. The business must always look for ways to drive revenue. Therefore, a business must improve continually to enhance and improve the processes in the value stream. So, how does a business use lean thinking to identify value?

- Understand the demands of stakeholders and customers
- Identify elements in the process that are waste contributors and those that affect the quality of the product

If a business is implementing lean thinking, it must eliminate processes that contribute to waste and those that do not add any value to the product or service. A business will view every activity that it performs and views the steps to see if each of them adds value to the final product or service. An activity is defined as a waste contributor if it adds cost and takes time to complete but does not improve the final product that is delivered to the stakeholder or customer. Every business focuses on how to shorten the timeline and how the value flow between the business and customer can be improved. The value is identified by becoming a faster, cheaper and better business. In simpler words, a business must always change its processes to produce goods and services that a customer is willing to pay for. Another way to identify value is by defining the internal customers or stakeholders. These internal stakeholders are members of each department that use outputs of one department as input to achieve their business goals and objectives. Regardless of whether a business is working with internal or external customers, it must focus on how the customers are satisfied rather how well they are satisfied. The fundamental of lean thinking then changes to the following – "if a process is improved, the value of the process is also improved." Most businesses are product-focused. These businesses cannot view the market or access the market to become the best. They also make the mistake of looking at the value of the product or service and how it will help the customer. Businesses must remember that the idea of value is abstract and there is no real definition. The business must always identify ways to create, identify and deliver value to its customers.

Ways to Add Value

Faster and Better

The business must identify ways to deliver products of high quality to customers either before the promised time or on time. Every individual is impatient and a person who has finally taken a look at a product will want it yesterday. If the business can deliver faster, more customers will flock towards the business since there is a direct perceived correlation between the value of offering and the speed at which it is offered.

Better Quality

The key is to remember that every customer wants products that are of better quality. Therefore, every business must develop products that are of greater quality when compared to the products of its competitors. A business must remember that the customer defines quality. A business must always find out what its customers want and develop products with high quality for them.

Always Add More Value

Always add value to the product. Most businesses in an industry deliver the same or similar products. For any business to stand out, it must offer something that other businesses do not offer. Apple is an excellent example of this point.

Increase convenience

You have to identify ways to eliminate processes that make it difficult for customers to place their orders with ease. There are issues when the customer needs to go through elaborate processes to place an order. If that is the case, customers will choose businesses where it is easy for them to place their orders. Lean thinking plays a key role here since the business will need to identify waste contributors and remove them thereby adding value to the process.

Improve Customer Service

It is important to remember that human beings are emotional and this is a factor that every business must include in its customer service. The business must identify a way to tap into the emotions of its customers by being warm, friendly, cheerful and helpful. A business must ensure that it always helps its customers regardless of how big or small the request is.

Changing Lifestyle

Businesses must identify how lifestyles are changing and how these changes impact customers. They must collect data and make sound decisions to improve the value of their products and services. It is important to understand that every customer has a different taste and a business must find a way to tap into those tastes and deliver products of excellent quality. A business can also have the ability to move into new markets and provide customers with better products and services.

Offer Discounts

Planned discounting will add value and wealth to a business. If a business has a surplus of products, it must identify ways to sell those products in higher volumes. Most supermarkets, like Costco, give customers the chance to buy large volumes of a product at a lower rate. The business can also pass on the savings to the customer and also make profits by selling more significant volumes of some products. When a business wants to identify ways to enhance the value of its products and services, it will look at ways to increase the speed at which it delivers products and also find ways to improve the quality of the products. This is when they begin to innovate and identify new processes that can maximize the value of a product for the customer. Businesses must always function with the customers in their minds since they define the business. If a customer believes that a business is honest and the products delivered are of great quality, word will spread across the market and more customers will switch to that business. Therefore, a business must always identify ways to enhance value for its customers.

Chapter 29
The 7 Principles of Lean Thinking

Lean thinking primarily started as a required practice in Toyota's manufacturing floor. The term "lean thinking" was first coined by James Womack and Daniel Jones in their book, Lean Thinking: Banish Waste and Create Wealth in Your Corporation.

All of their insights were a result of their comprehensive study of the Toyota Production System (TPS). They noticed that Toyota focused on creating system frameworks that makes manufacturing a lot more value-adding and efficient. Most lean strategies that you'll come across can be traced back to the wide success of the TPS. It remains the primary reference where most lean manufacturing methods are based.

Any business that is trying to get into the lean mindset will need to integrate the following principles into their processes:

Eliminating Wastes

Wastes found within the knowledge workflow are usually linked to the management and to the people doing the work, and not exactly on the production floor. Examples of wastes involved in the knowledge work are:

Context Switching: This occurs when people need to switch from one tool or platform to the other just to complete a single task. This may involve opening a ton of programs or apps all at once.

It usually requires a certain order to accomplish so it's prone to confusion. In a way, it overlaps with multitasking since your attention is scattered across various tasks.

Poor Appropriation of Tools: Sometimes, slow completion time can mainly be blamed on inappropriate tools. Oftentimes, when employees are forced to use a tool that certainly isn't the best for the job, the production flow doesn't move as quickly as it should.

Inefficiency of Information Systems: This is related to the previous point. If the workflow relies heavily on information systems, yet company reports say that these systems aren't helping like they're supposed to, you can't expect that things will be accomplished as planned. It's even worse when user feedback isn't integrated into the design — either before the system was launched or after a system overhaul had been made. Ineffective Communication Among Teams: The phrase "communication is key" isn't emphasized in many contexts for nothing. The lack of open communication and transparency is often the cause of many delays during the production process. Lack of Viable Market: Any factor in your product that your customer wouldn't be willing to pay for is ultimately considered a waste in the whole workflow. What's the use of something if nobody wants it?

Creating Knowledge

For companies to become a truly lean business, knowledge and learning must be integrated into the organization. When employees are constantly given the chance to learn the industry's best practices from experts, not only can they add more value to the work they do, but they also learn how to be valuable in other ways. This is typically done by:

Having retrospectives

Cross-training employees

Holding regular discussions about employees' work processes

When a company values knowledge creation, they will be able to perform their tasks with more value at a much faster rate. This is a way for them to constantly update their skills and competencies.

Integrating Quality

A company that envisions long-term growth needs to utilize systems that are as error-free as possible. Lean companies usually do this by automating tasks that are repetitive, mentally uninteresting, and prone to human error.

As a result, employees can pour their time and focus on skills that actually engage them mentally. This allows them to devote themselves fully to the pursuit of both personal and company growth.

Delivering on Time

Lean thinking is primarily driven by the idea that focus is the root of all high-quality outputs. When your work environment isn't conducive enough to maintain an uncluttered mind, this slows your work down. Top-quality work is hard to produce when an employee is constantly distracted. Lean systems always have steady workflows. This means that everything is delivered and accomplished on a consistent, predictable basis. A bad workflow, on the other hand, is always unpredictable because of unsustainable and unreliable work habits. Lean teams are always refining their workflows to optimize value at every level. They do this by greatly limiting their WIPs (works in progress) and providing a good work environment so nothing gets stuck in the workload traffic. Multitasking is prohibited because it only prevents people from finishing tasks on time.

Deferring Commitment

Careful planning is necessary to accomplish long-term goals. In lean thinking, however, it is discouraged to plan for a product's release way out in advance. This prevents having stocks that may only end up being useless. Instead, it recommends that you decide to pursue something at the last responsible moment — during the time when you've thoroughly considered all the factors that would help you come up with the best decision possible. This goes back to the main goal of all lean systems: eliminating wastes. Deferring commitment helps you decide more smartly by going over the data and reports that accurately reflect the current market situation. This prevents you from pursuing seemingly innovative projects that don't really translate into an urgent or even viable market need in reality.

Respecting People

The root of a lean system's success all boils down to one basic thing: respect. First, the concept of lean was born out of a desire to respect the customer's needs and preferences. Second, lean systems are able to thrive because their employees are well-respected by their superiors. They are provided with environments that encourage them to perform at their best. On an individual level, respect generally entails maintaining kindness and courtesy to everyone that you're working with — whether it's your superiors, your colleagues, your employees, or your customers. Respect is also often shown through:

Providing safe environments for idea sharing

Encouraging employees to develop themselves in whatever way they wish

Trusting employees' decision-making processes

Respect goes a long way in lean systems because trust is required to maintain good workflow. After all, building good relationships is the key to creating a stable system that produces high-value outputs.

Optimizing the Whole Organization

All decisions in a lean company must be made relative to the whole organization. For instance, decisions to optimize processes must not only involve one team — it must involve everybody else. Naturally, an improvement in one component can already be enough to see significant differences in the workflow. However, to become truly lean means to address all possible sources of waste. Building a lean enterprise all starts with creating a lean business. The next step would be to find others who also share the same lean ideas as you do. Maintaining collaborations among companies can already be difficult enough since each member will have their own goals and agendas. However, if all of you can work towards operating under the same lean system, then overall work and production is going to be a breeze.

Chapter 30
Kaizen

Kaizen translates to continuous improvement which is an important goal to consider when creating a Lean system that works for your business. The goal of this strategy is to get the entire team to focus on the idea that small improvements should be happening all the time. Everyone on your team will have different talents and specialties, the goal of Kaizen is to have all of that talent focused on improving wherever and whenever possible.

Kaizen is unique among Lean strategies as it is as much a general philosophy as it is a direct plan for future action. The goal of Kaizen should be to create a culture that supports improvement while also creating groups focused more directly on improving key processes to reach well-defined goals.

If you are already using or thinking about using a standardized work process, then it is likely you will want to take advantage of Kaizen as well because they complement each other nicely. Standard practices lead to current best practices that Kaizen can then improve upon.

Kaizen can be useful for essentially every process that your team uses with any regularity, but first, it is important to determine the goals of the updated process. After that, it is important to follow up and ensure the improvements work as expected. Consider using PDCA or DMADV for the same results.

Teaching team members to use Kaizen as a plan of action, simultaneously teaches them to apply it as a philosophy as well. The type of thinking that is formed habitually by constantly looking for paths to improvement also allows team members to approach their daily processes from new and innovative ways as opposed to simply sticking with what works. This mindset should be nurtured whenever possible as it only produces more fruitful results the longer it is active.

While constantly improving existing practices is a great place to start, it is important that the Kaizen your team is practicing does not only occur after the fact. When new processes are created, it is in everyone's best interest that they are held to the same stringent examination process as well. Hindsight is good, foresight is better.

Steps to better Kaizen

- Start by standardizing your process, not just the process that you are looking to actively engage in Kaizen, but all your processes to ensure future improvements are as beneficial as possible.
- Compare processes to determine what steps being used in some areas can be used in others. It is important to look at real KPIs and not anecdotal information during this step as it can be easy to get off on the wrong track without realizing it.
- Once you know where change should occur, work with what is available to determine easier ways of completing the process. Consider the beginning of the process and then its end, then simply visualize alternative ways from 'a' to reach 'b'. It is important to only move forward with useful innovations as innovating simply for the sake of innovating will simply create waste.
- Repeat, turn the innovations into new standardized procedures and begin the entire process anew. The only bad idea, when it comes to Kaizen, is resting on your laurels.

Create a Kaizen mindset

While it can be great to get your team together now and then for Kaizen centered events where everyone takes a look at a specific process and determines the best way to get to the solution. It can be more difficult to train your team to always be in a Kaizen mindset. The best way to begin to train them to this improved way of thinking is to start by making the elimination of waste a top priority. Keep this idea in the team mindset, every day and during every meeting. Once team members start noticing waste without thinking about it they will be well on their way finding ways to work around it instead.

From there, set aside time specially to allow team members to look at the processes they use most regularly and really think about them. The human mind loves pattern and repetition which is why it is so easy to follow well-worn steps regardless of their total efficacy. Providing your team with the opportunity to really think about their processes, instead of simply working through them, will push them into seeing the flaws that they may otherwise have been blind to for years.

Taking this exercise a step further can be useful as well. To do so, provide team members the time to talk to others about their processes which will, in turn, give each process a fresh set of eyes. This is also a great way to find logical blind spots in complicated processes, just be sure that everyone takes notes during the entire process to make sure valuable insight is not lost in the shuffle. It is important to emphasize that there are no wrong answers during this stage, a free and open dialogue can provide innovative solutions to problems you didn't even know you were facing.

Chapter 31
Six Sigma

Many times you may have heard of Lean Six Sigma, or even Six Sigma on its own, and you may be confused about what the differences are. It is possible to implement the Six Sigma methodology on its own, and it is also possible to implement the Lean process on its own too. You can also implement them together in order to get even better results for your process and your business. Let's take a look at the Six Sigma methodology and how it can work together with the Lean process we have been discussing in this guidebook.

Six Sigma is known as the shorthand name of a system that measures the quality with an overall goal of getting as close to perfection in the process as possible. If a company is using Six Sigma properly, then they are going o generate as few as 3.4 defects per million attempts at the given process. Z-shift is going to be the name that is given to any deviations that are available between a process that was completed in a poor manner, and a process that was completed to perfection.

The standard Z-shift is one with a number of 4.5, but the ultimate value that businesses are aiming for is a 6. Processes that haven't been viewed with the lens of Six Sigma are going to earn about 1.5. A Six Sigma level of 1 means that the customers are able to get what they expect from the customer about 30% of the time. If the Six Sigma level is at 2, it means that about 70% of the time, the customers are able to get what they expect. If you can get to a Six Sigma level of 3, this means that about 93% of the time, the customers are satisfied with what they are getting from you.

If we move up the scale and get to a Six Sigma level of 4, this means that your customers are satisfied with the level of attention and the quality of the product they are getting more than 99 percent of the time. this means that reaching a Six

Sigma level of 5 or 6 indicates that the satisfaction percentages with your customers will be even closer to 100 percent, or almost perfections.

In addition, you will find that the process of Six Sigma can be broken up into numerous certification levels. Each one is going to have a different amount of knowledge with it to help the individual know more about this process, how to implement it, and how to reach the near perfection levels that are required with it.

The executive level of Six Sigma is going to consist mainly of management team members who are going to be in charge of going through your company and actively setting up the Six Sigma method. A Champion of Six Sigma is someone who is able to lead the projects you set up, and who will be the voice of these projects specifically.

There are also white belts in this system, and they are the rank and file workers. These are the individuals who have an understanding of Six Sigma, but it is going to be more limited than the higher two levels. The yellow belts are going to be active members on the Six Sigma project teams, and they have the responsibility of figuring out some areas where improvements can be used.

Next, are the green belts. These individuals work with the black belts on some of the projects considered high level, while also working to run some of their own yellow belt projects. Then there are the black belts who will run their own high-level projects while still doing some mentoring and some support for the other tiers we talked about. The Master black belts are going to be those who the company brought in specifically to implement this system in the business, and who can help to mentor and teach anyone, no matter what level they are at.

Implementing

Giving your team some compelling reasons to work with Six Sigma can be so important to how successful the whole process is. To make sure that the Six Sigma process is implemented in the right way, you need to find a way to motivate the team. Explaining the Six Sigma process to them and discussing how important it is to implement this new methodology can be a great place to start.

One tactic that works with this is to use a burning platform. This is a kind of motivational tactic where you are going to explain the situation that the company is in right now, and why that situation is so dire. Then you can explain that implementing Six Sigma is the only way to get long-term survival to last for the company. Of course, before you make these assertions, you should have some statistics that can help you to make this point.

Ensure that the Right Tools Are Available

Once your team has gone through the initial rounds of training that they need, it is important that you set up a kind of program for mentorship along with some additional refresher materials ready for any team member who may need them. You will find that at this stage, one of the worst things that can happen is for someone to be confused about one of the important parts of Six Sigma, and then they are rebuffed because they don't have the right resources to help them out.

The more information that you are able to provide to your team, and the more opportunities you provide for them to learn and understand Six Sigma in the beginning, the easier the implementation of this process will be. You will be able to see that everyone is on the same page, that everyone understands the importance of this process, and everyone has the right training and knowledge to make this process happen.

The Key Principles

Now that we know a little bit more about Six Sigma, it is time to take a look at some of the key principles. This process is going to work the best based on an acceptance of five laws. The first is going to be the law of the market. This means that before anything is implemented, the customer should be considered. The second is the law of flexibility. This is where the best processes are those that can be used for the greatest number of disparate functions.

Then there is the third law, which is going to be the law of focus. This one states that a company that follows Six Sigma should put all of their focus on the problem that they are experiencing, rather than on the business itself. Then there is the fourth law or the law of velocity. This one states that the more steps that are in a process, the more likely that some of those steps aren't needed, and that the process is less efficient. For the last law, we look to the law of complexity. This one states that the simpler the processes are, the more superior they are for the business.

So, how do I choose the best process? When it comes to deciding which of the processes that you should use with Six Sigma, the best place for you to start is with any process that you know to be defective, and that needs some work to reduce the number of deficiencies that occur. From there, it is simply going to be a matter of looking for situations where Takt time is out of whack before you figure out which steps where the number of available resources can be reduced as well.

The Methodologies to Work With

When you are ready to work with the Six Sigma process, there are going to be two main methodologies that you can choose to work with. Both are going to be efficient and can work, it just depends on which kind of industry you are in and what works the best for you. The two main methods are going to be DMAIC and DMADV.

First, we need to take a look at the DMAIC. This is an acronym that is going to help you and your team remember the five phases that come with it. This is useful when it comes to creating a new process and fixing any processes that need some extra work to be more efficient and deal with less risk. The way that DMAIC works includes:

Define what the process needs to do. To figure this out, you need to get some input from the customer and then work from there.

Measure: This is where your team needs to measure the parameters that the process will adhere to. Once this is done, you can ensure that the process is being created in a proper manner by gathering all of the information that is relevant.

Analyze: Here you will need to analyze all of the information that you have gathered. You may be able to see that there are some trends coming out of that information or find out that you need to do some more research and analyze it before continuing.

Improve: This is where the team can take that information and the analysis that you did, and make some improvements to the process.

Control the process. You need to work to control your business process as much as possible. You can do this by finding ways to reliably decrease how many times a delinquent variation starts to make an appearance in your process.

In addition to working with the DMAIC process, you can work with the DMADV process as well. This is very similar to the method that we just talked about before, and the five phases are going to correspond with the DMAIC process as well. The five phases that come with the DMADV method will include the following:

Define the solutions that you want the process to provide. You can look at your own mission statement, how the product is supposed to work, and input from the customer to help figure this one out.

Measure out the specifics of the process so that you are able to determine what parameters need to be in place.

Analyze the data that you and your team have been able to collect up to this particular point.

Design the new process with the help of the analysis that you have.

Verify any time that it is needed.

Both of these methods can be very effective at helping you to see results when you try to implement Six Sigma into your business. Often they work in very similar manners. You will need to consider the situations around your process, what deficiencies you need to fix, and more to help you determine which process is the best one for you.

Is Six Sigma the right choice for me?

While this process is something that can work for many different businesses across a wide variety of different industries, and Six Sigma has something to offer for teams of all sizes and shapes, it doesn't mean that this process is going to be the best fit for everyone. This can be really apparent as implementing it successfully means that a number of specifics need to come into play. This will start with the conviction of those who are looking to implement the system in the first place, as well as the overall culture that is found in the business and how open it is to the new change.

This is why many companies decide to ease into the process and will start with the 5S method. This is seen as a lower impact method that can adjust the team to what you want to happen before you move into some more advanced techniques, like what you find with Six Sigma. Once the team has accepted what you are trying to do, it becomes so much easier to implement all of Six Sigma and all of Lean into the business and its culture.

When you are taking a look at the Six Sigma method and trying to determine if this kind of transition is actually something that you can do, you must make sure that no one in the business, especially upper management, sees this as a fad or a trend that the business is just trying out. In fact, Six Sigma, and the whole Lean philosophy needs to be seen as an evolution of the ideals that the company already put in place.

In most cases, the more involved you can get the leadership of the team right from the beginning, the more onboard the team will be, and the more participation you will be able to get out of everyone. This is why it is so important to get all of the employees on board, whether they are in top management or hold another important position within the company.

In addition, it is so important for the culture of your company to be seen as one that is in full support of this kind of positive change, and to remember that if your upper management, or anyone on the management team, isn't able to come up with a consensus on the new program, that it is better to hold off a bit to reach that consensus. Jumping in when not everyone is on board, especially if some of those are the upper management, means that the idea and the process will be dead from the start.

Of course, this doesn't mean that every single person on the team must be committed to the idea of Six Sigma or the Lean methodology right from the start. But it does mean that the changes that occur need to be seen as institutional. This ensures that the front that you send to the public shows that everyone is united under the ideas of the method.

Implementing Six Sigma into your business can take some time, but when you add it together with the ideas of Lean, then you are going to see a big shift in the company culture and so much more. But when both of these ideologies are used together, you will find that it results in more satisfaction with your customers, less waste, more efficiencies in the process, and more profits in the long term of your business.

Chapter 32
Deciding If Six Sigma Is Right For Your Company

While the Six Sigma system has something to offer teams and companies of all sizes and complexities, that doesn't mean that it is automatically a good fit for your particular business. In fact, implementing Six Sigma successfully depends on a myriad of different specifics including the conviction of those implementing the system, and the company's overarching culture. As such, understanding the concepts related to successfully implementing 5S will make the transition to Six Sigma much easier to accomplish.

Is The Leadership Involved?

When suggesting a transition to Six Sigma, it is important that it not be framed as another "fad" management style and instead be seen as an enhancement of what is already in place. As a rule, management is going to be opposed to the change which means it will be important to get buy-in from the person at the top and work down from there.

This doesn't mean that every person in the organization must be committed to Six Sigma, but it does mean that the change must be seen as institutional which means the public front must always appear united. The human brain is a creature of habit, especially when it is confronted with new systems that seem complicated which Six Sigma often does, if it is at all apparent that the new system is optional, most people will opt out every time. Don't give them an avoidance opportunity, do what you can to ensure that opposition is voiced in private.

Is The Correct Infrastructure In Place?

Six Sigma is founded on the principle of leaders mentoring those underneath them and in order to make Six Sigma work, this needs to be a full-time job for some people, at least until new, positive habits form. While it may not seem cost-effective to dedicate one or more people to the task of actively mentoring others on Six Sigma specifics, it is a sacrifice you must be willing to make if you want Six Sigma to be more than a flash in the pan with your team. Unfortunately, this will never be the case if the person who is responsible for mentoring others is also bogged down with additional work as that additional work is almost always going to ultimately end up in front of additional mentoring duties. Prior to implementing Six Sigma, it is important to ensure that you have the infrastructure to support it long term, otherwise, you are ultimately just wasting everyone's time.

What Will Cause The Rank And File To Fall In Line?

Once you have the support of management and have ensured that you have the infrastructure to support the undertaking for as long as it takes, the next thing you need to determine is if you have a way to motivate the remaining employees to stick with Six Sigma to the point that they internalize it so that it becomes second nature. Regardless of how their progress is tracked, it is vital that each member of the team feels an immediate and compelling reason to commit to the new program, at least at first. Companies are like any other body that is in motion, the larger the company, the more inertia it displays when it comes to making large changes, and for many companies, Six Sigma is a very large change. This is why a tangible incentive must be attached at every level of the company to ensure that everyone remains united in their drive to obtain the incentive. The side effect from this will, of course, be they are also internalizing the ideas behind Six Sigma without actively trying to do so.

How Common Is The Practice In Your Field?

While Six Sigma has proven value in a wide variety of fields, that doesn't mean that all of those fields are ready to adopt the process with open arms. While being a forward thinker is never a bad thing, if your industry has yet to adopt Six Sigma as a common practice, it is important to be ready for additional pushback from the institution when attempting to move forward with the change. Be prepared for resistance and stand your ground, using examples of successful companies who have already adopted the Six Sigma system will also help to silence naysayers. The research behind Six Sigma speaks for itself, be ready with specific examples of how it can help your company specifically and the facts will ultimately speak for themselves.

What Are The Objectives Of The Training?

Depending on the size of your company, training the team at the same overall level of Six Sigma may make sense. Eventually, however, the size of the team will necessitate the use of numerous training levels. If this is the case, it is important to consider the qualifications for each level as well as how training will be staggered for maximum efficacy. Don't forget to determine how the length of the training will affect other duties as well as the areas that will be focused on the most. Taking the time to identify the specifics unique to your desired training scenario before you start will make all the difference in the overall implementation of Six Sigma and should not be ignored. There are no one-size-fits-all options in this scenario, planning out the specifics of your team's training could very well make the difference between success and failure in the long term. What's more, it can help point out potential issues that may arise which may otherwise have not been visible until the training was already in progress.

Which Projects Are Going To Be Used As The Flagships For The New System?

Once Six Sigma training is completed, you will want to already have a few projects waiting in the wings that can be ultimately connected to the new system and pointed to as signs of success further down the road when the question as to whether or not it is a good idea to continue with Six Sigma arises. Your goal should be to increase the level of involvement surrounding one or more Black Belt or Green Belt projects and do whatever is required to ensure they are successful.

During this period, it is important to ensure that the initial round of Black Belt and Green Belt employees don't find themselves on so many projects that they begin to miss measurable objectives. Your goal above all others during this time should be to maximize success as much as possible. Take the extra time to ensure that the first round of projects has the appropriate amount of buy-in from management or other key stakeholders, again, there is nothing more demotivating than seeing projects fail after a new system has been implemented. Ensure that the management team is committed to making sure that doesn't happen. It is important that the projects chosen are not just "feel good" projects and are instead those that are truly beneficial to the company as a whole. If enough early Six Sigma projects are well-publicized but produce little of measurable value than the entire system is at risk of collapsing from the inside as it will be seen as a fad with little in terms of substance. Don't let this happen by instead choosing projects that have a clear value regardless of whether the person making the decision is trained in Six Sigma or not. Public opinion is crucial at this stage to allow everything to settle down to provide Six Sigma the time it needs to become a habit. In order to ensure that Six Sigma is properly implemented, it is important that you properly motivate your team by explaining how crucial the adoption of a new methodology really is. The most common choice in these situations is to create what is known as a burning platform scenario. A burning platform is a motivational tactic whereby you explain that the situation the company now finds itself in is so dire (like standing on a burning platform) that only by implementing Six Sigma is there any chance of long term survival for the company. Having stats that back up your assertions is helpful, though, if times aren't really so tough, a bit of exaggeration never hurt. Adapting to Six Sigma can be difficult, especially for older employees and a little external motivation can make the change more palatable.

Ensure The Tools For Self-Improvement Are Readily Available

Once the initial round of training regarding Six Sigma has been completed, it is important that you have a strong mentorship program in play while also making additional refresher materials readily available to those who need them.

The worst thing that can happen at this point is for a team member who is confused about one of the finer points of Six Sigma to try and find additional answers only to be rebuffed due to lack of resources. Not only will they walk away still confused, but they will have been rebuffed for trying and not rewarded for taking an interest in the subject matter. A team member who cannot easily find answers to their questions is a team member who will not follow Six Sigma processes when it really counts.

Give Priority To The Right Activities

In every situation, there are a number of potential outcomes when it comes to resolutions. While talking about Six Sigma is nice, it is important that team members see those in leadership roles commit to prioritizing the correct types of choices in every situation. It is important that determining criteria that are quality critical, listening to the customer and ensuring Six Sigma leads to measurable goals are all seen as vital activities for team members regardless of their level of Six Sigma certification.

Ensure The Six Sigma Initiative Is Owned By Everyone

When tutoring your team regarding Six Sigma it is important to make personal connections between it and individual team members so they feel more closely linked to the program's success. Whether it is by achieving buy-in from the team as a whole or making everyone in charge of enforcing Six Sigma principals, take the time to ensure that everyone feels connected to seeing Six Sigma succeed and the individual retention rate is sure to rise.

Ensure You Have A Way To Measure Results

Creating a realistic metric that can determine levels of success before Six Sigma was implemented, as well as after it is adopted, can provide you with the motivating data that you and your company need to keep it up over the long term. Alternatively, if it turns out that the system is actually ineffective in your case, the metric will be able to determine that as well. Either way, having a metric by which to measure aptitude is certain to come in handy. Additionally, it will be a reliable motivating factor (assuming the results are positive, of course) and provide yet another way to reinforce the benefits of sticking with Six Sigma until its processes become habits.

Reward Excellence

When all else fails, rewarding those who take to the Six Sigma system with the most ease will always motivate the rest of the team to work as hard as possible if only to earn whatever reward you have promised. The goal with this type of motivation should be to choose something that is valuable enough to be worth working towards without being so extravagant that eventually removing the external motivation would cause all forward momentum to cease. One common reason that Six Sigma implementation fails, is that many of those in management positions have never heard of the system and as such have a number of off the cuff questions or preconceived notions about it. Forewarned is forearmed, however, so many of the common critiques of Six Sigma, and their rebuttals, are listed below. Six Sigma is just a fad like any other flavor of the month management style In all actuality, Six Sigma can trace its origins back to the early 1900s where it was pioneered by the likes of Walter Shewhart, Henry Ford, and Edward Deming. What's more, it separates itself from the pack of related programs dedicated to continual improvement by being more focused on the use of data to make appropriate decisions that focus on the customer and ultimately always provide a solid return on any given investment. We don't have the resources or time to dedicate to teaching and learning Six Sigma Time is undeniably the most important resource that any company has as it is the only resource that is truly finite. Instead of considering the amount of time and resources that investing in Six Sigma will require, a better metric would be to determine what not adhering to a more effective system such as Six Sigma will cost in the long run. It is important to remember the story of the pair of lumberjacks who worked day after day in the forest. One man worked himself to the point of exhaustion every day while the other man spent the time preparing properly and at the end of the day both men had always chopped the same amount of wood. If your team has the opportunity to work smarter instead of harder, why wouldn't you provide them with the tools they need to make that the new norm. What's more, the cost of training the team in the specifics of Six Sigma can be mitigated over time by spreading out training courses as needed. While you won't start seeing the benefits from the higher levels all at once, training the whole team to Yellow Belt certification will still produce noticeable results. In addition, any funds put towards this type of training can also be seen as investing in the future of the business and should be considered accordingly.

We're Too Small For Six Sigma To Be Effective

Six Sigma offers up a new way of looking at the day to day business interactions that will increase productivity, and ultimately profits, regardless of the size of the team in question. Will a 10-person team need as many training sessions and resources committed to the project as a 50-person team? Of course not, but the individual results will be the same. In fact, for smaller businesses, taking the time to determine areas of waste and specific bottlenecks, can actually lead to greater periods of growth as the issues that have been addressed may not have otherwise been noted and, when left unaddressed, could have led to serious issues further down the line. Taking the time to streamline processes and improve customer relations is always the right choice.

Six Sigma Doesn't Apply To Us

While Six Sigma originated in the manufacturing sector, studies show that industries based around providing services are actually more likely to generate unnecessary waste, not less. This is caused by the fact that so much of what is provided is essentially intangible which makes standardizing processes much more difficult. However, all of the processes that are already in place to track the services being provided can ultimately be leveraged to implement Six Sigma successfully.

Six Sigma Involves Too Many Statistics To Be Used Practically

Despite its reputation for being all about the numbers, a majority of the tools and principles that are used in implementing Six Sigma require more common sense than mathematical formulas. For example, mitigating waste is one of the most important facets of Six Sigma, a facet, that only requires an understanding of the process in question and how to do it in the most effective way possible. Operating under Six Sigma is more about fostering a mentality that allows employees to get to the root cause of an issue, regardless of how long it takes. The formulas and mathematical equations simply justify it after the fact.

Lean Is A Better Fit For Us Right Now

Lean and Six Sigma aren't opposing processes, and indeed they work incredibly well together, so much so, that Six Sigma is often referred to as Lean Six Sigma. When used in conjunction with one another, Lean will improve the throughput and speed of your processes while simplifying and allowing the team to do the best with what is available. Six Sigma then takes those improved processes and makes them as high of quality as possible by reducing deviation and related defects. Combing the two will only lead to better results overall. Starting with 5S is recommended, after that there is no harm in combing Lean and Six Sigma for the best results.

We've Tried It Before And It Didn't Work

The Six Sigma system has a proven track record with some of the biggest corporations in the world including Starbucks and Coca Cola. This means that the reason for the failure is likely related more to the way the program was managed in the past as opposed to a lack of efficacy when it comes to Six Sigma in general.

Chapter 33
Methodology of Lean and Six Sigma

As defined in the very beginning, lean is "elimination of all forms of non-value-added work from the customer's perspective in business transactions and processes."

Lean Methodology

When we look at any business or process, different operations are the building blocks of them which combine to form that business or process. Some operations add value, and some do not. So, it is important to understand the concept of value from the customer's perspective so that lean can be applied successfully. The operations can be categorized according to the value they produce from the customer's perspective as follows.

Business Non-Value Add Activities

The operations or activities which do not result in any value addition or produce any beneficial outcome but are still necessary for running the company or organization are termed as business non-value add activities.

The most common example of it is the operations that must be carried out to achieve the regulatory requirements imposed by the government. These are generally the tasks that do not add any value from the customer's point of view but they still can't be eliminated.

Essential Activities

These are the operations, tasks, and activities which produce valuable outcome from the customer's perspective and the customer is willing to pay for it.

Wastes

The activities or operations which do not produce any beneficial outcome or result in value addition from the customer's perspective are termed as waste in the lean philosophy. In a typical business process, more than eighty percent of the activities can be classified as wastes or non-value add activities. This is indeed a tremendous amount of activity that produces nothing. The proportion also signifies that one can achieve an extraordinary edge over average businesses just by limiting or eliminating the non-value add activities. When you are able to control the amount of waste activities, you will be able to increase the proportion of activities for which the customer is actually willing to pay for. And this will make all the difference between your extraordinary efficient and profitable company against the average runt of the litter company. This calls for an increased scrutinization of the processes so that waste can be identified. After many years of efforts in finding various types of wastes, experts have boiled down their analysis of waste and found them to be of the following seven types.

- Motion
- Transportation
- Waiting
- Overproduction
- Inventory
- Over-processing
- Rework

Motion

It is the movement of the employee who is performing a certain operation. If an operation involves a lot of movement on behalf of the employee, it produces no such feature for which the customer is interested in paying, hence it is classified as a waste. Examples of such waste are going to different offices, going to the printer, searching for any missing information.

Transportation

This might come as unexpected to you, but any conveyance of a product is considered waste. Assembly lines, shipping or mailing move a product from one place to another, but they do not add any value to it. Transportation really does not transform or change a product; all it does is move that product from one place to another. Amazon is the company that has tremendously gained by curtailing this waste by building warehouses all across the United States of America. This greatly reduced the need for transportation to deliver the product to the customer which resulted in an extraordinary profit for the company.

Waiting

This is perhaps the most common form of waste in almost all fields all over the globe. Delay in the process or improper flow of the procedure results in waiting. The most common examples of waiting that the customer has to endure are waiting for clarification, delivery of the order and waiting to finalize the deal.

Overproduction

Overproduction is the waste which is a result of producing the goods or services in quantities which are higher than the demand for them. Overproduction generally happens when the planned production rate is based on a forecast of the sales rather than the present market demand.

Inventory

Any type of service or supply, raw materials, etc., which is kept in quantities higher than the minimum required to produce the product and get the job done can be termed as inventory. Inventory is something which also ties up the resources of the company as well as takes up space and demand special facilities in some cases. Too much inventory also results in unnecessary motion as well as transportation, in other words, it is a non-value-added activity which produces other types of wastes as well.

Over-processing

In many instances of producing a product, extra work is done which the customer is not interested in paying for. This type of work involves expenses but does not give any profit or revenues in return. If the product is made extra shiny but the customer is not affected about whether the product is shiny or not, then shining that product may be categorized as a waste because of over-processing. Of course, if the customer does care about whether the product is shiny or not, then shining the product should be classified as an essential activity rather than over-processing, in the end, it all boils down to the customer's perspective.

Rework

Any modifications or improvements in the product which are done in the product after its final step of manufacturing is termed as rework and is classified as a waste in the lean philosophy. Because lean stresses on doing the right thing the first time, if a product is not defective then it will not need any rework, hence rework is an additional step that can be avoided without affecting the quality or standard of the product.

Lean Tools

Many techniques and simple creative thinking are done to develop tools that help make the process and business lean. Lean tools, basically, are just a practical application of common sense in business management to make it more impactful, efficient and profitable.

Some tools of lean are enlisted below.

- The 5S
- Mistake-proofing
- Kanban
- SMED
- Andon
- Bottleneck analysis
- Continuous flow
- Muda (waste)
- Root cause analysis
- SMART goals
- Jidoka
- KPI
- Production leveling
- Gamba
- Hoshin Kanri
- Value Stream Mapping

Detailed description and analysis of the tools used in the lean methodology might require a separate book of its own, however, a brief discussion on some of the most important and extensively used tools of lean is done in the proceeding paragraphs.

The 5S

The 5S is basically a workplace organization tool. The 5S which constitute the following steps.

- Sort
- Set in order
- Shine
- Standardize
- Sustain

These are the guiding principles that, if followed, result in an efficient work environment.

Mistake-proofing

Mistake proofing is known as po-ka yo-ke in Japanese. It is a design approach that makes it impossible for a mistake to occur or once a mistake or error occurs, it becomes obvious right away. An example of po-ka yo-ke is the plug and socket having different shapes of each hole of the socket and leg of the switch so that they can be connected in a specific order.

Kanban

It is the lean approach developed by the pioneers of lean, Taiichi Ohno. The name, Kanban, is taken because of the cards used in this methodology. It is an inventory management approach focusing on the Just in Time (JIT) principle which Mr. Ohno introduced in the Toyota factory where he worked.

SMED (Single Minute Exchange of Dies)

It is a technique applied to significantly lower the time required to complete the change of equipment. SMED, short for single minute change of dies, focuses on converting as many steps of Chang over of equipment to "external" as possible. So that the process may continue while the changeover of the equipment is done. This approach streamlines the workflow and reduces downtime.

Andon

It's a management term that refers to the system to notify management, maintenance and other processes of quality and process problems. The workstation has an alert to indicate if a problem arises, it can be activated by a worker or by an automatic system. It informs the system that it may include some issues which should be resolved. The whole system is stopped so the issue can be corrected. It brings immediate attention to the problem so that it can be resolved.

Bottleneck analysis

A bottleneck refers to a process that causes the system to stop or delay the outcome of the system, a process that takes the longest cycle time. Bottleneck analysis should be done when the expansion of capacity is being planned. Only increasing the capacity of the other processes will not increase the overall output as they will still be limited by bottleneck processes. Bottleneck analysis identifies which steps of the process limit the overall throughput and improve it. It improves performance by finding the weakest part of the manufacturing process and strengthen it.

Continuous Flow

Continuous flow is the movement of the product or service through the production process to finish without hindrance. In an efficient continuous flow, the cycle time is equal to the lead time. Continuous flow can reduce the wastage of time when done properly and can significantly reduce costs. It lowers the inventory level. It improves the on-time delivery as there is no waste or unwanted goods piled up and only the right goods are moved forward through the system. It delivers high-quality products as mistakes in continuous flow only affect one part of the process.

Muda (waste)

Muda is anything in the process that does not add value from the customer's perspective and the customers are not willing to pay for it. The primary goal of lean manufacturing is to eliminate waste.

Root call analysis

It is a methodology to solve problems that begin by solving the problems related to the core of the system rather than fixing the problems on the surface which only give temporary solutions.

SMART Goals

SMART goals are the goals that are: specific, measurable, attainable, relevant and time-specific. It helps to achieve the goals.

Jidoka (Autonomation)

Autonomation is described as intelligent automation or automation with a human touch. This type of automation advises some supervisory functions instead of production functions. This means that if an abnormal situation occurs then the machine is stopped and workers stop the production line. And for this, the Jidoka follows the steps of the first detection of the abnormality, stop the process, fix or correct the immediate condition and find the root cause of the problem and install a countermeasure. Autonomation prevents overproduction, over inventory and elimination of the waste and focuses on solving problems and make sure they don't occur again.

KPI (key performance indicator)

The key performance indicator indicates how well the company is performing and effectively working towards the achievement of its goals. Organizations use key performance indicators at different levels to evaluate their success possibilities. High-level KPI refers to the performance of the overall organization and low-level KPI refers to the processes of the departments.

Production leveling

Production leveling, also known as production smoothing or, in Japanese, as "heijunka", is a technique used to reduce waste. The goal is to produce goods at a constant rate so that further processing can be done at a constant and predictable rate. It reduces the lead time and inventory by keeping the batches smaller.

Gemba

The term Gemba refers to the personal observation of the work- where the work is happening. Gemba is derived from a Japanese word Gembutsu, which means "real thing" or, sometimes, "real place". Observation in-person, the core principle of the tool, observe where the work is done, interacting with the people and the process for the change.

Hoshin Kanri (policy deployment)

It is a process that identifies the business's critical needs and demands and develops the capabilities of the employees, achieved by the alignment of the company's resources at all levels. Policy deployment increases the efficiency of the business. It focuses on achieving the company's goals by meeting the demands of the customers, employees, shareholders, suppliers and the environment. Policy deployment is an ideal report structure.

Value Stream Mapping

Value stream mapping is an amazing tool that helps to identify major non-value add activities (wastes), which must be removed from the process to make it lean.

What do we mean by a value stream map? A value stream map is a graphical representation of all the activities which constitute any process under consideration. The activities represented in the value stream map can be essential activities, wastes or non-value add business activities. It contains a lot of information regarding the process under consideration and is extremely helpful in understanding the flow of the procedure.

What do we get by drawing a value stream map? When a value stream map is constructed, understanding of the mechanism of the flow of activities and their significance becomes clear to the management and anyone studying the value stream map. It also helps to identify the nonessential steps in the process which must be eliminated from the process to make it lean.

Tips for developing a value stream map:

Value stream map is a simple tool for making the business lean. If applied efficiently, it can result in great value generation with minimal investment of time, mental capabilities and physical efforts. Some of the tips that might come in handy when you are developing a value stream map for your organization are discussed with you in the entailing paragraphs.

Use Sticky notes

Sticky notes are fun to work with, but that is not their main appeal or attractive feature. You can comfortably make changes in them and you can color-code them as well. For instance, you can designate green colored sticky notes only to be used for essential activities, red sticky notes for wastes, and grey colored sticky notes for non-value add business activities. This way, it becomes easy to identify the different types of activities when the value stream map is studied.

Make sure that your workstation is spacious

When developing a value stream map, things can become very messy very fast. If you are working on a value stream map in a congested space, it will become very difficult to avoid cluttering up different things. The more spacious the workstation is, the easier it will be to manage it. It would be much preferable if you work on a big whiteboard or a giant desk when you are developing a value stream map.

Don't develop the value stream map all alone

It is best to develop the value stream map with a team of professionals who are personally involved in the process. It eliminates or reduces the possibility of overlooking a step or classifying an essential activity as waste or vice versa. It also allows you to have an eagle's view of all the steps involved in the process and find the loopholes in the process.

Six Sigma Methodology

"Six Sigma is a statistical-based methodology used to reduce variations and remove defects in various processes and business transactions." We have already discussed the pertinent concepts of six sigma such as standard deviation, mean, upper specification limit and lower specification limit so we will not repeat those here. However, a concise discussion of variations must be done to continue the topic in an orderly fashion, so it is discussed hereunder.

Concepts and Tools of Six Sigma

Apart from calculating the mean, standard deviation, determining the upper specification limit and lower specification limit and finding the defects per million opportunities (DPMO), many handy tools are developed and utilized to reduce variations and minimize defects. These tools and techniques are termed as six sigma tools and some of them are listed hereunder.

- Fishbone Diagram
- Why-Why-Why Diagram
- Pareto Diagram
- Correlation Chart
- Punchlist
- Failure Mode Analysis
- Zero Defect

Detailed description and analysis of the tools used in the six sigma methodology might require a separate book of its own, however, a brief discussion on some of the most important and extensively used tools of six sigma is done in the proceeding paragraphs.

Chapter 34
The Motorola Case

The Six Sigma methodology gained traction in the 1980s after it was endorsed by Motorola. In that time period, Motorola had been trying to measure the defects their company was turning out on a granular level. This was quite the shift from previous methods, which had been measuring things on a much larger scale. Their hope, in putting their mistakes under the microscope, so to speak, was to reduce the amount of waste being created, while turning out a better product for their customers to use.

In implementing Six Sigma, the return on their investment was a massive increase in the level of quality in several of their products. Motorola even received the first Malcolm Baldrige National Quality Award, which is in its third decade of being awarded for performance excellence in United States companies. Shortly thereafter, Motorola shared their Six Sigma method with the world, causing several other companies across the country to start earning these awards in performance excellence as well. By 2003, the total estimated savings caused by the use of Six Sigma was topping out over $100 billion.

Chapter 35
How to Harness Lean to Foster Innovation and Develop New Ideas

There is a lot of talk about innovation and how companies have started to innovate their processes to work efficiently. But, what is the impact of using lean to foster innovation in business? The potential is huge, and it is essential that every business harness that potential if some criteria are met. The word innovation can either excite or terrify us. Many people are skeptical about the innovation of processes in their company. But, there are others who are embracing this innovation with open arms. The former group is stuck in their old ways while the latter are willing to unlock their creative potential to improve the business. However, there is one thing that is certain – the leaner a business, the easier it is to innovate the business. The debate on how lean thinking can foster innovation is one that has gained popularity. But, what is innovation? Innovation can be defined as the process of changing or transforming a process or an idea into something new, which will make the lives of the employees in the business more accessible. Regardless of what process the business is transforming – manufacturing technology, products, services, software and business models – any innovation should always lead to the maximization and creation of value for the stakeholder or customer. This means that the business should meet not only the needs and demands of the customer but also anticipate them. Apple is one company that has understood its customer group very well. I am sure you know where this is leading. Lean is one process that is customer-driven, and every principle and tool is based on the idea of freeing up the business's resources by removing waste and also maximizing the customers' value. This helps to include newer projects and also allocate some resources to those processes. Many people believe that a lean business can innovate processes since it encourages the employees to identify innovative ways to improve its processes. The business community has realized that lean thinking is one model that should be used to foster innovation in business. Many organizations have used lean thinking as a foundation to innovate their ideas and processes. Take Pixar, for instance, which is a company that has implemented feedback loops and team-based collaboration. This has helped employees overcome their creative block thereby triggering innovation. It is also important to remember that it is not only businesses that can benefit from lean thinking. Social, economic and environmental problems have become driving forces behind innovation. People and businesses should be respectful and mindful of the resources of our planet before they begin to innovate. This innovation should contribute to solving the challenges of our time. Toyota Automotive has taught the world that lean thinking improves the society. This is further proof that lean thinking and innovation are a perfect match. It has been proved that lean thinking is more superior to traditional manufacturing. But one has to remember that lean thinking is more about improving the management system and leadership behavior. Lean drives innovation and is an approach that is based on learning. However, certain conditions have to be in place for lean management to succeed.

Organizational Structure for Lean Innovation

An organization must have the right structure to foster innovation through lean thinking. Companies must always be inclusive in the sense that every stakeholder must participate in the decisions that the company makes. For example, employees, engineers, suppliers, scientists and customers must agree upon every decision that is made by the company to maximize value for the customers. Every function that takes place in a business must be included in innovation, and this is what lean thinking teaches us. The phenomenon of "open innovation" arises when every team in an organization is included in the process of innovation. This concept suggests that every innovative idea must be welcome even if it is coming from outside the organization. Businesses can take ideas that were coined by college students, scientists, young entrepreneurs and sometimes amateurs as well. A striking example of this phenomenon is Wikipedia. Any person who has additional information about a particular concept can make changes to pages in Wikipedia. Some traditional organizations are catching up and accepting products that were invented outside the organization. A company that is open to innovation must have a flat organizational structure since vertical structures have been known to fail. Business leaders must always identify the processes or layers in the structure that add value to their customers. There are a few strategies that a business can use to foster innovation through lean thinking in their organization.

How to Start the Process of Innovation and Experimentation

Understand why

Most businesses have started to innovate their processes. The ideas can be taken from outside the business. This does not mean that a business should always choose ideas from outside the organization. If the business is unable to sketch or draft an idea that can maximize value for the customers, it does not understand the process fully. Additionally, it cannot implement new ideas successfully if it does not understand how those ideas benefit the company and the customer.

Business Factors

The management must always look at the business factors in their business and their competitors' businesses. If the factors used to conduct processes are the same, no innovation has been made to the process. This reduces the competitive advantage that the business may have over its competitors.

Business Model Diagram

If there are any competitive barriers, they must be removed to start improving and innovating processes. The management must outline the key activities, partners, cost structure, revenue stream and value propositions and observe them keenly to understand if any changes can be made.

Value Matrix

If there are any products or services that the customers do not appreciate or want, these can be removed from the value stream to enhance the process. This allows businesses to invest in fewer resources and add more value to the products and services. Businesses will have the ability to elevate the elements of the business that are bringing in more value and also create different purchases that are in line with the demands of the customers.

Strategy Profile

Businesses must revisit their business strategies and their competitors to identify areas where they can innovate and newer areas of business that can be tapped into. This will help the business identify new areas of work and also develop products and services within that area of work.

Business Model Diagram

Businesses must always identify ways to solve problems and also identify new ways to develop and enhance customer relationships. There was one landscaping company that passed the following message to different households by flinging Frisbees into their yards - "We work on your neighbor's lawn. Let us work on yours too!" If the customer had never thought of hiring a landscaping company before, they might think about it twice since it will make their life easier.

Experimentation

Every business is allowed to fail. If there is a new concept that has been developed, the business should put it into action to see how the customers view it. There is a possibility that the idea may fail, but it is all right to fail. This helps the business identify what can be done better the next time an idea is implemented.

Renewal

Ideas that have been implemented should never be ignored. The business must revisit the ideas and see what can be improved to enhance customer experience. Always make upgrades to existing ideas since innovation is an ongoing process.

Chapter 36
How to Foster Learning and Experimentation through Lean

A learning organization is not different from lean management. Learning is a process that is embedded in lean management. An organization where teams learn from everyday processes and also experiment with innovations and changes made to a process is called a lean and learning organization. Every employee in an organization must learn every day about the processes and enhance their knowledge of the processes. This will enable the employees to cater to any problems that may occur during the process. Every employee must focus on the following questions:

- What have I learned today?
- Have I implemented any new changes to an existing process?
- Have I experimented with new processes?
- What is the data trying to tell me today?

Learning organizations are not the current trend, and there are very few businesses that have begun to learn about the processes and have tried to innovate those processes. What every business must remember is that learning provides the business with an environment where employees are given the freedom to think and also embrace the idea that solutions to work-related problems are found in their mind. The employee must always tap into his or her knowledge base and use that knowledge to develop concepts and ideas that will improve the process. In a lean business, learning is not restricted to training only. Training does help the employees develop some skills and also grasp and understanding of how the company functions. But, through learning, the employees will develop better skills and more knowledge that can enhance the profitability of the company.

Learning Model

The following learning model can be implemented in businesses to enhance learning.

Level 1

Every employee must learn the process, procedures, understand why a process is being done the way it is and also some essential facts about the process. This is a level of learning that applies to processes where only minor changes can be made.

Level 2

Learn new skills that can be transferred to situations at work. If the employee is in a new situation or has been shifted to a new process, he or she must have the ability to respond to changes in the process. The business can also choose to bring in outside expertise for this level of learning. There can be training that will help employees enhance their skills.

Level 3

Employees must always learn to adapt. This is a level of learning that applies to situations that are dynamic and where every solution must be developed. Experimentation and learning from failure are two ways of learning in this level.

Level 4

This is where an employee learns to learn. This is about how an employee can be creative and innovate processes. He or she can learn to design processes for the future. Knowledge is reframed at this level, and every assumption made by an employee is challenged. Learning organizations set employees free. They are not required to be passive players in the business but can learn to express their views and ideas and also challenge those ideas and their skills to improve the work environment. Employees can create an environment where they can create and achieve the results that they truly desire.

Learning Culture

It is difficult to establish a learning culture in organizations that are not lean since they are comfortable in old practices and rarely find the necessity to change their processes. That being said, it is hard to establish a learning culture in any business.

External or Future Orientation

Organizations that have external or future orientation can understand their environment. Some teams comprise of senior members of the organization who take some time out of their busy day to develop a plan for the future. Additionally, the business can also choose to employ advisors who can help them plan their business.

Free Flow and Exchange of Information

There should be some systems in place that ensure that there are experts available whenever needed. Employees must have the chance to expand their horizons and also network with employees or professionals from other companies. This will give them an opportunity to enhance their knowledge of different processes, which will help them become experts in the process.

Commitment to Personal Development and Learning

With the support from the top management, employees must have the chance to learn. Employees who make an effort to learn regularly must be rewarded. This act will ensure that other employees also step forward and learn more. The employees must also be given the time to learn and also be encouraged to think lean which will help to remove waste from processes.

Trust and Openness

Every individual must be encouraged to develop or create ideas that will improve processes. They must also be allowed to voice their opinion, even if it is different from what other employees think since that gives rise to diversity. Views should be challenged.

Valuing Employees

Any idea that is developed by an employee should be tried and tested. An employee must be valued, and his or her thought process must be stimulated. If the idea is experimented and fails, the employee must learn from that failure and develop an idea that overcomes any errors.

In simpler words, a learning organization does not only implement ideas developed by senior management. It also allows employees to express their views.

Lean thinking is about creating a learning organization

It is important to remember that lean businesses are not only about the processes, it is also about learning. Every process is a great tool to transform an organization into a learning organization. This should be the goal that every organization must achieve in the current market and economy.

The disruption, complexity and change are going to continue, and the rate at which these phenomena are occurring will only increase with time. The only competitive advantage that any business has in this economy is the ability to adapt, and the only way a business can adapt is by learning continually.

If a business wants to compete in the information-saturated economy, it is necessary for it to remain competitive, dynamic and to look for ways to improve its processes. It is essential to remember that change is the only constant in every organization and every business must rid itself of the traditional hierarchy that often averse to change.

A learning organization embraces change and creates reference points that help to rebuild the structure. Learning organizations are healthier since they:

- Increase the ability to accept and manage change
- Garner and encourage independent thought
- Improve quality
- Give employees hope that things can always get better
- Develop a committed organization and workforce
- Stretch and expand perceived limits

To create a learning organization the management or leadership must be effective. This means that leadership cannot follow the traditional hierarchy but must consist of a mixed group of people from different levels in the system.

The business must also accept that every employee can solve some problems that may occur in the organization. The business must give employees the benefit of doubt and encourage them to voice their opinion, which will help the business forge ahead and create a bright future.

An organization must never consider itself separate from the world. It is only when it connects to the world that it can build a learning culture and environment.

One of the biggest challenges that every business must overcome is the way it identifies people within the organization. Only when every employee is considered equal is there a possibility to develop a learning organization.

Conclusions

Thanks for downloading this book. It's my firm belief that it will provide you with all the answers to your questions.

Lean thinking is a way of business and not just a business project. There are only some businesses that have begun to use lean thinking to enhance and improve processes and also maximize customer value. The group of businesses that do not implement lean thinking is afraid of change. However, change is the only constant in the market and life.

Lean thinking requires a change not only in the processes but also in the management and leadership since the business has to be open to new thoughts and ideas.

Through lean management and thinking, a business can encourage its employees to identify ways to improve processes and also innovate or develop new processes that maximize value. This creates a sense of equality in the organization since every employee has the right to voice his or her opinion.

Section 3: Lean Six Sigma

Some things are that obvious - and that is a good starting point. It cannot also carry fluff and unnecessary baggage with it. That is what lean connotes, isn't it? So, we have bagged those initial marks; let us now find out what Six Sigma then is.

Simply put, Six Sigma is a method of working where you focus on minimizing wastage in whatever it is that you are doing. We have in mind the service sector; the manufacturing sector; and even the trading sector. Six Sigma helps you monitor, through observed data, how well you are doing. What you do in Six Sigma is analyze the data within your project and establish the degree of poor performance - and that is what you work on reducing.

Surely, you understand what we are essentially saying. For example, if you happen to be manufacturing a brand of alcoholic drinks, there is no way you will anticipate sending out to the market some cartons with empty bottles well corked. This is because your plan is not to short-change your customers and chase them away, but to supply them with cartons of full bottles of the drink. You do not also want to send out some batches with lower alcohol levels than stated on the label. Six Sigma is basically that - no complicated stuff. If you are running a salon, you want your clients to leave your parlor with their heads looking like the picture you both agreed on - or maybe close. And if your role is to supply materials to a manufacturing entity, you cannot surely afford to be that notorious supplier costing your customers hours upon hours of downtime because of your unreliable deliveries. You need to have set timelines within which to make deliveries after receiving the orders. In short, Lean Six Sigma calls for systems whose performance can be measured. And after gauging your performance against what is expected, you deduce where losses are occurring in terms of wasted inputs and so on; and then you correct that.

So what are the guidelines in Six Sigma?

First of all, you need to know what you would like to achieve: your intended specifications

Then you need to measure the results of your performance at every stage of the process. For purposes of credible assessment, you need to then get the average of various results that you get over a set period of time, and that is the figure you then take as your mean for purposes of calculations. Those two - your intended results and your actual mean results - must be as close as possible for you to speak of efficiency and impressive performance. The wider the variation between those two levels, the worse you are performing. In short, you do not want to deviate from what you planned with a big margin. You want to be as close as possible to what you initially planned. And you know what they call such kind of discrepancies? Well, they are called deviations. And that is because you are deviating from the planned results. You are deviating from the best way of doing things; the reason your performance is not optimum.

Your Expectations for Lean Six Sigma

At the end of the day, what you seek to achieve when you introduce this methodology of doing things into your organization is:

Alignment of projects with the organization's strategic objectives

This you do by having clearly defined roles for everyone involved and having set protocols for measurements

Objective assessment of processes

You want to know how ready the processes are to deliver the required output at the quality anticipated - and that is as close as possible to excellence

Modification or even overhaul of existing inefficient processes

The extent to which this is done, of course, is determined by the results of the processes assessment.

But how do we use Six Sigma to evaluate performance?

That is easy - always is, when you are using specific data and clear procedure. To help you gauge if you are doing well using the Six Sigma method, you are given an accepted deviation against which to compare your success. As such, if your mean performance is within the accepted standard deviation from your set goal, you can give yourself a pat on the back. Your performance, whether in production; in trade; or even in service provision can be termed good. But why, really, can you not be even closer to your goal than that; not deviating at all? What would happen if you smelt or even touched success; or the best performance possible? Would you not be the best rated in your industry? Would you not be reaping the most profits that you could? Would you also not have a well-oiled system where things work whether you are around supervising or not? Essentially, you would be utilizing every bit of input to its optimum and incurring no losses or waste. The implication of such efficiency is that every input and every effort contributes directly and unmistakably to revenue creation. No input is in excess and none is redundant. In the same vein, inputs are not insufficient in a manner to cause downtime or bottlenecks. Lean Six Sigma is about smooth running processes utilizing only inputs that are relevant and necessary to produce the desired results as per plan. That is the working of Lean Six Sigma when implemented by knowledgeable people: getting rid of the sticky stuff that lines the performance passage slowing it down. Think of the doctor's recommendation as far as your heart is concerned - clear the bad cholesterol that lines up your arteries, and if there is plaque do the same; and the blood will serve your body like you are just beginning your youth. That is what the call is in all spheres of life. You need to clear anything that slows down your performance.

Now, you will agree that you need to know exactly what this sticky stuff is in order to know what kind of brush to use to get rid of it. It is even important, before then, to ascertain if it is cleanable in the first place, because if it is not, a major decision will need to be made regarding the viability of the whole project.

Here are the eight categories of waste that you need to set your eyes on:

- Downtime
- Overproduction
- Waiting
- Non utilized talent
- Transportation
- Inventory
- Motion
- Extra processing

Shorten it as DOWNTIME, and you will not forget it. Wow! That technical sounding term - Lean Six Sigma - boils down to bringing down DOWNTIME as far as humanly possible...? It surely does; even when what is humanly possible involves using machinery and technical knowhow. It is essentially about making best use of resources at your disposal, and reducing redundancy all round. For those who know nothing about reducing DOWNTIME, waste within an organization becomes like a disease or a cultural weakness. Individuals do not tie their wasteful actions to the organization's end results. And that is what Lean Six Sigma seeks to clean up. Every move and every piece of resource has an impact on the organization's end results, and this is what every employee is made to appreciate when working within Lean Six Sigma projects. And since the processes are data based and all evaluations are clear at every stage, it is easy for individuals concerned to appreciate when they are doing well for the company and when they are doing the organization disservice through inefficiencies. Whereas the Lean Six Sigma way of working may seem to keep everyone on their toes, once they get the hang of it, it becomes a morale booster as great performers stand out through measurable results.

Chapter 37
What is the Lean Six Sigma Method?

Six sigma lean is a discipline which conveys client esteem. Not from the company's perspective, but from the client's perspective. It conveys client's value through productive activity, and quality. This implies that, lean six sigma conveys steady quality.

What is Lean Six Sigma?

Lean six sigma can be an idea of management, known for adequately improving job forms, in view of the mixture of the various tools of Sigma Six and Lean. Sigma Lean six is a procedure improvement technique intended to remove issues, eradicate inefficiency, waste, and improve working conditions to give a great response to client's needs.

It joins the techniques, instruments & standards for Six Sigma Lean all unto one prominent and incredible strategy for improving your company's activities.

Lean six sigma's group-oriented approach has shown results in amplifying productivity and increasing profits for organizations around the globe.

Lean manufacturing comprises 25 significant ideas, for example, proofing of error, SMED source of the quality, Kanban, 5s Balancing of Line, Cellular Manufacturing, Standard Operations, and Value Stream Mapping. A couple of associations put in a few years executing these wonderful guidelines into their organization. Six sigma includes a 5 phase approach DMAIC (Define, Measure, Analyze, Improve, Control), utilizing a few instruments all through the stages.

Incorporate the two strategies and these devices, and it is anything but difficult to understand the disappointment in activities. But on the off chance that the affiliation has the bent to manage the execution and help center the endeavors, the program transforms into a shotgun approach and is bound to come up short. Most affiliations couldn't withstand the perplexity and postponed costs without significant recompense.

The two six sigma and manufacturing of lean standards have been tested to work. Numerous organizations have expanded business, decreased costs, expanded throughput, and brought down process durations utilizing the two methods. It is reasonable to use all the tools that are available and accessible to get the most advancement possible.

It is basic for organizations to let the problem decide the tools that are required, as opposed to decide the tool and force it's utilization. Not many of the works shows plainly the assembling lean thought. In the occasion, if a machine has a short set up time and it is the bottleneck, by then a SMED undertaking is basic. It may be a straightforward SMED (Single moment trade of bite the dust) or a piece of a kaizen rush.

There are clearly various exercises which will be founded on a six sigma. For example, a clump strategy plant using 12 unmistakable fixings with various methodology at different temperatures, rates, and viscosities, would require a six sigma task to choose the best blend of machines and speed to get incredible results. A segment of the six sigma instruments used would be speculation trying, investigation of fluctuation, factual examination, and plan of trials.

There are different sorts of activities where both six sigma instruments and lean collecting would best loosen up the test. For instance, expect a bunch getting ready issue incorporated the different temperatures and speed. The best methodology may be a sure blend of machines, yet the best one has a 5 man bunch with a 2 hour course of action time.

It is the perfect open door for the lean gadgets to diminish the cost per man hour utilizing SMED, just as OEE (Overall Equipment Effectiveness). An average use of lean gear or devices in a six sigma undertaking is during the Improve arrange. The issue is being Define, Measured, and Analyzed by six sigma venture, anyway a lean gadget is essential to explain it. Another six sigma instrument/hardware will help Control it. In case the association simply used one of lean assembling or six sigma devices, the issue may not get unraveled.

The greatness of six sigma is the proficient method to manage conditions. The advantage of lean assembling mechanical assemblies is the speed of use. Right when the two gadgets are merged and used when important to settle business openings, the best result and most noticeable compensation will be gained.

What are DMAIC Cycles?

DMAIC are the information propelled procedure that are used to process improvement cycles. The abbreviation represents 5 indoor associated steps or stages that are; face has a particular purpose with a general objective.

In the Define face; an undertaking charger is made, to define the business issues, problem team, objectives, high project timeline, and target. The motivation behind the Measure face; is to decide the gauge execution of the procedure. This means that, we have to quantify how the procedure performs today. In the Analyze face; the group may break down information and the procedure stream to distinguish the main cause of waste, defects, and variation The Improve face; is tied in with creating and devaluating, to dispose of or lessen the recognized root cause. The major goals of the control face; is to get gains. This is achieved by creating or updating standard operating procedures, and ongoing managing of process performance based on a control plan.

The motivation behind the Control face; is to support the increases. This is accomplished by making or refreshing standard working methods, and ongoing managing of procedure execution dependent on a control plan.

DMAIC has gain credibility and reliability over the years, as an improvement technique that is simple to apply, reasonable for group, and efficient at conveying execution upgrades.

Who Are The Main Players?

While applying Lean Six Sigma, people all over the level of organization and business functions needs to play certain role towards a prosperous execution of this strategy.

The important ones are; Black or Green Belt, Champion, Project Team, and Process Owner.

Sponsor

The role of the executive sponsor is vital and important for the success of this initiative. The set of people are known members in a management or board members, and actively follow the implementation of sigma lean six. For the organization, they provide the resources and budget required for the program, and individuals for the projects.

Champions

These are probably the single most important role within the lean six sigma. They take the vision, and the directions from executives, and establish organizational objectives that need to be looked into by using lean six sigma. In addition, they also identify and prioritize project ideas which they assign to the black or green belt. As department head or manager of an area, champions are the ones responsible for the success of projects in their division. Once a project has been started, they provide motivation and consultation, and assist the black or green belt, and their team in removing any issue that might stop the project from being successful.

Green Or Black Belt

These are professionals that acts as project leader of lean six sigma projects. They also serve as teachers and mentors of the team members. The most important role and responsibility of a black or green belt is to deliver solution to business issues to the process owner.

Well, Black Belts sell mostly 100% dedicated resources to lean six sigma, and responsible for large scale projects.

Green Belts are traditionally only dedicated to part time within companies, and manage small to medium projects.

Process Owner

Another key player is the process owner. The process owner is a professional. This professional is the one meant for the procedure of business which are the goals of the lean sigma six initiative. One of the most important roles that the process owner has is to help for an execution prior for the problem solved that is brought about by the black or green belt, and typically control to improve procedure after the project has been closed. He also assist with the identification of future project opportunities, because he is the one that usually know the process intimately, and feels the pain of any issues we have in our processes.

The Team Members

The team members help the black and green belt to execute a project. They assist with things like, experiment, data or information collection, experimentation, and other duty related to executing the project. The reason why this people are incredibly important and need to be well selected, is because they provide the expertise needed to analyze a process appropriately.

When To Apply The Lean Six Sigma

When confronting a business issue, the accompanying criteria ought to be met to effectively be a part of this initiative.

These issues are connected from a dealed procedure: A business procedure is the tedious sequence of tasks or activities that produce a particular product or services for a specific client. The procedure runs often: This implies that the procedure happens all the time, and annually. The more often the procedure runs, the more advantage can be produced over a specific timeframe. There isn't a known answer for the issue: If you know the issue, you needn't bother with lean six sigma. Just take care of business. The underlying cause of the issue isn't known: Lean six sigma is a critical solving technique, concentrating on recognizing the underlying cause forgiven issue. It just bodes well to apply the apparatuses and ideas, if those jobs does not need to be finished. There is information accessible: Data availability and accessibility is basic to the achievement of lean six sigma and the speed. It is additionally the most basic condition to be met when applying lean six sigma. Without information, we can't gauge, and without having the option to gauge, we can't measure and devaluate the procedure execution, before and after development have been made.

This topic is the information driven procedure, used for adequately improve business forms.

Lean Six Sigma Methodology

These strategies pay attention to disposals. Waste incorporates utilizing too many staff individuals to finish a work. This makes a business spend an excessive amount of cash on work and even tries harder which can hinder, or slow production. Waste likewise incorporates making pointless buys on resources, assets or tools that you truly needn't bother with. One can figure out how to distinguish the waste and diminish it, just when you experience lean six sigma certification training. This can help a business reduce expenses, and also improve efficiency with workers. Congestion happen and hence hinder a business procedure fundamentally. At the point when representatives go attend lean Six Sigma certification training, they are instructed to recognize congestions inside a whole association right down to explicit procedures. Being capable of recognizing congestions offers your organization the chance to dispose them and amplify efficiency. Lean Six Sigma courses give brilliant training thinking basically and concocting imaginative answers for fix issues.

Another crucial part of lean six sigma is client loyalty and satisfaction. Clients are the place the cash originates from and in the event that you can't fulfill them, at that point you may not be good to go for a really long time. Organizations that have seen they have had an enormous loss of clients frequently send their staff individuals to Six Sigma Lean Certificate training in order to make something happen. Sigma Six Training will help workers get an in-depth comprehension and recognize the necessities of a client and how to meet their demand. This will surely help as a business accomplished and manufacture better client connections and expand your client base.

Lean Six Sigma techniques are designed for upgrading business forms in different ways. Your business can profit by removing waste, congestions, hindering efficiency, and improving client loyalty and satisfaction. These courses will profit the representative, and furthermore your business. You will realize that better productivity is an outcome alongside higher incomes at last.

Chapter 38
Introducing Lean Production

Lean is an end of the types of non-value added work from the client's point of view in business transactions and procedures. Lean centers on effectiveness; it limits delays, mistakes, and waste.

History Of Lean

Lean has its root traced back to the 90's of the nineteenth century. Frederick Taylor was an American mechanical engineer. He is called the management of scientific and was a primary administration consultant. Taylor started make out and see persons work techniques to find the most ideal approach to carry out each work. The outcome was institutionalized work, and time study. At that point, Ford Henry came into field. An American Industrialist and an Originator of the Ford Motors Industries he was. He presented auto-mobile, American industry, and revolutionized transportation. He formed the primary extensive assembling procedure. His island park plan generation by setting fabrication equipment in procedure sequence. The outcome was, a lot higher generation, and quicker production time.

In the 60's of a century ago, a man named Taiichi Ohno, created what is normally referred to today as the Management. He was a Japanese business person, and a supervisor for Toyota. Taiichi is the pioneer of the Toyota production framework. Which became lean Manufacturing in the US. Ohno perceived the role of inventory, and created functional strategies to execute the idea of "Just the nick of time". He likewise distinguishes the seven different ways, which should be disposed of as the focal point of lean, to increase profitability, and business forms.

As per Lean terms, reliably, esteem is described by the customer. There are three unique approaches to arrange esteem;

Squander: This is by and large alluded to as a non-esteem include exercises.

Basic Activities: These exercises are known as worth includes exercises for which the customer needs to pay for. There are a few activities that fall somewhere in the center. These activities are generally known as Non-Value Activities. The jobs can be finished, regardless of whether they are not customarily characterized as value add. A good example of a business non-value add activity, will be test required to meet administrative or lawful prerequisites. These activities are not characterized as increasing the value of a procedure from the client's perspective. In any case, they can't be avoided. In a regular business process, whether transactional or manufacturing, an enormous measure of the activities is non-value add. Most procedures are 3 percent to 5 percent value add, and possibly 10 percent to 15 percent non-value add. Be that as it may, most of procedure are the non-value add.

To comprehend the concept of Lean, of importance it is imperative of note is to understand the concept of what waste is. As a focal point of lean, is about the decrease of waste.

Lean gives the definition of seven kinds of waste. These are; Transportation, Motion, Inventory, Rework, Waiting, Over-processing, and Overproduction.

Transportation: Any movement of an item is viewed as waste. Mails and Shipping are move services and items, however don't add value. Transportation doesn't change an item or services. It just conveys it.

Motion: This refers to the real conveyance of an individual. This may be an unnecessary movement inside the work station, or movement in a task that takes much time and effort to finish.

Inventory: This is any sort of materials or provisions that are kept, over the base, to take care of job. Inventory occupies room. An excess of inventory in term of work in progress is a significant contributor to long live time.

Rework: Rework is any fix or repair, change to an item after it has been made, or any correction that was not done right the first run through. One of the essential part of lean is value, and something only have value if it was done well the first run through.

Waiting: This waste shows waiting for data or information. An absence of data or information, or the delay in the process is an instance of waste, and something we need to remove completely. The objective is to be able to respond to the client's needs, with no delay to goods or services.

Over processing: This waste is about activities that add cost, however no value. We do activities that the client couldn't care less about, or doesn't request. At the end of the day, over-processing just means, accomplishing things that are repetitive.

Overproduction: This implies delivering excessively, or too early. It is producing to forecast, rather than to request. Overproduction exhaust our assets with things the clients don't require, and has not requested. If we listen to the client's prerequisite carefully, we can respond with goods that satisfies those needs.

Stream Value Mapping

This can be seen as the most fundamental & amazing principle and tool of Lean. Value stream mapping helps to visualize and map the business procedures. A stream value covers entire plans and procedures, which can be needed to create an item, or service. Moreover, a value stream map ought to incorporate procedure data, to evaluate and exhibit the procedure execution in a graphical form. By making a value stream map, a typical comprehension of the present condition of the procedure is figured out. Most important, it distinguishes waste, opportunities for development. Data is what different a value stream map from a standard procedure map. The objective is to get as much data, in terms of process execution measurements as possible.

Value stream metrics are; cycle times, process times, rework rate or defect rate, and circle times. Now, that the process cycle is visualized, and customary execution measurement are visible, we have an ideal basis to recognize waste, in and between procedure steps, as this is the main reason of creating the value stream maps. It makes it easy and simple to point at weak points along the process. When talking about weak points, it means the seven types of waste.

Within this extent of the waste analysis, the procedure improvement group ought to research the value stream map, and in the process, trashs are recognized. To show kind of trash, issue area at a value stream maps. Graphic signs can be utilized and added to the map appropriately. This genuine mark areas is for development to concentrate on, when creating ways and answers to lessen the non-value time spent in a procedure.

Before you begin to make your value stream map, there are some tips to remember.

Use sticky notes

Instead of using a software tool to document your process, it's easier to make changes, and most important, it contributes to employing engagement and involvements.

Use enough space

Don't restrict your mapping activity to a single shit of paper. Find a large piece of paper, or a white board, to document your map.

Create value stream maps with a team

Really, only one person has all of the process knowledge, to make sure that the right amount of knowledge is given, you should answer the question of who was involved in the process. When building the team, in other to develop a business procedure to the eradication of waste may include some tools and principles.

Chapter 39
Introducing Six Sigma

Six Sigma is a known as a measurable based methodology used to diminish variety, and discard blemishes in business strategies and exchanges.

History of Six Sigma

Six Sigma has its initiation in the 20's of a century back. Walter Shewhart was an analyst, physicist, and specialist. He displayed the differentiation of unique sections basic reason variety, and the control diagram.

In the twentieth century, Six Sigma was exhibited by Bill Smith, at Motorola. Smith, who was an American architect, known as the pioneer of six sigma. As an administration thought, six sigma seem to improve the nature of system, by perceiving, and disposing of the reason for disfigurements, or errors, and restricting varieties in business techniques.

In 1995, six sigma ended up being prominent, after Welch made it a point of convergence of his business method at general electric. Welch was executive, and CEO of General Electric. He expressed, six sigma is the most huge activity General Electric has ever utilized, as six sigma is tied in with reducing variety, and clearing out imperfections. These terms ought to be clarified.

What is Variation?

Variety is the extent of complexity, between the measurable mean, and all information indicates that are used make sense of the mean. All things considered, it is how much methodology execution changes around the normal. In six sigma, variety is assessed by figuring the standard deviation.

What is an imperfection?

A deformity is a quantifiable thing or administrations characteristics that doesn't meet a customer essential. It is any methodology execution outside of described specs.

Imperfections, in six sigma are assessed by figuring the DPMO

DPMO is determined by separating the aggregate sum of imperfection, by the absolute units.

DPMO (Defects per million chances) is dictated by isolating imperfections by unit, by circumstance per unit, duplicated by 100.

Why six Sigma is called Six Sigma

Similarly, as imperfections unto million chances, the level of sigma is an extent of methodology capacity. Methodology limit reveals to you how extraordinary, or poor the technique is performing. The level of sigma is evaluated by deviations of standards from the system mean (or normal) to an objective, or a stipulation limit. Each sign parts associate to a related deformity for each million open doors esteem.

Chapter 40
Why You Should Use the Lean Six Sigma Method

Lean Six Sigma can be linked to the most diverse formations, not just to the engineering ones. Can only engineers take Lean Six Sigma training? Whenever someone asks me this question, I rebut with another question: "Do only engineering students learn statistics during college?" The answer is simple. Of course not, after all, even in a psychology course the student may have contact with statistics. So you mean that anyone can become a Green Belt or Black Belt? Before answering this question let's take a brief reflection.

Engineers are, by definition, people of logical reasoning who use mathematical calculations to turn numbers into efficient processes and functional products. Another ability of your profile is to transfer the ideas from the clipboard to the real world, but for that to happen you also need to have a good understanding of social and economic issues. What I mean is that in the market, there is a very thin line between different areas of knowledge. In practice, every profession has a little of each area, without exceptions.

Let me give you some examples that prove this. A biologist must have knowledge of the social sciences to deal with his patients. A journalist needs to be knowledgeable about the accuracy of interpreting numbers that will give credibility to a story. An engineer needs to know the numbers to understand the social impact of new technology.

And what does this have to do with the Lean Six Sigma methodology? It goes without saying that if you think that only an engineer or an expert in the field of numbers can learn a managerial methodology that involves statistical calculations, you are making a serious mistake. This mistake may cost a better job position in the future, as companies are increasingly looking for multi-disciplinary professionals who are able to solve problems and generate results.

The studies of the last decade have consolidated the definition of the term Lean Six Sigma as a managerial philosophy that allows companies to leverage their profits by improving operations, improving quality, and eliminating defects, failures and process errors. Because it is so broad, this is a methodology that is not restricted to only one area, not least because it is applied not only in the operational sector of companies but also in the administrative areas. Today we have several examples of good results that Lean Six Sigma has brought to the HR, legal, commercial, and even marketing areas of a company. So if in each of these administrative areas, I'm talking about employees with different backgrounds, that is, this methodology is suitable for managers, advertisers, psychologists, economists, engineers, and many other types of professionals. So, anyone can do Lean Six Sigma training? The answer to this question is YES. Anyone can learn and apply the methodology.

The only prerequisite to take on a Lean Six Sigma training is to be willing to face the challenge. It is necessary to know that in the course there is an extensive statistical section that is part of the Six Sigma professional training, but if you are interested in learning to apply the methodology and to face this challenge, you have everything you need to become a professional more valued by the marketplace. Look for stimuli! The ideology of planning is trained in psychology and worked at the core of Human Resources. So it's easy to see: not only engineers or people who work with numbers can learn and apply Lean Six Sigma.

How Can Lean Six Sigma Help Me?

To ensure the success of Lean Six Sigma and therefore ensure its great contribution to achieving results, it is necessary to train people with the appropriate profile and we have already proven here that this does not mean the need for specific training. Duly trained employees will become sponsors of the program and specialists in methodology and quantitative and managerial tools, which will have a great impact in their areas of action and in their chances of reaching new goals and paths. By committing to learning, the consequences will be visible in your activities. Lean Six Sigma can be a possible system for many, just by wanting and having willpower.

Lean Six Sigma in Government Operations

As problems do not distinguish businesses, they occur in the most diverse economic segments and sizes of establishments and in almost every company there is a need for improvements. In the food industry, for example, there may be bottlenecks in the production chain, which can increase the cost of the commodity and generate a number of negative consequences for the organization. In the financial services sector, the difficulty of doing the credit analysis of clients can be an obstacle even to the survival of the business, because this segment is very competitive.

Six Sigma in the Industrial Area

In the industrial area, a manufacturer of auto parts must have a high degree of accuracy to meet the needs of automotive factories. Otherwise, defective items will represent a major loss to the business. In a credit card company, a challenge may be to increase sales to ensure the financial health of the company. Therefore, practically any type of company lives in search of perfecting some process to leverage its own results. What many of them do not know is how to do it.

The differential of Lean Six Sigma methodology in the search for improvements is that it has a very structured method, capable of scientifically proving whether the changes implanted in an organization have in fact resulted in improvement of productivity and quality. Therefore, by having a method, Lean Six Sigma can be applied to different realities with satisfactory results.

When they do not have this methodology, companies tend to want to solve their own production system failures. However, many of them take very inefficient and costly paths to the business, such as putting pressure on employees to get better results. Another unsuccessful way of raising performance is to find scapegoats internally but without any scientific criterion of performance analysis. In such cases, the company walks in circles without finding solutions to its own problems.

By using an improvement road map and using statistical tools to prove or reject hypotheses, the Lean Six Sigma methodology seeks to combine efficiency and effectiveness in the search for better business processes. From the point of view of the projects, it is much more advantageous to invest in this type of work, to solve and to prevent problems, than to bear the consequences of perceived failures by the clients.

Six Sigma in Services

A service provider whose quality is evaluated during the execution of the activity can suffer damages due to defects in the processes. In the case of a bank, if the customer is dissatisfied with something, he can try to solve it at first by self-service, either over the internet or by telephone. If he cannot, he may consider going to an agency to talk to the manager. If this still does not resolve the situation, the customer can complain on consumer protection websites or file a complaint. If all this happens, the banking institution will create a great liability for the institutional image, not counting the possible sanctions of the supervisory entities. Therefore, it is much more advantageous to proactively decrease the rate of complaints than to learn to live with negative results.

Six Sigma in Health Organizations

Other companies that perform closely with their customers are those of telephone companies and those of the health sector. In these cases, the consumer already forms an almost automatic value judgment regarding the enterprise. Therefore, such organizations should be careful not to sacrifice their own business because of a lack of "listening" to complaints and the observation of opportunities for improvement.

In the case of the health sector, the needs of companies are increasing due to a series of factors, such as increase and aging of the population, growth in costs to maintain adequate structure and technology for care, risk of damages to patients, etc. Because this sector deals with the highest good for a person, which is life itself, the degree of excellence in business performance must be enormous.

Over the last few years, various applications of the Lean Six Sigma methodology in the health sector have shown that it is possible to improve three aspects of this area: the care of the population as a whole, the patient's experience in care, and the reduction of costs with the decrease of waste. As you may realize, the Lean Six Sigma approach not only considers economic factors but also customer satisfaction. In the case of the health area, it is not enough for the patient to get treatment for a certain illness, but he must also feel welcomed and cared for.

Six Sigma in the Public Sector

It is necessary to mention that even in the public sector it is possible to have applications of Lean Six Sigma. Entities and government agencies have a great history of dissatisfaction on the part of users of the services. Cases of friction between these parties are common.

In order to overcome this dissatisfaction in the public sector, managers must lead improvement policies in their respective areas of activity, to bureaucratize processes and speed up service delivery. It is clear that proactive initiatives presuppose a certain degree of political will on the part of those responsible for the operation of the public machine, yet they demonstrate that it is possible for Lean Six Sigma to operate in this sector. In Scotland, for example, the model of improvement is a state policy in the country, so it transcends the political plans of some rulers.

Chapter 41
Benefits of Six Sigma

Associations face increasing expense, and rivalry consistently. In particular, the demonstrated advantages are assorted.

Faster forms

With lean six sigma, associations accomplish quick procedures, by expelling all kind of non-esteem included work, as demonstrated by the seven sorts of waste.

Higher quality

Lean six sigma expects to accomplish higher caliber in term of procedure, soundness, and capacity, through the decrease of variety, and the end of imperfections.

Increased consumer loyalty

The essential wanted advantage of all procedure improvement exercises inside length of six sigma lean is a decrease for cost, by accomplishing stream line forms that are totally quicker, and all the more productively. Less assets are required, bringing about diminished cost. Moreover, less variety and imperfections prompts less

Cost of low quality incorporates cost that emerge because of the hole between the ideal and genuine item, and administration quality. Lean six sigma expands pay, by empowering an association or an organization to accomplish more with less assets.

Improved worker spirit and aptitude

Lean six sigma expands a worker's commitment, and adequacy. Lean six sigma don't just decrease cost, and expands income. It decidedly influences individuals by connecting with them in improving the manner in which they work. By including representatives in lean six sigma ventures, they increase a more noteworthy gratefulness for the effect of the work they do on primary concern business result. Too, as a thankfulness, or how crafted by different workers in offices additionally add to progress. When representatives get settled with lean six sigma scales, learnt through preparing or tasks. They can develop effectively, and keep on improving their business forms, in view of a genuine set up procedure.

The prime mandate of business: better, less expensive, and quicker. However, when squeezed for a clarification of what that truly implies, most administrators can just express the craving to get the most work, at all time, with the least individuals. When examined further on what's going on with their business forms, reactions are fluctuated however unsurprising. We need more individuals. The PC frameworks are lousy. The client's requests are unreasonable.

Most officials neglect to see the genuine issue. The genuine issue is the poor arrangement of the business procedure to the client needs and the abundance steps in the process that carries no an incentive to the client experience.

Other than consumer loyalty, putting resources into administration process improvement can rapidly add genuine dollars to the primary concern. It is settled that roughly 80% of an organization's contributed capital is the expense of individuals performing administration related obligations. So contributed capital is extremely the "Cost of individuals." Combined with observational information that has demonstrated that administration expenses are swelled by 30% to 80% waste, it bodes well to concentrate vitality on improving assistance side procedures.

How Lean Six Sigma Improves The Bottom Line

Services, typically encompass an organization's service framework, such as, Operations, Finance, Sales, Marketing, Human Resources, etc. A major characteristic of most service procedures is it that they depend on people to accomplish their objective.

Service process improvement is challenging for the following reasons:

They are moderate and costly on the grounds that there is in every case a lot of Work-in-Process (WIP). This is principally because of an inability to control WIP speed (for example work is pushed into the procedure regardless of work leaving the procedure).

- Less than 20% of administration procedure time includes worth or upgrades a client's understanding.
- The less obvious nature of administration procedures makes the procedure harder to track and issues harder to distinguish, measure, and fix.
- They have a convention of uniqueness, opportunity, and innovativeness.
- They are portrayed by an absence of significant information for basic leadership.
- People, your significant resource, are likewise the significant reason for process variety.
- Customers can't be dealt with like stock.

Sigma six lean for Services can be seen as augmentation of Sigma Six, not a substitution. Sigma six lean for Services & Sigma Six work pair.Six Sigma brings restrained, client driven, information driven devices and procedures to measures process mistakes, recognize changes, dispose of them, and bring the procedure under Statistical Process Control (SPC). Lean Six Sigma for Services centers around speed and productivity.

Lean Six Sigma for Services is ideal for improving help forms for the accompanying reasons:

- It isolates "esteem included" from "non-esteem included" work with Six Sigma devices to dispose of the major points of included non-esteemed exercises & (therefore) their expense.
- It gives a way to measuring and dispensing with the expense of multifaceted nature.
- Like its Six Sigma partner, it centers around consumer loyalty and quality by perceiving openings and wiping out client characterized surrenders.
- It perceives that variety thwarts the capacity to dependably convey top notch administrations.

- It requires information driven choices and joins a complete arrangement of value devices under an incredible system for successful critical thinking.
- It gives an exceptionally prescriptive social foundation for practical outcomes.

I have discovered that it is smarter to bring a procedure into measurable procedure control initial (Six Sigma), at that point take a shot at improving its ability (Lean). As it were, expel variety at that point raise execution level. At the point when a business procedure has been "Inclined" it has the accompanying qualities:

- The procedure is under factual control (for example assignable cause variety have been wiped out)
- The procedure works at a cycle productivity, more noteworthy than 20%. (Cycle effectiveness is known as the worth include time inside a procedure)
- It utilizes a draw framework where new work is discharged into the procedure just when old work has left.
- It utilizes visual controls to oversee and screen the procedure.

Lean Six Sigma for Services augments investor esteem by accomplishing the quickest pace of progress in consumer loyalty, cost, quality, speed, and contributed capital. It is a procedure, set of standards, and devices that attention on quickening the speed of all procedures over the endeavor by taking out waste and non-esteem included advances.

Organizations who have put vigorously in business process improvement have perceived a few crucial facts:

- Getting quick can really improve quality
- Enhanced quality can really improve speed
- Reducing unpredictability improves speed and quality

As you embark for improving business processes, stay focused on the above fundamentals using Lean Six Sigma for Services and you will see an improved bottom line.

Chapter 42
The Lean Six Sigma Method

It is not always easy to determine what to improve even when the organization decides to do so. There are so many things to check and many issues to point. It is always hard to know how to start and where to start. The Six Sigma approach is considered to be the best in the world as it answers all these questions. Keeping in mind the core principles of Lean Six Sigma, one can directly head towards improvement.

The Lean Six Sigma covers each and every step of processing in a systemic manner - here are its core principles:

Giving Priority To Customers

It is the first principle is related to customers in Six Sigma as they hold much importance in its functioning. The business advice of the past is considered true today that a customer is always right. Customers play a key role in the success of any organization. They are necessary for any business to mature. Therefore, no matter what business you do, you should give the first priority to your customers always. Keep in mind that without fulfilling the demands of the customer, your business might stop to grow further.

Each choice you make ought to carry your organization closer to conveying the greatest esteem. It's a good pre-practice to be sure about maintaining the degree of quality you have guaranteed your clients before making any minor or intense changes. Your new process implementation should focus on your goals without affecting or only improving the quality of your product or service.

Improving the value of the customer is the key thing. Lean Six Sigma offers companies and individuals the core principles to drive the business forward, a holistic view for the whole business, not just one component of it. It defines your proper goals and tells you where you must stand. Like trying to optimize the production process of some items that no one likes, it carries almost no value in doing that, rather than advancing the production process of products that people enjoy and want the most.

The PDCA cycle or Deming Cycle could be used here. It checks out the six sigma idea of continuously improving the quality model. An unmistakable idea of what comprises quality in your business shapes how you are willing to improve items and processes. You have to comprehend what your worth is and how it can be further improved.

The model PDCA Cycle has four logical and continuous learning steps that include Plan, Do, Check, and Act. Sometimes, it is also referred to as the PDSA Cycle in which 'Check' is changed with 'Study'.

If you are evaluating the production and supply process, remove the steps which don't contribute much profit; using this practice you can comprehend what is inefficient and what is not. Of chance, if you do not evaluate then you just cannot viably figure out what is inefficient. Hence, you can not make changes to improve.

Process improvements lead to ending what is not important and not ending the process and customer value gives a clear picture of it.

Six Sigma focuses on understanding the needs of the customers by using all means. Changes should be made for improvement, but the quality should be sustained.

Understanding The Heart Of The Process

Where your process is standing right now? Its evaluation is the only means to make the right decision and move forward. Designing of the value stream is what makes Lean Six Sigma special. It gives the complete idea of every step involved in your process and draws attention to the waste.

A couple of bits of plastic and glass on a mechanical production system, at last, become a LED TV? There is a value stream map for every progression that is involved in this process from buying all the necessary components, gathering them, running a quality inspection to dispersing the completed item. This stream map allows the organization to figure out which steps include more worth. Rest which does not work can be expelled from the procedure immediately.

Automated process mining is one of the core principles of Lean Six Sigma where whatever you do is process-driven. You can't simply leave things over a hunch, possibility, or any capacity because a process should be all smooth and practical.

All things considered, one of the initial steps is to make sense of and comprehend the issues.

The bottleneck seems to be the common and most clear inability to accomplish a smooth process stream. It is a zone of the process that is performed below the standard. It brings all levels down depending on it to its own level or the opposite of it where a zone of the process has the capability to perform far more than other levels.

When process mining is used during any process, programmed software is used according to the user's need; it can call attention to most bottlenecks as a feature of its analysis. Automated Business Process Discovery (ABPD) tools, in general, have the ability to recognize bottlenecks and bring them to light.

You can generally use the strategy of 5 whys to figure out the root cause. Usually, when the problem occurs, it is due to the malfunctioning of the system or when any process is lacking. The 5 whys are for only small operations. Here is one example that might help you – it is the example of your car stopped on a road.

- Why did the car stop? (First why) – The engine has seized.
- Why did the engine seize? (Second why) - There was insufficient lubrication inside the engine, it locked the crankshaft.

- Why was there insufficient lubrication? (Third why) - The oil pump on the engine is not circulating enough oil inside.

Using five whys technique lead to the root cause of the issue which can be solved using Six Sigma strategies.

Eliminating Waste Without Compromising Quality

When you have assembled your present value stream, you can distinguish issues with your work and tackle them. Remove activities that have no value at all. Lean Six Sigma philosophy is tied in with finding where issues emerge, fixing them, and averting future events. There is no need to showcase the sectors that are working flawlessly as it will diverge the attention from the main problem. Though it will make your employees happy to see the progress, but it is better to remain focused.

In an event where your value stream guide does not explain precisely where the issue lies, you can use a few different approaches, like logical result graphs, cause and effect graphs also called the fishbone diagram and any other statical method. They can assist you to look at another angle to find the root cause. Affinity diagram could also come in handy; you can brainstorm issues with it by taking help from the involved group to make things fast and more effective.

Anything that does not contribute towards production is a waste. Remove it out in order to prioritize the company's value.

Focusing on eliminating waste is called "Muda" within a manufacturing system. It is a Japanese word meaning uselessness or wastefulness. It is the basic concept of Toyota Production System (TPS); it gives insight on each level of production from raw materials to resources needed to mold materials into a complete product and improves overall revenue.

Under the TPS, seven basic Muda are identified as:

- Overpopulation (waste)
- Inventory (waste)
- Transportation (waste)
- Defected stock (waste)
- Over-processing (waste)
- Waiting (waste)
- Motion (waste)

Understanding the 7 Muda is easy but figuring out how to get rid of them as much as possible is a difficult job. Here are a few tips that are presented to eliminate waste for each Muda.

1. Overpopulation - Synchronize processes. Man and machine should work accordingly.
2. Inventory - Measure the waste and keep raw material and finished goods inventories clean.
3. Transportation - Utilize the most straightforward routes to reach a destination.
4. Defected stock - Be accountable, develop a system for quality assurance.
5. Over-processing - Get customers' standards and expectations on time.
6. Waiting - Be conscious, increase the reliability of processes.
7. Motion - Reduce travel time between stations. Decrease unnecessary machine movements.

When a specific classification of waste is identified, it's conceivable to execute techniques that will handle specifically that waste. The same goes for another Muda. Once it's identified which sector in the organization produces which sort of waste, you can take countermeasures to get the quantity of waste to near zero.

For example, you can counter waste overproduction through synchronizing processes (Man and machine). When things are accordingly, production will go smoothly with almost no waste. Or it can be encountered with Lean manufacturing techniques. On the other hand, One Piece Flow Assembly systems can be used to counter waste excess processing itself.

Having A Smooth Workflow

Nothing is going to change unless you take the first step. Make up your mind on how you want to fix or improve things, go for it. It's like the law of inertia. If a ball is rolling, it will continue to roll unless friction or some other force stops it. A body in motion tends to stay in motion and a body at rest tends to stay at rest. The same goes for any organization or company or even an individual. Nothing is going to change unless you induce a change.

Labor will continue to work or not work; they will continue the similar undertakings until someone from the management chooses something else for them. Convey new guidelines and practices to follow if you want the change. Be certain that every representative or worker gets proper training and look out for criticism. Otherwise, the problem will not be solved.

Lucid chart can be used to create a simple process map to convey to your workers what's new about their work process. Knowing about the change and its results can work like a force that will keep them motivated in doing the work.

The work must go smoothly. The obstacles should be managed beforehand to gain the best results.

Make The Change Acceptable Throughout

Lean Six Sigma requires a ton of progress and change. You have to welcome a change and ask your workers and labor to accept it too. If you'll put yourself in your labor shoes' you might fear or panic by hearing the news of change. As so much of work is now computerized, it could result in losing their job. Make things clearer from your end on how these computerized operations will help workers in making things much easier. Show them how convenient you have made their work.

As a major aspect of this move, your organization should consistently search for better approaches to streamline the process and counter waste. Watch out the data, examine it, and regulate your procedures where important.

Although directors and experts can settle on astounding choices looking down the workflow from where they stand, labor or workers involved are not behind. In each step, they might have a better understanding and significant knowledge as well because they are the ones doing the job.

The fact of the matter is, workers who are involved in the processes every day might have a useful opinion that would, in fact, result in product improvement. They know about machines and resources very well because they deal with them daily. Their contribution can improve the process and guarantee the company's growth. This is the approach adopted by Toyota.

It tells to go and see the work where it is actually happening as nothing can provide process details better than that.

Inside Six Sigma, various individuals from different teams liable for the improvement task are given titles:

- Process owner
- Process champion
- Black belt
- Green belts

All these titles have various duties, some of which can be about engaging with other staff and convey messages to representatives. Getting different groups in the organization to perceive the issue and to make arrangements to solve is an important aspect of Six Sigma job.

Including staff in the improvement process is the best way to approach a problem and to solve it. Running an association is not like coding a personal computer. People are included, you have to make things easier for labor to ensure the process runs smoothly. Six Sigma focuses on the team that is not burdened but relaxed while producing the top quality results.

Having A Systematic And Scientific Approach

On a basic level, the motivation behind why Six Sigma is so popular approach is that it defines a framework through which your company can improve its processes. It's the era of information; Six Sigma has a logical quality that takes advantage of the information drive world. It only seems fair to take the benefit of the collected data and use it for making enhancements and improve further processes through it

This same feeling goes right back to masterminds like Frederick Winslow Taylor and W. Edwards Deming who in real launched a logical way to deal with business tasks.

Ideas like the TPS are originated from Japanese culture with Deming being one of the minds behind it. He went to Japan after the 2nd world war and is credited with the process improvement of Japans' post-war interests.

One aspect of Six Sigma is using a scientific approach to achieve results is present in the form of the DMAIC process. It tells how to define the problem and measure the success rate even before the initiation of the process.

Chapter 43
Improving Customer Satisfaction

Six Sigma Strategies improve a business process or product. Its goal is to identify the root cause of the problem and find solutions to it so that the process or product is close to perfection. Sig Sigma eliminates any service problem or product defect to satisfy the customer. Using viable metrics, it focuses on monitoring progress to improve customer service.

A business can use a Six Sigma model that meets its needs in improving its present processes or create new procedures to serve its customers. It can measure its progress through the Six Sigma DMAIC (Define, Measure, Analyze, Improve, and Control) process. It can also use the Six Sigma DMADV (Define, Measure, Analyze, Design, and Verify) process to improve and execute the new process. The business must ensure that it finishes either of the processes to complete the Six Sigma.

One problem of using the Six Sigma model to improve customer service processes is to search for ways to measure improvement. Customer experience is not quantitative but qualitative therefore it is difficult to search for the right metrics to monitor progress accurately. As such, it is important that the company choose its metrics for its Six Sigma model.

Factors to Consider in Choosing Customer Service Metrics

First, the business must consider variability. It must be able to adjust its metrics to consider the differences of its customer service with the other businesses.

Second, the business must ensure that every personnel providing customer service is on the same page when it comes to measuring progress. It must create a positive environment within the department to effect the changes.

Third, the business must employ quantitative metrics, if possible. It can monitor the time spent by customers waiting for a customer service staff or the number of complaints received.

Fourth, the business must use sales figures by repeat customers in measuring customer loyalty. It can also use different metrics to measure abstract goals and customer satisfaction.

Fifth, the choice of metrics will depend on the customer service area that the business wants to focus on. As such, it is important that it is able to narrow down the processes to at most two at a time so that it will not overwhelm the customer service staff, as well as those who will supervise the Six Sigma process.

The identification of improvement areas in customer service is just one process of Six Sigma. A business must be able to monitor the metrics precisely and carefully so that Six Sigma will be effective.

Problems in Measuring and Improving Customer Service

Customer service is important in most companies. A business allots a large part of its operating margin in service processes. As such, most efforts of Six Sigma are in these processes to improve, modify, measure, and model them. The usual problems in these processes are in the choice of quantitative and qualitative measures that are right to the service process, in particular, and to the business, in general.

For example, a fast food business may see a need to measure quantitatively the time it takes to complete a process. On the other hand, a gourmet restaurant may regard fast completion as a negative indicator. It aims to offer a relaxing dining experience instead of rushing its customers to finish eating.

Another problem is how to balance the various qualitative aspects with the rates of response that the customers expect.

Most clients do not want to answer long surveys. They may decline or abandon them.

An issue in measuring the service processes for Six Sigma purposes is the characterization of defect, which can be quantitative or qualitative. Data measurement can be continuous or discrete, depending on the context. There must be a conversation from qualitative customer satisfaction measurement to its equivalent quantitative measure.

Usually, a business can rank overall satisfaction from one to seven. If the rank is below six, it can consider it as a defect if customer service is critical in the operations. On the other hand, it can be acceptable if customer service does not play an important role in the business process.

Lastly, defect can be context-sensitive. A newspaper delivery business must be able to bring the morning newspapers to its customers within the cutoff time. On the other hand, delivery of mail to the mailbox must be within the day for it to be timely. Customers of the Postal Service do not require delivery of their mails within a specific period during the day.

How to Make Sensible Measurements of the Service Processes

One way to measure service processes is to use the right measurement level. It is important to have the correct abstraction level in order to have a meaningful measurement.

Service processes also use the 80/20 rule, which means that 20% of the processes contribute to 80% of the time it needs to implement the service processes. The rule also means that 20% of customers account for the 80% of customer dissatisfaction. If it focuses only on some important elements, the business may be able to generate an excellent result. Detail usually does not create significant incremental value.

Another way to measure service processes is to take into account important variations in execution of tasks. For example, an underwriter in an automobile insurance underwriting can consider a regular car for a driver with no record of accidents as a regular case. On the other hand, it can consider a customized vehicle or motor home as a special case.

Assessments of the cases for Six Sigma purposes can differ significantly. Not all measurements are applicable for all cases. Therefore, it is necessary for the business to make the necessary adjustments in terms of deciding what and how to measure service processes.

It is also possible for a business to emphasize on quantitative instead of qualitative measures strategically. Some business can emphasize on qualitative measures when their customer service representatives have face-to-face encounters with their customers. On the other hand, they can put more value on quantitative measures if the service processes focus on quick service.

Lastly, a business can put emphasis on managing support and communication. There are large-scale service processes such as insurance claims processing that require various groups of people. As such, it is possible for these groups to resist any improvement in the processes through Six Sigma methodologies. These people may be doing the same process for a long time so they may feel confused about their role in the process improvement.

To remedy this problem, the company can offer information sessions to these groups in order to explain to them the bigger picture. This way, these people will not feel threatened. It is also important that the management provide significant support in the implementation of the process improvements.

The Customer Oriented Approach

Large companies like Motorola, Citibank, and General Electric adopted the Six Sigma methodology successfully because they adhered to the customer-oriented approach instead of the product-oriented approach.

Customer satisfaction, according to Hansemark and Albinsson, is the general attitude of the customer to the service provider. It is also an emotional reaction between what the client expects vis-à-vis what he receives. Customer loyalty, as defined by Anderson and Jacobsen, is the outcome produced by a business when it creates a benefit to maintain or increase the customer purchases.

The purpose of the Six Sigma methodology is to improve the business processes through quality improvement and elimination of mistakes. The customer-oriented approach has for major steps: quantifying customer satisfaction; gap identification between customer needs and the company's performance level; analysis why the gaps exist; and developing a plan to eliminate the gaps.

The customer-oriented approach gets rid of mistakes; improves product quality; and initiates product changes. To eliminate mistakes, it empowers the Six Sigma project team to offer solutions in important matters. It aims to encourage employees to do things right the first time.

For the service sector, it is important for the project team to understand customer satisfaction in order to eliminate mistakes. For example, improving doctors' scheduling of appointments in hospitals can produce significant results because it strives to understand customer satisfaction. Having to wait for hours is a significant issue for patients, after all. Thus, the Six Sigma strategy can devise ways to improve the scheduling appointments to minimize patients' waiting time.

For assembly line projects, an error can add to the cost of production and can affect product quality. It can influence customer satisfaction directly thereby affecting customer loyalty significantly. For example, if it employs the product-oriented instead of the customer-oriented approach, the Six Sigma model can make delivery time faster by changing the process of packing.

However, a change in the packing process can have an impact on product durability that can affect customer satisfaction. It is important for the Six Sigma project team to understand the customer preference in order to devise ways to improve product delivery without sacrificing product durability.

Chapter 44
The 5 DMAIC Phases

DMAIC is a strategy to implement Six Sigma into a business. DMAIC stands for:

- Define
- Measure
- Analyze
- Improve
- Control

It is a five-phase strategy that leads to solutions to the problems of unknown causes.

Define means to know the problem that is in need of fixing? Define means to get answers to some of the questions like defining:

- Who are the customers?
- What are their needs according to the product or service?
- What is the initiation point of the process of the problem?
- What is the finishing point of the problem?
- When will the problem be considered solved?
- In what direction and flow will the process flow?

Understanding the voice of the customer is important. Once understanding the need of the customer the team can then move to the next step of the DMAIC for further processing.

Measure means to know how the process is currently flowing. Measure means to collect data from:

- Multiple sources to know the defect and metric types.
- Comparison of customer surveys to know what is lacking?

Analyze means to make use of data collected from measure to determine the possible defects and how to solve them. Look into matters like:

- Identify gaps between the current process and the object to reach
- Know the different types of sources from where the data was collected
- Make room for opportunities for overall improvement

This is the most crucial part of the process as analyzing the root cause of the problem is very important. Failing to come up with root cause makes the process even more complicated and teams find it impossible to provide a solution to the customer's problem.

Jumping to conclusions without proper leaves a big question mark the whole time for the customer and the team solving the problem. No matter how many methods are implemented the solution doesn't seem to arrive.

Improve means to modify the secondary process by providing a creative solution to solving and preventing problems

- Make creative solutions to solve the problem
- Make and set up implementation plans

To improve is to refine the overall structure of the solution process here is the part where teams get to know the core reason for the problem and make it easy to counter it.

Control means to keep the improvements merged with the new process. Keeping the new processed maintained is demanded from the team and it does so by monitoring the plan to track the plan's success. Once the process is considered a true success the current process is updated to the best solution available.

The systems and structures are modified to the latest solution and are referred first to the future problems. The 5Ss are used to keep the process at its most efficient level.

Tools used in DMAIC

DMAIC stands for Define, Measure, Analyze, Improve and Control. The DMAIC comes under the methodology of implementing Six Sigma. Knowing what tools can be used in the five phases of DMAIC makes it easy to implement the methodology.

Define

Define phase can be used in a step by step process:

- Describe the problem by building a Problem Statement
- Describe the objective or goal by making a Goal Statement
- Describe the process using Process Map
- Describe types of customers and what they need
- Make it clear to others involved in the Project process

The following tools can be used in Define phase to outline the steps:

- A3
- Swim lane Map
- Tree Diagram
- Project Charter
- Relationship Map
- Value-stream Map
- Voice of the Customer Translation Matrix
- SIPOC (Supplier, Inputs, Process, Outputs, Customers)

Measure

Measure phase can be used in a step by step process:

- Know the current state of the process
- Build a plan on collecting data
- Make sure data is from a reliable source
- Collect the data from point zero
- Modify the project charter

The following tools can be used in the Measure phase to outline the steps:

- Check sheets

- Project charter
- Data collection plan
- Operational Definitions

Analyze

Analyze phase can be used in a step by step process:

- Carefully observe the process
- Display the data collected in graphical form
- Look for the root cause of the problem
- Verify the reason(s) the problem occurs
- Modify the project charter

The following tools can be used in the Analyze phase to outline the steps:

- 5 Whys
- Box Plots
- Run Charts
- Histograms
- Pareto Charts
- Project Charter
- Fishbone Diagram
- Value Stream Map
- Root Cause Hypothesis

Improve

Improve phase can be used in a step by step process:

- Brainstorm the possible solutions to fix the problem
- Select the solution which is practically implementable
- Develop Maps of Process depending upon the various solutions
- Choose the best solution(s)
- Apply the Solution(s)
- Measure to make sure there is an improvement

The following tools can be used in the Improve phase to outline the steps:

- To-Be Map
- PDCA/PDSA

- Plot Checklist
- Benchmarking
- Brainstorming
- Swim Lane Map
- Value Stream Map
- Impact Effort Matrix
- Implementation Plan
- Weighted Criteria Matrix
- Classic Lean Improvements

Control

Control phase can be used in a step by step process:

- Make sure the process is properly monitored and managed
- Make the document of improved process
- Make modifications to other sectors
- Celebrate and share your success
- Make continuous improvements to the process using Lean production principles

The following tools can be used in the Control phase to outline the steps:

- Control Plan
- Gallery Walks
- Control Charts
- Documentation
- Monitoring and Response plan
- Innovation Transfer Opportunities

Chapter 45
Lean Six Sigma Implementation Method

Sigma's six principles use statistical and numerical methods to reduce the number of defects in the output. They emphasize the simplicity of the process, the quality of the parts and the logistics, and the responsibility of the employees to achieve the promised results.

Key Points to Implement a Project

There are some key points which are necessary for the implantation of project. Mandatory are as follow:

- Project
- Training
- Team
- Plan
- Execute
- Evaluate

Choose Project

The best way to implement the Six Sigma program is to start with a pilot project. You can identify a company process that is usually causing production problems or having other problems.

The process of identifying the pilot project involves the workforce involved and their input needs to be considered. Six Sigma only works when everyone is involved.

Training

The person who guides the implementation of the Six Sigma project should know six principles and principles of Sigma. In Six Sigma's terms, he should be a "black belt" expert.

In small businesses, a black belt is usually sufficient for a pilot project. A qualified new employee in the business can hire or train in the ranks. Training can be an overlap for Black Belt certification and pilot project implementation.

Team management

Once the company has chosen a Black Belt Team Leader, it has to assign team members who will assist in the process.

The company has to consult the workers involved in the pilot project. The team needs good staff, but also to run the Six Sigma Pilot Project after implementation.

Make plan

The team plans to implement it. The aim is to have an organizational structure that simplifies the production target preparation process to minimize defects.

Projects Manager (Black Belt holder) identifies areas of the problem, and workers at work assist with the solution. The project describes the steps the team has proposed to reduce team waste, increase worker efficiencies and eliminate barriers.

Execute

Six Sigma requires initial effort and then it is a continuous process. The pilot project will have to take preliminary steps and keep the organization in place for permanent application.

The team makes the necessary changes according to the plan and then wears a black belt to run it. The Green Belts support the new project and take on specific aspects.

Evaluate

Upon completion of the pilot project, an evaluation describes what worked and where the problems were encountered. The workers involved are a key source for diagnostic standards and parameters.

Assessment is the basis for permanent application in other areas of the Company's work. In a small business, the second round might include all the rest of the production activity.

Beneficial Tips

Without understanding what is being done and why, there will be very limited scope to improve Lean and Six Sigma. So, let's take a look at the top 10 tips for successful implementation of Lean and Six Sigma.

- Change in behavior
- Make Lean Six Sigma Compulsory
- Strong Platform
- Top-Down Approach
- High Profile Identification
- Right Measurement Systems
- Awareness of cultural Difference
- Having Communication Channels
- Perfect to start Lean Six Sigma (σ)
- Communities or Forums

Change of behavior

Industry experts believe that change of behavior is essential for effective implementation of change. This tendency in people is to work around it rather than to solve a problem, and this is where Lean and Six Sigma's willingness to permanently eliminate problems arising in the business process.

Even when people pledge to change their behavior, the tools will be added seamlessly. Training your manpower in Lean & Six Sigma is one thing, but without a change in attitude, the whole process will be educational only with no practical implications.

Make it Compulsory

Incorporating Lean & Six Sigma as part of the organization's goals and core strategy is one of the key components to its successful implementation.

And without it, the entire initiative will have a short-term life where people reject the process even before it is properly established in the organization.

Moreover, when an organization has a basic mechanism for the center of everything, combining lean and six sigma increases its chances of success.

Strong Platform

Strong platforms make a good impression on any customer. Which naturally inclines you towards it. A robust platform acts as a backbone for any organization.

Top-Down approach

Organizations around the world can apply Lean and Six Sigma to a bottom line. But industry experts believe that trying to involve senior and middle managers before ways to improve the process is worthwhile.

Their involvement in implementing Lean and Six Sigma towards improving key business processes will strengthen other affiliate practices that will also help increase adoption by others. Without the involvement of senior and middle managers, it is a difficult task to successfully adopt Lean and Six Sigma throughout the organization.

High Profile Identification

You need to choose projects that are endorsed by senior and middle management that passionately care about bringing people faster results.

This increases overall confidence in the lean and Six Sigma approach and will lead to widespread acceptance in the organization.

Right Measurement Systems

Practitioners can use data to make informed decisions and decide on baseline performance with the proper measurement system in place. And when people understand the potential of lean and six-sigma, plans will quickly improve.

Awareness of Cultural Differences

Each organization has its own distinct culture, and experts believe that the culture is different between different geographical areas and different types of organizations such as local, corporate, small or medium, public, private and government.

It is better to avoid the assumptions about how you need to adopt lean and sigma and avoid the use of jargon unless this organization wants it. Doing so will facilitate the smooth implementation and integration of the lean and six sigma procedures between the two entities.

Having Communication Channels

Keeping open communication channels in an organization is an important aspect of timely completion of lean and six sigma projects.

On many occasions, addressing a small group or talking face-to-face to discuss important things is more effective than mass email communication.

Perfect to Start Lean Six Sigma

It is better to start with just a handful of people who will take over the leadership and responsibility of Lean and Six Sigma implementation and tell them that this will work for them, rather than just wasting their time and energy on skeptics or unbelievers. The word will spread positively through the networks of internal champions.

Communities or Forums

Knowledge management plays a key role in sustaining the growth or improvement of key business processes through lean and six sigma practices.

Lean and Six Sigma practitioners play an important role in knowledge management techniques to ensure learning from each other's experience, improving their capabilities with respect to the Lean and Six Sigma principles and tools regularly used in an organization.

Steps for Successful Implementation

There are 8 major steps in order to implement a successful project management. By following them, you can easily win a project management & can be applicable for a successful project implementation.

The steps are given below:

- Burning Platform
- Keep resources in the place
- Teaching
- Prioritize Activities
- Ownership
- Right Measurements
- Govern Programs
- Recognition

Burning Platform

To implement or think about lean or six sigma modes, we must have a burning platform. A burning platform can take many forms.

For example, some common or rare are like:

We are experiencing huge quality losses and this accounts for more than 45% of our cost

Our competitors are gaining 12% of our market share every quarter

By this, organizations are rarely motivated to implement continuous improvements to TPS (Lean) or Six Sigma or TQM or any improvement. With the completion of this task, ever since Six Sigma became a visionary in the organization, everything else began to fall into place. So in order to increase organizational vision and value across our workforce, customers, partners and suppliers, we need to leverage our key leadership towards a common vision.

This ensures that the organization's environment is viable for change and capable of driving change, leveraging innovation and technology as key tools.

Finally, we need to take steps to achieve our vision. This ensures that we have visibility and strong support from the leadership. Leadership sponsors make sure we meet our organization's vision, thereby achieving excellence.

Keep resources in place

It is important to know what to look for in potential resources. Resources don't just help us succeed. We need to deploy them as a team, and this team must act as a change agent.

As an organization, we need to emphasize taking the initiative to empower the team, so we need domain expertise and knowledge. We also need to take care of our resources in terms of wages, and also have the resources to fit and realize the common vision.

Teaching Methodology

Lean Six Sigma Organizations need to train their team members as powerful change agents in order to survive. Yellow Belt, Green Belt and Black Belt training can help increase organizational awareness with skilled teachers. Employees identified for training should share the organization's vision.

Prioritize activities / Tasks

We need to know what to ignore and where to take the risk, and the question here is whether we can meet the key expectations of our organization's goals in terms of risk mitigation and expectation management.

Organizations should make it a top priority:

- Listen to the customer
- Identify quality standards by quality
- Ensure that the Lean Six Sigma efforts are aligned with business goals

Ownership

This includes setting up a committee to determine who is responsible for the entire team.

Ownership feels empowered and proud, and team members who are more committed, responsive and committed.

Right / Accurate measurements

Practitioners can assess baseline performance and use data in objective decision-making and variable analysis by setting up a measurement system. The key to measurement is to correct the right price.

Govern Programs (Making Reviews)

A proper governance structure can help maintain the momentum of a program. Poor governance or excessive governance can cause vision to fall apart.

For example, setting up a Business Quality Council (BQC) can help remove any obstacles that can slow the project down, and allow the project to follow timelines.

Appropriate governance also helps practitioners create a best practice sharing forum, which helps to redesign plans and highlights common challenges.

Without regular scheduled, fruitful meetings or review meetings, the program can halt courses and employees may lack guidance.

Recognition with Contributions

Rewards and recognition play a vital role in ensuring team members are satisfied with their role. They can help create excitement from the top to bottom and from the bottom up.

Rewards and recognition can also help drive innovation across the organization. Proper rewards and recognition ensure consistency in achieving excellent performance. Let me present my personal example of reward and recognition at the grassroots level.

Chapter 46
Tools to Use with Six Sigma

There are many tools that you can use in order to make Six Sigma work for you. These tools are there to ensure that you are providing good quality management to your business and some of the tools are so successful that they can be used outside of a Six Sigma application as well. Some of the main methods that can be used include:

5 Why's

The 5 Why's is a technique that is there to explore the cause and effect relationship of a problem. Each answer is going to form the basis of the following question. The 5 in the name derives from the idea that it takes about five iterations in order to resolve the problem, but depending on your particular issue, you may need to use more. Not all problems though are going to have one root cause. If you would like to figure out more than one root cause, this method is going to be repeated by asking a different sequence of this question each time that you use it. In addition, the method is not going to provide any hard rules about what lines you should explore with the questions, or how long you need to continue your search to make sure you find the root cause. Thus, even if you follow this method closely, it may not give you the outcome that you want.

An example of the 5 Why's includes the following:

My vehicle is not starting:

- Why? The battery is not working.
- Why? Because the alternator is not functioning
- Why? The belt on the alternator has broken off.
- Why? The belt should have been replaced a long time ago, but was not.
- Why? The vehicle owner did not follow the required maintenance schedule for the vehicle.

This helps to show why there was an issue with the vehicle, and you can easily choose to take it further into some more why's until you find the solution that you are looking for.

Axiomatic Design

The axiomatic design is a systems design methodology that is going to analyze the transformation of the needs of the customer into design parameters, functional requirements, and process variables. The method is going to get its name because it is going to use the design principles that govern the analysis and decision-making process. The two types of axioms that are used with this process include:

Axiom 1: This is the independence axiom. It is going to help you to maintain the independence of your functional requirements.

Axiom 2: This is the information axiom. This is going to help you to minimize the informative content of the design.

Cost-Benefit Analysis

Cost-benefit analysis, or CBA, is an approach that is meant to estimate the strengths or weaknesses of varies alternatives. It can be used with project investments, processes, activities, and even transactions. It can be used to determine, out of several solutions, which options will provide the best approach to a business in order to achieve benefits while still saving the company money. To keep it simple, the CBA method is going to come with two main purposes. These purposes are:

- To determine if a decision or an investment for a business is sound. This means that the benefits will outweigh the cost. You also want to look at how much this is. If the benefits do not outweigh the costs much, then it is probably not the best option to go with.
- To help provide a good way to compare projects. This can involve comparing the total amount that you expect each option to cost against the benefits you expect to get.

The benefits, as well as the costs, are going to be shown in monetary terms, which makes it work well for Six Sigma.

Moreover, they can be adjusted in the formula for the time value of money. This ensures that all flows of costs and those from benefits over time are expressed with a common basis. The simple steps that you will follow when you are working on a cost-benefit analysis include:

- You first have to define the goals and the objectives of the project or the activity.
- You can list the alternative programs or projects that you may be able to use.
- List the stakeholders
- You then select the measurements you want to use in order to measure all of the elements when it comes to benefits and costs.
- You can also work on predicting the outcome of the benefits and the cost of each alternative over a period of your choosing.
- You can then convert all of the benefits and costs into a common currency to help them compare better.
- Make sure to apply any discount rates
- Next, you can calculate the net present value of all project options.
- Perform a sensitivity analysis: This is going to be the study of how the uncertainty of the output from a mathematical system can be shared to different sources of uncertainty in its inputs.
- After you have all this information, you can then pick out the option that is the best.

Root Cause Analysis

A root cause analysis, or RCA, is going to be a method to help with solving problems and it focuses on finding the root causes of the problem. A factor will be considered the root cause if you can remove it and the problem does not recur. Essentially, there are going to be four principles that come with this type of method including:

- It is going to define and describe properly the problem or event.
- Establish a timeline from the normal situation until the final failure or crisis occurs

- Distinguishes between the casual factor or the root causes
- Once it is implemented, and the execution is constant, the RCA is transformed into a method of problem prediction.

The main use of the RCA is to identify and then correct the root causes of an event, rather than just trying to address a symptomatic result. An example of this is when some students receive a bad grade on a test. After a quick investigation, it was found that those who took the test at the end of the day ended up with the lower scores. More investigation found that later in the day, these students had less ability to stay focused. In addition, this lack of focus is from them being hungry. So, after looking at the root cause and finding it was hunger, it was fixed by moving the testing time to right after lunch. Notice that the root causes are often going to come in at many levels and that the level for the root is only going to be where the current investigator leaves it. Nevertheless, this is a good way to figure out why one particular process in the business is not working the way that you want and then finding the best solution to fix it.

SIPOC Analysis

If you are talking about process improvement, a SIPOC is there to be a tool that can summarize the inputs and then the outputs of at least one process and then shows it in table form. This acronym stands for suppliers, inputs, process, outputs, and customers and these will be used to form the columns on your table. Sometimes the acronym is going to be turned around in order to put customers first, but either way, it is going to be used in the same way. SIPOC is presented at the beginning of a process improvement efforts or it can be used during what is known as the define phase of the DMAIC process. There are three typical uses of this depending on who is going to use it including:

- To help those who are not familiar with a particular process a high-level overview.
- To help those who had some familiarity with the process, but may be out of date with the changes in

the process or those who haven't used it in a long time.
- To help those who are trying to define a new process.

There are also some aspects that come with this method that are not always apparent. These include:

- The customers and the suppliers are sometimes external or internal to the organization that is trying to perform the process.
- Outputs and inputs can include things such as information, services, and materials.
- The focus of this method is to capture the set of inputs as well as outputs, rather than worrying about all the individual steps that are in the process.

Value Stream Mapping

When it comes to value streaming mapping, we are talking about a method that is there to analyze the current state of a business and then designing a new state to use in the future. It is meant to take a service or product that a company offers from its very beginnings all the way through to when it reaches the customers. The hope is that the process is used to help reduce lean wastes, especially when compared to the process that the business is using right now. The value stream is going to learn how to focus on any areas of a business that helps to add in value to the service or product. The purpose of this is to learn where the waste is in the business and then remove or at least reduce it. This can increase the efficiency of the business and can even increase productivity. The main part of this process is to work on identifying waste in the business. Some of the most common types of waste include:

- Faster than necessary pace: This is when the company tries to produce too much of their product that it can damage the flow of production, the quality of the product, and the productivity of the workers.
- Waiting: This is a time when the goods are not being worked on or transported.
- Conveyance: This process is used to move the products around. It can look at things like excessive movement and double handling.

- Excess stock: This is when there is an overabundance of inventory. This can add on storage costs and can make it more difficult to identify problems.
- Unnecessary motion: These wastes mean employees are using too much energy to pick up and move items.
- Correction of mistakes: The cost that the business will have when they try to correct a defect.

This process is used often in lean environments to help look at and design flows for the system level. This is often something that is associated with manufacturing, but it can be used in many other industries including healthcare, product development, and even software development.

Business Process Mapping

The idea of business process mapping is going to be all activities that are involved when you try to define what a business does, who is the person or persons responsible, and at what standard a process in the business needs to be completed. It can also determine how the success of the process in the business can be measured. Business process mapping is there to help a business become more effective. A clear business process map will allow even outside firms, such as consultants, to come in and look to see where improvements can be made, such as what can happen with Six Sigma, to help the business. This mapping is going to take a specific objective of a business and they can measure and compare it to the objectives of the company. This makes sure that all processes that are done can align with what the company holds as its capabilities and values. A good way to do business process mapping is with a flow chart. This can help you to see how the business does a certain process and can even include who is responsible for each part if that is important. These are just a few of the options that you can choose from when it comes to working with Six Sigma. All of the options above can help you to make informed decisions while finding the process that is causing your business the most trouble at the time. Pick one of these options that go along with your biggest issue and find out how you can make smart decisions that will turn your business into something even better.

Chapter 47
Lean Six Sigma Certification

Lean Six Sigma improves quality control & different business forms more rapidly and more productively than standard Six Sigma. Along these lines, there are numerous individuals who are currently keen on getting their own Lean Six Sigma Certification so as to enhance their own organization or to enhance the eventual fate of their vocation. Lean Six Sigma Certification is gotten when an individual finishes Lean Training. Lean standards are now and then observed as only an augmentation of the ordinary Six Sigma process. Hence, some data and examination utilized for the Lean Certification is fundamentally the same as customary Six Sigma Training and Certification. The thing that matters is in the genuine procedure and ultimate objectives. To become familiar with the additional standards of Lean, you should know the Six Sigma Methodology, else you won't know the essential nuts and bolts. A representative with Lean Certification will have the option to help in squander decrease, disposing of procedures and sub-forms in the business that are never again required, squandered developments of numerous types, just as end of sat around idly. These individuals will be extraordinary for any organization and will find that they are truly necessary for some applications. Those with a Certification will have the option to spot overproduction, any unnecessary stock, and might have the option to help move workers who are not understanding their maximum capacity at their present situations in the organization to different positions where they will be better utilized. Lean applications for a business will be centered around the speed of the procedures and their proficiency, however there is a contrast between this speed and the general timetable of the organization. Those with Lean Certification won't attempt to fit a bigger timetable into a littler time period, they will work to streamline the entirety of the procedures so more can be fit into a day. Lean Certification is an extraordinary thought for the individuals who as of now have their standard Six Sigma Certification, as it will be a legitimate augmentation of their insight base just as a resource for any organization they may decide to work for. Lean Six Sigma Training and Certification courses enable a person to work at their own pace, in spite of the fact that there is normally a set time limit inside which one should complete their Training. The online Lean Six Sigma Training and Certification courses are finished at assigned occasions and days that are foreordained by the Training supplier. Lean utilizes the way of thinking of applying pressure for speed and quality in the assembling universe of business. This has advanced from a little to an enormous scale quality activity to dispose of deformities in business and creation by disposing of varieties in a procedure or administration. This was first utilized in the United States by GE. At that point came Caterpillar account, just as Lockheed Martin. The Lean ways of thinking and apparatuses for administrations are utilized as a strategy for improving business, utilizing the best pieces of the Six Sigma ways of thinking. This gives investors more worth, yet in addition gives the organization a quick pace of progress with regards to speed, quality, cost, capital, and consumer loyalty. The contrast among Lean and customary Six Sigma is that the lean strategy acknowledges and encourages that you essentially can't just concentrate on speed or quality, however the general organization must be adjusted so as to enable the organization to be as well as can be expected be. Lean Six Sigma causes organizations to improve their administration quality, which clients consider as worthy. Without clients, a business is basically a fantasy. The thought behind Lean Six Sigma Trainings &Certification in a business is to concentrate on what the client sees similar to item or administration, in general expenses, and working. In the event that an organization must pass on expenses to a client rather than assimilate them, the client may not utilize this organization or administration. Lean Six Sigma finds and trains methods for assisting with decrease of the utilization of significant cash-flow to help keep away from this circumstance. Lean can manage forms, improve speed and diminish capital required, just as lessen cost of intricacy for the business.

The six sigma accreditation is granted after a person's abilities required for the particular organization are confirmed. The organization has a progression of steps characterized by which the work intensity of an individual is estimated all through the work procedure. On the off chance that they are sufficient, an accreditation is granted by the concerned position.

The Lean Six Sigma can be seen as used for outline the administration approach towards estimating the business execution. Lean sigma and the six sigma join together to frame up the Lean Six Sigma. It is equipped for taking care of complex issues with the assistance of its administration strategies to improve the general execution of the association. It is a productive procedure with quick improved results. It is a procedure to create viable administrations and thoughts for the welfare of the clients and the association.

Preparing

Learning the six sigma requires broad preparing and endeavors. You can experience the preparation guides accessible for the tests of the American Society for Quality (ASQ) and the International Association for Six sigma (IASSC). The aides contain different connections from which you can access significant themes and necessities of the test. Completely perusing the guide will demonstrate productive for you to accomplish a superior outcome for the six sigma assessments.

Expenses

The cost for the accreditations change far and wide. The establishment truly matters from which you are getting the confirmation for which you will need to pick the best one among the others. You ought to know about the outcomes if there should be an occurrence of any loss of installment for giving erroneous individual subtleties to the foundation.

The International Six Sigma Institute causes you meet to the expert prerequisites by its broad preparing process. The procedure is directed by the Six Sigma standards and technique. The foundation has effectively granted in excess of

187,000 affirmations all around the globe with radiating the Green Belt, Black Belt and Master Belt grants to its clients. They help people and organizations to deal with their business just as expert needs. The enlistment technique is simple and very straightforward. You can enlist yourself for the accreditation online for the necessary program and an Exam access code will be sent to you. Lead the online test whenever and area which you like. After you breeze through the test, the affirmation is granted to you in a flash at the online entrance. The organization offers a 100 percent unconditional promise on the off chance that you neglect to finish the six sigma affirmation test. The program is believable all around the world as the accreditation is given by the International Six Sigma foundation. You shouldn't go to the entirety of the study hall trainings and instructional exercises though the establishment centers around self-perusing of the expert without anyone else's input. The accreditation has a lifetime legitimacy with unlimited potential outcomes in the building procedure. Premium preparing can likewise be benefited free of cost through the online gateway of the establishment. This is a useful asset to finish out your Six Sigma test.

Lean Six Sigma Belt Online Training & Certification

Web has made some amazing progress in a matter of a brief timeframe. For the individuals who are needing Lean Six Sigma Black Belt Certification who can't discover an opportunity to get their preparation in a conventional setting, online courses are an extraordinary spot to turn. Getting on the web Lean Six Sigma Black Belt Certification manages numerous advantages and focal points to the individuals who pick it, including more comfort and decision in the projects that are taken. At the point when you are thinking about online courses, it is fundamental that you set aside the effort to look at all of your alternatives and ensure that you are getting a total Lean Six Sigma Black Belt Certification course from a legitimate organization and not only a 'program' from some organization who has no clue what they are instructing.

Online Lean Six Sigma Belt Certification will bear the cost of you the advantage of finishing the real task required for confirmation alongside the internet preparing in a similar measure of time. Contrasted with the common longer calendar of preparing offered by most workshops and on location courses, this can be an immense improvement. The data that you learn will all be equivalent to it would nearby when you pick a certified program to work with, and you'll have the option to do it on your time, whenever the timing is ideal, and without having the problem of voyaging or going to classes when you could be accomplishing different things. Lean Six Sigma Black Belt Training can help an assortment of associations and businesses. A large number of them are looking for the Lean procedure due to its speed. In the event that the procedure offers a snappier goal, shouldn't preparing be less difficult and quicker, too? Online courses offer that speed, yet at the same time assist you with adapting about Lean squander decrease standards and procedure improvement methods that are made through the waste disposal as a rule. By taking Lean Six Sigma Black Belt Certification on the web, you'll have the option to speed up your prosperity and demonstrate to your manager that you are submitted and arranged to deal with a Six Sigma Project in a shorter measure of time. In the event that by chance you're not a mechanically propelled individual or you aren't especially web insightful, don't stress! Web based Lean Six Sigma Black Belt Certification courses are very easy to use, and frequently accompany a help group you can email for help - regardless of whether it be inquiries concerning the Six Sigma course material itself, or what your secret word is in the event that you overlook it! Simply realize that when you're needing to prepare in Six Sigma, speed isn't simply all the while yet additionally in the preparation through the accessibility of online Lean Six Sigma Certificates.

Conventional Lean Six Sigma Certification Vs Lean Six Sigma Certification

Speed is the essential contrast between customary Six Sigma and Lean Six Sigma Certification. Lean Six Sigma confirmation is a speedier rendition of customary Six Sigma. Lean Six Sigma focuses on accelerating business forms so as to make an organization or association run better and smoother. The procedure isn't upgraded by basically turning up the dial and running the machine at a quicker speed. Lean strategies recognize issues in center forms and wipe out the hindrances backing them off. Expanding speed additionally doesn't mean shortening your center procedures or pressing your conveyance plan just to get the item out of the entryway quicker. It is just about eliminating abandons in the framework, which hurt conveyance and quality. Lean Certification implies the individual has become equipped in searching for approaches to streamline the work procedure. Affirmed people have Six Sigma apparatuses that they use to concentrate on the center procedure by making it work all the more easily. It likewise implies the individual comprehends the fundamental orders required for accelerating forms, shortening learning cycles or information creation, just as postponing responsibility. A lean Six Sigma Certification shows that the individual has aced the factual abilities and devices with which to achieve organization objectives for streamlining the center procedure. Lean Six Sigma encourages that speed and quality come at whatever point there is more information creation as opposed to learning replication. Learning creation consistently brings about stream improvement, bringing about better assistance. Issues do emerge inconsistently when task chiefs mess up the works by front stacking a venture. As it were, making the task fit as opposed to giving the undertaking a chance to uncover how it functions all through the procedure. Front stacking is settling on all choices about the undertaking before it hits the gathering belt or machine. In a working lean Six Sigma venture run by a guaranteed lean Six Sigma individual, the procedure is contemplated as opposed to constrained. Considering the center procedure opens up more alternatives for taking care of business. Lean Six Sigma accreditation empowers the laborer to successfully tinker with the center procedure empowering a smoother stream with less or no issues. Lean Six Sigma and Six Sigma affirmation contrast here too, in light of the fact that Six Sigma includes layers of technique that may not directly for your center procedure, some of the time making it increasingly slow. Lean, then again, empowers the person to perceive the issue, dissect it and use the accessible devices to expel the barricade in a sensible measure of time.

Speed is straightforwardly attached to greatness in process, as attested by Lean Six Sigma confirmation and preparing.

Improve the procedure stream by disposing of deviations or blunders, and you will naturally accelerate the procedure, conveying better quality, and improving your association with customers and clients. Having an accreditation in Lean Six Sigma implies that you can take a gander at the procedure and find the hindrances so as to turn out better items and administrations all the more quickly. Speed doesn't mean truncating or crushing your conveyance plan for request to get the item out more rapidly. What it means is disposing of slip-ups that delayed down or stop the procedure, in this manner harming quality and conveyance. Utilizing Lean Six Sigma implies that you have gotten skillful in searching for chances to streamline your procedure. It implies you can recognize your center procedure, and you have the apparatuses expected to concentrate on making that center procedure run better and all the more easily. Having a Certification in Lean implies that you comprehend the two fundamental orders for accelerating the procedure; short continuous learning cycles or information creation, and deferred responsibility. Being Certified in Lean Six Sigma likewise implies that you have aced the measurable apparatuses and abilities with which to achieve your objectives just as those of your association. At whatever point the task incorporates data creation rather than simply learning replication, speed and quality will start from improving the stream, and Lean procedures tell senior organization that you have the right stuff to achieve this objective. Some undertaking chiefs are now and then blameworthy of gumming up the procedure by constraining early decisions and lessening the quantity of conceivable outcomes, as opposed to tuning in to their Lean experts. As it were, the venture administrators are blameworthy of task front stacking, where they settle on all choices forthright as opposed to permitting those ensured to run the procedure to uncover what is correct and what's up in the application. Lean Six Sigma confirmation means having and understanding a huge number of choices essentially by taking a gander at the center procedure itself, which is the thing that Lean Six

Sigma laborers have been affirmed to do. Tweaking the procedure as you travel through it will limit the procedure into a smoother stream that normally accelerates in light of the fact that the issues have been killed. This is the distinction of Lean Six Sigma Affirmation Lean Six Sigma. Layering in Lean Six Sigma incorporates rehearses that are unmanageable, and not directly for your focal procedure, making it moderate, just as not tolerant to change.

Lean Six Sigma Certificates Using Lean Six Sigma Training

Lean Six Sigma confirmation courses likewise give a portrayal of the framework expected to get the best results just as stress the necessity of perceiving varieties from the plans that reason lower quality administrations. Lean six sigma preparing centers around benefiting as much as possible from process speeds, gives instruments for investigation of stream and times, focuses on esteem included and non-esteem included work, for example, squandered ability, surrenders, stock issues, holding up times, overproduction, and transportation costs. Lean six sigma preparing encourages the member to understand that individual segments don't make quality, however there must be a reasonable procedure set up to finish this. Lean six sigma preparing/affirmation courses will cover the examine stage which incorporates such devices as stream graphs and conceptualizing, while the measure stages will cover FMEA. The characterize period of the courses will cover partner investigation's and arrangement decreases, techniques for disposing of blockage or postponements just as Kaizen. Kaizen can be considered as continuous enhancements. The aftereffect of Kaizen is aggressiveness and achievement of organizations wherever that utilization it. Most organizations stress advancements to change business, yet Kaizen rotates around proceeding to turn out to be better and not depending just on new ideas to work. Kaizen pushes that HR are the most significant resource an organization has, and enhancements must be founded on a measurable assessment of execution. An alum of the Lean Six Sigma preparing or accreditation will be a pioneer in their general vicinity.

Chapter 48
Lean Six Sigma Certification Levels

The Six Sigma is divided into different levels:

- White Belt
- Yellow Belt
- Green Belt
- Black Belt
- Master Black Belt

These certifications are obtainable by getting accreditation from a body like ASQ (American Society for Quality).

Six Sigma White Belt

The most basic or entry-level certification deals with basics of Six Sigma concepts. White belts are helpful for an organization's change management and involve with company's problem-solving teams who help with projects.

Six Sigma Yellow Belt

This level provides Six Sigma's specifics, how and where they are applicable. You will be able to help project teams with problem-solving.

Six Sigma Green Belt

This level of advanced analysis is understood and helps in resolving problems regarding quality. Green belts lead the projects and help black belts in gathering data and analyzing.

Six Sigma Black Belt

Black belts are the professionals and experts of change. They provide training along with leading the projects.

Six Sigma Master Black Belt

The highest level of Six Sigma achievement is the Master Black Belt. This level professionals design strategies, develop key performance indicators, coach green, and black belts, and act as a consultant.

Is Six Sigma really that important? The idea of this can be best understood from case studies of different who adopted Six Sigma which is given below. Six Sigma process helped General Electric to put $350 million in savings back in 1998. Motorola allocated its highest savings by 2005, of $17 billion. After a decade GE was able to increase that amount over $1 billion.

Six Sigma Certification Benefits for Individuals

The Six Sigma certification isn't just another addition to your resume the certification comes with a lot of advantages for companies and individuals.

Improve business processes and durable quantity improvement.

Once done with Six Sigma certification you will be investigating the manufacturing and business processes of a company and take actions to improve them. You will be able to do a complete evaluation of company's current procedures and assess how they affect the quality.

The certification displays that you are able to reach the durable quality that the firm is looking forward to. Keeping check of processes carefully to make sure that there isn't any deviation from the meanwhile taking right actions to bring projects back online which were deviating from path.

Having value in every industry

Being a highly demanded methodology in industries. Six Sigma techniques are useful in electronics, aerospace, telecom, financial services, IT, marketing, banking, HR and various industries.

Industries certified in Six Sigma have knowledge in many different methods which can be opted to streamline business processes, reduce costs, improve employee acceptance, and increase revenue, all these lead to an improved bottom line in any industry.

The Six Sigma certification earns an individual the title of a change agent in any organization. Working alongside teams further refines the leadership skills and adding more value to the individual.

Ensure Compliance

Six Sigma requires extremely high-quality standards. This is the reason a noteworthy number of procurers, vendors and oversight organizations use Six Sigma Standards when reviewing products. Individuals with Six Sigma certification can help their company with profitable contracts and working with international standards.

Rise to higher positions

Once done with Six Sigma certification an individual gets a clear picture of how to make maximum profit from any Six Sigma project. The certification helps individuals in getting financial management and risk assessment skills. These types of skills are always in demand for top-level and middle-level managerial positions.

Greater Salary

Six Sigma Certification is not easy to get, there are lot of studies, and the exams are tough. Furthermore, getting from one belt level to another requires years of actual work. For this reason, Six Sigma Certified individuals are the highest paid professionals in the world having pay bracket above $100,000.

Get practical experience in Quality Management

The Six Sigma training program provides individuals with practical experience on industrial projects and making use of theories in real-life workplace. Getting started with Six Sigma Certification gets an individual a valued knowledge even before working with a team. The professional acquiring such a certificate is refined to take strategic decisions and tackle the obstacles causing delays in processing.

Six Sigma Certification benefits for Organizations

In 1995, Jack Welch introduced Six Sigma as a key component to General Electric's Business Strategy. From that time, firms have put up Six Sigma to use with major success, the benefits can be seen below:

Higher Productivity

Engineered for the space industry for making new products, Allen medical implemented DMAIC methodology and lean tools for overall improvement to production of Arm boards. The new methodology allowed them to save 45 seconds per arm board production, hence increasing the arm boards produced per hour from 5.3 to a bit over 6.

Lower Costs

Decreasing defects reduced and minimized wastage resulting in overall lower production cost with greater profits. Failing to produce a quality product can get costly. Developing a poor service or product can greatly reduce the cost which is the true meaning of cost of quality.

Raising the client's confidence in one's business

Using Six Sigma can reduce processing steps and increase customer satisfaction. For example, through the use of cross-functional process mapping (CFPM) methodology, Citibank removed the unnecessary steps from their process which resulted in higher customer satisfaction.

Gaining reliability and shareholder's trust

Customers and shareholders trust a company where employees are relatively qualified. A company having a significant number of Six Sigma certified employees it means that quality is expected from that company. A company having quality is competitive in the market and inspires confidence in partners and investors.

Reduce training costs and employee turnover

The DMAIC methodology is applicable to be used in HR management. Research shows that in a multinational company losing millions of dollars because of employee turnover of 35% each year wanted to reduce the numbers to 25%.

After applying Six Sigma methodology, they came to know about few contributing factors which were: low compensation and poor career prospects. The solution was to make use of new hiring processes and training new employees. The outcomes were great reducing the turnover by 10% and saving $1.1 million as a result.

The Six Sigma Progress

The numerous cases of Six Sigma implementation success can be studied from all over the world. It is an internationally accepted standard that can be used in small to high profile organizations. The methodology is a logical and structured approach to develop a chain of continuous improvement.

Six Sigma isn't a destination that stops after accomplishing single milestone instead it is a journey of continuous improvement which doesn't end. The outcomes are excellence and higher customer loyalty with bottom line profits. Implementing Six Sigma is worthwhile for any organization in search of reaching near perfection.

Once the road of implementing Six Sigma has been taken by an organization it doesn't want to get off it. The company sees for itself the benefits of the process as it solves the complexity of the production processes and resolves issues arriving one after the other. The smoothness inflow of the production process is what inspires any company to opt the methodology in very first place.

Criticism of Six Sigma

There are multiple reasons why a business might not be adopting Lean Six Sigma. A few of the reasons can be stated to be valid, a lot can be stated as a misconception, while some stand as pure fictions. The ten common reasons observed over the years are:

Fear of the unknown or failing

The one reason which we can all agree to is the fear of the unknown. The effects of such fear can be paralyzing in the real world and in the business world it can also occur. The fear prevents a business from growing and making it stuck with the same old procedures and outcomes.

Not able to afford Six Sigma

The reason for not adopt the methodology is the fear of finance. It is not a process requiring large capital instead it should be looked as an investment which will give turn your results 5 to 10 times better in a year. A business can get started with Six Sigma after obtaining the Yellow belt certification. However, hiring an external black belt certified professional for training will be a good idea to grow. A business can also buy projects and statistical management software.

Never heard of Lean Six Sigma

This seems to be a valid criticism as Lean Six Sigma is growing in popularity but still, it isn't a part of the normal business language. Many small organizations mainly are unaware that it is present which keeps them behind.

Lean Six Sigma is a trend which will fade away

The presence of Lean Six Sigma can be found since the 19th century with business and quality leaders like Toyota's Shigeo Shingo, Henry Ford, Western Electric's Walter Shewhart, Edwards Deming, Taichi Ohno, and Joseph Juran. Six Sigma has grown over time and is different from other kaizen programs. People think that it might fade away with time, but the improvement techniques are something that an organization always want. The customer's choice is well focused on Lean Six Sigma techniques. So there's little to no chance that it may get lost in time any time sooner.

Lean Six Sigma is too much calculation and statistics

The truth is a lot of companies don't even need advanced mathematics and statistics to get benefitted from Lean Six

Sigma. A lot of principles of Six Sigma can easily be applied in any business.

The most powerful amongst all tools is to know the wastes in the process and their types. Planning out a map to point out all the bottlenecks, and gaps in the process. If the employees can understand what the customer needs then arriving at a solution to solve the problem won't be that difficult.

The employees don't necessarily need to be engineers; they can be front line supervisors and trained to work and understand the needs of the customers. Proper training will play its role again and again till the perfection that is expected is reached by the employees.

Don't have time to dedicate to Lean Six Sigma

A company that is not being able to identify the cause of the problem will always be stuck to it. No matter what is done to solve the issue, when the root cause is not defined, the problem will appear again. The only solution to make things right is finding where the problem has been initiating from.

The biggest waste a business can make is of time. The businesses do it so often that they don't even regard it as a waste. They take it for granted.

Every material waste can be salvaged but no amount of time can ever be salvaged once it is gone it can never come back. The truth is Lean Six Sigma can help a business put the time to efficient use, so understanding the methodology is a smart choice for any business. The outcomes will be rewarding for any business making a business reach its maximum output with minimum wastage.

Our Business is not that big

The most common voice raise against Six Sigma by Mid and Small-sized businesses is that they consider that their organization is not a large corporation to implement Six Sigma. The solution here is that Six Sigma won't be applied in a day and show the results immediately. Following its principles will show benefits sooner and an improve infrastructure will come forward. Six Sigma will make it easier to understand customers' needs and work according to it.

Once the key wastages are identified in any business it becomes easy to use them in the DMAIC framework. Time management gets easier to handle tasks that were taking longer periods of time. It is to understand that Six Sigma methodologies are there to improve the overall processing of the company by utilizing every material and reducing waste. The size of the organization doesn't matter at all as it benefits all.

We aren't manufacturing anything

While the Six Sigma methodology was born in the manufacturing industry it has left a greater impact on services and transactions environment also. Many people think that its parent organization is a manufacturing company thus it can produce the results only in the manufacturing environment. This is a total misconception as the Lean Six Sigma methodologies can equally be used in the companies that offer services only.

The services industries need it more than anything as their product is intangible and the work done is in a repetitive process in a large volume. Delivering, invoicing, order processing, employee onboarding, accounts payable, all of this can become smooth to handle with the help of Six Sigma methodology.

We used Six Sigma in the past but the results weren't good enough

Defining success here is really important and finding the reasons for Six Sigma failure are more important.

- Were the processes tracked and shared properly?
- Was the communication between managers up to date?
- Were the employees were trained to use the tools?
- Were the leaders committed to the program?
- Was the program internally driven?
- Was it in the context of people or technology?

- Were the employees aware that you were launching such a program?
- Were the goals realistically set?
- How the projects were chosen?
- Were the projects managed carefully?

Before raising the question against Six Sigma, evaluating the reasons for adopting Six Sigma are more important. Six Sigma methodology will work efficiently according to the efforts of the people implementing it. It is a commitment amongst all the levels of a corporation including front line supervisors. Six Sigma is a culture that is adopted gradually by the whole organization. It is not something that should be the duty of one sector only. Failure to accept the change could be one reason of malfunctioning.

We find Lean more appropriate for our business than Six Sigma

Six Sigma and Lean production complement each other running side by side along with other concepts. Where lean simplifies business by eliminating waste and getting more from less, Six Sigma refines the process making it near perfect. The Lean can be stated as an efficient method, the Six Sigma can be stated as an effective method. Combining effectiveness and efficiency a company can get great results. With the use of Lean production only you are sacrificing the perfect quality while adopting Six Sigma only you reduce the chance of efficiency. Hence, both concepts run side to side complementing one another.

Chapter 49
Criticality of the Lean Six Sigma Method

Many people in the business world have been talking about Six Sigma and how great it has been for them. Many of the organizations who choose to implement this method have found that it can improve their processes, services, and products. Having the ability to reduce their defects has helped these companies to increase their profitability, customer satisfaction, and productivity.

However, there are going to be some obstacles that can show up, and these will often stand in the way of being able to implement Six Sigma properly. You need to make sure that you recognize some of these hurdles and that you know how to address them if you want to be able to make Six Sigma work for you. Here are some of the common issues that sometimes come up when you are implementing Six Sigma and how you are able to fix them.

Lack Of Commitment From Leadership

Six Sigma is not a methodology that you can read about once, hand off to the employees, and hope that it goes well. There needs to be a big effort among the whole company to make Six Sigma work, and getting commitment from everyone in management is one of the most important steps.

A true test to see if a company is truly committed to working with Six Sigma is going to come when the management decides which employees it is going to dedicate to the new Six Sigma project. It is always best to go with your top talent on a Six Sigma project, rather than just picking out whoever is available.

If you just choose to use some random people in the business who are available but do not have the right training, then you are already starting the project off on the wrong foot. Moreover, this can reduce how likely it is that the project will be a success. A successful Six Sigma project is going to require leaders who have the dedications to provide money, talent, time, and resources to this new endeavor.

You will find that taking your top performers and reassigning them from their current work so that they can work with the Six Sigma project is going to be the best bet. Sure, you may have to make some short-term sacrifices to make it work. However, in the end, you will end up getting the most benefits out of Six Sigma, which can greatly improve your business, when you choose to do this.

Not Understanding How Six Sigma Works

It is hard to get a methodology to work well if you do not have a complete understanding of how it works. Some organizations try to do it simply because they think they should. Some do it because they see that someone else was successful, and they want to be successful too. Others just rush into the project because they are so excited, but they do not have a firm grasp on what it requires to implement Six Sigma successfully.

The first thing to understand is that you should never implement the Six Sigma methodology just to keep up with the competition. You should also not waste your time on it if your only reason is to impress the shareholders. If you are only planning on using Six Sigma as a cosmetic change, or you implement it without giving it all the resources that it needs, then you are just inviting failure into the project from the start.

The best way to overcome this kind of obstacle is to commit to the process fully from the beginning. You can make sure that you employ and support the Six Sigma experts on your team to ensure that the new process starts working, rather than just bringing it on to use the terminology.

These experts, who may work for the company or not, are there to keep the project focused on the areas where they can make the biggest difference. Do not waste your time or the time of your team by using Six Sigma to help with simple changes that will not make that much of a difference. Six

Sigma can do some amazing things for your business, but you have to be willing to take on the big tasks, the ones that really need to be changed, rather than the smaller options.

Poor Execution

Even if you have some expert guidance to help with this process, there are times when the project is not going to go well because it was not executed properly. This poor execution will happen when the improvements are not aligning with the goals of the organization. It can be an issue when the project is reactively solving problems, rather than meeting strategic objectives. Alternatively, it can be when the quality improvement project focuses too much on the outputs of the project rather than focusing on the inputs.

When companies that use Six Sigma are able to understand that these methodologies are not there to act inside a vacuum but are there to work while aligning to the objectives and goals of the organization, they will find that it is easier to stay on target.

If you are working on Six Sigma and find that you are not getting the gains in productivity that you were hoping for or the savings financially, then it may be time to look for a reason. The reason is not going to be that the methodology of Six Sigma is ineffective. Instead, it is going to most likely come from a lack of effective leadership and the fact that the project was not managed in the way that it should've been.

When the leadership learns how to be committed and completely on board with the methodology of Six Sigma, they work to assign the top talent to their teams. They put the project through all the right steps, including the formal selection and the review process, and it provides the required resources to all people in the process. The odds of seeing success with Six Sigma are then going to increase quite a bit.

If Six Sigma is used in the proper manner, you are going to see some amazing results. You will be able to cut out wastes, help your customers out better, and make more profits in the long term. However, there are times when a business will take considerable resources to work on Six Sigma, and they will not see the results they had hoped for. Making sure that these top issues are not a part of our project can increase your chances of seeing success.

Chapter 50
Why Companies Are Not Taking Advantage of Lean Six Sigma

Do you recall the mention that Lean Six Sigma helps companies reduce expenses and thus end up with increased revenues? Well, Praveen Gupta, a consultant who is also an author and who has had occasion to teach matters of business at Illinois Institute of Technology, says that no other methodology of management comes close to creating great savings for an organization like Six Sigma. He says that the amount of savings companies using Six Sigma are making is in the range of billions of dollars.

Of course, as you have already read here, Six Sigma is a management system whose main focus is on customer satisfaction in terms of the appropriateness of products and services that the customer receives. And you also strive to minimize variations in agreed specifications as well as defects. To achieve this, you must be looking at processes that are consistent, and as such, predictable.

Now, when you bring in the strength of Lean to complete the methodology that is Lean Six Sigma, you are bringing in a management arm that is also centrally targeting the customer - using data to determine objectively how close the organization is to meeting the customer's demand and hence to make necessary process adjustments. Here, you look at functions that you want added to your processes but use data to establish if they are worthwhile or not - how worthwhile being a measure of the customer's willingness to pay for that added bit of work. Likewise for the product or service - you check if it is worthwhile adding a certain feature by the willingness of the customer to pay for the extra expense. However, there are some cases when you will not look at the issue from a compensation point of view. Rather, you look at how much of a competitive edge your additional feature or function is likely to give you.

- Does the change result to shortened delivery times?
- Does it lead to decreased costs that allow for a drop in product price?
- Does the adjustment lead to decreased number of defects?

Just to recap then, when you are weighing whether to take up or not to take up Lean Six Sigma in your organization, you need to be aware of the main benefits at stake:

- Improving the quality of products or services
- Improving the customer experience
- Increasing your bottom line

Those were the principle targets of the pioneers of Lean Six Sigma as exemplified by Henry Ford of Ford Motor Company and Taiichi Ohno of Toyota; and they are the same principle targets that continue to guide this methodology as is evidently clear when you consider the case of General Motors and Volkswagen. In fact, Toyota has been consistently on the list of Fortune 500, and a number of times within the Top 10.

Why, then, are some companies still not applying Lean Six Sigma?

Lack Of Relevant Information

Well, for one, this methodology has not penetrated the general market. It is safe to say that it is still with the pace setters. So the reason some companies who would otherwise make huge strides in growth do not even talk about Lean Six Sigma is sheer lack of knowledge. In fact, apart from coming across the term when trying to Google something, or hearing it from word of mouth, there are few other sources of information on this cutting edge methodology.

Believing Lean Six Sigma To Be A Fad

There are many Doubting Thomases, so to speak, the reason some companies lead while others follow. Some companies that are yet to implement the Lean Six Sigma methodology have heard about it and its advantages. However, often you find CEOs who are close minded and not willing to do anything that seems to challenge the status quo. That is why you find sudden structural overhaul of a company's top management by the board when some forward looking member introduces the idea of change of management style. In short, there are those who dub the relatively new management style a fad simply because of the fear of implementing something new.

Time Management That Is Wanting

Have you ever taken into consideration the fact that time spent, no matter how well or poorly, cannot be salvaged? This, of course, as opposed to an exam failed - you can always do a re-sit. Even a product not well completed - final touches can usually be made later. Anyway, some executives who know about Lean Six Sigma keep it at bay citing lack of adequate time to implement it when really it is a shortcoming in time management.

What such people miss out is the essence of the methodology which is not to become an addition in the organization but rather a modification of the existing methodology; and if necessary, replacement. In any case, if the worry is on the issue of time to train your workforce, there are professionals who are already versed in these matters, as has been indicated before in this book, and they even bear relevant certification. If you hired one of those, they would help you out without the inconvenience of stopping any of your production lines for any significant duration.

The Expenses Involved In Lean Six Sigma Implementation

Do you think you need millions of dollars to begin implementing Lean Six Sigma? No way! In fact, some companies that are not heavily endowed but who happen to appreciate a good thing when they see one have delved into the process of implementing the methodology by giving their key personnel the Yellow Belt training. That is just two days at most. How big, really, is such a cost compared to the doubling and trembling of returns that you are looking at if you implement Lean Six Sigma in full?

Underrating The Size Of The Organization

This business of ours is too small for big methodologies! Do you think you could be too tiny for a fat bank account? If not, how then can you dismiss an improvement tool that does not come as a whole mass but as a combination of implementable principles? If you are small or just medium size but you acknowledge that reducing product defects is worthwhile and you are ready to use reliable data to improve your processes in a way that can be objectively assessed, then you are ready for Lean Six Sigma. In short, you could embrace Lean Six Sigma but implement it in phases. In fact, your most fundamental step no matter the size of your organization is to be able to pinpoint the specific needs of your customer.

Not Being Involved In Manufacturing

Birds fly - fine. Do airplanes fly? Yes, they do as they have what it takes to fly. That is the same case with Lean Six Sigma. Where was it that this methodology was first tried out? In the manufacturing sector - and this was with the likes of Motorola. Does that mean that only the manufacturing sector needs to cut down on losses? And are customers of manufactured products the only ones that need great products? Of course, not! If you want a service, you surely want the best and as per your specifications. And the business enterprise providing the service wants to make as much money as possible by cutting down on costs. In short, there is no business, irrespective of whether it is in the manufacturing sector, the service industry or even trade, that does not wish to be as profitable as it can and to please its customers.

The Massive Statistics And Advanced Math

Have you also misconstrued Lean Six Sigma to be all about big math; statistics and probability? Well, it is not. You can still make a big improvement in the success of your business entity without involving yourself with complex figures. Even a business that deals with customer care and not anything like engineering can do with reduction of waste. It can also do with happier customers. Can you identify obvious duplications and redundancies in your organization without holding a calculator or mathematical table? Yes, you can. Can you identify obvious wastage without doing number related calculations? If it is a yes to both questions, then you surely can apply Lean Six Sigma without having to employ a statistician and still reap higher revenues.

Planning To Embark On Six Sigma Or Lean Methodology First

Do you take the two - Six Sigma and Lean - to be mutually exclusive? Of course, they are not. Both Lean and Six Sigma have the customer's satisfaction as their main focus. So you need not delay your endeavor to transform your enterprise as you try to determine which of the two methodologies is best to begin with. That is the main reason you will be talking of Lean Six Sigma projects and not Lean and thereafter Six Sigma down the line or the other way round.

Having Tried Lean Six Sigma Before And Not Succeeded

Can you identify the reasons you failed? What, exactly, failed you? Was it the technology you used; the people handling the processes; or the processes themselves?

In short, wisdom lies in you learning from your experience even when that experience involves failure. You fail and then you try yet again - not quit because you once tried and did not make it. In fact, you have great role models in instances of turning failure around to become exemplary success. Think of Henry Ford, he of Ford Motors Company, and the number of times he failed before actually succeeding.

Chapter 51
How to Embark on Implementing Lean Six Sigma

Ever heard someone warn that saying the ram is fat is no proposition that it be slaughtered? If you have not, no worries - in any case, that saying is organically African. But here, you would not be exercising prudence if you let a good system go untried. You have seen that Lean Six Sigma cuts operation costs drastically; involves virtually every team member thus making everyone feel valued; makes revenue figures somersault eliciting wide smiles from shareholders; and basically makes everyone happy. Why then would anyone with this valuable information not embark on implementing it? Please say you are not too mesmerized to begin.

Identify A Champion

Champion...? Well, a champion leads, right? And here in Lean Six Sigma you are looking to building a team. You are also looking to soliciting resources. There is also the building of some kind of working structure - call it even your modus operandi (Let them know you know some Latin, why not? Or some legal jargon...). Anyway, all these fundamentals need someone to structure how they are going to happen. And hence the need for this Project Champion.

When To Bring In The Project Champion

The Project Champion is the one to take the project from the ground. So you need him or her like yesterday. In fact, even before you know what shape the Lean Six Sigma project is going to take, it is important that you have this guy. If there is anyone to pull hairs to baldness, it is the project champion - convincing top management that the project is worth the paper it is outlined on; and even laying its groundwork. In fact, do not lose sight of the grim reality that some organizations still have those old guards - wise alright - but still with the 18th century thinking. And without their signatures on the check you are not going to get any funds.

The Basic Role Of The Project Champion

Coming up with the project

You know if you come up with a project that gets stakeholders wondering if your organization has been bought out you will be digging your own grave. So the project champion needs to be able to come up with a project that is relevant to the operations of the organization. A project that draws attention to the organization's increased efficiency rather than superficial changes is what you want.

Gauging your project against your organization's strategic objectives

After all the good work of sourcing materials and engaging everyone in cost cutting is done, you need to emerge from the same end of the tunnel that the organization envisaged long before your project came to being. If, for instance, the organization looks forward to serving the region in 5yrs, you need to have that in the picture even as you improve efficiency. In short, you could be termed unsuccessful if you attained 98% efficiency but ended up serving only your country by that time.

Liaise with the very top

For every penny that gets out of the organization's bank account, the top leadership must give their blessings. That goes for other major decisions like altering employees' working schedules and so on. That is mainly why you need to have a project manager who does not freeze in the presence of the big guys and who also does not have a tendency to grow horns when given important responsibilities.

Pinpoint key project personnel

The Project Lead

Project Finance Certifier

I hope that tells you outright that the Project Champion is not the guy for the dirty work. Challenging, yes – bumping onto each other with regular team members on a day-to-day basis, no. And even the sensitive role of saying the team is justified to request this and to spend that the Champion delegates to someone else.

This underlines the importance of the Champion's role; being able to observe the overall picture of the Six Sigma project. For this reason, it is presumed that the Champion is capable and willing to appoint the two main officers for their competence and competence alone. Obviously, anything with the semblance of biases or prejudices being a factor would be jeopardizing the success of the project.

Analyzing Project Performance

Of course, you must remember reading that the project is assessed periodically. Now the person to give the project the green light to proceed to the next stage is the Project Champion. If, for any reason, he feels dissatisfied with your product at that stage, then the relevant parts would have to be redone. And if it is to do with provision of a service, even that would be reviewed and if farmhands have to be replaced, then that would happen.

Whereas the Project Champion may come across as the boss with both hands in the pocket, his is not such an easy job. To be a Project Champion comes with great responsibility because at the end of the project, the buck stops with him or her. However, seeing a Lean Six Sigma project to its successful completion is an additional feather to the Champion's hat; a real boost to the Champions resume.

Who Qualifies For The Position Of Six Sigma Project Champion?

Me! Me! Oh, no. This position is not filled in a haphazard manner. Just like the Champion is expected to be diligent when appointing a Finance Certifier, so is anyone in top management when it comes to supporting someone for the role of Project Champion. This is not one of those offices where you sit and rock the chair all day long waiting to append your signature onto something that nobody will ever inquire about. So, here are the criteria:

Be part of senior management

Do you know the reason?

It is unlikely that you left college and found yourself in a senior management position. So, naturally, you have gone through muck to get to where you are. You have, for example, witnessed firsthand the reality of employees being all smiles today and tomorrow they have placards with your name on it – and in negative light, for that matter. Having survived such challenges, you now know how to run a team.

Your time climbing up the ladder has given you great experience that is necessary for such changes that would be seen to be radical.

Being one with the top management puts you in good stead when it comes to lobbying for resources.

Having held a similar position before

Obviously, if you can truly say, been there and done that, you are very well placed. You know what challenges to anticipate, which means you can put measures in place to cushion your project and your team; you have an idea how resources become necessary along the way as incidental costs and hence you can provide for them; you are aware how tight employees schedules can become a handicap and so you can psyche the top management to expect requests for flexible working hours; and so on.

A bonus if you have been a Project Lead before

You see theory and practical are two different realities. Please... Isn't that really obvious? Maybe; but in some areas, once you know the theory the practical part is a smooth ride. But there are positions like this one of Project Lead that you may not exactly understand until you enter those shoes.

At times you may find yourself dealing with clients who like giving verbal specifications and you are not worried because you scribble down as they speak. But then the danger is that they have no qualms denying those specifications when the product is finally complete. And they make you look bad. Not to mention you have to face the reality of the organization losing resources on your watch. How can you empathize with your Project Lead unless you have been in such a situation yourself? How would you bring yourself to tone down criticism on your Project Lead when team members fail to attend meetings having been derailed by their department heads?

Yet for there to be a healthy working atmosphere, empathy and support are necessary amongst team members; between the Project Champion and the team; between the Lead and team members; between the team and the client; and even between the Project Champion and his appointed assistants - the Project Lead and the Finance Certifier. In fact, it can be very frustrating, for example, for the Project Champion to trash particular demands for funds just because of the timing, without understanding that it is very difficult to anticipate all expenses.

Be aware of the tools to measure quality

How else would one tell if the quality has been met unless with clear knowledge of the relevant tools of assessment?

Be alive to the strategic goals of your organization

Why is this, yet the Project Champion is not becoming the CEO's equal? Well, he or she is not getting any more senior than he or she already is, but then it would hurt the organization to have the Champion working towards divergent goals. Remember that everything happening under the organization should be geared towards achieving the ultimate goals of the organization.

In fact, it is in this light that the Champion will identify the Lean Sigma Project to undertake. The strategic goals will determine too how the Champion lays down the resource allocation structure.

Chapter 52
Why Use Lean Six Sigma Systems For Your Small Business?

The Lean Six Sigma revolution is systematically carrying more non-manufacturing businesses in small and medium-sized organizations. IT, telecommunications, banking, promotion, insurance, health, and construction organizations have looked into the advanced lean six sigma approaches to boost their own quality and standards in handling their clients, providers, and customers. A slender six sigma system enriches every location of your business with just one, only system. It eliminates and reduces value-added activities and waste in your enterprise. In general, it provides you with a competitive advantage by lowering operating expenses and improving productivity.

It defines a job route for many individuals, diminishing wasted labor and emphasizing specific elements of this project. It gives tools to enhance worker efficiency and boost their efficacy, quality of output signal, confidence and motivate them into enhancing performance degrees. It generates process improvements through the duration of the job flow procedure. You learn how to classify many items and expel the people not linked to the procedure. This permits you to concentrate on what ought to be executed on an everyday basis. On top of that, it elevates the career of one's business in the market. It's merely good sense. Why waste substances? Why spend time searching for funds? Why waste space saving surplus stock? Get outcomes. Employ lean-to your factory or administrative procedures. Or create it an above-mentioned option and expand it into a supplier and sub-contractors.

The tiniest lean execution might impact your own workflow as well as your bottom-line. You want to compete. Your organization has gone going there at a worldwide market that's less money to pay off. Why should anybody choose your service or product? As you've made sure that your products or services are your very best. Lean six sigma may help reduce waste, in addition to expel the sources resulting in waste. It highlights a successive operating system which focuses solely on those degrees demanded and just once they're required. This method was developed particularly for small to midsize organizations that are attempting to boost their endurance throughout the operation. Expert advisers in thin six sigma can jumpstart your own business progress. Or you could possibly get training online or at live training classes.

Be mindful that there are a few gaps between the original six-sigma machine and the lean six sigma system: Generation I is targeted on defects, Generation III centers around value. Generation I puts focus on the provider, while Generation III puts concentration to the customer and the provider. Generation I experts are called Black Belts, Generation III pros are White Belts. They make results quicker because of thinner focus and also a thorough schedule. Rather than earning its principal attention on the decrease in prices, and Generation III is targeted on the invention of value. This really is a huge advancement in plan, specially for its small and medium-sized organizations. The objective would be always to get a business provide services and goods of optimum price, at the ideal location, punctually, while in the ideal amount, and at the best possible price. This also boosts the view of consumers, analysts, investors and workers equally. Everyone else is on board working toward aims everyone plays a role in achieving! The actual beauty of thin six sigma is you may tailor the procedures to fit your company as they aren't adjusted methodologies which need to get utilized in a given purchase. Today, employers, irrespective of their size, will benefit from the advantages and potential offered by the lean six sigma procedure.

Challenges And Problem Of Lean Six Sigma Improvement Teams

Organizations which cannot supply because of consideration for the particular aspect, frequently don't exploit the entire potential of little implementations and thus begin whining that 'Lean Six Sigma doesn't work'. They don't appreciate that the issue isn't with little theories; their failures are the result of the inherent inability of their execution team to overcome the usual difficulties and challenges.

Pinpointing Implementation Issues and Challenges

For making sure the achievement of Lean Projects, the execution team should try to recognize the common difficulties and challenges that it may encounter throughout the execution period. For that, the team should use time tested Sigma tools and processes such as 'Procedure Records' that highlight every single event, functionality, and also sub-processes of this provided process selected for advancement.

But as it's not achievable to start looking into each and all aspects of this given business method, the team needs to concentrate on just those aspects which can be critical to the most important procedure. In consequence, the team needs to pay attention to pinpointing potential issues in mere people sub-processes which may be donating significantly more than 50 to 60 per cent to the delivery of the last outcome. That is essential because when issues occur in significant sub-processes throughout the execution period, the small business will lose its productive efficacy, something which is likely to produce a mockery of 'Lean' goals and targets which involve improved efficiencies that are sustainable.

For greater results, they ought to search Input from individuals like floor managers, managers, process managers, along with many others that may possibly be needing viable understanding in regards to the provided business procedure. When required, top and middle management may be asked to supply their valuable inputs and suggestions.

Overcoming Challenges

The project is stated to be 'half done' because soon while the difficulties have been identified, however, the execution team must not lose its attention at this point since it has to complete the rest of the half, i.e. beating the recognized challenges and problems. That is the toughest part, as not even the very experienced professionals like Black Belts will guarantee the achievement of initiatives required for beating execution issues and challenges.

The very best that the execution group certainly can do afterward would be to use Seven Sigma simulation software, that could create predictions that are very accurate. Simulations enable a whole lot since they have the ability for that team to make use of the 'hit and trial' system without fretting about real reductions, physical or monetary. Employing the 'hit and trial' procedure, they can then readily choose an initiative which most suits the requirement of beating implementation issues and challenges.

Besides placing their faith in Six Sigma tools and methods for overcoming challenges and problems, they ought to attempt to boost innovation and creativity as some times merely these skills may save a job from certain failure. Constant motivation, guidance, and comprehension are all good methods of promoting innovation and creativity on the list of Lean Six Sigma implementation team associates.

Keep Costs In Check With Six Sigma

While Six Sigma can maximize various other procedures as a way to squeeze more from these, a lean manufacturing procedure can pay attention to reducing the expenses specifically related to transporting and manufacturing, from raw material into finished product.

Here are some ways by which Six Sigma Contributes to lessen costs.

Implementing the Principles of Six Sigma

As Six Sigma is mainly geared toward Increasing the return on investment [ROI] and absolute client care; activities from Master Black Belts or Black Belts in specific areas could lead to cost-saving measures like process inventions and product upgrades.

This is done so as to catch a larger market combined side high degrees of consumer care. By executing Six Sigma, Black Belts could pull on a bigger yield from assorted endeavors by making certain every one of the tools are useful to the fullest.

Six Sigma may additionally identify different risk factors which empower businesses to produce counter-plans on how best to market them. It can offer necessary data to find out if certain projects will need to be left in favor of the others that may possess more potential.

Using Six Sigma in Numerous Procedures

After you employ Six Sigma to different procedures, like stabilizing manufacturing procedure and moving towards zero rejection, you can perform enormous savings as your cost of production has been paid off radically.

By paying heed to a clients' complaints concerning the accessibility and level of one's services and products, you're able to make certain you maintain your work and production centers at probably the most perfect levels.

Get Lean and Mean

From the production process, Lean Six Sigma may lead to lower transportation prices, faster processing of orders and material and preserving ideal stock amounts, averting over-or-under-processing of products and orders.

By making sure that workers are Producing at optimal levels, waste might be curtailed, which translates into reducing costs and high economies. By employing minimum resources like raw material, machines and labor - and - from getting the full process right first time round - associations may get minimal wastage of resources that are available.

While price cutting the substance Side is very predictable, finetuning the wave lengths of a high quantity of employees to execute cohesively is quite troublesome - which really is where adapting and embracing six-sigma can create effective outcomes.

Generally, employing a mix of Six Sigma and lean production procedures which are always monitored by Master Dark connectors could lead to substantial cost cutting edge and coast up the main point of their company, hence helping to survive and flourish in the face of demanding competition.

It'll take some time and Decision to make certain that all method merges effortlessly into a while decreasing wastage at precisely the exact same period - however, that the upshot of such efforts might be extremely rewarding.

Rightsizing Lean Six Sigma Teams

It's quite true that brains mean more processing power, the concept doesn't find prefer when choosing team size as what exactly is even more essential is communicating - a thing which becomes a massive problem when significantly more than the requisite amount of employees is invisible to the Lean Six Sigma implementation crew.

Therefore, rightsizing Lean Six Sigma Teams ought to really be the initial priority for most organizations that are looking sure to the victory of 'Lean' endeavors and realize the entire potential of such endeavors.

How Does a Small Business Make Means for Rightsizing?

Within their attempts to decrease the group size, most organizations frequently make the error of inducting 'top-rated' workers, so believing they will compensate for the size of their 'Lean' implementation crew. Organizations don't appreciate that a lot of 'top-rated' employees are respective actors and they could possibly not have the capacity to present their utmost when asked to behave like a team. In addition, since celebrities generally have enormous egos which could result in conflicts and maybe not cooperation, it seems sensible to not include them at the 'Lean' team.

The group size may vary depending on the complexity and vastness of this 'Lean' job, however, for an ordinary job, organizations should start looking for a group of three to four associates. When choosing associates, direction should start looking for employees who could have worked for no less than five to ten decades and demonstrated consistent operation through recent years.

Since keeping appropriate communications is among the major responsibility of 'Lean' execution teams, the direction must gauge the communication and social skills of possible applicants prior to inducting them at the team. Ability to consider this package, solve issues, view things in the ideal view, and also motivate the others are a few of the additional qualities which the direction should keep an eye out for when selecting 'Lean' execution team.

Great Things about Rightsizing Lean-six Sigma Teams

The real advantages of rightsizing might differ based on the sort of 'Lean' job and also the sort of company, however, a few basic benefits which each company could aspire to derive from rightsizing comprise the next.

Increased communications amongst implementers, direction officials and other things connected with all the 'Lean' task

Better liability on a part of the team members because actions and decisions taken by the group could be tracked right back to members

Reduced cost of operations since lower the amounts, the less are the number of tools employed for doing the exact jobs and responsibilities

Higher efficacy in solving complicated problems and problems since workers would know the Precise individual to contact should they experience difficulties throughout the execution stage

Less likelihood of self and conflicts issues because the size will stop the creation of subgroups within the crew

These advantages are sufficient to prove the significance of rightsizing and rightsizing is your thing to do for associations seeking to eventually become 'Lean' and then enhance their efficiency and endurance.

Chapter 53
The Six Sigma Infrastructure

One other Significant change initiative needs an obviously defined encouraging infrastructure to induce the application. Coding means the inherent base and basic frame of supporting and personnel systems necessary to guide Six Sigma installation tasks. Because every component of a provider engages in Six Sigma tasks, the infrastructure has to be clean, consistent, and comprehensive.

A successful infrastructure eases the maturation of the core competency that'll establish and connect Six Sigma project teams into (1) projects, (2) financial goals, and also (3) the tactical plan. These project teams will probably be multi-functional and certainly will be needing multi-functional aid to perform the projects. If six-sigma has any potential for achieving success, the infrastructure may interval from the CEO and his leadership team to both industry leaders and also to those executing the projects. Remember we heard early in the day that you of Kotter's eight stages of pioneer shift is "Produce a Guiding Coalition." Thus, there's the objective of the Six Sigma infrastructure.

The infrastructure makes a solid network on the list of the executive team, the Six Sigma Champions, the Belts, and also the serves and companies. This is logical since the CEO's leadership team holds the responsibility for executing the organization's strategic plan, and Six Sigma projects are instrumental in proceeding together with the tactical plan.

One learning obstacle of a Six Sigma Deployment entails training the Six Sigma project teams. The individual resources on such teams must discover what is a Six Sigma team. A fresh road map and also a brand new group of tools, and an even more different focus on job liability, enhance the fluctuations faced with a business when designing a Six Sigma environment.

Equally more significant and complicated is the learning barrier of these senior executives. Teaching the direction team to master to direct a home-based organization is imperative to tactical and long-term success. Because the execution of this plan is a very clear responsibility to the senior executives that are more liable, it follows becoming a lively team leader over the Six Sigma installation which will encourage the tactical efforts.

Implementing a fantastic strategic plan involves the manipulation of multi-functional internal pursuits. Mature executives must figure out how to take care of a multi-functional stadium as opposed to the conventional functions. A huge selection of Six Sigma teams started simultaneously could be that the results of an exceptional installation of Six Sigma. All those teams want at minimal

- Clear purpose for your Six Sigma team structure.
- Clear six-sigma app expectations.
- Six Sigma job charters.
- Six Sigma infrastructure monitoring the Number of clubs.
- Centralized repository for job results.
- Six Sigma team objectives.
- Six Sigma team monitoring mechanism.
- Recognition and reward orientation.
- Six Sigma development and training plan.
- Six Sigma team operation measures.
- Deployment management of Six Sigma teams.

To achieve all the previous requirements requires a thorough infrastructure together with encouraging systems. Preexisting tools are largely utilized to staff of that particular infrastructure. Deploying a Six Sigma application, but will not assume that a requirement to put in outside resources at lots of fresh places. The extra costs will normally need related to the outside consulting group you hire.

By way of example, the sole real resource that Larry Bossidy inserted when he started Six Sigma to Allied Signal had been a corporate application pioneer. Larry Earned Richard Schroeder out of ABB to push the app. The rest of the tools for AlliedSignal's Six Sigma program existed within the provider. Even a few additional tools were inserted with the organizations as needed. Because liability reflects the sign of successful Six Sigma deployments, specifying the Six Sigma staffing and infrastructure and training that the infrastructure players should come about early at the Six Sigma setup. Training is vital as you need to "understand the courage of this initiative" In addition, he adds that key members of the leadership staff should know the courage of this initiative. Historical leadership training is a standard area of Six Sigma deployments to permit the app leaders to know that the courage of six-sigma until the app becomes too far over.

Assessing the Six Sigma infrastructure is just somewhat catchy. There ought to be a tiny centralized unit to guarantee consistency and cost-efficacy of Six Sigma tasks round the functions and businesses. There should likewise become a decentralized procedure which makes it possible for each small business and be capable of tailoring the Six Sigma installation for its special wants. There's a difference in deploying Six Sigma into the hour work when comparing to deploying product development and R&D. Thus, our advocated infrastructure includes both centralized and decentralized elements in it.

Initialization and Developing an Infrastructure with Lean Six Sigma

Infrastructure preparation could be learned in a Six Sigma training curriculum in less than a day or two having some work help with. You are going to discover to process launches of endeavors, maintain and assess the accomplishment of performance improvement programs, and initialize or supply the outcome of their company vision to some solid action program. Once you walk off from a slender Six Sigma class you may truly have a good base of how you can work a whole operation improvement program and you'll have the ability to reach Six Sigma results.

When someone goes throughout the Initialization and development part of the Lean Six Sigma app, they are going to discover to roll out and convey the particulars of a job's installation to every one of the personnel. You are going to discover just how to successfully gather a realistic deadline for the whole job, for example training and proceed live customs. You may see about the significance of a Six Sigma green belt, yellow belt, black belt, and also other degrees of Six Sigma expertise.

All instruction inquiries will probably be replied here because this really is actually the initialization and installation period. After you undergo Six Sigma training, then you are going to have the ability to answer questions regarding how training will happen. It's crucial that you be aware of the form of training that'll function as the most reliable for staff. Can be an off-site classroom that is the ideal option or even on the web may be your very best means for your own category to master.

Prioritizing tasks for your organization is just another component of lean Six Sigma you are going to see. It's vital in order to recognize projects which may forge the business into a success, maybe not bogged down a wealth of productive employees while hardly making a profit. Once you finish a Six Sigma black belt certificate, you're going to learn precisely how to spot and find the worthy projects which are going to soon be successful for that provider.

The Lean Six Sigma app or the Six Sigma classes are intended to assist you to know about initialization and installation for a personal infrastructure. Become familiar with about building an infrastructure in the vertical building, deploying an eyesight during a business, discovering successful jobs and training, plus even more.

Six-sigma As A method to Develop People

Some of the numerous benefits of Six Sigma is the way that it will help to build people. This cultivate excellence in not only product quality and also benefits but also from the data, confidence, and caliber of the men and women in your own organization. Individuals are, after all, your businesses' most valuable assets. To preserve and always improve, a business should develop its own people. Six Sigma helps develop your visitors in 2 different areas: it grows leaders plus it enables people to become more knowledgeable and valuable contributors to this company's success. Every company needs people with leadership qualities. Leadership skills are necessary at each level of the company. Ongoing Six Sigma training and execution from the executive degree online supervisors can help grow leadership in your own organization. With Six Sigma, you can find various chances to build leadership abilities and leadership qualities at all levels from the company. Six Sigma certificate training and also the hands-on real-world training of leading Six Sigma projects cultivate direction abilities.

Six-sigma attempts to mature leaders at a company through its training programs. Individuals who've completed Six Sigma practice develop a Belt name. It denotes their amount of wisdom and responsibility. A greenbelt is someone that has completed fourteen days of training over the Six Sigma road map and fundamental elements of statistical methods encouraging Six Sigma projects and who's part of a Six Sigma process improvement crew. A Black Belt is someone that has completed four weeks of practice concentrating in the Six Sigma road map and extensive statistical methods and also can be experienced at directing cross-functional process improvement teams. Black tutors become pioneers of Six Sigma project teams plus they mentor other employees to help them grow. Six-sigma values direction, however in addition, it protects participation in employees at all levels of this company. In case everyone could possibly access the origin of an issue and help solve that, then it isn't important where the concept comes out of. Six Sigma needs to own absolute commitment and support from all levels of this company. Six Sigma requires purchase from everybody involved with the commercial procedures which can be quantified. This condition actually will help develop a better company.

Involvement from all degrees of employees comes around by the Six Sigma plan of construction project types. Continuous improvement procedures, such as Six Sigma, means, for example, people, gaining their participation, after which encouraging what they have been attempting to achieve. Six-sigma requests input improvement solutions from all employees since it acknowledges that the worth of creative methods to issues in all sources. The easy reality is that workers know some matters the higherups do not. Frontline employees know the customer better than anybody. Businesses that solicit thoughts from line workers can discover innovative methods to conditions which may never be discovered by detached investigation. Involving people through six-sigma additionally results in enabling people. Six-sigma's data-driven methodology supplies people appropriate feedback regarding the procedure and quantities of advancement that they have been achieving- exactly what they did well and exactly what they needed poorly. Throughout Six Sigma, the folks receive real methods to get rid of the actual root causes of issues. Plus, it provides the comprehension of the data, where, and whys as the info is not there. So, Six Sigma helps develop the awareness, confidence, and caliber of individuals in your own organization.

Further, the Six Sigma helps encourage a civilization of confidence that everybody else's energies will be led to favorable and constructive work. This kind of civilization contains including people, providing them with the tools that they will need to ensure success, a proper amount of control and influence, and being offered together. As confidence builds, people begin to receive are more involved, become committed, accept greater empowerment, and more profound levels of confidence grow. Teamwork, coordination of tasks and also hoping that one of the teams get the method to attempt of Sigma successful.

The end result of doing so well is Professional growth, improved morale and favorable attitudes toward combined efforts. Six Sigma will turn into one of those facets which perhaps not merely fuels stunning excellent advancement on your employees but also creates a workplace that is exceptional.

How To Use Lean Six Sigma In Your Business.

Businesses competing at a complicated international market place face enormous pressure to keep up functional excellence. Applying Lean Six Sigma, the standard control technique utilized to decrease waste, eliminate product defects and enhance client care, involves focusing on customer desires and in-depth data analysis to be able to meet that challenge. Shifting your own company to work with better procedures is dependent upon executive livelihood and trained employees. Employ Lean Six Sigma methods not simply on your manufacturing processes but also your ceremony and also other business purposes.

- Teach your employees on Lean Six Sigma Theories in order that most employees can notice that Six Sigma methods improve customer care levels by reducing flaws to no further than 3.4 per thousand. Lean manufacturing methods reduce ineffective actions as a way to boost product progress. Together, they allow you to conduct a far more efficient and profitable company. The Motorola internet site offers complimentary courses on six-sigma topics. The American Society for Quality offers a certificate to qualified applicants because of a blackbelt, an average of accountable for job management or greenbelt, frequently accountable for team donations.
- Identify procedures requiring improvement Predicated on non-performing usable metrics. By way of instance, if customer satisfaction levels for a specific product always fall, inspect the support logs to isolate the issue, for example as raw material employed in fabricating or even a defect at the original layout. Conduct focus groups or interviews with clients, production specialists along with also other employees to collect information.
- Utilize resources, like a Fish-bone Diagram, to demonstrate the reason and effect of all people, techniques, equipment, substances, data and also the surroundings on the creation of one's service or product. To earn a fishbone diagram, then draw an arrow from the left on the best in the middle of a

webpage. On left end, draw lines above and below the point, such as fish scales, also list the complexities. On the best, clarify the issue or effect. Add extra lines to list sub-causes. Use this advice to work out just how to successfully cover the issues.

- Concentrate on reducing prices by optimizing your own processes. Get a grip on process inputs and that means that you may expel flaws. Monitor and track your own progress achieving those aims. By way of instance, to apply Lean Six Sigma processes to human resources activities, correct your procedures to decrease the time that it will take to recruit, and orient a new employee by standardizing your procedures and training employees effortlessly. Employ Lean Sigma for a fund company through the elimination of unnecessary approval workflows, reducing the time that it requires to accomplish trades, like paying vendors or calculating your own payroll.
- Give attention to reducing mistakes by Streamlining and simplifying the procedures of completing work. By way of instance, centralize your database surgeries to ensure if your earning team goes in order, strains pre-populate with existing customer info, available inventory and also the purchaser's credit line. Catch awareness for debugging client service calls into a database accessible with service employees therefore that your service teams can lower the time that it requires to fix customer issues.
- Inspect and audit procedures frequently, for example, in a yearly basis to keep a high amount of quality on your own systems.

Conclusions

Now that you understand what the Lean Six Sigma method of management is, you can start living it every day. Start with implementing the various aspects of waste reduction. As you get all the respective aspects of process improvement working, you will see a definite change for the better on the overall performance of your organization. Wastage will be a thing of the past; or it will, at least, be reduced to negligible levels. And since waste constitutes a big part that eats into revenues, your bottom line will automatically shoot to impressive levels.

There is also the aspect of problem solving that you have learnt in the form of DMAIC. As you embark on practicing those systematic steps of problem solving, your processes will be improving and your revenues will be increasing as a consequence. That will show you that, evidently, cutting waste and solving problems in the way prescribed by the Lean Six Sigma approach gives fast and progressive results. And you will also see the benefit of having more of your people trained in matters relevant to Lean Six Sigma.

The next step is to go back over the book as needed. At the same time, observe the systems existing in your organization and see where they require modifying. Once you take those initial baby steps leading to more efficient processes, you can easily change your employees' old mindset and help them adopt a new one where they feel in-charge and accountable for their actions. That, in turn, means that they will revel at the success of the organization. What this effectively does is give you a motivated workforce that is eager to save costs for the organization while doing everything to make the organization succeed and beat competitors.

With this powerful knowledge, the ball is now in your court. Work towards helping your organization reach its potential and do not hesitate to congratulate yourself for a job well done when you are finally the leading light in your industry!

AGILE PROJECT MANAGEMENT

HOW TO MASTER SCRUM, KANBAN AND ALL AGILE TOOLS TO OPTIMIZE THE ORGANIZATION, PERFORMANCE, QUALITY AND RESULTS. INCLUDES KAIZEN GUIDE TO GROW STEP BY STEP AND ACHIEVE GOALS

JACK LEAD

This book is composed of three parts.
The first one explains the Agile method, all its tools and its implementation. Among them also short introductions to Scrum and Kanban which will be dealt with in dept in the second and third parts of the book.

Jack Lead

Part 1: Agile Project Management

These days, it almost feels like agile project management is on everyone's lips. The term gets tossed around with so much ardor (among those who are for it and those who are against it) that we have almost lost its meaning altogether.

Agile is about a lot more than just hanging out in circles every day and playing little games when it comes to splitting larger tasks into smaller ones.

Agile was born with a reason — but even more than that, it was born in a time and for a time that needed a drastic change in approach.

Although agile methodologies (like Kanban, for example) have been practiced for many decades already, agile project management — in its raw, official format — was born a little under two decades ago.

In many ways, it feels like it's been ages already — and that is mostly due to the fact that agile has changed a lot. Its very foundation stays the same. But in terms of adaptability, agile has won the long-term game, and it is now one of the rulers in the world of project management.

How much of a ruler is it, really?

Studies show that about 30% of projects use a clear agile approach, while approximately 40% of them use a traditional/waterfall approach. The remaining 30% use a hybrid approach (Getapp, 2019) — which, contrary to what some may believe, doesn't show that waterfall has won the race, but that it needs agile adjustments to function in the modern world.

We invite you on a journey of learning and discovery, at the end of which you will discover which version of agile works best for you and for your organization.

History of Agile

Agile project management was born out of sheer need. Together with the advent of modern technology and computers, a lot of things had to be done — and more importantly, they had to be done fast, accurately, and within the budget.

Agile methods started to take shape as early as the 1950s, but it wasn't until five decades later that the famous Agile Manifesto was laid on paper.

Sometime around the mid-'90s, most of what is now known as agile project management began to be contoured. At first, it was all dispersed — there was RAD (Rapid Application Development) in 1991, Scrum in 1995, and Feature-Driven Development two years later.

In 2001, it all came together, as if to offer clarity to a world that was getting ready to make a full jump into the one channel that rules them all today: the Internet. Sure, web connections had existed before, but it was at the turn of the millennia when things started to really take off.

On this background, seventeen brilliant software development minds got together in Snowbird, Utah. That meeting would go down in history, as this was when the actual concepts of agile project management took their official form.

We would be very curious to know exactly how that meeting went. We do know it didn't come out of the blue (you cannot simply expect the forward-thinkers in software development to just accidentally come together in Utah, can you?).

And we also know that the Snowbird meeting set the grounds for everything that followed in the world of agile project management. We would go as far as to assume that a lot of the amazing software tools we use today on a recurrent basis now would not have existed — they would have lingered somewhere, still in development.

Agile project management was born because there was a dire need to alter the project management landscape in software development. Back in the '90s, when the demand for software increased, traditional project management methods proved to be inefficient (at best) and downright disastrous (at worst).

In fact, it is frequently mentioned that most of the (major!) software development houses had (equally major!) lag when it came to their releases. On average, software development was lagging by approximately three years. For large projects, the lag extended further, up to 20 years.

It sounds preposterous, and it is.

But that's just what waterfall did to these projects. The very nature of software development is ever-changing, so it made no sense at all to stick to a management approach that focused on spreadsheets, more than the very core of what these projects did.

Agile project management has succeeded in removing those parts of waterfall that might have been bottlenecks in the development process.

Furthermore, as you will see throughout the entire book, the waterfall-agile hybrids have also ensured the streamlining of the waterfall processes, taking the best of the two worlds and providing organizations based on heavy documentation with an alternative to traditional project management.

Agile project management was born at the right time to become the backbone of the tech industry before it boomed completely.

From the Silicon Valley to China, and from Iceland to Australia, agile has become a household name in project management. Even more, it has expanded well beyond the borders of software programming and is now used in pretty much every industry you could imagine. Hospitals, schools, governmental and non-governmental institutions, marketing, translations — everyone can embrace agile, precisely because it is so flexible and adaptable to multiple situations.

History is rarely written when we expect it.

We don't know if those seventeen minds actually knew the kind of impact their meeting would have — but we do know that software development and agile are so intertwined these days that it seems almost impossible to completely separate them.

Chapter 1
What is the Agile Method?

Agile Project Management refers to a way to manage projects. In short, it is a way to handle a project to help achieve its goals. This can include early delivery of a specific task and continuous development of project processes and products. In addition, Agile Project Management focuses on creating a flexible scope and ensuring that products are tested to reflect the different needs of a customer.

Without these factors, it becomes difficult for a project to be successful. All software projects have a goal and a goal. In addition, each project has determined the time for completion.

Agile Project Management has various techniques that help improve the way to manage a project. As a project leader, it is important to keep abreast of the Agile approaches to project management. It is also useful if you understand a history of project management and the common problems that can be associated with it.

The Start Of Modern Project Management

Projects have been around since the invention of the printing press to the building of the Chinese wall. Projects have been present, small or large.

Project management, however, began in the mid-twentieth century. It was during this time that most researchers were looking for important developments and changes in the computer industry. To ensure that these researchers complete these developments, they have decided to set up effective ways to manage and complete projects. In the beginning, these mechanisms were based on a systematic procedure, so people in the programming and computer areas passed most of these processes.

One reason for this is that all computers were primarily dependent on hardware. The software is set to expand. During this time, software even represented a small part of the computer. Remember that part of the history of computers consisted of computers built with thousands of physical tubes and only a few lines of code. That is why the production process used in this period has led to the development of the Waterfall method.

Why Go Agile?

Now that you have a basic knowledge of agile, it is better to know how agile works, which roles are agile and why agile becomes.

In the beginning, we had defined Agile Project Management as a way to manage projects by delivering value to customers and the organization. In other words, this gives project managers the opportunity to offer work with high priority and high quality in the various projects.

Agile Project Management is a dynamic approach to managing projects that takes into account every type of change that is coming. Agile Project Management will embrace change even late in the development phase. This allows you to create the right functions that have the best value. With Agile Project Management, one is sure to deal with real-time information and to deal with scope, time and costs.

The most interesting thing about managing projects with Agile practices is that it is simple and efficient. It will help reduce complexity by ensuring that it shortens the time required to compile requirements for the entire project. It will further help in building the entire project and testing to discover multiple product problems.

Why Do You Have To Worry About Agile Project Management?

Suppose you have started applying Agile practices and you find it much more complex, chances are that certain things will not go well. Maybe some components are missing. In this case it is advised to inspect the implementation process. What everyone needs to know is that implementing Agile correctly will always be successful in the delivery process. In general, a positive improvement must be noted, both in the value delivered to customers and in the product.

With Agile Project Management, time and costs are an important aspect. It continuously examines these two elements that are the key to any software project. Moreover, it provides quick feedback to the team. It further helps the team to adapt and apply a QA practice. This will help to deliver first-class service and output. Project managers who control Agile practices are concerned with real-time delivery, proactive and the total flow. The general goal is to have the minimum costs of a project and a working product on time.

Examples Of Agile Project Management Software

Monday

Monday was formerly called DaPulse. It focuses primarily on social communication and the sharing of internal information. Monday has given priority to top choices in Agile project management. Collaboration is achieved by a board that indicates what is being worked on within a certain time. Teams can then continue to respond to the work of other teammates or add the required files. There is a mobile or desktop application that allows real-time notifications. Monday is great software to use for basic and business plans.

Wrike

It is SaaS project management and collaboration software. Wrike is designed on the basis of a minimalist user interface. It has a project management feature that allows you to monitor dates, project dependencies, and manage assignments and resources. It features an interactive Gantt chart, a sortable table, and a workload view that you can customize to save project data. The Wrike collaboration functions help with team members' discussions, decision-making and activation. These include Wrike's Live co-editor, tools to attach documents, track changes, and discussion threads. Wrike has an "inbox" function and browser notification to remind users of updates to their dashboards about pending tasks. It is available in both iOS apps and native Android.

Asana

This is web-based software designed to improve collaboration. This allows users to mainly manage projects and online tasks without using an email. Asana supports team sharing, organization, planning and monitoring the progress of each member in a simple style.

Taiga

This is an open source Agile Project Management platform designed for smaller teams of project managers, developers and designers. It facilitates project collaboration, time registration and task management. Taiga has customizable Agile functionality such as Kanban boards and arrears. This software supports web-based implementations that are flexible with many operating systems. The system is accessible as a free self-hosted model where projects are public. There is also a paid plan where projects are private.

Plan box

This supports members with different business functions to collaborate, plan and create Agile projects. It has a Scrum methodology with iterations, Scrum roles, arrears, sprints and story points. Planbox has a four-level platform that includes tasks, projects, initiatives and items. This supports, among other things, dragging and dropping priorities, task lists, messages, bug tracking and reporting.

Smartsheet

This is another SaaS-based application that supports collaboration and work management. Smartsheet has an interface similar to that of a spreadsheet to keep track of projects, manage calendars, monitor progress and manage other works. Files can be linked to each row in the Smartsheet, the discussion board is linked and e-mails are saved. While information is being updated, another

Smartsheet that monitors the same task is automatically updated.

Trello

It is web-based project management software and a well-known brand that exists. With a free account, everyone has the possibility to use most functions, while a premium account has complex functions. Trello has a design that depends on the Kanban method. Projects are seen as signs with lists. Each list has a progressive card that supports drag-and-drop functionality.

Chapter 2
Agile Manifesto

It's just hard to imagine how software and activity came from "The Agile Manifesto." Before this 'Manifesto', software development was not a fast process. This copy usually resulted in many projects in the pipeline being canceled due to a change in business need.

The Agile Manifesto is the most important basis of the Agile Movement. The use of Agile that goes beyond software development has been achieved in the production, collaboration, communication and rapid development of granular functions under the overall plan's control.

Agile Manifesto History

This manifesto was released after frustration in the 90s. There was a big gap between the delivery of a product and the needs analysis. This led to the cancellation of many projects. It was during this period that business requirements and customer needs changed, and the result was that the end product did not meet current needs. The existing software development methodologies did not realize the requirements.

Later in 2000 the Agile Manifesto and the 12 principles were released.

Values in the Agile manifesto

There are four core values of the "Agile Manifesto and the 12 principles" that support this. Each of the Agile methods is based on these principles and values.

Individuals and participations above tools and processes

It is the first value in the Agile Manifesto. It places more emphasis on people than on tools and processes. This is because people are the ones who respond to the needs of a business and drive its development. If the tools or the process are spearhead development, there is a good chance that the team does not actively participate in the changes and that this has a chance of not satisfying the customer.

Operating software through detailed documentation

Traditionally, a lot of time has been spent creating a document for use in product development and delivery. Technical requirements, specifications, test plans, documentation and approvals were required. This extensive list caused delays in software development. Agile does not eliminate documentation, but offers a much better way to help the developer know what to do. Agile documents are created as user stories that are sufficient to help with software development. The Agile Manifesto has respect for documentation, but also much more respect for working software.

The customer's partnership on contract negotiations

Negotiation refers to the point where a customer and product manager sit down to come up with project details. In a software model such as the Waterfall model, customers discuss the requirements of a product in detail at an early stage. In this case, the customer acts as a participant in the development.

However, they do not participate in product creation. The Agile Manifesto offers a customer a platform to collaborate in the entire product development process. That is why it is easy for the team to meet customer needs. The Agile methods can involve the customer during different periods of the demos, but it can still involve the end user in the daily development. This ensures that all requirements are met.

Response to change in a subsequent plan

The traditional method for software development regards changes in software as an additional release. As a result, no changes are made. The goal is to make a comprehensive plan with a collection of functions. In this plan all functions are marked with the highest priority. There is also a high degree of dependence on helping a team work on a puzzle. However, with a short iteration, Agile methodology makes it possible to transform priorities from one iteration to another. In addition, new functions are integrated in the following iteration.

And so Agile offers a positive response to change. A popular example is the Method Tailoring method. This method means that people determine the developmental approach of a system through various changes. With Agile, a team can change the process and ensure that it reflects the needs of the user.

The 12 Agile Manifesto principles

These principles describe a culture in which change is accepted and the customer is central. These 12 principles include:

- Satisfy the customer through frequent software delivery. This means that customers should feel happy when they see the progress of their projects instead of waiting for the time of release.
- Resist changes in requirements throughout the development process.
- Constant delivery of working software.
- A partnership between developers and business owners throughout the project.
- Providing trust, support and motivation for all people involved.
- Provide face-to-face interactions.
- Working software is the basis for measuring the progress achieved.
- Agile processes to promote the subsequent speed in development.
- Focus on technical specifications and design to improve agility.
- Deliver simplicity. Make products the right way to ensure that everything runs smoothly.
- Self-organizing groups must promote better architectures, designs and requirements.
- A follow-up meeting to ensure that the right product is made.

The aim of Agile is to ensure that both development and business needs are up to standard. Agile projects are customer-friendly and motivate the customer to participate in the development. That is why Agile has proved to be the game changer in software development.

Chapter 3
Stages of The Agile Process

The objective of agile is to deliver shorter development cycles and more continuous item discharges than traditional waterfall project management. This shorter period empowers project groups to respond to changes in the customer's needs more successfully.

You can utilize a couple of various agile project management structures—Scrum and Kanban are two of the most well-known. In any case, each dexterous project technique will pursue a similar essential procedure, which incorporates:

Project planning

Like with any project before starting your group ought to comprehend the ultimate objective, the incentive to the association or customer, and how it will be accomplished.

You can build up a project degree here, however, recall that the motivation behind utilizing agile project management is to have the option to deliver changes and increases to the task effectively, so the project scope shouldn't be viewed as unchangeable.

Product guide creation

A guide is a breakdown of the highlights that will make up the last item. This is a critical segment of the arranging stage because your group will fabricate these individual highlights during each sprint.

Now, you will likewise build up a product backlog, which is a rundown of the considerable number of highlights and expectations that will make up the final product. At the point when you plan sprints later in.

Release planning

There is one execution date that comes after a whole project has been created in traditional waterfall project management, When utilizing an agile project methodology, notwithstanding, your project utilizes shorter improvement cycles (called sprints) with highlights discharged toward the finish of each cycle.

Before commencing the project, you'll make an elevated level arrangement for highlight discharges, and toward the start of each sprint, you'll return to and reassess the discharge plan for that element.

Sprint arranging

Before each sprint starts, the partners need to arrange for what will be cultivated by every individual during that run, how it will be accomplished, and survey the task load. It's imperative to share the heap equally among colleagues so they can achieve their appointed tasks during the sprint.

You'll additionally need to outwardly report your work process for group straightforwardness, shared comprehension inside the group, and distinguishing and expelling bottlenecks.

Day by day meetings

Hold short day by day meetings to enable your team to achieve their tasks during each sprint and evaluate whether any progressions should be made. During these groups, each team will quickly discuss what they achieved the day preceding and what they will be dealing with that day.

These everyday gatherings ought to be just 15 minutes in length. They aren't intended to be expanded critical thinking sessions or an opportunity to discuss general news things. A few groups will even hold these meetings are rising to keep it brief.

Sprint review and retrospective

After the finish of each sprint, your group will hold two meetings: first, you will hold a run review with the project stakeholders to show them the completed product. This is a significant piece of keeping open correspondence with partners.

A face to face or video conference meeting enables the two groups to fabricate a relationship and examine item gives that emerge.

Second, you will have a sprint review meeting with your partners to talk about what worked out in a good way during the sprint, what could have been something more, whether the assignment load was excessively substantial or unreasonably light for every part, and what was cultivated during the sprint

If your group is new to agile project management, don't skirt this basic meeting. It causes you to measure how much your group can handle during each run and the most productive run length for future activities.

These are the most essential and significant parts of an agile project methodology. As you progress your team to an agile methodology, these procedures, jobs, and standards will assist you with changing your mindset and start cooperating to be increasingly adaptable and adjust to ridiculously.

Chapter 4
Agile Vs. Waterfalls

In modern times, smart project management has become an important tool for companies. Smart project management is the reason why companies run smoothly without challenges in their processes. So far, any company, small or large, uses technology and better project management tools to ensure that it builds the right software and delivers the right software. Whether it is team collaboration, the use of these tools has improved the software development process. In fact, it has done everything so well with the least challenges.

Although there are different approaches to applying when managing a project, the most striking approach is Agile Project Management, because it is flexible and practical. Agile practices offer someone several options to perform different tasks. This is one of the reasons why it is very popular. Below are some of the differences between Agile and the traditional approach.

Traditional

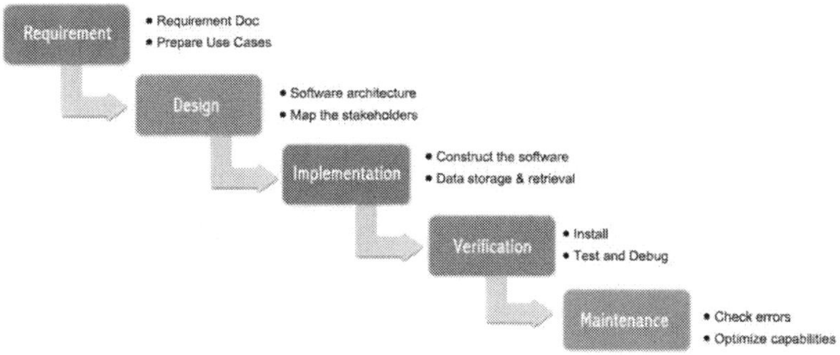

Agile

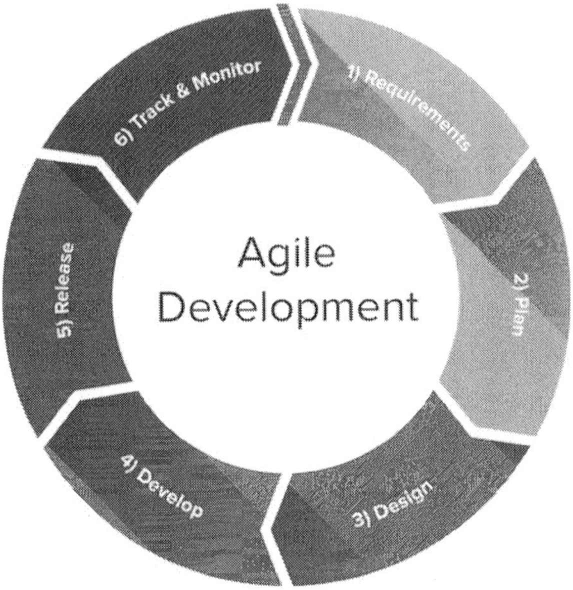

Overview Of Agile Versus Traditional Project Management

Define traditional project management

Much has been discussed about Agile Project Management and how good it is for project managers to use in their software creation process. However, to properly understand how good it is, one must first understand how traditional project management works.

The traditional approach is also called the waterfall model. This name is based on its shape. This approach assumes a linear pattern in which each phase of the process takes place as a series. The basic idea of the Waterfall model is predictability. Predictability refers to predicting experience and used tools. Every project is based on the same life cycle. The phases involved include planning, design, testing, feasibility and production support.

With the waterfall approach, planning takes place early without room to change project requirements. This approach is most focused on time and costs, but the project requirements remain the same. This is one of the reasons why projects made with the waterfall model have challenges in terms of budget and timeline. The table below summarizes the differences between Agile and traditional project management.

Features	Traditional	Agile
Project Scale	Large-scale	Small and medium scale
User requirements	Defined clearly before any implementation	Interactive form of input
Organizational structure	Linear	Iterative
Client Participation	Low	High
Development process	Life cycle model	An evolutionary delivery process
The cost of restarting	High	Low
Model of development	Fixed	Dynamic
Testing	Done after coding	Each iteration
Requirements	Standard and known at the start	Emerges with rapid changes
Architecture	Generates current and predictable requirements.	Generates current requirements

Why Do We Prefer Agile And Not The Waterfall Approach?

Agile is preferred by many developers and project managers. Let's take a look at some of those reasons:

Project complexity

- Agile

This is the right method if an organization wants to find a solution for a complex project. An advanced project can contain several phases that have been merged and each phase can depend on other phases instead of just one phase. This is the reason why most project managers prefer Agile for large and advanced projects.

- Traditional

For small projects that do not have complex functions, the traditional approach can best be used. However, it is still to be recognized that unexpected changes in the project or certain complexity can occur that can affect the entire process and force someone to go back to step one.

Adaptability

- Agile

Agile is popular because of the adaptability that it provides for project development. Complex projects have multiple phases that depend on each other. Because Agile methodology offers adaptability, one can take a risk and change something at a certain stage.

- Traditional

In the Waterfall approach, the concept is that when a specific phase is completed, there is no turning back. In short, there is no adaptability in the traditional approach. In the event that a customer requests sudden changes, it becomes difficult to change. The only option is to navigate back to the first step. This can really waste a lot of time.

Reach to receive feedback changes

- Agile

When it comes to feedback about a certain software product, Agile Methodology is the best in this sector. This is because it has a flexible process that includes feedback as soon as a product is released to users. Feedback helps to improve a product and resolve any problems. Flexibility in the Agile method is the main reason why most organization managers choose to use it. Software developers who code using this methodology can respond quickly to customer requests because they perform small tasks in the large project.

- Traditional

In the Waterfall model, each step is defined in detail before implementation can begin. This approach cannot handle sudden changes or feedback that may require rapid responses. In most cases, the traditional approach has both a fixed time and a budget.

Characteristics of the Agile project development

Breaks project into smaller parts

Agile works by dividing a project into smaller chunks called iterations. The iteration is then sent to the customer for assessment. The success of an Agile project depends on what has been achieved after each iteration.

Organize yourself

There is a parallel management model in Agile development. This is where company employees are not only managed by one person, but by a group. Agile projects generally consist of three parts:

- The owner of the product
- The scrummaster
- The team

Customer participation

When it comes to Agile development, the customer comes first. The customer is very important in the construction of every iteration. The role of the customer is to assess the iteration and provide feedback. As soon as the feedback has disappeared, the right action is taken.

Agile is generally the leader in the project management system. When you compare it with other approaches, the functions of Agile are paramount. That is why it is the leading methodology for software project management.

Chapter 5
Benefits of the Agile Method

Is it possible that there are clear-cut benefits from a philosophy without processes or tools? Although you could read through the manifesto in an almost Doctor Seuss like fashion, it's a very serious document. The Agile Alliance didn't craft the manifesto to put some ideas out into the world without knowing that a few results would happen nearly every time. The ideas, values, and principles, which make up Agile do set the stage for many great things. Of course, you'll want to ensure that you're using Agile properly. Don't try to implement Agile and expect all of these benefits if you're not working in software development. Compliance departments would not be happy if their team turned in a half-finished report, with working increments. In most departments, you need to deliver finalized versions of whatever you're working on, not just a functional version of the deliverable. There are times also when Agile isn't right for your approach because of limited access to customers or clients. If you're developing blind, then it's best to release your absolute best, rather than to release the functional version and then improving it.

The many benefits of Agile hit home for software developers, and they include:

- Predictable delivery of milestones
- Opportunity to implement change
- Focuses on customers or users
- Transparency
- Risk Reduction

Predictable Delivery of Milestones

About the only predictable aspect of Agile is the increments, or in Scrum the sprints. It's not difficult to keep track of various tasks and goals within the project either which is a little bonus of this benefit. The delivery of milestones in one to four week periods helps everyone, even those not involved in the development team, know that they're on track. It means that they can release or test the software well ahead of time. It also means that each smaller division of the software is known to work and work well before moving forward. There is no giant risk for companies to put in months of work to learn that something is causing the entire thing to fail repeatedly.

This benefit comes from face-to-face communication and the high-frequency of communication. It is possible to implement predictable milestones without Agile; however, you've probably seen first-hand the requests for extensions or blatantly missed deadlines. The reason why milestones work so well in Agile is because the methods involved break down the tasks and small goals for the team rather than for each person.

To see this in action, we'll present this example. In a Scrum meeting, the sprint goal could be something like, "map out user interactions for registration feature on paper, begin drafting design." Whereas in a normal project management meeting, that same goal might sound more like, "Jim, work on the user story and preferred interactions. Anette gets back to us with feedback from last week's milestone. Jody, test the user design when it's ready." See the disconnection here? When the managers in charge assign tasks to people rather than to the team, there's no guarantee that each person is using their skills correctly. From the above example, Jody, or Jim may have better connections to obtain feedback, but because the task was assigned to Anette, those resources will go unused.

Delivery of milestones largely rests on the structure of a self-organized team. The team identifies what work they're capable of delivering, and then figures out the best way to do that work. With all of this in mind, the milestones become much more predictable.

Opportunity to implement change

Change adaptation was the onset for the Agile Alliance formation and the drafting of the Agile Manifesto. The crisis, which plagued the software development community throughout the late 1990s, came from the inability to pivot and adapt to change in internal and external conditions. Agile allows that to happen, and this benefit is the leading reason for adopting Agile values. Through each iteration, it's possible for the entire team to recognize the need for change and alter their plan accordingly. It's also important to note there that documentation does play a key role in realizing many of the benefits of Agile methodologies. Where may teams only rely on a backlog, that one bit of documentation allows the entire team to reprioritize primary concerns when faced with change. It also allows them to implement changes to the backlog items that are set for the next sprint or iteration. That means that changes can happen in days or weeks rather than months.

Focuses on customers or users

The ability to focus on customer satisfaction is a huge payoff for many companies. When working with an Agile team, the focus on working software and improvement with every release or sprint. It can extend the product lifecycle by releasing the product earlier and keeping the product relevant for longer. It's also possible to keep customers more engaged throughout the process. The focus on customer or user satisfaction is something that stems from traditional product development expectations.

A side-effect of this benefit is that your clients have access to the functional parts of the software earlier. So, when the customer can use and begin developing training for the software earlier, it means that the release will come in tandem with comprehensive training materials or troubleshooting. Ultimately the product is of higher quality and improved usefulness for the end-users.

Transparency

Saying that transparency is a benefit is a bit of a risk because it only works as a benefit if the members of the team exercise it properly. Essentially, it only works if the team makes it work. However, if the team members are working with an understanding of the Agile principles, then it should go without saying. Transparency isn't just about communicating openly, though; it's about making sure that the goals are obvious and making it difficult to stray from those original goals. Working with transparency will also require different levels of communication. In one example successful transparency would include the communication between the Product Owner and the administrators in the company, while the Scrum Master must ensure that the Product Owner knows the progress of the project and help the team stay on task with their goals. It's a very difficult aspect of project management to manage, but it has a huge payoff. With transparency, everyone has realistic expectations, everyone is on the same page, and when it's necessary, people can ask for help. Without a doubt, transparency is a huge issue in traditional software development methods. In the waterfall method, it was common for no one to know what was going on with the development unit the development team believed that they were ready for testing. Then that often led to many people involved feeling as if they were misled or that the team failed in one way or another. Agile transparency starts with contract negotiation, customer collaborating and bringing together the team. Ideally, the concepts of transparency would be on the mind of anyone assembling the development team. Then, the team would work with the contract negotiations in an open and honest manner. They would provide what information or insight they could and be forthcoming when it was unrealistic or when the team wasn't sure of the information. Agile isn't about following a plan; it's about communicating what the product and the customer's need. Transparency is a must if you want Agile to work, and the presence of transparency makes the entire project more satisfying for everyone involved. In fact, it's so important that transparency is the one area of Agile that has tools in every methodology.

In Scrum, the task-board is the presence of transparency in that anyone could walk up to the board and see the stories, work in progress, and finished task. A Kanban board shows the backlog tasks, their status, and what is in testing or finished. Scrum meetings and sprint retrospectives also boost transparency. These meetings and face-to-face communication are built-in aspects of Agile that people often overlook. There are many methodologies, but each of them centers upon making sure that each member of the team can access what they need and communicate where they're at with their work.

Risk Reduction

Risk reduction is a huge deal for businesses in any department. Agile confronts the issues of risk head one by insisting that teams act transparently. But other aspects of Agile methodologies help reduce risk as well. For example, working in sprints such as with Kanban or Scrum, the small batches make it easy to identify and mitigate risk in real-time. Rather than working on a giant chunk of the development to learn of a gap in security or progress. The small batches reduce the risk of outrageous costs, while the work in progress reduces the risk of wasted time. Transparency helps reduce the risk of low-quality, and the prioritization of the backlog reduced the risk of lost value for the company. The risk reduction for Agile methodology is outstanding, and it makes it imperative for software developers to understand how to implement Agile whenever possible. Using Agile can help you protect your relationship with your customers as well.

When deciding if Agile is right for you, make sure that you look at the big pictures. Are you using agile to accomplish one specific thing, or are you looking for a development method that looks out for your customers? The benefits of Agile are big-picture aspects because Agile operates on the big-picture level. It helps companies ensure that the final product is something that their customers want, and something that they need.

Chapter 6
Disadvantages of Agile Method

Having an Agile approach to software development is hardly any terrible thing. However, there are a few disadvantages to many of the Agile methodologies. They can impact developers, the business people involved, and even the customers at times. Ultimately it comes down to the management of the project and the team, and how you accept various trade-offs of using different methods. For example, using Kanban when there are few members of the team who understand Kanban will likely lead to a severe loss of time to adjust for the learning curve. The disadvantages of Agile are many, but nearly all of them are avoidable or preventable, and it depends solely on the team's approach and understanding.

Major drawbacks of Agile can include:

- Longer projects
- Many demands on clients and developers
- Lack of design effort
- Resource planning
- Done and finished are different things
- People get sidetracked
- Technical debt

Too Long Projects

The sprints are short, but the projects are long. That extent of commitment, the many face-to-face meetings, and close cooperation makes for long projects. While a sprint surely won't run longer than one month, a two-month project can quickly become a six-month project. However, it's not just meetings, which extend the projects out. Remember that these meetings are vital for the software to meet user needs. The issue is that the close cooperation and the agreeable nature towards change make it so that the developers will often add numerous features or aspects to the software. The goal here is to ensure that the user expectations are met and that the team creates the best software that they can. However, the time and energy involved aren't always necessary. Teams need to take a step back and identify if what they're doing is necessary. Refer back to principle seven, "Working software is the primary measure of progress." Many teams lose sight that there's a focus within Agile on the goal of working software. Adding in the unnecessary can make a better product, but it can also lead to a much longer project. Working in increments, which is standard for nearly all Agile methodologies including XP, Scrum, and even Lean, can make it easy for a project to feel short when in actuality it's gone long past its completion date.

To avoid doing projects unnecessarily long, ensure that everyone on the team avoids adding aspects to the project, which aren't necessary. It's entirely possible for the development team, which stays on for updates and new rollouts to bring in advanced features and ideas in the months following the initial release. Then it frees up the rest of the team to work on other projects.

Too Demanding

Is it possible for any development project to be too demanding? Yes and no. This problem is not limited to software development, and it is specifically a problem for any team responsible for creation. It's also a problem of perception. What is too demanding for one person is a normal amount of work volume for another. The underlying root of this issue comes from one or two-person Agile teams. If there is more work than people, then it's not fair on anyone and the purposes of Agile will extend the life of the project, put more strain on the developers, and more strain on the clients as they rush towards a release. Clients then must learn the software and determine if it's of a quality that they can support.

The best way to mitigate this issue is to focus on collaboration early into the project. Scrum is one of the top methodologies in Agile because of this issue. When working with Scrum, the team meets at the beginning of the project to design the scope of the project. Then the development team breaks that into sprints, and the full team meets at the end of every sprint. Even with very small teams, Scrum can help Product Owners and clients understand what they're getting and what their team is working with in terms of staff.

Lack of Design

This perceived problem does come with a set of disadvantages for the Product Owner and the clients. Although the foundation of Agile is trust, it is very difficult to execute. Asking your client's to trust a team they've never worked with before is hard for anyone. The Product Owner must also trust the team and for them working with the administrative side of the project can be difficult. Before Agile, with heavyweight software development, teams used the waterfall method. With that method, the administrative side was able to see the complete design before the work started. They knew exactly what they were getting, and they had an idea of what the final product would look like. However, when it comes down to Agile development that is not the case. The design is done per sprint, although the development team will often have a very rough sketch of the final product.

The solution to this issue is communication. When the administrative side of the Agile process worries, they should convey that to their development team. Make requests, ask questions, but mostly, ask if they're confident in their product. Trust is vital, but that doesn't mean that you can't communicate. As a client or Product Owner, Agile allows you to have a level of involvement. However, that doesn't mean that you can't communicate, and many Product Owners or clients involved in an Agile project don't understand that aspect. There is not a lack of design, but often a lack of communication about the design as it unfolds.

Resource Planning

Where other disadvantages are just veiled minor issues, resource planning is a major issue. Imagine if someone in the Marketing department approached their managers and said that they could develop a winning marketing strategy. But they had no idea what it would cost in terms of acquiring sales copy, ads costs, or the time to complete it. That is essentially Agile. While Agile's flexibility makes way for many opportunities, the primary issue that teams face is resources planning. Companies do not like operating this way, it makes executives uneasy, and essentially, only big businesses can get away with it. What is worse is that the bigger the project, the more unknown the needs for resources. There is very little to do to prevent or mitigate this problem other than to go with the flow. If you're working with an Agile team, you will need to trust that they are doing their best with the resources available. However, if you are part of the Agile team, you need to ensure that you're using the available resources wisely carefully. It's on every team member to not waste resources. If you're looking for ways to sharpen your resource handling skills, consider opting for a course or two in Lean processes.

There are many overlaps between Lean and Agile, and learning both could be useful for everyone on your team.

Done and Finished are Different Things

The phrase "Definition of Done" or DoD gets thrown around a lot in Agile discussions because it presents a unique problem. There is no such thing as finished. Because these teams release software in increments, customers or end-users are likely using the product well before it's actually "done." Most users don't mind or care, or sometimes even notice because they have a working software, which just keeps improving. Often improving at a rapid rate, releases of patches, updates, and additional features make it so that these projects can last forever. The fragmented output approach makes it extremely difficult to know when to throw in the towel. Then you have the aspects of keeping the software up to date with other software and the hardware that users rely on daily. For example, the release of the Microsoft Office 2019 suite happened on April 9th with version number 1903. However, on May 14th, barely a month later, another rollout happened with version number 1904. The system was available, functioning, and users were happy. However, developers weren't done, so they kept working. Updates on 2019 continue, and with Microsoft track, record developers will likely continue refining the coding and tweaking small things until the next Microsoft Office suite release. Essentially, a Microsoft Suite will never be finished. It's largely on the development team and Product Owner to know when to decide that a project is done. This method of working is one of the things that comes up repeatedly as a disadvantage. If you're looking for a way around this, then consider using Kanban. With Kanban, you'll have a visual representation of the many moving parts of the project and the initial aspects as well as the added features, which came up at various moments during development.

People Get Sidetracked

This problem is present in nearly everyone's workday, but for software developers, getting sidetracked can cost the company a fortune. It can derail the team, the timeline, and on a small scale, it can derail the sprint. The problem comes from the combination of welcoming change, a core Agile outlook and having a minimalistic plan. Many blame the high-availability of getting sidetracked on a lack of processes. However, when you look at the many methodologies involved, Scrum offers a lot of structure for teams and does help them stay on track. It even gives some window of involvement for a horizontal check-and-balance with the Scrum Master and the Product Owner. If you're on a team that gets sidetracked easily, then resort back to the Agile principles and meet with everyone face-to-face. Focus in on the aspects that are sidetracking the team and identify why the team is getting off-track. Now, if you're the Product Owner or Scrum Master, then ensure that your team is working productively. Bring the focus back to the customer, not just what changing elements within the tech environment make it possible in term so features. Don't allow the surrounding environment to rule over the productivity of the team. Always come back to principle seven; the proof of progress is in working software. That is the goal, working software.

Technical Debt

Technical debt is a hot topic because although it is a disadvantage, it is not inherently a bad thing. There are times when technical debt is necessary to prove that the team should make a change or just to move the project forward. Technical debt is comparable to monetary debt and often cannot be repaid. Essentially, it's feeding into software entropy to accomplish a more urgent goal or solve a more urgent problem. There are two types of technical debt, and both are drawbacks, but at certain times, both are necessary parts of Agile software development. The two types include deliberate and inadvertent. Deliberate technical debt is almost always taken because of release date constraints or due dates. Often the tagline is, "We'll release now and deal with the consequences later." While inadvertent technical debt, is well, inadvertent. Often it goes unnoticed until someone on the team can identify the software entropy. Often if a team has to ask which team member is taking care of something, then they already have inadvertent technical debt. For example, if someone asks, "Who's layering?" then it's clear that something was missed or not planned for during the Sprint Planning. The best way to avoid inadvertent technical debt is to use Kanban or Scrum, although neither will guarantee that there is no opportunity for inadvertent technical debt.

Although Agile does have its drawbacks, they're not anything that is more or less noteworthy than the disadvantages of other project managing methods. As a philosophy, of course, there is a lot of room for error. It all depends on the application, and in true Agile form, it depends on the people involved. It's easy for anyone to step in and say that Agile leads to waste, or that Agile projects take too long. However, there are many Agile teams, which are waste-conscious and choose to work with the Lean-Agile methodology. There are also many teams who reach their definition of done on time, or even ahead of time. Whenever you're looking at disadvantages of Agile, it's vital that you look at the human elements of that team. Then you can decide for yourself if the team was responsible for the project failure of if the project failed because Agile doesn't have strict processes.

Chapter 7
How to Implement the Agile System

How can you start implementing agile methodologies? It depends on where you are in your work. As well as the condition of your environment and the construct of your team. For example, if you're working indirectly to your software development team, then you may adopt some of the Agile principles but not necessarily the Agile methodologies. If your team is built up of people with clear communication problems, who cannot respect the Agile principles, then it may not be the right time to implement Agile. You need to put a careful focus on how you will go about implementing agile methodologies and how you can best approach the topic with your team. Keep in mind that Agile teams utilize self-organization, and there must be no strict titles among the team outside of Scrum Master and Product Owner.

Additionally, each person within the team must understand the values and principles of Agile. They should also be able to showcase these principles in action. These concerns don't mean that you can't or shouldn't begin to bring in Agile methodology.

To start bringing Agile into your workplace, give a brief survey. Look around and see how clear the communication is between the administrative and development teams. Also, take a close look at how the members of the development team interact with each other. See how they approach each project. Many of the development team may be already familiar with Agile principles and terms. However, keep in mind how often people claim that practices or methods are Agile when they are not.

If you've decided that Agile is right for your team, then you should bring together a meeting or training so that you can get everyone on the same page. Use this meeting to lay out a foundation for your team. During this meeting or brief training, you will want to address many of the Agile misconceptions so that people don't come into the next project with any unclear aspects of their role. Explain how and why self-organizing teams work so well in software development. Also, look at how the team should operate within a time frame. Do you have a team of people who often meet deadlines, or does your software development team request extensions again and again? Then evaluate the core of the extension requests. Does the team need extensions to complete their work? Or is it to adapt to changes that were made late in the process? So many aspects go into compiling an Agile development team. Many managers or Product Owners will often use the transition to Agile methodologies to put together a new team. Ultimately as you transition, you will need to work with your team to set new standards and expectations. The Agile process, principles, and values are so people-driven that one toxic or rebellious person on the team could derail the entire process. Work with your higher-ups to address personnel issues or concerns that you have before you begin your first Agile project.

There are a few things that you can do to put together an Agile team that's primed for success. While there isn't a specific formula that leads to success, there are many prevailing aspects of a team, which leads naturally to success. Creating an Agile team is not an easy process, so strap in and get ready. Before you start bringing together your team, you'll need to lay out a few key aspects for personnel selection and strategies to set attainable expectations or standards. Work with the Product Owner, or if you are the Product Owner, identify the person most likely to take the mantle of Scrum Master. Together you will need to flesh out what aspects will be most important to upholding the Agile principles and value. Most leaders end up with three pieces of documentation, a checklist of virtues and values, a very detailed job description, and a team agreement.

The checklist of virtue and values should outline the standard values from the Agile Manifesto, your company values, and the virtues from the Agile principles. Some values and virtues that you might consider adding to your checklist include:

- Patience

- Adaptability
- Willingness to self-reflect on failures
- Willingness to receive criticism and feedback
- Positive mindset regarding change
- Positive mindset regarding simplifying processes wherever possible
- Communicates with priority on respect

You can craft this checklist in a few different ways. Some employers look toward the team members to fill in answers to questions that allude to these virtues. For example, instead of deciding for yourself if someone communicates with respect, you can ask a potential team member, "Is it more important to be right, or to be kind?" This can give you insight into how they would prioritize their own communication methods.

Moving past the checklist, you'll want to focus on the job description. Revisiting the job description for a software developer can be an arduous task. It requires going to HR and dealing with many people along the way. However, when you have the opportunity to include things such as, "communicate changes to the technology environment immediately," or "deliver sprint goals on deadline consistently," then you have more room to govern your team. From a Product Owner or Scrum Master standpoint, it is very difficult. Many people don't trust others on their team to do their job, and much of Agile relies on that very basic level of trust. However, that distrust does come from a place of experience. How often have managers heard excuses? How often have you personally heard someone say, "That's not my job," or more directly, "That's not in my job description." The power of including very specific language in a job description, specifically for self-organizing teams isn't about control. Governance isn't about telling people what to do; it's about laying down clear expectations. With the job description, you are telling team members that if they take the position, they must meet these expectations. Self-organizing teams often have these expectations and can still function to the best of their ability.

Team agreements are another thing to consider drafting. However, you and the Product Owner or Scrum Master may want to evaluate if it's necessary. A team agreement, from the view of many people, doesn't fit into the Agile motif of having less documentation. However, many project managers believe that if there is any question about the personalities on the team that a team agreement is necessary. Team agreements are social contracts, which help teams, perform at higher levels because it sets the tone for the project. Team agreements usually are the first thing that the team will work on together, which gives the Product Owner and Scrum Master a chance to see how the team can collaborate.

How can you get your team together to write a team agreement? After you go through everyone and have your team come together, schedule a meeting. Then divide the meeting into five segments. These segments will be to decide the tone, create a memory that the team will share, look for themes and connections, set priorities, and summarize the events of the meeting. Some of these will overlap with other steps of the project planning and dividing everything into sprints if you're using the Scrum method. However, this meeting and this agreement focus more on the elements of the personalities and communication abilities within the team. Allow the team to come together but ask that they set a time limit for each segment so that the meeting remains productive and short. Again, many people argue that there is no need for a team agreement because the Agile Manifesto should stand as a team agreement for anyone working on an Agile project.

Ultimately, the biggest obstacle that you'll need to overcome when implementing Agile in your company or department is trust. If you are the manager or supervisor, then you need to trust your staff to perform in ways they haven't performed previously. You'll also need to trust the others in your company on the administrative level as well. Your self-organized team that should operate on unbelievable levels and with high reports of job satisfaction relies on your trust. Give them that trust.

When you go through and have your team together with any documentation in place, then you can go to your next step. Consider working with your team to create a succinct list of the tools you will use. And decide which methodology within the Agile family is right for the project and get ready to release your team. The executives at hand may feel comfortable throwing around Agile terms but may not necessarily know what they mean or how to use them properly. Let these go and revert back to the principles of communicating respectfully and focusing on delivering working software. While it is vital that everyone on the team knows what is going on and how to use Agile appropriately, it is not your job to teach the entire company about becoming Agile.

Starting your first Agile project can be nerve-wracking for everyone in the company. It can cause a lot of unease, and the only advice that can be given to help in this is to over-communicate. Invite the Product Owner or concerned executives to watch a Kanban or Scrum meeting. Fill them in on how quickly your team responded to a team, or how the Scrum Master worked to bridge communication with the Product Owner to take a new step. Showing Agile in motion is the only way to help those who don't understand the process ease up and begin to trust the development team the way that you do.

Chapter 8
Scrum Methodology

Scrum and Agile are general terms in the field of engineering. They are sentences mentioned by technicians. It is as part of their language. However, this language can be frustrating for someone who is not used to it.

Scrum and Agile: what is it?

Things may not be easy when you think about starting with Scrum and Agile. The two words can confuse everyone, because you can eventually use them interchangeably. However, do not get confused because both words have different meanings.

Until now you know the meaning of Agile. You do not have to define it here. What about scrum?

In summary, Scrum is a framework that is used in Agile development. An example to illustrate the difference between Scrum and Agile is the difference between diet and recipe.

A person who eats vegetables has prepared a diet based on certain methods and principles. A recipe for cooking vegetables is the framework used to make a diet for a vegetarian. This analogy attempts to explain how Agile and Scrum are related.

Who can benefit from using Scrum?

It is wrong to think that Scrum was built for engineers and developers only. In fact, this framework can be used to build any other project. Scrum can be used in any type of project, whether in the market sector or in another type of industry. Scrum is the right framework for collecting ideas and organizing a project team.

Parts of a Scrum

To understand how Scrum works, one must know the parts of the framework and the people involved. The best thing about this is that experience is not necessary.

You do not need any prior knowledge before you can start using Scrum. The only requirement is a place to help create ideas. That can be a whiteboard or software such as Trello. Below are the parts of Scrum.

- Product owner. This is the person who has the best interest of the user and can say what he or she wants in the end product. The product owner is responsible for creating a backlog. A backlog represents a list of requirements or tasks for the end product.
- Sprint. This is a timeframe in which a team must perform various tasks.
- Daily Scrum. This refers to the daily updates provided by the teams.
- Retrospective.

This should help you realize that Scrum is very easy to learn because you do not need any special tools. The only trick lies in controlling the lingo and following the guidelines.

Basic Scrum Framework

Remember that no previous experience or special training is required to use Scrum. You can teach it to yourself. It is easy to learn the basic principles of Scrum. The most difficult part is mastering the techniques. Experts from Scrum believe that you can learn the rules of Scrum in 10 minutes, but it would take years before you become an expert in Scrum.

The principles of Agile

There are 12 important principles that can be used to manage a project. These principles work best with Scrum.

- Customer satisfaction is the main objective and is achieved through a continuous and fast delivery of a product or software.

- Changing environments or circumstances are embraced at any time at the stage to deliver the best product to the customer.
- A service or product is delivered at a higher frequency.
- Stakeholders and developers work hand in hand every day.
- Both the stakeholder and the team members must remain inspired to guarantee the best results in the project.
- Physical meetings are the best way to track the progress of a project.
- A final functional product is the general measure of success.
- Sustainable development is achieved through an Agile process in which both the stakeholders and the development team can maintain a constant pace.
- Agility is achieved through a subsequent focus on technical excellence and correct design.
- Simplicity is an important aspect.
- A self-organizing team usually develops the right architecture and designs to meet the requirements.
- Regular meetings help improve efficiency and tune a product.

Best Scrum master skills you need to know to help drive digital innovation in the company

A scrummaster is an important person in the entire Agile process. This person is responsible for guiding the team in applying best practices and removing obstacles. Although there is a 'master', these people are not really masters. They are a serving leader and help the product owner and service team. This means that a complete change of mind will be needed. To advance digital innovation, the best Scrum Master skills that anyone should have is the ability to change and to be constantly ready to improve both yourself and your team members.

Master these 3 Scrum Master Skills and become a Scrum Hero

Listen

Typically, Type A personality enjoys taking leadership and leading people in what they should do. There are times when you have the feeling that you have to get up and give instructions to make things go well. For example, you can be the first to speak and give directions for the scrum meetings. You may already be aware of the best way to achieve things, and sometimes you just know.

But the focus of Agile development is on the team that finds a common goal and delivers the end product. The most important thing is to let the team work in the best possible way both effectively and efficiently. It is difficult to achieve your goal if you cannot listen and learn from the team members. It is very important that you listen to some of the problems the team encounters, the suggestions they make and some of the improvements they want to introduce.

- How to listen effectively

Most people are not natural listeners and the best way to start is to act as a good listener. Make sure you don't speak until the other person has made his point. Do not interrupt a person while speaking. Second, stop arguing with others in your head or plan how you are going to respond. Finally, try repeating everything they said to make sure you understand everything they wanted to say. Practice your listening skills every day with a one-to-one conversation and then you can continue to the scrum meetings.

Coach

The team that guides and leads you is the most important body of the Agile process. That is why you have the responsibility to ensure that every individual in the team grows and develops. Whenever you encounter a developer who is struggling, do not polish it under the carpet. Come out and help them. Using tips, guide them through each problem and help them achieve whatever they do. Use a one-to-one time in the meeting. This style of coaching has proven to be important at the start of a project. It also helps to prevent problems that may occur later in the project. If you find a person on the team who is causing a particular problem, you must resolve this problem early. Don't be afraid or shy to talk about it. To remember. A small problem that is ignored today can become a bigger problem tomorrow.

- How to coach people in the most effective way?

The purpose of coaching is to generate feedback for team members and individuals. Do this as often as you can. Has a developer or the whole team done something good? Well, praise them privately or publicly, depending on their personality traits. Do you find something that can improve a person? Tell the members. Start by mentioning what went wrong and creative suggestions to make it right. When you learn to give suggestions or feedback every time, team members learn to expect and appreciate this. Although feedback becomes a habit, team members start taking it personally or even shying away from it.

Facilitate

Some of the goals of a scrummaster are facilitating meetings and coaching people in the right way. This means that you are not supposed to point out to other people what they should do. The team must work together at every meeting. The best facilitators are those who notice no one that he or she was present in the meeting.

- How to facilitate in the most effective way?

Good listening skills are one of the most important skills of effective facilitators. They ask brilliant questions to help them understand everyone's perspective and steer the group forward. Good facilitators remain neutral and do not give preference to someone's opinion. They have a lot of faith and believe in themselves. They believe that an agreement will be reached and solutions will be found in the group. It is important to know that no one is born as a facilitator and therefore everyone can learn to be a great facilitator.

In short, a Scrum master has to work hard. Moreover, it is always great to see a team work together and realize the results faster. Although the above skills are important for Scrum Masters, each individual has the role of facilitating, listening and helping others.

Chapter 9
The Scrum Members

Scrum works to form cohesive Teams to maximize efficiency and produce high-quality deliverables. However, the composition of the Team must be carefully considered to ensure successful Sprints. Scrum works when all Team members are committed to the methodology and the project, but don't worry! Scrum has specific roles for some Scrum Team members to work toward each Team member's buy-in and clear understanding of the Team's goals, to be discussed in depth below.

At a high level, the Scrum Team is composed of between three and nine individuals who are assigned one of three roles. There is one Scrum Master, the Team's expert on ensuring that Scrum processes are followed and a key obstacle-remover. A complementary position is the single Project Owner. Their role is to make final decisions regarding the order of the items on the Product Backlog and to maintain communications with the client. Everyone else is part of the Development Team, the players who possess all the skills needed to self-organize and create the desired product.

Creating The Best Scrum Team

In many industries, 'teams' are organized around common roles that they play, not the projects on which they work. Those who manage clients sit together and report to one another, while programmers do the same, as does IT, as does marketing, and on and on. Each 'team' works on multiple projects at a time, jumping between them to attend meetings, put out fires, and chip away at the work demanded by each project when they can.

Sound familiar? Unless you've worked in Agile-oriented organizations before, this was likely the setup of your office and the organization of personnel.

As aforementioned, Scrum organizes differently. This method includes two Team members who are in specialized roles: the Scrum Master and the Product Owner. Let's start, though, with the role that most will fill: Development Team members.

Choosing The Best Members

Let's imagine a team of folks organized in a more traditional organizational setup. Say that a client has hired a market research team to send customers quality surveys a month after they purchase a dishwasher. This team will consist of members who fulfill several roles, which could include client managers/liaisons, survey programmers, data programmers, reporting platform specialists, and quality assurance.

Many companies organize their personnel by the type of work they do, not the project that is their main focus. Commonly too, employees will be tasked with working on multiple projects, wasting substantial time by switching back and forth between tasks and projects throughout their days. Management will likely be structured over each specialization, with a client management manager, a programming manager, etc.

But, consider what you already know about a Scrum Team – that it is composed of no more than nine members. Could nine survey programmers take on a quality assurance survey program singlehandedly? Or nine client managers? Of course not.

In fact, it would likely become apparent quickly if you were to reorganize Teams by project than by function – and if you were limited to a maximum of nine Team members - what personnel you might need to maintain an ongoing customer survey project. Perhaps one of most of these specializations would do: one survey programmer, one data programmer, one reporting platform specialist, one quality assurance specialist, and perhaps two client managers to form a Team of six.

Depending on the size of the project, this may seem small. "Do you know the amount of data a single project handles?", you may ask. The number of specialized roles and functions?

We have three or four personnel in each of those roles who contribute to a single project.

Yet, consider the communication between that many team members. Picture a meeting in which you may sit, for an hour or more, with ten people related in various ways to the project, only to realize that Marina was the one who had the particular information regarding that particular data stream for that backfeed. She's the one who holds some knowledge we need to address this issue. And she's not in this meeting, but rather is tied up with work for another project for the next day or two.

When an organization implements Scrum, they structure themselves by project. Whoever is assembling the Team must have a strong knowledge of what component parts exist for building or maintaining the project, aware of what functions or specialized knowledge must be present within the Team.

Potential Team members should be resourced when assembling a Scrum Development Team too! Especially if the project is an ongoing one that is already underway, and the organization is shifting to Scrum. Team members should have some input into the composition of the Team, considering that member's confidence in their ability to work within the Scrum structure is key to success when adopting Scrum midstream.

Functionality Of The Team

So, we have a newly assembled Development Team, about to embark on a project for a new client. Now is the time to assign titles, according to many management models. To set up the internal hierarchy and reporting structures, siloing each member into their specialized role and ensuring they stick to what they know.

Yet, in Scrum, Development Team members are just that - Development Team members. Not Senior Programmer Kevin, Research Analyst Swaita, and Vice President Desiree. Instead, titles are stripped to simply note that everyone is a Team member.

This does not mean that there are no final decision-makers. The Scrum Master and Product Owner hold unique positions to be discussed in detail shortly, although neither of them fills the role of a traditional manager.

Because what is a traditional manager? All too often, by the very role they are expected to fulfill, they become an impediment to the team. Because who decides the direction of the team? The manager. Who decides what must be done to go in that direction? The manager. Who decides how it should be done, by whom, and when? So often, it's that same manager.

In this setup, we find some team members sitting around with little work while others are swamped. New ideas for products or process improvements are never heard because the manager doesn't have time to consider them, much less do the planning work to implement them. In some organizations, they may be cc'ed on all or most email communications across several projects - making the amount of email they receive alone enough to overwhelm any one individual.

Within the Scrum Development Team, no one holds this manager role, and the Team is self-organizing. This self-organization is supported by the Scrum Ceremonies, including Sprint Planning meetings, Daily Scrums, Sprint Reviews, and Sprint Retrospectives. These Ceremonies facilitate the kinds of communication and teamwork needed for the Team to organize itself around the Scrum's goals.

To be clear, this doesn't mean that roles flip and anyone on the Team does anything. Programmers communicate with clients while client managers try to write code - that would not improve efficiency or create high-quality products.

But picture a self-organizing Team tasked with updating a web-based survey with a new question at the client's request. Within a Sprint, the whole Team gets together to decide how and when to complete the task at hand. The survey programmer has the strongest grasp on how to code the survey updates, and the client managers have the best idea of what the client is seeking and how they want it to look on the user end.

Yet, within this Sprint's task, other voices are needed too. The reporting platform coder needs to develop how to pipe in the new questions from the surveys into the reporting platform, so results are viewable by the user. Quality assurance must be present to test the updates, within the new survey version and within the reporting platform, ensuring best practices along the way.

So, are those the only people needed to be involved in this task, then, perhaps not the whole Scrum Team? No, because consider this: have you ever seen the way Team members in a different department were working, the details of which are not in your knowledge base but thought to yourself - why are they doing it that way? Or, why are they doing that at all?

Let's consider an example. Perhaps the client has told our quality survey Team - we want to begin to see U.S. customer data identifying which state they live in, to see if that impacts the issues they report with the product. On a non-Agile team, the client manager and survey programmer would get together to discuss how to do that. Should we have a box where the customer types in the state? Or a drop-down menu with all 50 states listed? Should this be searchable to be more mobile-friendly?

Development continues, pulling in the reporting platform specialist to pipe the data into the platform and with quality assurance testing the end results before rolling it out to the client after a week or two of work.

Yet, a month later, the data processing programmer seems surprised that this survey question has been added. 'We get that data from the dealerships on our incoming feed,' she says. 'We have their city and state, in fact. We could just pipe both of those right through to the reporting platform with a 100% response rate for that question, without the possibility that the customer won't respond.'

On a Scrum Team, the data processor is in the room as the Backlog is created and prioritized, sharing her knowledge about the data feed before more than a week of work is wasted.

Facilitating Team Work

In any organization, there are negative impacts on productivity if team members hoard their information. This is what makes me valuable, knowing this piece of the process, their logic goes. It's why I have a job. If I teach everyone else, what is my value?

So that person – or many people – becomes a gatekeeper to processes, with everyone else on a project held up as they wait for this person's knowledge or skill in order to proceed. Not only is this clearly inefficient, but it's also awful for team morale, where members are competing against one another to seem the most valuable to their managers, instead of working together to remove obstacles from one another, creating an amiable work environment.

Within Scrum, Development Team members cannot hoard information, and in fact, information saturation is the goal, for each member to have a strong grasp on every other part of the process. The stripping away of hierarchical roles and titles can facilitate this sense of teamwork, as well as the servant-leader style guidance of the Project Owner and the Scrum Master.

Chapter 10
Kanban Methodology

Kanban is a method of managing work that is focused on continuous delivery while at the same time, avoiding overburdening your team. It was first developed and implemented initially by Toyota at their manufacturing plants, but it is now being used by people across all industries to plan and manage tasks. Some teams have used Kanban to organize tasks in an exciting way that helps them define new workflows, features, and categories in the ideation process of new products or services.

Kanban relies on the use of a Kanban board to help teams visualize and improve their current and future workflow. Whether physical or digital, its most basic form is defined by three columns; To-Do, In Progress, and Completed. Team members should add their tasks to the board and move them through from left to right as a way to keep track of their performance.

The word "Kanban" is a Japanese word that translates to "Signboard." A board used to state the amount of work available. This points out how the Kanban method profoundly relies on the visual organization of a board to generate a sense of order and promote a team's understanding of tasks, bottlenecks, and opportunities for improvement.

There are many reasons why companies such as Spotify, Zara, and Pixar use Kanban to help them with their operations.

Maximizing Time And Resources

Kanban helps project managers see both the overall scope of workflows and processes at the same time as the work being performed. It aims to identify bottlenecks to become cost-effective at an optimal speed. Identifying problem areas quickly provides the opportunity to fix them and plan accordingly reducing the waste of resources in time.

Kanban allows companies to offer their products or services sooner while swiftly modifying them to satisfy unforeseen market conditions which provide the potential to grow faster. It encourages collaboration with clients thanks to the necessity of getting their feedback to complete a task. This enables closer bonds with clients, which will ultimately result in referrals and repeat business.

Kanban Is Good For Team Building

Each team member becomes aware of not only his role in the workflow, but also that of others by continually reviewing the Kanban board and understanding others' tasks are dependent on his own. Kanban promotes constant communication and feedback among team members to be able to achieve the goals that have been set while making sure nobody is overwhelmed with work.

Team Benefits Of Using Kanban

Some of the most significant benefits Kanban adds to project management is how it stresses the importance of having a solid human perspective beyond the process. It entices organizations to reap the full benefits of Kanban by promoting teams, project managers, and team members to internalize certain behaviors. Avoiding multitasking, limiting work in progress, and inviting workers to solve issues as teams, are the types of actions that allow organizations to culminate their projects successfully.

The pull don't push system helps control the flow of work by allocating only the necessary resources to the available demands; this means you get to avoid wasting or overusing them. One of this framework's main goals is resource efficiency since it is pulled along the pipeline only as it is required. Kanban cards work as a signaling system that enables you to control the flow of resources visually.

Chapter 11
Kanban Essential Principles

At first glance, Kanban might seem complicated. However, its main principles are clear and easy to understand. Let's take a look at those core concepts that Kanban was built upon.

Principle 1: Visualize Your Workflow

Since its inception in the manufacturing industry and subsequent introduction into the software development landscape, Kanban was meant to be visually appealing so you could use it to map out your process and workflow. Proper visualization allows us to identify opportunities for improvement while also remaining a practical resource to communicate the state of projects, operations, and inventory.

Principle 2: Limit Work In Progress (WIP)

Kanban's general goal is also to let you manage every bit of work from beginning to end by moving it through stages with as little friction and waste as possible. This means you will be required to limit the amount of work in your pipeline to something reasonable to achieve in a specific time frame. Kanban's approach helps balance the input and output of work so teams do not commit to too much work as it is never pushed forward but pulled, avoiding bottlenecks.

Principle 3: Focus On Flow

If the principles are appropriately set in place, workflows seem to run smoothly and freely; therefore, any interruption to that flow becomes a top priority. A stop of that work will give you an excellent opportunity to revise your workflow and find new ways to improve your processes. Additionally, if a task has been completed successfully, you then need to pull the next most important thing right into play.

Principle 4: Continuous Improvement

Kanban promotes a never-ending cycle of learning, improvement, and collaboration while at the same time encouraging constant monitoring and analysis that aims at finding opportunities to improve. As circumstances, conditions, and requirements change over time; you too should be assessing your workflow to alleviate friction or remove blockers.

Kanban In Your Daily Life

Kanban is more than a project management methodology; it is a way of thinking about organization and planning for business and regular life chores. A personal Kanban board can help you manage everyday projects with the same benefits it offers to corporate projects.

For some strange reason, multitasking is praised in our current day, even though there is enough evidence to suggest that it takes a toll on your brain. We all have that tendency to overestimate our capacity and how much we can achieve during short periods. By limiting yourself with work in progress limits (WIP), you have a better chance of achieving your goals.

Different solutions have been proposed to help you complete larger than life To-Do lists, but Kanban is by far the most effective. One of the reasons is that it helps us overcome that feeling of having too many things to do.

Just like a regular Kanban board for businesses, its core principles can be applied to daily life; visualization of your workflow and limiting your work in progress are things you should still aim at. However, the book Personal Kanban: Mapping Work — Navigating Life, suggests you take a slightly different approach.

You should have a board divided into three vertical sections, each for different columns; one for Options, another one for Doing, and the last one for Done.

Here's what's different when compared with a conventional Kanban approach; the first column represents a stage in which you should identify how to tackle tasks since it allows you to see everything that is available on it, and assess what's manageable. This step will help you understand if you should delegate or hire another person, whether temporarily or permanently.

The second column is used to represent at least two of those things we are working on at the moment. Here's where avoiding multitasking takes place. If you start many tasks, you will get overwhelmed by the inner mechanisms of your cognition; keep it as simple as possible.

The very existence of the third column, Done, is self-evident. Completing tasks is self-assuring in and of itself. This column becomes a record of your personal successes that can boost you up even if just a little.

If you stick to a personal Kanban board, you will gain self-awareness of your behavioral patterns. In a way, this tool, otherwise reserved for working environments, can help you find yourself. This is a feature that not many are aware of. The level of clarity this method could bring to your life adds deeper nuance and value to it.

Project management solutions like this are not only meant to increase productivity; they can also allow you to have a break, breathe in, and evolve according to your circumstances.

Chapter 12
The Relationship Between Kanban And Agile Project Management

To be able to define the relationship between Kanban and Agile project management, we must first speak a little about the latter. Agile is a set of principles and ideals designed to help managers adhere to a goal. Agile promotes continuous iteration of development and testing via something that is known as the Software Development Life-Cycle (SDLC). It heavily relies on constant feedback to provide a good product.

The Agile approach understands that developing products can be a daunting volatile task and provides a framework to self-organize teams and allow them to respond to change. It is currently used by almost all companies planning and delivering products which have made it an essential approach to use if you plan to stay afloat in today's competitive world.

Kanban is itself one of Agile's two most popular methodologies along with Scrum. Scrum is a project management methodology created to structure projects beginning with the ideation of a product. The product's requirements are translated into features and put in a backlog. A time frame that is usually called an iteration or sprint is set. The product features and specifications are split into these sprints so they can be focused on.

The goal Scrum aims to fulfill is the creation of learning loops to gather and integrate feedback. Scrum users take on specific roles and hold regular meetings to keep things moving forward.

Kanban And Scrum's Main Differences

Even though Scrum and Kanban seem to tackle similar principles and goals like helping you build better products and services smoothly, they do have some philosophical and practical differences.

Scheduling

Scrum is entirely reliant on time frames. Since the team decides on a prioritized list of things to take on during a sprint, anything outside of that scope will be relegated to the next iteration. The idea is that after each sprint, the team will discuss ways of optimizing their processes and become more accurate when estimating and planning future sprints as they have already assessed their capabilities and blockers. Kanban, on the other hand, does not focus on sprints. However, it is iterative by nature since continuous improvement is something to be expected. Limitations found in the workflow are considered early in the Kanban process.

Roles

At least three roles need to be assigned for Scrum to work appropriately; product owner, Scrum Master, and team members. Each one of these roles has its own set of responsibilities, which should ultimately result in an efficient workflow. No such roles are predefined under the Kanban framework. It does make sense to have some type of hierarchy within a team using Kanban, but these roles should theoretically be defined when the need arises.

The Board

Even though very similar, a Kanban board and a Scrum board are different. A Scrum board is labeled after the different periods that make up a sprint. After a sprint's retrospective meeting, the board should be cleared to be available for the next sprint. On the other hand, the Kanban board is labeled after different workflow states while also acknowledging the number of stories allowed at each column during the same time. It is intended to enable the team to enforce and determine their limitations in advance. There is no real need to reset a Kanban board since it has a limited number of stories that can be placed under one column at a time and it does not work on sprints. Work here will continue to flow as long as there is any.

How Kanban And Scrum Overlap

Both methodologies allow teams to break down a large number of complex tasks and complete them efficiently. They place the utmost value in continuous improvement and optimization of the work and processes. Both also rely on almost exclusive visual elements to define a workflow that keeps all team members in the loop of what is and what will be.

Kanban and Scrum are valuable each in their own ways. This might be making you feel like you need to choose one of them. However, your decision doesn't need to be so black and white. Many teams are using a hybrid of both frameworks. The best thing to do is to become familiar with both and experiment using elements from both in your working environment. Working with your own structure is one of Kanban's main principles.

Kanban And Scrum Hybrids

If you plan to use both, some writers have suggested that you start working with Scrum as the structure that holds a team together until you reach a point where the time-boxed meetings mandated by Scrum are not necessary. This goal can only be achieved through testing and optimizing.

Other variations of the Kanban/Scrum hybrid are based on moving past removing fixed time frames. You can also use Scrum's approach as a way of actually executing tasks while at the same using Kanban as a lens through which you engage and improve your work. This model suggests having sprints if crucial, and it also suggests implementing specialized teams and functions.

Several organizations use Kanban for teams whose tasks are more responsive (like support teams), and Scrum for groups that get to plan for the future due to the nature of their work (like software development teams). It all depends on the context.

Where To Go From Here

It can become a pretty difficult task to create a global definition for Agile methodologies when one of its primary features is that you can adapt it to each working environment. What's important to keep an eye on is not a textbook definition to start with it. What matters is that you use structure and discipline as a cornerstone on which you can build your processes around.

New teams will benefit from Scrum as it offers them more structure. Organizations who require Scrum's learning and framework along with the continuous flow provided by Kanban will benefit from a Scrum/Kanban hybrid.

The terminology might vary between them, but they heavily focus on reviewing and improving the workflow, just as all Agile methodologies. You need to understand the main concepts behind both, define, implement, and continuously reflect and improve.

Kanban Visualization, Clarity And Its Benefits

Project managers are usually as busy as could be, they have to keep track of team performance as well as the quality they are putting out. You might already be using visual aids like Gantt charts or Excel spreadsheets, but larger projects specifically require different approaches. They might be too complex to fit in a single document, which in turn does not help with an overall workflow visualization. Visual project management tools like Kanban are here to do just that: facilitate your work.

Project management comes down to making ideas a reality. Doing that will be even more complicated if you do not count with the right information to make accurate decisions; it is essential to have that information displayed memorably. Additionally, if team members can't access the same information and understand it, they can't cooperate efficiently and collaborate.

A visual management tool helps you avoid that as it relies on fundamental concepts of perception to ease data consumption and processing in the brain. Kanban helps you:

Save Time

You are probably spending most of your time on communicational activities like messaging, joining meetings, and reporting. You might be spending even more time on them than you feel comfortable with.

These types of activities usually slow you down and rob you of the time and energy that should be spent on actual work that gets things done.

With a Kanban board your team has the chance to share all information concerning a project in one single place, which makes it easier for them to access it, helping you move past those long hours of attending unnecessary meetings, back and forth conversations, and responding emails.

Increase Problem Solving Speed

Every team leader's goal is to solve issues as fast as possible and then move on the next. Being able to identify bottlenecks as soon as they appear on your workflow is going to help you do that.

With a clear Kanban workflow, you will be able to figure out if a task is not moving as fast as it should be. This allows you to find timely solutions for bottlenecks, issues, and blockers as soon as possible.

Improve Efficiency

For any business, efficiency is equivalent to the best use possible of resources. Kanban helps improve productivity through WIP limits as they help you reduce waste of resources.

It also helps workers focus on single tasks rather than jump from one to the other, avoiding multitasking, and enabling them to complete tasks sooner. In the same way, your organization will be benefited with the quality they manage to put into their work.

Increase Accountability

Kanban promotes accountability across businesses; it enables workers to make their own decisions and act as driving forces on the outcome of a process. Team members feel more motivated to add more value when they see themselves as leaders.

The visual layout of a Kanban board allows each team member to define and pull their work according to their circumstances, making them more accountable for their progress and resulting in more engaged individuals with higher productivity.

Improve Team Performance

Since Kanban encourages you to improve your workflow continually, it encourages team members to share feedback on time. The visual representation of your progress helps teams learn from each other daily.

Your team's performance will improve over time, leading to better products and even happier customers.

Successfully implementing Kanban goes far beyond having a board and adding columns to it. It comes down to how transparent and easy to understand it is, so that team members find it helpful and add more value. Adopt a Kanban board to make it happen.

Chapter 13
XP Methodology

In practice, the Agile Methodology is highly applicable in all sorts of projects; not just those that involve coding and programming. If you have a project that involves something that needs to be developed prior to mass production, then you can use various Agile frameworks to guide your production and development process. This is irrespective of the fact if that end product has to be made on a work bench or a desktop computer.

However, the Agile was designed primarily for software development and this all the more apparent with its software-focused variant, Extreme Programming (or XP for short). XP is an Agile framework whose core purpose is to improve the quality of the software as well as the work process of which the development team is to adhere to. And if the process and the end product is improved, then needs of the customer are satisfied or more.

Core Principles

Extreme Programming is a framework by nature. As such, its success is utterly dependent on its implementers adhering to 5 basic values which are as follows:

Communication - The XP framework demands that the development team maintains an open, transparent, and effective channel of communication within each other and with people outside. The exchange of ideas, concerns, and other crucial information must be so clear and direct so as to minimize confusion and waste of time.

Simplicity - Reduction of waste is a strong focus in the XP framework. This, in turn, can only be possible if the team adopts a system that is straightforward and a software design that focuses on the basics. This way, the team can put all their efforts into creating important features, addressing the most pressing of issues, and creating a product that is easy to produce, monitor, and maintain.

Feedback - There is no doubt that feedback is integral to creating a good product. However, the XP framework takes things a bit further and demands that feedback be not only constantly given but also immediately acted on. This will help the team quickly identify where they can improve on and make important changes to their development practices.

Respect - The XP framework understands that each person in the team plays a crucial role in the success of the project. Thus, their personal needs have to be respected and the members must bond with each other both at a professional and personal level. A more cohesive team will be able to achieve the project's goals quickly and more efficiently.

Courage - The XP framework encourages everyone involved to be courageous. And by courage, the framework needs everyone to speak out when they feel something is not working or something might negatively affect the quality of the product and the efficiency of the development process. Alternatively, they must be courageous enough to face criticism or feedback of their work and improve on their methodologies accordingly.

When is it Applicable?

Due to the unique nature of the framework, XP is not exactly applicable for all types of projects out there. The general characteristics, principles, and practices promoted by this framework is best appreciated in projects that revolve around or deal with the following:

Changing Software Requirements

Software development processes were meant to be short because technology changes at a blistering pace especially in recent years. The Video game Duke Nuke Forever, for example, was announced somewhere in the mid-1990s but was released in 2011.

Aside from the usual development problems and corporate issues involved, one major element that impeded the game's release was the changing of technology especially with graphics processors. In fact, the game had to be overhauled by no less than 3 times in a span of a decade as graphics engines and corresponding hardware developed quickly especially during the early 2000s.

Moreover, despite all of the efforts and money pooled into the project, the end result was disappointing to many as the conflicting engines and design philosophies ultimately lead to a jumbled mess of a game.

Time-Related Risks in Using New Technology

If a project were to capitalize on a new piece of technology, then it goes without saying that the product needs to be released while that technology is still relevant.

Longer development times run the risk of certain technologies being incorporated in the software being replaced by ones that are more efficient. This means that if such shift were to happen mid-development, then the team has to do everything all over again. This constant doing-over can cause a lot of time to be wasted as well as production delays. Ultimately, the end product released is but a compromised version of what the client intended in the first place.

Small Development Team

The XP framework was designed to take advantage of smaller development teams. A small development team means that communication lines are smaller, more direct, and easier to manage. It also means that issues get addressed quickly while feedback is near-instantaneous.

This even works across multiple subgroups so as long as they are co-located or are working in the same vicinity.

Autonomous Program

The technology that should be used in the project must allow for automated unit and functional tests. This is because the team should be given the chance to fully focus their efforts on developing the software or improving on existing ones.

Automated tests do speed up the testing and maintaining phase which shortens an already short development period. If incorporated right, the team should have no problems moving from one phase of the project to another.

What's the Advantage of XP?

So what should you expect if you are to apply the XP framework in your projects? The answer to that could be different from one project head to another. However, let us just say that XP is something that is not definite in the advantages that it offers to its users.

What it does offer, however, is the chance to do away with some of software development's more infuriating issues, which include the following:

Slipped Schedules - With a focus on shorter development schedules, XP allows a project team to deliver something tangible and of value to customers on a regular basis. This also means that they can get to finish tasks on time without overexerting themselves.

Cancelled Projects - Ultimately, it is client dissatisfaction that kills projects. Whether something gets delayed for several times or the client itself is disappointed with the end result (or a bit of both), there is a high probability that elements in the development process will result in the entire project being canned or put on hold. Either way, everybody wasted their time for something that won't see the light of day.

Change-Induced Costs - In the XP process, ongoing and extensive testing makes sure that changes are implemented into the program without compromising its base functionality. A running and working system always ensures that changes are accommodated and given enough time and attention at in order to be properly incorporated into the main code.

And the best part is that the team can adjust their work accordingly without losing momentum.

Production and Delivery Defects - Constant testing and integration will expose flaws and bugs in the design which the team can then address to the best of their abilities. With these tests, the structure of the code is thoroughly cleaned which means that the team can now shift their focus on "enhancing" the product post-launch instead of "fixing" what is inherently wrong with it that users have to discover for themselves.

Misunderstandings – More often than not, projects result in failure because of a failure of communication. It is either that the customer was never given the chance to constantly communicate or, if they do, the developers never fully understood what the latter wanted out of the project.

By making the customer an actual part of the team, communication is now direct and clearer. If the exchange of ideas and information is faster and more transparent, the end product will be a more accurate reflection of the customer's vision and intention for the project.

Business Changes – Change is always inevitable but they are often detrimental to the team. After all, there is nothing more damaging to the morale of the entire group than to tell them to start everything over again.

In the XP framework, not only is your team more open towards change. They can also be more anticipative of it. This means that they conduct their work in a manner that allows them shift gears in the instance that they need to do so. And while doing this, the team must never lose sight of the goal which is to complete the vision of the customer to the best of their abilities.

Constant Staff Turnover – As a result of delays, technical issues, and interpersonal conflicts, a team's roster can change frequently which affects the quality of the end product. The XP framework puts a strong focus on team collaboration and communication with external people.

On paper, this should promote transparency and goodwill with everyone involved in the project. If everyone identifies with the project and has a strong sense of ownership over it, they can contribute 100% of their effort in completing the project.

XP in Practice

Aside from values and principles, the XP framework is dependent on you adopting new practices. These practices, in fact, were made to be interconnected with each other through the framework provided by XP. They are the following:

The Planning Game - XP addresses two key questions in software development: what must be done before a due date and what needs to be done next? The emphasis, then, is on directing the project instead of predicting what needs to be done and how long. As such, the Planning Game can be done in two strategies.

Release Planning - Here, the customer presents the desired feature to programmers who, in turn, estimate how it should be done and how difficult each feature is to incorporate. With cost estimates at hand and with knowledge of how important each feature is, the Customer essentially laws out the project. All that the development team has to do is to follow the specifications and produce the desired results to the best of their ability.

However, release plans may change and those project estimates are never definite. Even if the initial release plan is manageable, the XP team must revise the plan regularly to fit in changing development conditions.

Iteration Planning - In this strategy, the team is given direction of what needs to be done every two weeks. Essentially, the project is divided into what we now know as "iterations".

As this is the more Agile-ready strategy, developers are given the option to determine for themselves what needs to be done for every iteration and commit to completing the same within that time period. The point here is that they must be able to produce something functional at the end of that period.

But what should you and your team talk about when doing planning sessions? Here are a few issues that need to be tackled by the business and management people in the team.

Scope – How much of a problem must be solved in order for the system to be better? The upper management, customer, and the coach are in the position to determine whether or not enough effort has been done to address issues and where the team should focus on next.

Priority – With all the tasks that need to be done, which ones need to be completed first? Yes, the team ultimately decides what they want to do with each task but it is the leaders who should determine what stories are ultimately important to the end product.

Release Composition – How much (or how little) needs to be done before the business improves with the software than without it? This is something that a leader can only determine as a developer's intuition as to how the business is going to benefit from the completion of the project is not as accurate as that of a management-trained person.

Date of Releases – When should the end products be released to the public? And if they are released on that date, would their presence be welcomed in the market or even have a huge impact on it?

The overall impression of the public to the software upon release is something that managers and project heads are more capable of identifying than developers and software technicians.

These are management related issues but what about the more technical stuff? Your development team can also discuss issues that it can handle such as:

Estimates – How long will a feature take to be implemented? This is something that developers can determine based on their combined skill sets and expertise.

Consequence – There are some strategic management decisions that can only be made if the management folk are fully aware of some technical consequences that could arise from such. If strategy A were to be used, what would happen next? And if B was used, what detriment would it serve to the company?

The development people need to explain this to management so they can make better informed decisions in behalf of the entire project.

Process - What is the organization of the team for this project? What is the workload for each member? The team must be a perfect fit not only for the specifications of the project but also the culture for which they are to operate under.

The reason for this is that the end product will reflect the overall cohesion of the team. If the team functions well, then the software should have a stable structure with all of its promised features properly implemented.

Schedule - Within a planned released, what stories should be included? The developers should have the freedom to schedule the most labor intensive and riskiest segments first so as to reduce the overall risk for the entire project.

Of course, this in-team set of priorities must be reconciled with the business's overall priorities for the project. If done so, this reduces the chance of important features being dropped just to meet deadlines.

At a glance, you should realize that the planning process should be a joint collaborative effort by the development team, the business persons like upper management, and the customer.

Small Releases - In XP, teams do small releases in two different ways. First, the team releases running and tested software to the customer in every iteration. The customer can use this software for any purpose that they have in mind. The goal in this strategy is to give the user something tangible and useful for every iteration.

The second option is to release something to end users as frequently as possible. This means that an initial product is released and the team continues to build (and fix) that product over a period of time.

Metaphor - Teams following the Extreme Programming framework must develop a common vision of how the program should look and function which is the "Metaphor". The best definition of this metaphor is that it is an accurate description of what the end product would be like after extensive development has been done on it.

This metaphor, as the name would imply, does not need to be technical. It can be poetic or it can be dramatic as the framers would like. The point here is that the metaphor is an expression of the vision of the entire team which points them to a general direction when starting a project.

Simple Design – The XP framework puts a lot of focus on software with a design that is simple but is adequate. The project starts with something simple and, with further programming and testing, ends up with something that is still simple.

As such, the Team must keep the design suited for those conditions. Needless elaboration is a waste of motion which complicates the value of the product.

However, designing is not a one-time affair in XP. It always occurs in the project to meet new needs and address current technological shifts. Also, there are dedicated design phases in each iteration. With this, the software changes for the better in each cycle but stays true to the notion of simplicity.

Testing – XP is largely focused on feedback which can only be acquired through constant testing. Good XP teams practice what is called as "Test-Driven Development" where they work in short development cycles, add a test run, and make things work.

However, there is a difference between setting up a good test and running it. Your team must do test runs correctly once they release new code to the repository. Also, you have to make sure that the test covers 100% of the new code. This should provide the feedback of which your team relies in determining what needs to be done later on.

Refactoring – Also known as Design Improvement, this practice focuses on delivering value to the customers in every iteration. To accomplish this over the entire project, your team must abide by the Refactoring process, which focuses on improving several key issues of the design.

First, the team must detect and remove duplication all over the code, which is a telltale sign of poor software design. After this, the team must then work in improving the cohesion of the entire code and ensuring nothing is fundamentally broken.

On practice, this allows the team to start with a good and simple software design and build on that in every iteration. This reduces the chances of the team having to start from scratch in every cycle, streamlining the development process even further.

Pair Programming - All production in the XP framework is built by two programmers who work at the same code at the same time. This should ensure that the code is reviewed, tested, and implemented by two different people who understand how it works line by line.

The act of letting two people what one can do on their own might sound impractical but programming seems to be the deviation of the norm. Research has shown that paired programmers produce code that is more functional and easier to implement than singular programmers. To put it simply: Two heads are better than one.

Aside from resulting in better code, pair programming also helps in communicating information to the team in a more efficient manner. When working on a shifting basis, every pair involved in the development process can get to learn what the others have been working on and where they specialize in.

The more a programmer learns from their peers, the more valuable they become to the team. In essence, Pair programming helps your team evolve as a self-sufficient group without having to add new talent every cycle.

Collective Ownership - On an XP project, any pair of programmers can improve on the code on their shift. This means that the code itself gets the benefit of being attended to by many people, which reduces defects and improves its overall quality.

There is also another, more important, benefit. When everyone has ownership of the code, they are more invested in making it work. Singular ownership of a code can result in features being replaced or written over when a new programmer replaces the old one. The result is that the code becomes too complex or, if functional, a major deviation of the customer's initial vision.

Of course, Collective Ownership can make people work blindly on a code without fully understanding what it must do. This can be easily avoided through tests and constant communication. This way, improvements are delivered when they are requested and everybody on the team share the same knowledge on how to complete the product for each iteration.

Continuous Iteration - The XP framework is all about optimizing work. In other methodologies, daily builds are seen as irrelevant or, in some cases, weak. But the XP method understands that daily builds are not only integral to producing good product but can be done multiple time in a day.

To understand what this means, think of the software development process as building a car. Each team might work on some part of the vehicle like one team focuses on the engine and transmission while the others focus on the electronics, interior, and fuel intake.

All of their work is necessary to the completion of the product but there is still the challenge of making everything cohesive during the actual process of assembling the car. Some parts might be well made but don't fit the overall design. Some might fit the overall design but could negatively impact the overall functionality.

Software integration faces the same problem. Your team might find that some lines of the code are not compatible with each other or, worse, create bugs in the system. Of course, errors in the system means that your team has to work double the time in fixing them while delivering on the software on the promised date.

With continuous integration, your team can correct on its mistakes as they are made as you make sure that each part complements one another as they are being developed.

This way, the overall software is cohesive and major, program-crashing errors are eliminated before the software gets mass produced. After all, it is easier (and less stressful) to fix problems while the project has not yet been shipped.

The 40 Hour Work Week - The XP framework directly addresses one of the major criticisms of software development: it's reliance on Crunch Times. What we know as Crunch Times are basically periods in the development process where people have to invest more time in delivering the promised features on a due date.

The XP framework recognizes that crunch times are not only unnecessary, they are detrimental to the health, sanity, and overall wellbeing of the developers. The team must commit to delivering the features on time but they must not over-extend themselves.

In essence, they must give100% of their effort for 8 hours and 5 days of the week. Nothing less and nothing more. This could be done by distributing the tasks over several iterations and making the team prioritize on what needs to be done for that specific iteration.

This way, value is provided in every cycle and your team members are not left severely exhausted at the end of each segment.

The On-Site Customer - The team using the XP framework must coordinate their efforts with a representative of the client as closely as possible. This "on-site customer" gives the team an impression of what the end client wants from the project.

Also, they are the tones that primarily test the product at the end of each iteration. Here, they can provide feedback which gives the team an idea as to what to do and improve on the software in the next iteration.

Coding Standard - IF people work on the code by pairs, how is the XP framework going to ensure its cohesiveness at the end of each iteration? This is done by making the team follow a common coding standard.

Basically, the team must adhere to a set list of principles and specifications when working on the code. These principles and specifications are, in turn, based on the information provided to them by the on-site customer.

By adhering to the standard, the development team can create code written as if only one person has been working on them. The specifics of the standard are not exactly important here. What is more important is that the end code, all of the parts that comprise it, would look familiar in support of the notion of collective code ownership.

Chapter 14
DSDM Methodology

It's the original Agile method, and it's still present among many teams today. DSDM is an abbreviation for Dynamic Systems Development Method. DSDM was first seen in motion way back in 1994, and that project was part of a Rapid Application Development strategy. Ideally, the DSDM would have given software development teams governance and discipline to work in a way that allowed them to focus on value instead of the many other aspects of daily work. People still choose to use DSDM because it allows them to clearly define their goals and act on real benefits for the business. Benefits for the business is one reason why Product Owners will urge their teams to use DSDM methods again and again.

DSDM does come with its own set of principles, and they all align clearly with the twelve principles of Agile.

The eight principles of DSDM include:

- Collaborate
- Deliver by the deadline
- Don't compromise quality
- Focus on business needs
- Build incrementally from foundations
- Develop iteratively
- Continuously communicate
- Control

As DSDM rose and the use of it spread outside of software development teams and into systems development as a whole the term changed. Now, DSDM does not specifically refer to the original Dynamic Systems Development Method, but instead will often have "Driving strategy, delivering more" attributed to the acronym. The "Driving strategy, delivering more," has become the mantra for DSDM as Agile teams have proven, this method allows them to work more collaboratively and flexibly than many other Agile methods.

People often choose the DSDM Agile approach because it deals with the entirety of the project rather than only the communication or only the planning. DSDM is also applauded for its scalability and working effectively with both large and small teams. Given the governance of rules, DSDM also provides a bit more structure than alternative Agile frameworks.

To use DSDM, you want to start by segmenting out the business requirements and making them user stories. Understanding how different aspects within the business will impact the customer or user can help guide decision making. DSDM projects will constantly refer back to the business requirements and user stories for decision-making purposes. When experiencing change, the question will often come back to, what is the business requirement. This method relies heavily on not working unnecessarily, and by reacting to change quickly with one consistent method of change response.

After establishing the business requirements, the team will work together to set their priorities. Usually, the priorities will apply to the business need and industry demands. For example, the preexisting demands of user security and regulations, which require certain levels of security, will take priority over design. Then, the team will come together to work on the project in chunks while interacting consistently with the Product Owner. They will deliver, test, and provide the software for acceptance within a relatively small span of time. After each acceptance or milestone, the team will collaborate with the end-users or customers to identify any necessary changes. The DSDM loops with transparent feedback and necessary adjustments until the project is complete, the user is satisfied, and the software is ready for launch. DSDM focuses exclusively on the project, rather than looking at the lifelong needs of the software.

If in the case of FDD the name is quite suggestive of the nature of what the methodology employs, DSDM may appear to be a total enigma when you first look at it.

We understand why it might sound downright confusing and why you might not be that open to learning about it if you are at a beginner or even intermediate level of agile project management. However, we must mention that DSDM is far easier than it sounds.

Like all the methodologies we have approached in this book, DSDM too abides by the general Agile Principles. As a result, it too can be defined as an agile, iterative, and incremental project management methodology. Like many of the other methods we have described here as well, the Dynamic System Delivery Method started off as a framework pertaining to the world of software programming. In time, however, some of its concepts and principles have transferred to other industries as well.

The DSDM approach has been largely developed upon the foundation laid by RAD (Rapid Application Development), a method that lies at the confluence between agile, adaptive, spiral, and unified project management. In essence, RAD is another way of approaching agile project management, but one that comes with its own set of principles and specificities that make it look like it pertains to everything nontraditional in the field of project management in general.

The delimitation between RAD and agile are very hard to make, and, as such, most of the theoreticians are happy to include RAD (and its offspring, including DSDM) under the wide umbrella term known as agile project management. It's not wrong to do this, as the principles are congruent, and there is a common anti-traditionalist factor to the entire point of view in both the case of agile project management and Rapid Application Development.

In many ways, RAD represents just a slice of agile when you compare the core of the methodology. It focuses a lot on the speed of production and on delivering working software, and it doesn't focus on procedures and documentation.

What RAD lacks as compared to the other agile methods is the focus on the human element of a development project, as well as the mindset behind it. In this respect, RAD and FDD are quite similar, but it is important to note that DSDM has come as a solution to this because it includes the human element in the entire process and places it at the center of its main principles.

Dynamic System Development is a methodology that sets out the time, the costs, and the quality of the final delivery from the onset of the project. In order to make sure it sticks to the plan, this method splits tasks into four main categories according to their priorities:

- musts
- shoulds
- coulds
- won'ts

One feature of DSDM you might find interesting is that its handbook is available for free, online. Furthermore, multiple resources and templates are also available for download, for those of you whose curiosity might be stirred after reading about the basics of DSDM.

Before we dive into the specifics of Dynamic System Development, we would like to take a moment to analyze its eight main principles: the guiding light of the entire methodology and the core ideas according to which everything DSDM happens.

In short, the DSDM principles you should be familiar with include the following:

- Business needs are very important. It is crucial to understand the specific business need behind the project to be able to deliver what the customer needs.
- The delivery must be made on time, as this helps keep the project on its right course and allows you to keep the customer happy.
- Collaboration is a core value of the DSDM approach, same as in the case of all the other agile project management methodologies out there. You should be able to properly collaborate as a team, as well as with external and internal stakeholders (including the customer).

- The quality of the product should never be compromised. At the end of the project, this is what brings business value both on your end and on the end of your customer, so it is essential to make sure the product abides to the highest standards of quality possible.
- You should build incrementally, but it should all start with a proper, solid foundation. Without that, the "house" will crumble, so take your time in ensuring that the foundation is solid enough for you to start building on.
- You should deliver iteratively, same as with all the other agile project management methods. This allows constant feedback to be properly incorporated into the development process, so that the final product is suited to the client's needs in all respects.
- Communicate at all times. You should be able to communicate clearly and continuously, both internally, as a team, and externally, with your customers and/or other external stakeholders.
- Demonstrate that you have control over the entire process. As a DSDM adopter and as an agile practitioner, you should be on top of the changes that come along the way, and you shouldn't allow them to spiral out of control.

Furthermore, aside from the core principles behind Dynamic System Development, you should also keep in mind that this method is characterized by a series of specific techniques one should use. They include the following:

Timeboxing. This concept is quite interesting because it will provide you with a mindset that will help you prioritize tasks. In DSDM, the time needed for delivery and the budget needed for delivery are fixed variables. As such, the only flexible variable you are stuck with are requirements.

This means you should prioritize the requirements according to the importance they have in the overall functionality of the product. If you run out of time or money, you should leave the least important features out of the iteration and deliver the working product as such. As long as the essential 20% of the requirements are satisfied, you can consider your iteration delivery a successful one.

Do keep in mind that this does not mean you are allowed to deliver an unfinished product. However, the requirements left out of an iteration should be seen as a way to improve the product throughout the future development process.

MoSCoW is an acronym for: work items and/or requirements can be prioritized according to whether or not they must be done, should be done, could be done, or will not have to be done.

Prototypes are an important concept in DSDM, as this method advocates for the creation of system prototypes early in the development process. This will allow you and your team to discover any kind of shortcomings your system may have and do it early in the development process, so that amends can be applied as soon as possible.

Testing is another crucial concept in DSDM (one that is common to most of the agile project management methodologies, actually). Continuous testing and feedback allow for the creation of a better product in the end.

Regular workshops that bring together the different stakeholders of a project are also encouraged. These workshops allow the stakeholders to discuss the requirements, the functionalities, and the specifics of the project and ensure that everything is crystal clear for everyone involved.

Modeling is a concept that is somewhat common to FDD but with a lack of emphasis on feature modeling and more of a focus on visualizing business domains so that you can improve your understanding of the product and its requirements.

Configuration management is a practice that helps managers handle multiple deliveries at the same time, at the end of each timebox.

As you have probably noticed thus far, DSDM is a pretty prescriptive approach in the world of agile project management (at least as compared to other methods in the same spectrum). Thus, it makes sense that it comes with a set of predefined team roles as well:

The Executive Sponsor (also known as the "Project Champion") is on the side of the user organization and has the power to divert funds towards the development of the project.

The Visionary is the person who initializes the project and draws the basic requirements earlier on in the process.

The Ambassador User is the person who connects the user community and the project and makes sure that essential information reaches the development team.

The Advisor User is a user that is actively involved in providing feedback and ideas with relation to the product being developed.

The Project Manager is either a user or a member of the production/IT Team who is assigned to the management of the project.

The Technical Coordinator is a person responsible to create and design the system architecture and ensure the technical quality of the product.

The Team Leader is a person whose main purpose is that of leading their team and making sure that they work effectively and efficiently.

The Solution Developer is a person charged with the interpretation of the system requirements and their modeling.

The Solution Tester is the person responsible for checking the correctness of the code, as well as raising the issue when defects are spotted.

The Scribe is responsible for the collection and recording of the requirements, agreements, and decisions of every workshop. In general, another member of the team will be temporarily assigned to this task.

The Facilitator is the MC of the workshop—the person who makes it happen and ensures that discussions stay on track.

In addition to these roles, some DSDM projects will also include specialist roles, such as that of the Business Architect or System Integrator. These roles are not prescribed but recommended under certain circumstances, depending on the complexity of the product and on the complexity of the project in general.

It is also quite important to mention that the DSDM method also ascribes certain factors to the potentiality of success. In short, there are four main points that make a project successful:

Senior management must accept and support the implementation of DSDM as a project management method. This helps ensure everyone is motivated throughout the entire duration of the project.

End-user involvement is crucial as well, and for this to happen, you must make sure that higher management is willing to get them involved as well.

The team must include skillful members. But maybe even more importantly, the team must be constantly empowered, not just in the sense of putting them in the right mindset but also in the sense that obstacles should be removed from their way. For instance, the team should not ask for approval for every small change. Instead, a delegated person in the team should be empowered with a certain level of decision making. This way, time and effort will not be wasted by running paperwork through the management chain of the organization.

Customers and vendors should maintain a supportive relationship based on communication and collaboration.

In very brief terms, this is what DSDM is all about. Combined with the specific practices of this method's lifecycle, these principles and rules make for what is generally known as the Dynamic System Development Method.

As you have probably noticed, most of these concepts are congruent with agile project management. So, if you are familiar with its general ideas and Principles, you will find that internalizing the innerworks of DSDM is quite easy.

Let's take a closer look at the Dynamic System Development Method lifecycle and everything it entails.

Feasibility And Business Study

The first stage of the DSDM lifecycle consists of two main phases: the feasibility study and the business study. They have to happen in this specific order because the feasibility study will provide you information for the business study as well.

During the feasibility study stage, you should study how feasible (or how possible) your application idea is. If it is deemed feasible according to specific criteria, you will have to look into the available team and the available budget. At the end of the stage, you will have to prepare a report on how the product meets the feasibility criteria (time, budget, resources, etc.), as well as a prototype (model) of the project.

During the business study stage, the business experts and the technical experts are brought together to discuss the main issues that might arise throughout the development of the product. The problems will be listed and documented for further reference. Together, the business and the technical experts will determine if they have the business and the technical capabilities to handle the project successfully. If the result of the discussion is a "Yes," the meeting (or series of meetings) will be concluded by a list of requirement priorities, as well as diagrams of the application and product infrastructure.

Functional Model/Prototype Iteration

Once you have all the requirements set in place, the data collected during the predevelopment phase (the first stage of the DSDM lifecycle) is pulled together in a functional prototype of the product. The model will include all the requirements, and it will organize them incrementally.

The prototypes will be further studied and split into smaller substages, including:

- The identification of the functional prototype—the key functionalities you want to include in the prototype.
- The creation and acceptance of the plan and of the schedule.
- Creating the functional prototype: bringing in the programmers and asking them to create a prototype of the product based on what has already been identified and planned in the previous stages. It is important to include a testing phase here as well. Just because this is a prototype, it doesn't mean that it shouldn't be perfectly functional.
- Reviewing the prototype. Once the prototype of the product is ready, it is time to place it in the hands of the end users and ask them to test it. Their feedback and comments will be taken into consideration for future iterations, as the product prototype will continue to be grown and improved throughout the entire duration of the project.

Design and build iteration

The third phase of the DSDM lifecycle is all about building on the prototype and ensuring that it is a continuously improved product. From the prototype, you and your team will move on to developing specific functionalities (also known as individual units) and integrating them into the system.

It is worth mentioning that in Dynamic System Development, there is no clear distinction made between design and build; both of them are handled during this stage of the DSDM lifecycle.

Furthermore, it is important to mention that this stage is also split into four smaller substages, as follows:

- The identification of the design prototype, which includes the requirements that have been decided upon in the prototype/model and then prioritizing them.

- The acceptance of the plan and scheduling. Once the requirements have been planned and scheduled, they need to be agreed upon with the team.
- The creation of the design prototype. Same as in the case of the functional prototype, this stage will deal with the actual development and testing of the design prototype.
- Reviewing the design prototype. At this stage, you will allow the design prototype to be tested and ensure that it is correct and congruent to what was initially planned. Any changes will be implemented in future project iterations until the product is ready for a full release.

Implementation

If the previous stages of the DSDM lifecycle were more about planning and developing small pieces of the product for the purpose of observation, this stage is all about actual implementation.

This is all about watching the live action unfold: putting the product in the hands of the end users and allowing them to fully test it and see if all the business requirements are met.

The Implementation phase is (perhaps unsurprisingly) split into four substages as well:

- Getting the user's approval and offering them guidelines on what should be tested more specifically
- Training users
- Implementing the feedback, you receive from the users
- Reviewing the business needs and whether or not the product meets them. If any new valuable features are identified, they will be further implemented in the product.

Like all agile project management methodologies, the Dynamic System Development Method is based on multiple iterations, so the steps will be repeated for as long as necessary to ensure that the product satisfies all needs and that it is fully ready to hit the market.

DSDM might sound overly complex at first, but once you nail down its basics, you will understand that this specific method is, just like FDD, a very suitable one for organizations that are more focused on structured planning and documentation. For you as the DSDM project manager, the emphasis will lie on delivering working products. For your organization, however, DSDM and FDD can provide you with plenty of structured information and reporting to keep higher management sound asleep at night.

As you have seen, all agile project management methodologies are more or less variations on the same topic. All of them abide by the Agile Principles. And all of them aim to deliver quality, timely, and budget-friendly products—in software development and every other industry that has embraced agile at the core of their functionality.

Chapter 15
Crystal Methodology

While you may have heard about Scrum, Kanban, and even Extreme Programming, the Crystal Method might be more of a mystery to you if you are new to the agile project management world.

Indeed, the mainstream agile methodologies have migrated past the borders of their agile world, and they are now common even in companies that deem themselves as adhering to a traditional waterfall approach.

When it comes to the less popular methods, however, things get a little more complicated. Methods like the Crystal one is incredibly powerful and useful for a wide range of situations, but they tend to be less prescriptive and thus less adaptable to teams that are new to agile. As a result, the Crystal Method has not yet made the leap into the mainstream agile project management framework.

We want this book to be a comprehensive overview of the main agile methodologies employed by worldwide organizations. As such, we have decided that we will include the less popular, but still extremely valuable, methodologies here as well. Crystal falls in this category because, as you will see later on, it can provide you with a lot of benefits.

As mentioned in the introduction of this book, we do not claim that the entire book encompasses everything all these agile methodologies are. You might be surprised to find that Crystal makes a lot of sense, and you might decide that it is the right direction for your team and organization too.

Even if you don't choose Crystal to guide you through the intricacies of the agile world, we still believe there is value in learning about it. The more you know, the more in depth you can go with your agile approach and create a "program" that allows you and your team to perform at your maximum capacity!

What Is the Crystal Method?

This is a lesser-known fact, but the Crystal Method (or the Crystal Methods, as the approach is frequently referred to) was born in one of the biggest and most resilient IT companies in the world: IBM.

It sounds odd to think that one of the least known agile methodologies out there was born in one of the most famous IT businesses, but the low-prescriptive, very lightweight nature of Crystal explains why it isn't one of the more popular choices for companies these days.

In addition to this, Crystal is one of the first agile methodologies ever developed, at the beginning of the 1990s. Come to think of it, there was a one-decade gap between the moment Crystal was developed and the first official Agile Principles were laid down in Utah, so it makes quite a lot of sense that the Crystal collection of practices has been left behind in the fog of time.

This doesn't make Crystal any less valuable. On the contrary, we believe that it can be a very good approach, especially for teams that are already at least somewhat used to agile project management.

Sometimes, it takes going way back to the roots to discover the true essence of something that has evolved over the years, and agile project management is no exception to this general statement. The Crystal Method might be exactly what you need to rediscover the true roots of agile and why it was such a groundbreaking, earth-shattering framework when it first started to trespass the closed world of high-end software project management.

The Crystal Method is very simple in essence, and yet, applying it with no limitations whatsoever can be quite tricky, precisely because it leaves the door open to a world of opportunities in terms of the specific practices you may or may not want to employ with your team.

The complications of Crystal arise when you try to understand the fact that its value lies in the lack of prescriptiveness and the ways in which it can be adapted to teams that are wildly different in nature.

In other words, Crystal is only as hard as you make it. Beyond the basics, Crystal is nothing more than one of the incipient agile methodologies. It relies on the same basic Principles; it's just that they are less polished, less prescriptive, and less limited at the same time too.

If we had to summarize the Crystal Method, we would simply say that it is a collection of primordial agile practices adapted to the specificities of various types of teams. Although incipient and apparently dated, these practices continue to make sense in today's environment, particularly as more and more companies are looking to scale up the agile methodologies they have been using to date.

How Does Crystal Operate

When he first analyzed the dynamics of teams at IBM, Allistair Cockburn noticed that there are two main tenets that make them more efficient:

- the ability to streamline and optimize their own processes according to the workload
- the adaptability they have when it comes to the uniqueness and specificities of each project

Later on, these two concepts became the foundation of the Crystal Method in a way similar to how the Agile Manifesto rules over the entire agile framework.

While he was developing the Crystal Method, Cockburn also noticed that there should be a clear differentiator between methodology, technique, and policy. This helped IBM understand where Crystal begins and where it ends, and it continued to help organizations everywhere delineate between what their project management approach is and what other regulations of their businesses are.

In short:

- A methodology is a set of elements (such as practices and tools, for example).
- A technique is related to skill areas.
- A policy is related to what must be done in an organization.

Furthermore, Cockburn also stated that the new set of methods he was developing would be focused on six main areas:

- the people
- the interactions between the people
- the sense of community people gets at work
- the skills people have
- the talents people have
- better and more efficient communication between the people

As you can see, the Crystal Method is a clearly human-centric view on project management. By far and large, what Cockburn developed back at the beginning of the 1990s might have set the foundation for the first point of the Agile Manifesto later on, in 2001.

Same as the Agile Manifesto and its adjacent Principles, Crystal says that processes are never more important than the people. In fact, according to Cockburn, people should come first in all circumstances, and processes should come second. The team, as Cockburn puts it, is the core of the project because they are the ones holding the skills and the talent, and as long as these are abundant, processes follow after.

Additionally, Cockburn also identified four main behaviors people have in relation to work:

- People are meant to communicate and crave for proper communication. It is worth mentioning that this is a concept all agile methodologies support. But it is equally important to mention that this concept was perceived differently back in the 1990s and the beginning of the 2000s, when online communication had not yet reached the level of accuracy and real-timeness of today's technology.

- One of the main issues people have is being consistent over the course of a longer period of time. As such, the project management approach should be built in a way that keeps the team continuously engaged and supports software development in a sustainable way.
- People are not constant either. They have good days and bad days, they may or may not perform at their best in one place or another, and they will always be the same. As such, the processes behind the project management approach should adapt to this type of change as well.
- People are inherently good. They want to be good citizens, they want to take care of their peers, and they want to do a good job. If you enable them to be their best, they will be, and as such, they will perform better on their day-to-day duties at work.

Although this might sound odd coming from one of the largest corporations in the world, the Crystal Method is one of the easiest ones to adopt in terms of the rules it brings forward precisely because it has designed mini-frameworks for a variety of situations.

More specifically, Cockburn split the entire Crystal Method into several categories, organized according to five major criteria:

- the size of the team/ project
- comfort
- discretionary money
- essential money
- life

The first criterion is pretty straightforward: the size of the team influences how it should be managed.

The other four, however, are related to the impact the system could have on the mentioned verticals if it doesn't work:

- how it will impact comfort
- how it will impact the disposable income of the user

- how it will impact the essential income of the user
- how it will impact the life of the user

According to these five criteria, Cockburn has categorized the Crystal family of Methods into five color-coded groups, as follows:

Clear: for teams of up to 6-8 people, low to no impact across all verticals

Yellow: for teams of up to 20 people, low to medium impact across all verticals

Orange: for teams of up to 40 people, medium to high impact across all verticals

Red: for teams of up to 80 people, high impact across all verticals

Maroon: for teams of up to 200 people, very high impact across all verticals

Aside from these five basic categories, you might also encounter adjacent Crystal Methods used in specific contexts:

- Crystal Orange Web (used for web products)
- Crystal Sapphire and Crystal Diamond (used for large-scaled projects that can have a dangerous impact on human life, like aircraft software, for example)

It is also essential to note that there is quite a lot of flexibility when it comes to how each category applies to your team and project. However, should the team grow over time, it is recommended to upgrade to the next color-coded category, rather than continue to apply the same methods and try to scale them up.

This might all sound very prescriptive, but it is quite the opposite in most respects. At the same time, keep in mind that this methodology was not born in a small software development house. It was born in a company that was already a mammoth corporation by the time Crystal came into play. As such, you should see the lack of prescription through the prism of a company that was very well-grounded in traditional approaches too.

One of the areas in which this is more apparent is the way in which Crystal Methods assign specific roles to team members and stakeholders. While you will encounter a pretty deep level of role-defining in Scrum as well, the very nature and the names of the roles assigned in a Crystal project will most likely be more familiar to those coming from waterfall approaches.

Some of the roles you will encounter in a Crystal project include the following:

- Project Sponsor (customer or internal stakeholder)
- Senior Designer/Programmer (the equivalent of team leads)
- Designers/Programmers (Business Class Designers, Programmers, Documenters, etc.)
- Architect
- Requirements Gatherer
- Coordinator
- Business Expert
- Project Manager
- Design Mentor
- Lead Design

... And so on.

We will not dwell too much on the specific differences between the different roles assigned in a Crystal project. For the most part, they are quite self-explanatory and quite similar to traditional roles you will encounter in many other software programming projects.

Furthermore, we will not dwell too much on the differences between the different Crystal family members either. Each of the colors is assigned to a type of project. Different specific methods are meant to be employed according to the criteria.

If you want to take a specific Crystal approach, we highly encourage you to go in depth with your knowledge on that specific family member. Same as in the case of XP, even if you don't end up using that particular approach, you might still find practices your team is congruent with.

Crystal Method Characteristics

The basic characteristics of the Crystal family of Methods might be easy to understand. However, for the purpose of clarity, we feel the need to also relay the specific characteristics that bring all Crystal Methods together.

Things are quite simple in this sector. There are three main characteristics the Crystal Methods have in common:

They are all human-powered. Manpower lies at the very core of the Crystal methodology. People are the blood and veins running through projects and making them come to life, and, as such, all Crystal Methods (regardless of the color they were assigned) put massive emphasis on the importance of the human resources. They are ultralightweight. All agile methodologies are lightweight, but methods like Crystal take this up a notch and become ultralightweight. What this means is not that team members are allowed to do whatever they please, but that documentation and reporting are less of a point of focus in Crystal than they are in other methods. This is also why implementing Crystal from a waterfall standpoint might not be as easy as it is generally believed by those who go through its basic principles and M.O. They are adaptive. Like all agile methods, Crystal methods are adaptive. They embrace change as a natural part of the process, and they embrace the differences between the different teams as an equally natural element. As such, Crystal Methods are adaptive, flexible, and interchangeable down to their very core. That's it. These are the characteristics that bring all the Crystal Methods together and tie them to the larger world of agile project management.

Properties of the Crystal Method

The Crystal Method has a very stable set of properties as well. As you will see, these properties are similar to the Agile Principles. So, for the most part, they will most likely not surprise you.

The seven main properties of the Crystal Method are as follows:

Frequent delivery. Same as all the other agile projects, Crystal projects should be delivered in smaller increments, rather than larger chunks (or entire products at the end of the project). This will help you ensure that you don't put a lot of money and energy into a product that will not be well received (by the customer or by the end market). Reflective improvement. Constant and continuous feedback lies at the foundation of agile in general. So, it makes all the sense in the world that Crystal would adopt this principle as well. The more feedback you get and the more you reflect on how to improve your product, the better the end result will be. Osmotic communication. This might sound very fancy, but it refers to a very high level of communication among team members. For smooth projects, you need to constantly encourage people to talk to each other and communicate their issues, opinions, and suggestions. Personal safety. As mentioned before, Crystal is one of the most human-centric approaches you will ever encounter. As such, it puts a lot of emphasis on personal safety as well. This is not so much related to personal safety in the sense of ensuring a lack of life-threatening conditions at work (which goes without saying, right?), but in the sense that people should be encouraged to speak up. Yes, this means they should speak up even when they don't agree with the majority. Focus. This property is twofold. On the one hand, it speaks about each team member's ability to focus on one task at hand and how to deliver it better. On the other hand, it speaks about the focus of the entire project, defining clear objectives and goals and ensuring the entire team is on the same page in all respects. Easy access to expert users. In Crystal projects, you are encouraged to always get feedback from the end users. Focus groups and surveys might help with this, but do keep in mind that you might need interdepartmental cooperation for this.

Technical environment focused on test automation, configuration management, and frequent integration. The more automated your processes are and the better your management and tracking tools are, the more likely it is that your team's skills and talents will be focused in the right direction. As such, the final product will be better from all points of view.

Why Is the Crystal Method Useful?

All agile project management methodologies are useful in their own way. The Crystal Method makes no exception in this area either. Overall, the Crystal Method is considered to be useful for the following reasons:

- It's fairly easy to implement, both due to the high level of categorization it includes and to the high level of flexibility it allows.
- It's easy to implement its specific practices with other agile and nonagile methodologies.
- It focuses on people and communication, and in a world that seems continuously disconnected from its human nature, this is a big advantage.
- It allows continuous integration and incremental deliveries, which helps deliver better products in the end.
- The processes are configurable, and you don't have to worry about documentation too much.
- It actively involves the end user, and this means that you will get better, more accurate feedback that suits the actual market.

The lack of specific guidelines can be quite confusing when it comes to the Crystal Method, but it is more than worth mentioning that Crystal was not meant to become a policy or a set of actual techniques from the very beginning (this is specifically why Cockburn made the distinction between the three terms).

At the end of the day, Crystal can provide you with a mindset at the very least and a pretty good ultralightweight methodology at the very most. It is up to you and your team what you choose to do with the basic information you have been given!

Chapter 16
Feature-Driven Development (FDD)

Together with Crystal and the Dynamic System Development Method, the Feature-Driven Development approach (FDD) is less popular as a methodology per se.

This is largely due to the fact that FDD tends to be associated and annexed to some of the more popular methods, instead of functioning as a standalone methodology in its own right.

This is not to say that Feature-Driven Development is not important or that it cannot function on its own, on the contrary, actually. It can and you can definitely try it out.

Rather than debating whether or not FDD is popular or relevant, or whether or not you should actually implement it as a pure methodology, we want this chapter to be an informative one that will set things on a clearer path for you and help you understand not only what FDD is and where it stands in the world of agile but also how you can incorporate it in a unique and personalized approach to agile project management in general. At its very core, Feature-Driven Development is not much different than many other agile project management methodologies. The one quality that differentiates it from the rest of the agile methods is the fact that, as the name suggests, it focuses on making progress on each feature. Basically, the importance of the "story" delivery you know from Scrum is transferred to the importance of each feature. Sometimes, a story might coincide with a feature, but this is not a must.

Developed at the end of the 1990s for a project that aimed to deliver a short time-spanned project for the banking industry in Singapore, FDD is nowadays used quite widely. Many people automatically incorporate it in their Scrum or Kanban approaches, but it is important to note that just because this is common, it doesn't mean FDD and Scrum are one and the same (or that FDD and Kanban are, for that matter).

Feature-Driven Development is one of the more prescriptive agile methodologies out there in the sense that it works based on a clearly defined life cycle, and it assigns clear roles among the different team members.

The FDD life cycle is defined by five main stages at which the product is developed:

Developing the overall model. At this stage, the team gets familiarized with the high-level scope of the entire project and system, as well as the context it comes from. Further on, the team will split into smaller groups, and each area of the system will be modeled then presented for peer review. The model(s) that are deemed a better fit will be selected to act as a domain area model. In time, all the domain area models will be merged into the larger model. Building a feature list. Once the knowledge has been collected throughout the first stage of the development, all the information will be used to identify the list of features. The domain area will be split into multiple subject areas, according to the functionality of the features representative of the area. It is important to note that each feature should be identified through the prism of the value it provides the user with. Planning by feature. Once you have the entire list of features at hand, you will be able to start planning the development per se. During this process, you will assign the feature sets as classes to the programmers in your team. Designing by feature. Each feature of the product comes with a design package that will be handled during the fourth stage of development. This will be handled by a chief programmer in a team, who will initially select a set of features to be developed over the course of two weeks. Together with the class owners associated with these features, the chief programmer will create sequence diagrams for each of the selected features and use them to refine the model.

Building by feature. Once the prework has been done and once the design inspection is ready, it is time for the team to move on to the actual programming, then test and inspect the code to ensure the feature is complete. Once that happens, it can be incorporated into the system.

As for the roles encountered in FDD, they are quite clear, and they may include the following:

- Domain Manager
- Language Guru
- Build Engineer
- Release Manager
- System Administrator
- Tester
- Technical Writer

In some respects, FDD and XP are quite similar to each other. It is very important to note, however, that the major difference between the two comes with the introduction of a "class ownership" concept. Collective ownership is one of the particularities in Extreme Programming. In Feature-Driven Development, however, this ownership is transferred to the class owner who becomes responsible for its functionality. The most notable tip of information you should keep in mind when it comes to how FDD functions is that instead of focusing on more or less random chunks of the project, it approaches development on a feature-by-feature basis.

Same as in the case of the other agile project management methodologies, Feature-Driven Development is associated with a series of best practices too.

Domain Object Modeling

Domain Object Modeling is one of the most important best practices associated with FDD. This practice basically consists of both exploring and explaining the domain of the problem at hand. Once the domain object model is generated, the team will have an overall framework to use when adding features, one by one, as they are developed.

Developing by Feature

As mentioned before, this is one of the main tenets of Feature-Driven Development (as the name of this methodology suggests a well). There is one important rule associated with the concept of developing by feature: if a function is too complex to be developed and implemented in two weeks, it will be split into smaller functions until each of the resulting subproblems is small enough to be considered a feature in the full sense of the word. This allows for better control of the changes that might appear along the road, be they related to changes in product requirements or changes related to bugs and/or lack of functionality.

Component/Class Ownership

What class ownership means is that different pieces or groups of pieces of code (called "classes") are assigned to specific owners. Each of these owners is responsible for the code on multiple levels:

- consistency
- performance
- conceptual integrity

Feature Teams

Same as most agile methodologies, Feature-Driven Development prefers working with small teams. As such, feature teams will be assigned for the development of each feature.

A feature team is a small team formed dynamically to develop a small activity. Together, they work for each design decision, and they evaluate their options before they choose a particular one.

As you can see, there's quite a lot of trust placed in each and every member of these teams, as well as in how they can work together and cooperate for the success of the entire project.

Inspections

According to FDD's best practices, you should run regular inspections of the design and code, so that you can detect any defects in due time (and so that you can apply the changes necessary to improving these defects).

Configuration Management

Configuration management is quite important, especially when new team members join in or when you are adopting FDD for the first time. However, it is a best practice that should be maintained regardless of where in your journey to Feature-Driven Development you may be.

Basically, configuration management will allow you to identify the source code for everything (all the features) that have been developed to date. This will also allow you to keep track of the class changes while feature teams work on their enhancement.

Regular Builds

The concept of "regular builds" is similar to that of "continuous delivery" in the general Agile Principles. What this concept refers to is ensuring that your system can demonstrate, at any time, that integration errors have been fixed early on in the process. This allows the customer to maintain trust in you and your team, and it allows you to actually keep track of all the issues, whether or not they are repeat offenders, and whether or not they have been successfully fixed.

Visibility of Progress and Results

This concept is quite similar to the Scrum and/or Kanban board in the sense that the progress and the results of your team's efforts should be visible at all times. FDD may not employ an actual board for this, but the FDD project manager needs to ensure that all reports are frequent, accurate, and appropriate both from the internal point of view (team, internal stakeholders, higher management, etc.) and from the external point of view (customer).

Feature-Driven Development is a less common methodology on its own. However, it is quite essential to remember that it can be easily integrated with other agile methodologies. In fact, the first two stages of the FDD development cycle are almost entirely congruent to the initial envisioning model of Agile Model Driven Development, showing that FDD belongs in the agile family just as much as Scrum, Kanban, or

Extreme Programming. Indeed, there is less focus on people in FDD (as compared to Scrum, Kanban, XP, or Crystal, for example), as the main center of this approach lies on the actual feature and how the people around it help with its harmonious development. However, this doesn't make Feature-Driven Development any less agile in nature. At the end of the day, FDD abides to the general Agile Principles just as much as any other methodology in the book. It is easy to dismiss the lesser popular agile methodologies out there, including FDD, especially since there seems to be less information and a smaller number of tools that are designed specifically for this approach.

However, what you do have to keep in mind is that methods like these are more of a supporting system to the more popular methodologies that focus on mindset more than specific approach.

FDD can work in combination with most of the project management methodologies we have described so far, with the exception of Extreme Programming (where the concept of class ownership and that of collective ownership will clash).

Same as in the case of Crystal, we thoroughly encourage you to learn more about FDD as well. Aside from the five main stages we have described here, each of them is associated with specific substeps that will allow your entire plan to be more structured. For this reason, FDD is one of the agile methodologies that seem to be more of a better fit for very structured businesses (like large corporations, for example).

As we have emphasized throughout this book (as well as the first installment of the series), we thoroughly believe in the fact that every business should find their own agile path. For some, the "traditional" Scrum or Kanban may be enough. For others, however, a more complex combination might be needed. Experiment and see what work for you!

Chapter 17
Common Errors Behind Agile Failure

Just as Agile methodology comes in many forms and flavors, so do its failures. While Agile projects typically have a much lower failure rate than their WaterFall counterparts, unsuccessful projects still happen; these are defined by a lack of delivered projects, insufficient customer satisfaction, exaggerated expense, or carelessly allotted calendar space. The reasons behind these failures have a pattern to them, typically stemming from four fundamental issues within a team or organization. The reasons for these failures are a critical lack of support, broader organization or communication problems, project speed, or inadequate training. If a team can overcome, prevent, or reinvent around these four problems while running authentic Agile, the project has an infinitely better chance of landing a stamp of approval from each stakeholder involved.

Lack of Support

Organizing a support structure behind an Agile team is the core functionality of a project manager. This means giving power and decision-making authority to a group of professional programmers rather than following a more traditional hierarchy. Organizations can achieve this through executive buy-in at the highest level—if the CEO of a company pledges their unwavering support to the efforts of an Agile team, they often have little trouble parting the sea of corporate bureaucracy.

However, this support means more than gracing a team with the leader's presence at the start of a project. Agile projects need resources and funding upfront, two things that executives control. They also need access to information and people, two more things that executives control. Executive buy-in means granting reasonable access to the things the team needs to complete the project on time and budget, and then trusting them to handle the resources with care.

A common expression of this pitfall is underwriting executive support to another person without proper authority. A local manager may grant access to rooms and whiteboards, but they cannot allow a significant hardware investment within one iteration. Furthermore, they do not represent the support of an executive team, which is arguably more critical than resource allocation. The fastest way to have a project fail is to have an executive kill it. Period. If someone on the executive team does not clue in to the real vision and impact of the project on the customer and the benefits for the company, they can get in the way and sabotage the entire effort, reducing weeks or months of a team's effort to nothing.

Even though this may seem extreme, you need to understand that Agile practices often threaten the internal culture of a company—hierarchical and traditional in exchange for something more spontaneous. This cultural shift directly threatens the executives' power structure, specifically affecting those who act as managers rather than leaders. Beyond shifts in the organization's direction, disorganization and a lack of respect for the process, some executives may think their jobs, position, status, and identity are being threatened. Undermining the efforts of an Agile team, especially a new one, is, therefore, in their best interest. This manifests in support for a WaterFall method and a company philosophy, which is at odds with the Agile methodology.

Look for an executive looking outside the organization and toward the future and prosperity of the company. They will see the value of Agile in a rapidly changing world as an opportunity rather than a threat. At some point, projects and efforts become political within a big enough company—leave this piece to the executives supporting a team's efforts instead of focusing on it more than necessary.

Broader Organizational or Communication Issues

As unique and independent as Agile teams may feel once inside, they still operate within the larger organizational space. Systemic weaknesses negatively affect all parts of the systems, no matter how Agile. These are much larger, organization-specific issues that the team must consider before implementing an Agile project system. Is the organization culturally ready to accept a shift to a more independent framework? Will those outside the Agile team readily accept or outright reject it? Are the communication systems in place strong enough to support the demands of an Agile team?

There are things a project manager can do to address these questions and the many more that, if left unanswered, may undercut the efforts of an Agile team. One of these is executive buy-in, but general buy-in can be just as critical. Involving mid-tier managers by keeping them informed, asking what questions they might have about the process, and understanding huge reservations is key to breaking the ice of a project. Moreover, it leads to an understanding of the Agile team's demands, communication, or requests for information. Poor communication is seldom malicious at this level, preferably an initial miscommunication of important information. To prevent that or other problems that may arise externally, you should include them in conversations early in the process, explaining their significance in the functionality of the team's success.

A more robust method, especially for a team starting with an Agile process, is to create a level of value for those teams and engage them in the system's success. Organizations typically apply Agile methods to software and development projects, they have a wide range of applications beyond those worlds. If a manager has never heard of Agile practices, speak with them about it, and see where those principles may fit into their world. From there, test principles within the first Agile team and report back to the manager: "This worked, that was a problem, these are the solutions I used." Not only does this engage the rest of the organization with the individual project, but it also works to "infect" the culture of an organization with a single suggestion: there may be a better, newer way to approach organizational problems. From there, the organizational culture loosens and becomes open to addressing the issues of a system more broadly.

Going Too Fast

The move to an Agile system, especially if it carries the expectation of a "solution to all our problems," can be exciting. While jumping into Agile unprepared is a bad idea, speeding through the process is just as dangerous. Often, issues of speed management stem from poor coaching, processes, or tooling. These core issues present themselves in three flavors:

Not defining a process to absorb issues regarding multiple dependent or distributed teams

Defining a project without the entire consideration of all relevant stakeholders undermines effectiveness. However, Agile teams can often work around this oversight with executive authority or team restructuring. If a dependent squad has not been adequately accounted for, it halts the entire progression of a project, ripping through the process like a malfunctioning crane on an assembly line. If a team does not define a method for addressing this potential fault before it begins, it becomes, by definition, impossible to move forward and continue the project. Often, a desire to rush into a project creates this oversight, which is the result of little consideration rather than lack of foresight—take the time to build the structures a project needs to succeed.

Scalability issues with core Agile tools

Though this quote is often wrongly attributed to Abraham Lincoln, the wisdom encapsulated by it extends into the software development world through Agile implementation. Agile tools are designed to automate and support larger systems; they act as a strength multiplier just as the axe does. When developing tools to help a broader functionality, we might be tempted to jump straight to the functionality rather than further invest in the tools themselves. The rush to produce often produces a base tool, which becomes inaccessible after its first use. Do not rush through the fundamental development of tools for the sake of production—this will cause more retooling down the line or, worse, a functionality that does not live beyond a development tool and results in failed implementation.

Furthermore, team members must use tools consistently. The inconsistent use of a tool can cause faulty metrics, overall incorrect builds, and flow or quality issues.

Extending tools to the wrong processes like testing or business collaborations

Retooling and artifacts are the key to making an Agile system even more efficient; however, that mindset leads to the temptation to reuse tools inappropriately for the sake of speed and convenience. Extending a means to address issues it was not built for, such as a general deployment, testing, or other business collaborations, may cause a more significant failure down the line, when proper tools are finally in place. This is a small detail that often causes a lot of havoc within an Agile team. Proper retooling usually means recoding and an in-depth understanding of a tool's more substantial functionality; as a project manager, encourage an Agile team to ask, "In what ways can this tool be better for this application?" before reusing a tool, then retool it based on the answer.

Teams do all of this by experiencing pressure and cutting corners because speed is the focus, not quality. Finding the balance between speed and quality is never easy, but consistently undercutting quality for the sake of speed is a critical ingredient in the Agile project failure soup.

Poor Training

Insufficient training is a common reason for failure, which occurs in three forms: nobody receives training, not everyone who needed it got it, or the training wasn't great. While the first two can be solved through proper scheduling, the third directly results from having a poor coach. Why is finding qualified Agile coaches so tricky? Many people are unsure of what to look for in an Agile coach. And this goes beyond trusting a certification, history, or experience.

The first strategy is through formal training experience. Within the software community, there are loose definitions attached to programs or people themselves. A "software developer" might be someone who attended a graduate program, and developed skills in years of practice with complicated problems and projects. Then, there are self-taught, new hires, whose experience consists of a few personal projects and a cluster of YouTube videos. While an inexperienced software developer can still develop good software and often find new and unique ways to do so, a coach does not have that luxury. The Agile coach needs to experience coaching and being coached over the years to be effective.

The first step to clearing a coach is to get references and understand how deeply their experience extends. This applies both to coaching and Agile skills independently. Apprenticeship under another Agile coach is a great way to establish these skills, though there are a variety of legitimate Agile coaching organizations available. These organizations not only focus on how to coach Agile specifically, but they go deep into Agile skills and knowledge. This leads to a second requirement. An Agile coach knows Agile. This seems like an obvious requirement, but a coach may claim to know Agile without truly understanding the principles. Years of experience do not guarantee a deep understanding of all aspects of the Agile Lifecycle. Delivering an excellent coaching experience means coaching all parts of a team, including enterprise architecture, data management, and portfolio management. Finally, an Agile coach should have experienced a context that is similar to an organization's project. This not only applies for the project, but also for organizational realities. Coaching a team that is centrally located and coaching a team from a different time zone on the globe are two different experiences. Even clearer is the difference between a modern startup whose team might include the majority of the company's personnel and a large organization in which the team is barely a percentage of the company's payroll. A good Agile coach should have sufficient experience in any given context, or at least possess transferable knowledge that he or she can apply to specific situations. Context is relevant.

By following these steps, you will ensure that the common pitfalls of Agile implementation and management are avoided successfully. Good luck!

Conclusion

Every Agile project manager that ventures with a project into the world is driven by a desire to solve complicated problems. There is also a broader dissatisfaction regarding the way we address new challenges with old methods, though.

Agile is the modern way to address current problems. The reality accompanying the 21st century is one of constant deployment, innovation, and technological shifts. It affects every industry, from news and fashion to B2B companies. Companies are faced with a question—resist the wave or learn to ride it to shore. For many problems, Agile management acts as the surfboard that allows you to navigate this crazy, fungible world.

The data are there to support the core processes of Agile methods. The software world has extensively analyzed the difference between traditional, hierarchical approaches and dynamic, Agile ones. As it turns out, 86% of conventional projects are failures. About half of those failures produce no working software and zero product delivery. The people involved in the system demanded a radical change, and Agile was the response.

Not only does Agile produce a final product more often by reducing the failure rate to under 10%, but it also increases the quality of delivered projects. This happens systematically, as the relevance of a project to the overall system is no longer determined by shifts in the external environment. This reorientation from determination to adaptation is highly critical. If the project requirements change, it is up to the project team to shift with them. Agile management allows for that shift to be systematic, thus encouraging and developing applications that are relevant to the end-user.

An Agile approach also ensures higher customer satisfaction. Incorporating a customer in the development process introduces aspects of accountability with buy-in. The level of customer interaction in Agile settings allows teams to evolve with the demands, threading the needle between consistency and flexibility. Overall, there are significantly more chances to make sure the customer is happy. It's as simple as that!

There is also a gripping sense of control that comes with Agile. It stems from the way a team organizes its work. Work is not a list of process requirements and neither does it involve dictating terms and directing an entire team through the descriptions of a document. It verbalizes the complaints from the mouth of the only person who matters: the customer. Rather than handing in a to-do list, the customer pleads with the team to help them. They provide constraints and a problem. From there, it is up to the team of experts to determine the most effective solution and implement it. Agile provides room for expertise, nuance, and creativity to become assets rather than risks. This is a powerful shift for both the customer and the team, motivating each to be diligent and inquisitive rather than working to deliver a list.

The metrics show all of this too. Not only do Agile approaches reduce the risk of project failure, but they also create a faster ROI for the company and customers alike. Agile projects commonly come under-budget and ahead of schedule. With the disparity in quality also accounted for, what more could a system provide? Agile methodologies are better for modern problems that require iterative problem solving and solutions.

These benefits would be bare offerings without the methods, allowing incorporation into the companies. Agile methods rely on a few core tenets: planning, communication, and team development.

The foundation of an Agile system is the people within it. In a world of automation and computerization, Agile methods are uniquely, perhaps ironically, human. The shift from a hierarchy-driven organization to a self-organizing team, with its power and structure, is a challenge to overcome. It requires leadership rather than management, executive support, and internal determination. But from that shift comes the rest—it is the effort to see the field that begets the benefits.

Shifting from plan to planning is often the most challenging step for one reason—it's the first step. The initial instinct of every traditional organization is to develop a concrete plan; shifting that perspective is a cumbersome task, for you also need to move the accompanying organizational inertia. But the benefits outweigh the apparent disadvantages, because in exchange for the effort you get an adaptable, functional team that continually betters and evolves.

That is, unless poor communication squanders those efforts. In a traditional organization, money is the blood that leads to project success. With Agile projects, it is information. Apart from internal, functional communication, there is a communication of vision that needs to take place. Most jobs don't require sustained buy-in and commitment, but Agile projects do. The only accurate way to do that is by inspiring the right people.

This book provided a bird's-eye view into the world of Agile. But there is much more to dive into, should you choose to adopt this approach. Not only are there more in-depth investigations of how we apply Agile, but there are also more ways and systems where we could use Agile methods. Each Agile system has its nuances. We can use each application with diverse problems and ensure success. Finding a system that works best for each company is a matter of education and consultation. Hopefully, this book introduced you to a few questions and terms that you can use.Apart from terminology and questions, this book also introduced a critical idea: complex, modern problems demand modern systems. There is no quick answer or set of rules to change. These problems will not go away with excessive working hours or dollars. They are problems that demand a modern solution—a system—to address them. They require a shift in perspective and understanding rather than resources. That shift needs to be malleable, in line with the times, and easy to reorganize when called upon for a different problem. It is a high bar to satisfy our modern times. But thankfully, Agile systems allow us to do just that.

PART 2: SCRUM

This book aims to provide a step-by-step guide to the agile project management process while setting out a historical overview and discussing the philosophical underpinnings of the school of thought. There is a large variety of schools of thought that are available and effective in the realm of project management as a discipline. This book advocates the modern usage of agile methodology in the software development space but also considers how it can be applied as a process to various industries while looking ahead at the future of agile as a discipline.

Agile project management was primarily used in the software development space in its earliest form and underwent most of its transformation as a framework in this industry. As the industry grew and technology evolved, the requirements for efficient software development changed, and so too has the agile framework. This book outlines the fundamental terminology that will enable you to apply the framework to your organization while adhering to the fundamental principles of the discipline. Any framework has its strengths and weaknesses, and no system is flawless, which is why the agile process is continually evolving. One of the biggest challenges to the agile framework is the larger global organization with geographically-segmented team members and much larger team sizes all working toward the same goal. As such, agile project management was scaled to cater to these needs and there have been many revisions of the system, all centered around the core Agile Manifesto.

Through this adaptation of the agile process, the application of agile has become much diversified and is no longer restricted to the software development, building, or testing process. Regardless of the industry your organization is in, the size of your team, or the number of project tasks you may have, there is an agile framework you can use. This book discusses the multitude of options at your disposal while teaching you to apply agile not only to work, but to your thinking as well.

What Does Scrum Mean?

So how does Scrum specifically fit into all of this? There are different approaches to Agile Framework; different types that you can use, depending on what fits best with you. It would be like trying on different brands of jeans and picking out the one that feels the most comfortable. Each approach (or type of agile framework) is considered "lightweight", meaning all rules and practices are kept at the bare minimum. Each approach also ensures that the main focus is on empowering developers to collaborate and make decisions together. It's important to note that each developer has a different background, which allows the group to work more quickly and effectively. You don't want everyone to know how to do the same thing. What if they come across a problem that they can't solve because they all have the same background? Having people that can do different things will help create a more cohesive team, and in turn, the team will create much more amazing things. And remember, the big picture of the Agile development ideology is creating applications in small increments. Each individual increment is tested before being considered complete, which assures the product is built with quality at that specific time, instead of figuring out the quality at a later date.

To summarize, an Agile Framework is a process that the developmental team can follow to ensure positive things happen. It's designed so that all parties, including the customer, can provide feedback while the project is currently being developed. Doing so cuts out problems later on and makes it much more efficient in the long run.

And while the Agile Framework has several different choices for software development approaches, the most popular one is Scrum.

Scrum is a type of Agile Framework that has a broad application, which allows for managing and controlling iterative and incremental projects of different types. It's useful when there are many different types of projects and helps complete each project in a timely manner while ensuring the value of the product doesn't change. It has a strong collaborative and connective philosophy, which also helps each project to be completed in the best possible way. In order for this to be done, there are different roles in the Scrum process, and each person must take their role seriously. If one person doesn't do their job correctly, then the process will fail. Again, Scrum is all about team-work and connectivity.

Breaking it down even further, Scrum has three basic principles:

Transparency

Inspection

Adaptation

It's all about seeing things how they are and making sure everyone knows what is going on at all times. It's important to be clear and concise and keep everyone informed. You might feel like hiding a mistake, but that will make things much worse in the long run. It's important to be transparent throughout the entire process. Inspection ensures that there is a sort of accountability involved. Each Sprint requires a sort of inspection, so that everything is shown to be on track. Without it, the team could be working on a product that might not even be working! And adaptation is probably one of the most important principles. Things change, that's just how it is in life and in the working world. It's important for the Scrum Team to be able to adapt to all the different changes the process will go through. The customer could change their mind, the Scrum Team could change how they want to complete a task, and the Product Owner can easily make changes to the Product Backlog. Each product goes through so many changes throughout the process, and it's important to be adaptable. Otherwise, the product will fail to be created, and the entire system would have to be reworked.

Chapter 18:
The Scrum Method

What Is Scrum?

Scrum is one of the various Agile Frameworks that is mostly used in developing complex projects. Initially, the Scrum framework was formalized to be used in software development projects, but it can now be applied in any innovative and complex project.

Scrum is a control and management process which cuts through the challenges and complexities of project development to develop a product capable of meeting the business needs. The Scrum Teams are allowed to deliver working products in an incremental manner. Scrum can be seen as a simple framework which provides an effective team collaboration during the development of complex products.

Scrum isn't a technique or a process for development of products, but it's a framework in which one can employ many techniques or processes. With Scrum, the efficiency of product development and management processes can be made clear for project development teams to be able to show improvements.

The framework is very simple, and any individual or organization can choose to implement it easily. The framework can be adopted by anyone, including those with limited knowledge in project management. If your organization develops projects, this is the time for you to adopt this framework. The framework is scalable and flexible, making it applicable to various kinds of projects. If you are developing a project for the first time, this is the right framework for you due to ease of use and ease of adoption. Other members who will be participating in developing the project will also find it easy to learn the framework.

It is essential for the Scrum Team to have the ability to adjust to each of the various changes the procedure will go through. The buyer may change their mind, the Scrum Team could improve just how they wish to finish a job, or the product owner could make alterations on the product backlog.

Each product goes through a lot of changes throughout the procedure, and it is crucial to be adaptable. If you can't adjust, the item is going to fail to be created and the whole system will need to be reworked.

It's useful when there are many different types of projects to complete each project in a timely manner while ensuring the value of the product doesn't change. Scrum has a strong collaborative and connective philosophy, which also helps each project to be completed in the best possible way.

Scrum Principles

Evade formality on Agile projects

Scrum project teams that see the most success are those that embrace creativity and spontaneity in their processes, as opposed to formality. Remove formality in your processes by eliminating and rooting it out where possible. This will be achieved if the team looks for ways to make their activities less formal. For example, instead of having to wait until the daily scrum to ask some questions or discuss issues that can be resolved easily, it is easier to walk over to a team member and ask the question directly.

Act and think as a team

Team members work for the benefit of the entire team and hence should work towards ensuring that the team as a whole is productive. Whenever individual performance metrics are introduced in a team, collaboration, communication, and performance go down. Instead, team members should seek to work as a team through failures and successes. In a Scrum project, the responsibility of working towards the goal of the project, defining the scope, and sticking to the assigned time should be the responsibility of the entire group, not individuals.

Visualization over writing

Visualization works better than writing in boosting thought and memory. This is because retention improves when you visualize compared to when you write. Successful teams use drawings, diagrams, and modeling tools to help their members conceptualize the project. The goal is to make the material as visually consumable as possible.

Visualization makes it easy to process raw data into information. Simply reading reports on the progress of a sprint is ineffective and unlikely to demonstrate the progress fully. However, adding a visualization such as a burn-down chart increases the ability to retain information and allows the team to measure the project against trends and timelines. It is also easier to identify problem areas at a glance than having to read about them.

Scrum uses

While Scrum was initially used to develop products, for nearly 30 years it has been used in a wide variety of industries to do things like:

- Determine viable markets, products and technologies
- Identify products ripe for refinement or enhancement
- Iterating and producing new versions of products or additions as quickly as possible
- Sustain existing operational environments and create new ones including cloud environments
- Renew and sustain existing products

Due to its rapid iteration process, Scrum has been used extensively when it comes to developing hardware, software, embedded software and the like. It has also been used for almost everything, including autonomous vehicle creation, governments, schools, marketing strategies and organizational operations too numerous to mention.

While it was created nearly 30 years ago, as the interactions between environmental, market and technological complexities have grown, Scrum has proved its utility when it comes to dealing with life's complexities on a near daily basis.

It has also proven especially adept at improving processes related to incremental and iterative transfers of knowledge.

Scrum Values

Scrum values are the values upon which the Scrum framework is formulated. These values relate to ethics, which makes scrum from a social perspective, a value system. The values are commitment, focus, openness, respect, and courage.

Courage

Scrum members work together as a team and feel more supported with all resources available to them. As such, Scrum teams can undertake even the most challenging tasks. It is through courage that the Scrum team can see change as a source of innovation and inspiration. Training, resource provision, and support are essential for any team to remain courageous.

Commitment

They are committed to show an improvement and deliver a working product. Scrum teams are self-organized, and this requires a lot of commitment. A committed team has a higher chance of achieving a goal.

When team members commit they commit to the team, to quality, collaboration, learning, the sprint goals, self-organization, excellence, and doing the best they can. They also commit to coming up with working software, constantly improving it, adhering to the Scrum framework, creating value, finishing the work, inspecting, and adapting. Challenging the status-quo and transparency are also critical commitments in Scrum project implementations.

Openness

Due to the empirical nature of Scrum, openness and transparency is very important. It helps the team inspect the facts as they are so that appropriate solutions can be developed. The work, progress, problems encountered, and lessons learned changes in a project due to the unexpectedness and unpredictability of the world.

Openness is encouraged in Scrum projects, particularly in regards to how Scrum teams should work together and express to each other how they are doing. Any team which faces concerns should raise them for handling. Inspection should be done on what is real so that any adaptations made are sensible. Scrum teams should also be open and ready to collaborate with other teams even from other disciplines within the organization.

Respect

Scrum teams work together and share their successes as well as failures. They help each other in times of challenges and this brings about respect. Each member in the Scrum should be ready to respect the background and experience of other Scrum members. Diversity in the team should be embraced and respected. Respect should be accorded to the project sponsors by developing the right product. Money and time should not be wasted doing things which were not initially planned for. Any changes to be made to any aspect of the product under development should be communicated to all stakeholders.

Focus

Focus is paying attention to the most important aspects without being bothered by sideshows, even when they may prove to be important. It is important to focus on what is clear now rather than on other changes and adaptations that may or may not happen in the future. The now is important because it resolves problems that consumers are experiencing at the moment. The future is highly uncertain, and the best lessons for tomorrow are best learned from the issues of today.

The Scrum team should focus on few things each time so that they can work together in a bid to produce excellent products. Due to the iterative and incremental approach of

Scrum, the Scum team should be focused. At any particular time, the Scrum team has to be focused on what is important without being worried about what will be important at some time in future. The future is uncertain, so the team should focus on what they know currently. This helps them learn something so that they can show an improvement in the future. The Scrum team has to focus on their work to get things done.

The above values are related to the Scrum ethics. They give direction to the kind of work done by the Scrum team, as well as how they behave and act. Anything done in Scrum, whether implementing changes or coming up with new decisions, should reinforce and uphold the above values instead of diminishing them. Each member should commit themselves towards upholding them.

Scrum Rules

No project methodology can be successful without rules, and Scrum is no exception. Scrum rules are the glue that binds the Scrum Team to the roles, events, and artifacts within the overall Scrum Framework. While some methodologies have extremely rigid rules that govern them, what sets Scrum rules apart is that they are more inclusive and flexible in nature.

While some of these rules are guidelines for adopting Scrum best practices, others take the form of general norms that should be encouraged within a project setting. Together, these rules and norms will then govern the interaction between team members and stakeholders.

Here are some key Scrum Rules that Scrum practitioners must be aware of:

- Sprint lengths should be of the same duration
- No Sprint should exceed 4 weeks in length
- Teams shall not take inter-Sprint breaks (Sprints must follow a continuous, unbroken cycle)
- Each Sprint must start with a Sprint planning meeting
- Sprint planning meetings must be time-boxed (2 to 3 hours)

- Each Sprint review meeting should then be followed by a Sprint Retrospective, which all team members must attend
- When prioritizing Product Backlog Items (PBIs or User Stories), no two items can have the same priority
- If there exist any defects in the previous Sprint (Iteration), those must be prioritized for resolution at the highest level in the upcoming Sprint
- Team meetings must be open and fair, with all members (and stakeholders) allowed to express their points of views
- When a team member is facing a challenge delivering his or her commitments, he or she shall actively seek out assistance from others who can support him or her
- Scrum Team members who complete their assignments ahead of time must actively volunteer for additional tasks from the "Open" list
- While rules will certainly help bring order and discipline within project teams, no number of rules can actually prevent chaos - unless everyone on the team abides by the rules.

The key principles behind Scrum Rules are:

- Everyone must be consulted before a rule is proposed
- All Team members and stakeholders must agree to abide by the rules
- The rules must be well publicized
- There should be consequences for not following a rule

Ultimately, these rules and norms are high-level guidelines for project managers to refer to when managing their projects. Common sense should be used when adopting them, and they should be tailored to adapt to a specific project's needs if required.

Transitioning to Scrum requires adjusting to cultural changes and hence new mindsets. And like all change, it will not come easy; but we assure you from experience that as teams fully commit themselves to Scrum they discover a new sense of creativity, flexibility, and inspiration which leads to better and more efficient results.

Chapter 19: Scrum for Agile Project Management

The History of Agile

Throughout history, there have been many great human achievements, and in some respects, they may have been achievable through project management. To understand the basics of agile project management, it is necessary to start with the history of agile and where its core ideas and principles originate. Agile itself, as a project management framework, stems from the manufacturing industry. Around the 1950s, Western companies were fascinated as to why their Eastern competitors were able to achieve a much faster turnaround time for product delivery. Toyota, in particular, was a company that was able to produce many more vehicles than most other manufacturers who were in business at the time. It was observed from Toyota's manufacturing process that standardization and the elimination of costly and unnecessary processes led to greater output in comparison to the other leading automobile manufacturers of the generation.

Some years later, following the lean approach, around 1980, was the invention and introduction of the Scrum project management framework, created and pioneered by Hirotaka Takeuchi and Ikujiro Nonaka in 1986. Takeuchi and Ikujiro observed that the way certain industrial companies, like Toyota, were able to set themselves ahead of competitors was because they used an operating procedure that largely resembled a game of rugby. As opposed to a more procedural framework, these early scrum practitioners were passing information across teams and across production and project processes while incorporating feedback and decisions from all hierarchies to achieve the end goal.

Agile operates on the basic principle of "Kaizen," which is a Japanese word for constant improvement. This principle stems from ancient Japanese philosophy that affirms to do things effectively, you need to be constantly changing. The direct translation of the phrase "kai" and "zen" is essentially good change, simply put, and change for the good. This means that fundamental to the philosophy is that if things change from their original plan or the traditional way of doing things, you then customize the process to your needs and adapt to the situation or environment that you find yourself in.

Between 1987 and 1998, project management theory had been centered on the synthesis of all the established practices with the addition of a few more approaches. Earned Value Management and the PRINCE method appeared in 1989, followed by the CHAOS report in 1994, which was essentially a compilation of reported errors to date that have arisen in the software development space; 1996 saw the revision of the PRINCE method, which emerged from Europe and was upgraded to PRINCE2, which became a more generic and widely applicable project management approach compared to its earlier version that was limited to Information Systems and Information Technology application. Lastly, in 1997, Critical Chain Project Management was founded by Eliyahu Goldratt incorporating algorithms to distribute resources and maintain task and project schedule evenly.

Sometime later, following the establishment of the scrum framework, 17 software developers invented the foundational principles of agile, which was established as an approach to software development in 2001, which is now known as The Agile Manifesto. Since this first iteration of the theory, the process has been adapted in various ways, and the applications of agile have been customized to the user's needs and revised in the following years.

The Agile Manifesto favors certain components of the software development process over others and has established four core values that need to be adhered to in order to follow the true Agile process.

In these four core tenets, the founders acknowledged that there is indeed value in the components to the right of the word "over," it is the items to the left of the statement that are the most valued and considered the most agile adjacent in the typical software development process. Furthermore, Kent Beck and his colleagues state there are 12 principles that underpin the manifesto and give more clarity to what makes the manifesto such a concrete approach.

- Ensuring your customer's needs are satisfied by delivering software in both a timeous and consistent manner is considered the most critical priority.
- Regardless of the stage of the development process, always accept alterations in customer requirements. Agile embraces change to turn it into an advantage for the customers to help them stand out from the crowd.
- Aim to produce functional software regularly while seeking to deliver as quickly as possible.
- All team members, regardless of role, need to collaborate daily.
- Ensure team members are motivated, have sufficient support, and have an environment conducive to achieving project completion while having faith they will get things done.
- The most valued form of communication in a development team is face-to-face conversation as it is the most effective and reliable communication channel.
- Producing functional software regularly is the primary gauge of project goal completion.
- Truly agile processes are able to produce consistent and high-quality work regularly without fail.
- Critical and detailed working habits increases team agility.
- Eliminating unnecessary work in a project is the key to simpler design processes.

- Self-managing teams produce significantly higher quality work.
- Team members should regularly assess project progress and evaluate how to adapt processes to become more efficient going forward.

What does it mean to be Agile?

At its very core, being agile is essentially flexibility, which is oddly enough the dictionary definition of the word. This flexibility is the idea that as work evolves so, too, does your approach to solving problems and getting processes implemented through the project management cycle. Agile disregards a cookie-cutter approach to each project and embraces that there is no singular, universal way to implement a project, but it can be adapted to the goal of the project, the employees skill set and the company's goals while encompassing ongoing feedback from your customer and team members.

At this point, having discussed the core values behind the agile process, let's discuss traditional project management and its core values.

What is Traditional Project Management?

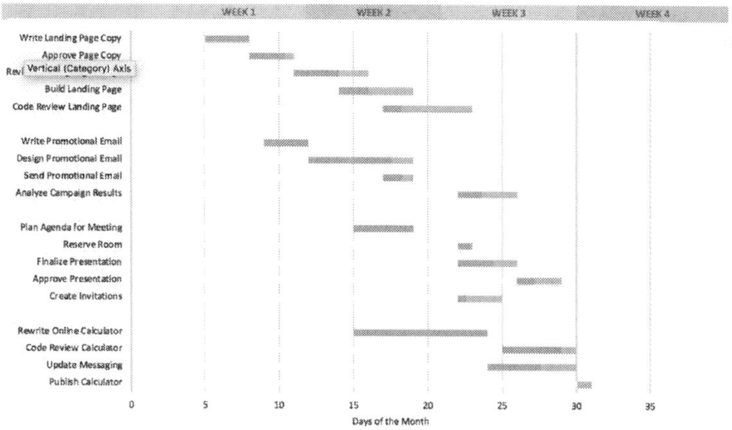

Traditional project management is similar to following a recipe. You are fully aware and have a very clear goal for your result and can rely on tried and tested steps to get you to that end goal. For project management, this encompasses your ingredients, so planning what resources are required to reach the goal, estimating how much time is needed to complete the recipe and, finally, controlling activities during your cooking time to reach your end goal. The reason these strategies are applied is to reach the company's product goal within a specific timeframe, while controlling expenditure and making sure that your customer is happy with your deliverable. The concept of traditional project management was initially practiced from around 1950 by Henry Gantt but has been applied throughout history, some suggest dating back to the Pyramids of Egypt. In 1917, Gantt developed a means to visualize the project timeline in the means of a chart to represent the task sequence as well as the time needed to perform certain tasks until the project is complete. As such, he is considered one of the forefathers of the traditional project management approach, and his charts are still used today for practitioners of the traditional approach. Refer to the diagram below for an example of a Gantt chart.

In the above diagram, we can see how the task sequence is broken up as established in the project plan, as well when certain tasks were initiated and how long they took for completion. As mentioned before, traditional project management is used when your development process is largely sequential in nature, and we can see from the progression of the chart the list of tasks are generally reliant on the completion of the previous task to move on to the next step of development.

Having a clear visual representation of the project process is vital; however, in this current format and layout, any development processes that require numerous sets of subtasks will render the Gantt chart too complex to understand. Additionally, one bar as a representation of the time elapsed is useful; however, it does not give a clear indication of the quantity of work that is required to complete the project.

Typically, a traditional project management approach is largely sequential as tasks are always completed in the same order. Again, the reason the same sequence is followed is because the methodology has been tested and established as the most cost-effective, time-efficient, and organized project process.

As such, there are five stages of traditional project management.

- Initiation:

  In this stage of the project process, the team sets out what the end goal of the project will be, what are the customers' requirements, and outlining potential difficulties that may hinder this process.

- Planning:

  At this point, how the project is divided into specific tasks if formulated as well as how long these particular tasks will take. In conjunction with this, the amount of resources required to complete the project is determined and finally documenting what the final plan of the project is.

- Execution:

  Following the establishment of the project plan, the plan is then followed step-by-step while at regular intervals, assessing the quality of the project and distributing the information that is needed.

- Monitoring & Control: At this stage, the quality of the project and the costs are closely monitored, making sure that project plan is closely adhered to.

- Closing:

  The final step is making sure the client is happy with the final product and send out a report to the team of how successful the project went.

As the modern world of work evolved, and project requirements evolved too, the traditional project management approach needed to be refined and progressed. There are many instances where traditional project management approaches may be more appropriate based on the type of work needed to be done, for example, in construction. Most notably, one of the first projects noted to have used a Gantt chart to map progress was the construction of the Hoover Dam in 1931. In this particular instance, the work is mostly sequential where later building stages can rarely be completed before the preceding phases.

Within a software development industry and the progression of technology, a project management framework is needed that can respond and adapt to these demands. Agile project management is considered to be one of the framework evolutions originating from the more traditional project management approach.

Scrum

Scrum is a process structure that can be adapted to various kinds of work but was formulated in a product development setting. Scrum can be defined as a tool used to formulate a hypothesis of how projects work. In a typical Scrum suited work environment, projects are broken up into two to four-week iterations before a project is completed. The framework itself adopts all of the principles of Kaizen discussed before and can be implemented in your projects through various practices.

The first term is known as a Sprint. A Sprint is defined as a timeframe in which the team will produce a deliverable. The Sprint could be the life cycle of one project, provided an entire project typically takes four weeks from start to finish. Alternatively, your full project lifecycle can be divided into a subset of Sprints to reach your final project goal. Before the Sprint starts, the team decides which components of the project each team member will take responsibility for and plans an estimate of how the tasks or subsets of tasks are divided and how work is done. Also, the team needs to define what is considered as "done," meaning what criteria would tasks or subsets of tasks need to fulfill before they can be marked as complete or done. Once this is agreed upon, the tasks that have been finalized from the planning process now becomes the product backlog. Items or tasks within the product backlog can be prioritized as the team sees fit and then worked on throughout the duration of the Sprint. Throughout the Sprint, it is important to have short daily scrum huddles, where the team comes together for less than 15 minutes and outlines what tasks will be worked on for the day ahead to maintain the project goal. The daily scrum should not be too long a meeting and should not be centered on problem-solving as this is the core focus of a retrospective. A retrospective is a meeting where the team gathers and sits down at the end of a Sprint and addresses any problems that became apparent in the Sprint and discusses how these can be resolved going forward before starting another Sprint.

The Scrum framework is synonymous with agile project management as a whole as it embraces the key events as outlined above and makes use of further processes to ensure that your team reaches goals.

Kanban

Kanban is another word that has been borrowed from the Japanese, which directly translates into "sign board." A kanban board is essentially a visual representation of the entire work process from start to finish. It also further details the steps being taken, which team members are responsible for these processes, and in which stage of completion that particular task is in.

Further, in the kanban approach, there are five core values that should be applied for the process to be effective.

- Envisage workflow
- Limit the amount of work-in-progress
- Manage the flow of work

- Detail processes clearly
- Collaborate

The most accurate visual representation of a Kanban board is a Post-it Note and a white board. Written on the white board is generally three columns running from left to right that read: Backlog/To Do, In Progress, and Done. Refer to the following image.

As mentioned before, team members would then add Post-it Notes to the to-do list and move them along each stage of the process. As such, the Post-it Notes represent one task or one step in a production process, which is moved from column to column as the task is completed. For example, take the task of reading a book as well as the other tasks in the above diagram. Before you start reading the book, you label the Post-it "Read book" and place it in the backlog column. This indicated that the task has yet to be started but is also not yet in progress. Any tasks that need to be done can then be placed in the backlog as they arise. It's important to observe that each Post-it Note doesn't need to be a singular task, but it can also be a series of related tasks that have a common theme in your particular project. Please refer to the accompanying image.

The image shows that one task can be broken down into a subset of incremental tasks that need to be completed as a project progresses from inception to completion and delivery to your client.

The fundamental goal of a Kanban board is visibility. Once production processes are visually manifested, it is easier to identify what is actually being done as well as track how far certain processes are and what is yet to be started or completed. Another advantage of the Kanban board is team member accountability. As tasks or project chunks are added to your Kanban board, it is also possible to add employees who will then be primarily responsible for completing the task or set of tasks. As the working process unfolds, it is then very easy for employees and managers to visually determine how far certain processes are and what still needs to be done to complete the particular project in progress. Also, as processes are made visually available to all team members, it's easy to transfer processes. Task transferability is easily facilitated, and should an employee who was working on a certain process suddenly fall ill, it would be very easy for another team member to resume the task. The task or process has already been made very clear on the Kanban board and the team member can assess what has been done and carry on with the project, which does not halt production in the long-term.

Chapter 20: Agile Manifesto

The Agile Manifesto was produced in 2001, within which were written the 12 principles and 4 core values of leading an organization to agility.

12 Principles of Agile

Agile guides project teams to follow 12 basic principles that help the teams to implement a project that produces a high-quality product, within a reasonable timeframe. A project executed with agility allows for fast, efficient adaptation by expecting and embracing change.

1. Customer Satisfaction

Customers are more satisfied because the Agile way ensures they are getting software releases in more regular intervals. They can view their product as it evolves instead of having to wait for months or even years for the complete product.

2. Harness Change to Gain a Competitive Edge

The nature of Agile development welcomes change throughout the project even at a late stage of development. This allows the team to harness change in order to give the customer a competitive advantage.

3. Deliver Quality Software in Frequent Releases

The goal of the Agile way is to deliver working releases at short intervals that span from 1 week to 4 weeks, with a preference for the shorter intervals.

4. Developers and the Business must Work Together Daily

Daily collaboration at all levels from the stakeholder, manager, customers, end-users, and the project team should meet frequently face-to-face. This ensures the customers, management, stakeholders, and end-users are up to date on all the latest issues or progress.

5. Empower Team Members by Trusting They Will Get the Job Done

Agile works by assuming that the team members are capable of getting their jobs done and do not need to be micromanaged. The Agile way empowers the team, motivating them to get the job done by ensuring they have everything they need to work, including a healthy working environment.

6. Value Face-to-Face Conversations over Documentation

Although there is minimal documentation, Agile works on a daily-face-to-face conversation, finding these to be a lot more efficient and productive than reams of endless reports and documents.

7. Build every iteration as a Working Module or Feature

Being able to bring each iteration into an operable state marks positive progress and value for the project.

8. All Parties Involved in Development Must Maintain a Constant Pace

All parties involved in the development must be able to commit to seeing the original development through as well as continuous improvement to the system. They must commit with the same vigor throughout production and maintenance of it.

9. Pay Constant Attention to Technical Excellence and Dynamic Design

The development team must constantly be working on ways to improve upon the design of the product and the process of developing it. This enhances the product, process, and developer's skill.

10. Simplicity Equals Value

This means weeding out the features that are "nice to have", "not essential", or "just in case" gets a developer closer to being able to prioritize and develop the essential features and requirements of the product first. This is important for agility in a project to show its true value.

11. The Best Results Come from Self-Organizing Teams

Developers are like artists: they create magic with their coding. When you give an artist a directive but with free reign to create, you are going to get amazing authentic work. Give a developer the canvas and requirements along with the trust to self-organize their priorities, and you are going to get their best efforts.

12. Evaluate, Fine-Tune, and Adjust To Become More Effective

The project team is constantly collaborating on how to fine-tune the process and the product, then adjust parameters to achieve their goals.

The 4 Core Values of Agile

During the development of the Agile Manifesto, the team found that they did not always agree on matters. They were, however, in agreement that through helping others develop software faster, more efficiently, and increase the quality of their work-life, there were 4 core values all were agreed upon.

1. Individual Interactions are More Valuable than Tools or Processes

Agile values teach that individuals should have more value to an organization than tools or processes. The processes and the tools may drive the software development process, but it is the individuals that do the driving of those tools. Without skilled individuals, the tools and processes are not worth much as they cannot drive themselves.

Valuing tools and processes over individuals makes them feel undervalued, with the result being an unhappy workforce.

2. Working Software

Agile is a streamlined process. As such, it calls for less documentation in order to put more time and attention into creating quality working software. It is why they call Agile light on documentation, as it does not eliminate it entirely. It instead uses tools to help automate the document process and make it more visible to all parties involved in the development.

3. Customer Collaboration

Customer collaboration over contract negotiation is valued because it means that the customer is constantly involved in the project from start to finish. As the customer is usually invited to demo's and product reviews, they get to watch their product being developed. This way they can instigate changes throughout the project, which means when the project is delivered it fully meets their requirements.

Historically, the customer was only involved in the initial part of the project where the scope of the product would be discussed. Once this was done and the customer was in agreement, the project went ahead. The next time the customer got to review the product was upon completion. For the customer, this meant that they may not be getting exactly what they wanted. If there were changes to be made they would get tied up in a lengthy change request process.

What this method meant for the team was more long hours and fixes that would have to be traced back through an entire program of code.

4. Responding to Change

Responding to change instead of following a plan gives Agile its agility, as it is designed in short iterations which means changes are easily made and quickly adapted. Features and priorities can change from iteration to iteration, which is why the Agile way embraces change in view that it is what improves a project and adds value to it.

Historically, when a project was designed it was with rigid blueprints that steered clear of change. If the change was necessary it was costly for both the customer and the organization designing the software.

Getting Started with Agile

Agile means having to change the way the business works in terms of having a set purpose and being methodical. Think in terms of a vision that you can inspire the business to align with. In order to change the way others think or work, those who are on a journey towards agility need to emulate that persona themselves.

But that is just the beginning part of the Agile journey. There are a whole lot of steps in between that need to be taken care of as you start to steer the business towards agility.

Understanding the Organization or Current Process

The best place to begin any story or journey is at the beginning, as let's face it: a Captain of the ship does not just wake up one morning knowing all about his ship, how to sail, and then expects a crew to just go on a merry journey with him.

No, he goes through the rigors of getting to know all about boats and how everything works. He needs to know what makes up a sailing crew as well as all the legal, compliance, HR, finance, etc. matters that a leader needs to know.

A great captain would spend some time getting to know exactly how each of the positions on board worked, from the deck cleaners to the bar staff, to the administration, all the way up to the second in charge.

Well, if you are about to take on the challenge of implementing Agile in your organization, you are about to embark on your first voyage to Agility. It is time to make sure you know the organization as best as you can.

One of the keys to moving towards agility is collaboration and the sharing of knowledge. Think of this as the first step to implementing change as you learn the ropes from people who know the ropes.

This includes all the policies, standards, processes, systems, software, departments, and so on. You may not have any impact on them, but you still need to know what function they hold within the business.

Gathering all the Information - Become the End-User

Once you can confidently say you understand the business, it is time to start gathering data to find out the scope of the challenge that lies ahead. When a company first identifies a need for change it is usually because their business product, process, or service is just not meeting customer demands or they are having problems keeping up with market trends. In order to stay afloat in this fast-paced world of ever-changing technology, a company has to move with the times. Especially as customers realize technology can give them more, companies need to keep their products fresh and up to date.

Historically when there was a system upgrade, a full specification of what was required would be drawn up, usually by a team or project manager that had been given the requirements. Following a methodology such as the waterfall method or the V-shaped method, they would go about writing up the product justification, do a cost analysis, start getting a team together, etc.

Once the specifications and team had been signed off, the project manager would go about drawing up an in-depth project plan, complete with job specification, sections of the project each member of the team would be working on, and milestones that were to be accomplished.

The project was looked at as a whole and the customer or business only ever got to see the product once it was finished. Teams were not only bogged down with having to code but all the paperwork that went with it, sit in lengthy team meetings, etc. For all involved in the project, this meant long hours which usually lead to errors from the team members being overtired.

The thing about this method of project management is it usually did not have the outcome that appeased the customer and left an unhappy burned out project team. With the advent of Agile, businesses look at managing a project in a different way.

One of the qualities of Agile was the way the developers of the Agile guidelines thought to look at how software was being designed and developed. They realized that there were two ways to look at any system. One was from the user's point of view, the other from the developer's point of view.

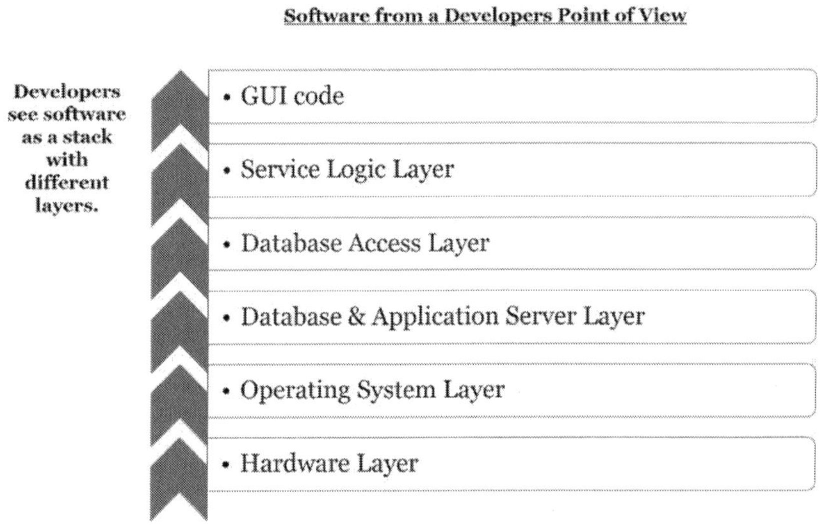

Software from a Developers Point of View

Developers look at software in a series of layers or as a stack.

- GUI code
- Service logic layer
- Database access layer
- Database and Application Server
- Operating system

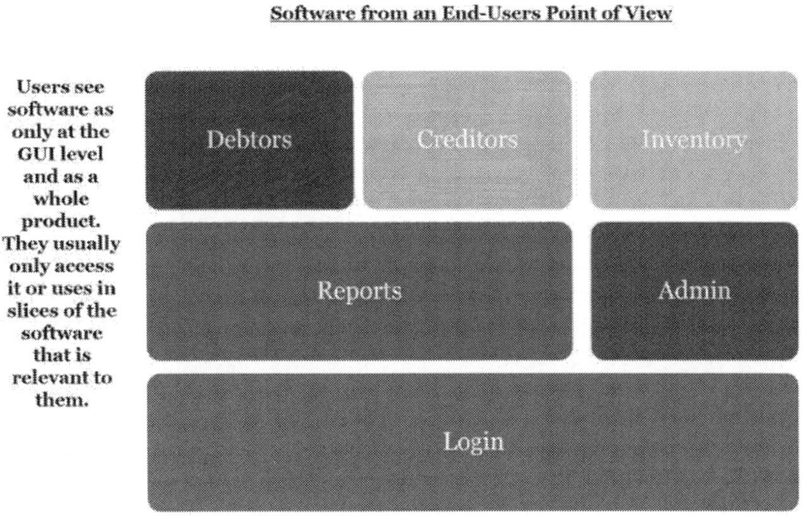

Software from an End-Users Point of View

Unlike the developer, the end-user only sees the software as a whole finished product. Although they are aware that there is a lot more going on behind the scenes of the program, their interest is the part of the software they mostly use.

For instance, Dan is a Debtors clerk so the only part of the software he uses is the Debtors section. Whereas Mary is responsible for inventory and reporting so she is only interested in the Inventory and Reporting parts of the software.

It's Time to Stop Thinking in Layers and to Start Thinking in Slices

If we think of software in terms of a six-layered cake, the developers would be the bakers that had to design, bake, ice, and make sure the cake was perfected before presenting it to the customer. The end-user would be the customer, although they knew there were six different layers to the cake, each with a different frosting, all they are really interested in is their slice of the whole cake they are going to eat.

In order to better develop software of value and be Agile, you will need to look at the software from the user's perspective. Agile teams will have to reprogram the way they think only in stacks and start thinking as the product in slices. The good news is that code is not like building a house or baking a cake. It is not bound by the same physical aspects that say it has to be structured from the base up. In order to know the program or look at it from the end-user's point of view, you need to get to know the software the way they do.In order to understand the software 'slices', you need to become that key user and find out how they do things. Think of it as living the user's story. Take notes, ask questions, and while you are working with them you will be able to start to form a better vision of the way the software needs to develop. It will also help you to better slice up the user's stories when the time comes to break the product down into iterations.

Slicing Up and Iterating User Stories

Although a user-story is not exactly only part of Agile, we use them to describe the user's needs. These stories are usually gathered by the Product Owner or the person that is responsible for the product as a whole. Historically this was the project manager. A user story is a user requirement or wish list for the way the user envisions the product should function so they can do their job to extract value from the software being developed. These can be short, from needing a drag and drop function or a login screen to a long, long list of requirements. For an online store, there may be a need for a catalog, shopping cart, each item needs a detailed page, a checkout feature, payment facilities, order tracker, and maybe even a weekly blog. These are the requirements the person who is responsible for ensuring the application is designed correctly — the Product Owner — will have gathered during their investigations as they collaborate with the key users. It takes a skilled, experienced developer to know how to break a product down into small slices. That is, small slices of the product that could potentially be used as a stand-alone part of the product. Most of the Agile frameworks or methodologies beneath its umbrella are designed to deliver the product in release worthy iterations that take no more than 2 to 4 weeks to complete. So, not only do you have to divide the user stories into workable portions, but they have to be workable portions that take no longer than 2 to 4 weeks to complete. At first glance, you may think, "Okay - so that does not seem like it would be too hard!" But it actually is just a bit more complex than it first seems to be. When the project is scoped and all the requirements are in, the development teams go over all the user stories or requirements. Understanding how the users work and how the modules need to coexist in order for them to perform their daily tasks is an important key to breaking the project down. Non-Agile methods would scope the project and then assign it to a fixed budget for the project as a whole with a suggested timeframe. Any changes would have to go through a change request and the cost would be worked out from the time, effort, and scope of the changes to be made. It also may mean that the entire project plan would need to be adjusted. Tasks would need to be re-assigned affecting the customer's budget and expected delivery dates.Making changes on most projects will probably affect both the delivery dates and costs of a project but it does not have to be on the scale it once was. One of the principles of Agile is: "Simplicity - the art of maximizing the amount of work not done is essential." It is also all about empowering the project team and trusting them to get the job done. Frameworks, like Scrum Framework, believe that learning from the past is the only way forward. Hence the need for experience when it comes to sifting through the user stories in order to group and prioritize. Once they have that, each iteration needs to have an effort level assigned, and then it needs to be time-boxed. Something you will hear often when setting out to a project with agility is at the start, only commit to developing the first iteration.

Why? Because as skilled a developer as a person may actually be, there are many factors that surround creating the iterations. It is not only just the code! There are a whole lot of other variables that need to be considered. Until that first iteration has been developed a person is not going to know how it is all going to work out until it starts.

Chapter 21: Advantages of Scrum Implementation

Advantages of Scrum Implementation

Enough with the praises, though!

If you are reading this book, it is quite likely that you have already heard about how great agile is and the "miracles" it can bring about.

What makes agile project management so good, specifically?

There is a long list of benefits that bring agile project management to everyone's attention — specifically those in software project management, but most definitely not exclusively so.

Better Quality

One of the main tenets of agile project management is that it promises a better product quality.

To get things straight, it's not that products developed via waterfall project management lack in quality. It's just that it is far more likely for an agile-developed product to be qualitative by the point of its full release on the market.

There is very strong logic behind this.

On the one hand, waterfall project management tends to be too strict within its own limits. This means that it is far more likely for mistakes to:

- Be noticed too far out in the process (and waterfall will not allow the team to reiterate the same feature/part of the project)
- Be noticed when the product is already on the market/in review by client

Agile project management is *very* focused on continuous improvement. As such, a product has a much higher chance of actually getting better throughout the development process.

Or, in other words, instead of sweeping all those small (or not so small) mistakes under the rug (as you would do in waterfall project management because you have to follow the *plan*), you will just *deal with them there and then*.

Sounds much more feasible, right?

Better Customer Satisfaction

Another reason that makes agile so advantageous is related to the fact that, by the end of the project, customers tend to be far more satisfied.

How so?

There are a few verticals to consider when it comes to customer satisfaction, and agile makes sure that all of them are properly met. For instance:

- Agile will allow you to change the requirements as per client feedback.

- Agile will force you to release bits of the project as you move along, ergo, it will allow your customer to provide you with input that is easier to implement (due to the small size of the actual bit they are testing).

- Agile will help you deliver a better final product

Given all these factors, it makes all the sense in the world that customers will be happier — throughout the project, as they will be able to request the modifications they need and, at the end of it, as they will receive a product that fits their requirements, purposes, and desires.

Do keep in mind that the same stands true in those cases when the "customer" is an internal stakeholder — such as, for example, when you are managing a software development project meant to be used internally.

Better Transparency

This agile benefit is very tightly connected to what has been mentioned already. When you can ensure better quality and better customer satisfaction, it all comes with greater transparency.

This transparency will manifest itself on all the verticals of project management. You will see better transparency in your team.

You will also see better transparency within the organization, regardless of whether or not the upper management uses the same project management approach as you do.

Finally, you will see better transparency between you and your customer (be it an internal one or an external one). When you constantly ask for feedback and continually improve the product to suit your customer's needs, you create a more genuine relationship with them. You start to truly communicate, rather than engaging in nothing more than ping-pong emails.

Better Control

For those of you used to the premises of waterfall or traditional project management, it might seem that agile is anything *but* control-focused.

In fact, it very much is.

Agile project management allows you to control your project at a granular level, precisely because it encourages (and downright forces) you to split your project into small, bite-sized bits and pieces.

Waterfall project management forces you to lay it all down on paper before everything begins. At the same time, though, it also forces you to stick to the plan even when things go south. And yes, they will eventually go south, one way or another: the client's requirements might change, you might realize something is taking longer than planned, your product might be bugged, or the costs might end up exceeding your expectations.

There are a million things that could go wrong, especially in software project management (where things tend to be more experimental than, let's say, oil drilling, for example).

When you can manage all these things that could go wrong *as* they happen, you gain control over the entire process. Even more, you can use your (bad) experience to improve the process, as well.

Don't take this the wrong way. *Control* is not one and the same as *micromanagement*. You don't have to constantly look over your team's shoulders and manage each tiny detail every step of the way. That would just ruin the bridge of transparency, honesty, and self-discipline you are trying to build between yourself and your team.

Better Predictability

Again, this might seem like it's the exact opposite of what agile project management is all about.

But when you take a closer look, you will realize that agile projects can be better predicted precisely because they are managed step by step.

Let's compare this with baking a cake.

When you buy the boxed mix, you can easily and accurately predict what you are going to get — a decent cake batter you can then personalize according to your tastes. However, you don't know all the ingredients in that boxed mix — and, although the short-term result might be easy to foresee, it might be a bit more difficult to predict what will happen to your body if you continue eating boxed cake every week, for decades on end.

That would be the waterfall project management approach. You are using a mould and hoping that everything in your project will fit that ideal, very predictable format. However, long-term, you have no idea if your project plan won't go against you.

When you bake a cake from scratch and you know where each ingredient comes from, how many calories it has, and how many nutrients it provides your body with, you can predict its effects on your body if you eat the same type of cake for an extended period of time.

Plus, as long as you accurately measure each ingredient's quantity, you will be able to accurately predict how your cake is going to look and taste like. It might take a bit of practice until you learn how to do this correctly but, once you learn its tricks, the cake made from scratch will be more predictable in every single way!

That would be the agile project management approach. It might seem totally unpredictable at first, but the results will become more predictable once you have the right tools and the experience to accurately measure and approximate everything.

Better Risk Management

One of the major downfalls of waterfall project management is connected to the fact that it remains confined within its own tables and spreadsheets.

Waterfall project managers plan everything out at the beginning of the project. Agile project managers do the same. The main difference lies not in *whether* they plan, but in what happens when things don't go according to that plan.

As mentioned before, waterfall tends to sweep risks under the carpet — or, at least, estimate them poorly and through an idealistic point of view.

Agile, on the other hand, doesn't do that. It faces the problems head-on, tackles them, removes them from your path, and then allows you to draw honest conclusions.

As a result, your risk management will improve, as well. When you stop hiding your head in the sand, you can see things more clearly. As such, you can manage any potential risks with more accuracy, as well.

Better ROI

Put every advantage we have already discussed throughout this chapter one on top of the other and you will understand why agile project management tends to lead to better ROI.

Better products + happier clients + better risk management cannot go wrong.

It's a universal formula for success. The more you can manage your money and put out better products, the more likely it is that customers will:

- Come back to you
- Pay on time
- Evangelize and recommend you to other potential customers
- Leave great reviews for your company on various channels

Sounds like a dream?

We prefer to call it *agile*.

Better Metrics

This advantage circles back to the fact that agile won't allow you to just sweep problems under the carpet. It will make you have a face-to-face conversation with these issues, get to know them in-depth, and then tackle them from a stance where you actually know what to do.

Plus, agile project management is a team effort in every respect. From the moment you start splitting your project into smaller chunks, your team will be involved in the process. They will be able to give you real-life estimations on how long everything takes.

Finally, agile project management will allow you to track what is *genuinely* going on, rather than what you idealistically projected to happen.

All of these aspects will eventually lead to better, more accurate, more realistic, and more useful metrics when it comes to team performance, ROI, and time management.

Better Collaboration

If there is one thing absolutely everyone loves about agile project management (aside from the apparent chaos, which, by the way, can become addictive) is the fact that teams just tend to work better when they are managed under an agile method.

Agile project management fosters an environment that focuses on self-discipline, honesty, and taking responsibility. When you have these three ingredients, you create *true* team spirit — the kind where people naturally understand and empathize with each other, where they genuinely want to help each other, and where various types of frustrations and bad feelings don't even take root.

Agile is all about collaboration. The way you collaborate with your team, the way your team members will collaborate among themselves, the way your product manager will collaborate with the client, and the way you will collaborate with other stakeholders and upper management within your company — this will all change for the better.

This is not an empty promise. It lies at the very foundation of what agile is and what this approach aims for.

Better Work-Life Balance

We won't lie.

Not all people who work in agile project management have a great work-life balance.

But, then again, not all people who work in *anything* have a great work-life balance.

It is generally believed that those who work in agile project management (meaning the project managers *and* the teams) tend to have a better work-life balance because they learn how to efficiently manage their time. Therefore, they are much less likely to slack off and prolong their workdays into work nights and work weekends.

They are more likely to get their job done in the time it is supposed to be done — so that in their off hours, they can go back to their families, hobbies, and spare time.

Overall, this can lead to nothing but better, happier, more productive employees.

And we all know how happy *that* makes management, HR, and every single part of your organization, right?

You don't have to take our word for it when it comes to all these benefits. You just have to look at those companies that have embraced agile as part of their structures — they have plenty to say about it and how it has drastically changed their entire way of doing business.

These are just some of the advantages. You might experience all of them, a few of them, or more. In any case, you will definitely enjoy a noticeable, realistic improvement in the way your projects are managed!

12 AGILE PRINCIPLES

01 Our highest priority is to satisfy the customer through early and continuous delivery of valuable software.	02 Welcome changing requirements, even late in development. Agile processes harness change for the customer's competitive advantage.	03 Deliver working software frequently, from a couple of weeks to a couple of months, with a preference to the shorter timescale.
04 Business people and developers must work together daily throughout the project.	05 Build projects around motivated individuals. Give them the environment and support they need, and trust them to get the job done.	06 Agile processes promote sustainable development. The sponsors, developers, and users should be able to maintain a constant pace indefinitely.
07 Working software is the primary measure of progress.	08 The most efficient and effective method of conveying information to and within a development team is face-to-face conversation.	09 Continuous attention to technical excellence and good design enhances agility.
10 Simplicity – the art of maximizing the amount of work not done – is essential.	11 The best architectures, requirements, and designs emerge from self-organizing teams.	12 At regular intervals, the team reflects on how to become more effective, then tunes and adjusts its behavior accordingly.

The Main Principles of Agile Project Management

Agile project management did not come out of the blue.

Those seventeen people didn't just sit down over beer and chips and lay out whatever crossed their minds.

As we have already mentioned, each of them had already experimented with various forms of what they called "lightweight project management" (the term "agile" was more informal at that point, rather than official).

Some had experimented with Kanban, others had experimented with Scrum, and others had experimented with other types of agile project management over the course of the '90s.

When all of it came together, these bright minds came to a conclusion and created what is now known as the *Agile Manifesto*.

There are four main points to the Agile Manifesto — and all of them are mirrored in the *12 Agile Principles*. Together, the Manifesto and the Principles make up the "bible" of agile project management — the nearly sacred rules that lie at the foundation of everything agile under the sun.

We won't dwell too long on either the Manifesto or the Principles, as they will both be emphasized and explored in-depth.

Chapter 22: Criticality of the Scrum Method

Difference between the Project Manager and Scrum Master

Clear meaning of jobs, with regards to a scrum group, is amazingly basic. Numerous organizations tragically mix up such jobs and this prompts a disappointment of the venture. For example, one of the most widely recognized missteps that pretty much every association has is to make no effect between the scrum-ace and the venture administrator.

In all actuality, these two substances are totally extraordinary. They have explicit jobs to perform and once these "work duties" have been recognized and point by point, it can prompt a colossal level of progress.

Arranging as opposed to encouraging

A scrum-ace is the facilitator while an undertaking supervisor is the organizer. The previous is really a "go-between" with regards to the client on one side and the undertaking on the other. However, it is the activity of the undertaking director to take every one of the choices and to do all the arranging that is required for the group and fruitful task the board.

Both these regions require an entirely unexpected range of abilities. A scrum boss will never get into the low down of dealing with the group. While, a task director needs to get every one of the subtleties of the equivalent.

Extent of the board

Regularly, an undertaking administrator will get concerned distinctly about his task and the manner in which it is advancing. It is the activity of the scrum-ace to take a bigger perspective on things and go about as the correspondences conductor between the item proprietor and the task administrator.

Accomplishing things like arranging and audit gatherings and itemizing client experience and in any event, giving input about the usefulness of the item is the activity of a scrum-pioneer.

Distinction in attitude

A few associations pick a scrum-boss from a pool of task administrators. This may not be a fruitful undertaking as a result of the distinction in mental make-up that is required. Ordinarily, a venture chief must be excessively explanatory and very organized in his way to deal with work.

While, a scrum Master may need to manage a great deal of smoothness and dynamism so as to be an effective communicator. Being the guide to the venture, a scrum Master must have the option to consider building connections and critical thinking too. What's more, these are territories that don't loan themselves to an organized methodology!

Not taking certain choices

With regards to choices about the result of the undertaking, at that point the scrum Master will basically not be engaged with the equivalent. Actually, one of the signs of effective scrum undertakings is the way that it has kept these two people totally separated.

Along these lines, on the off chance that the scrum Master is discussing item or task choices, at that point it's anything but a fruitful or powerful scrum approach.

Instructions to Sell Scrum to Your Organization

Reasons why the scrum master role works

1. Devoted bulldozer: Unlike different structures, the job centers one individual around evacuating deterrents. This implies the group can focus on taking care of business.

2. Devoted mentor: The job gives one-individual obligation regarding instructing others. Nobody can "pass the buck" on this. In this manner, one individual has the focal point of helping all individuals from the association to comprehend the system.

3. Fair-mindedness: A scrum ace can be as useful to a group as an item proprietor (see beneath) without picking sides. The main spotlight is on ensuring the system and undertaking is fruitful. This can help take care of issues and increase trust.

4. Duty regarding structure not conveyance: This is practically turn around brain research. The scrum ace is just worried about ensuring the system is completed as the scrum standards state. Separating from the obligation regarding the structure from the duty to convey implies that the individual in question can focus on ensuring that guidelines are pursued which thusly makes a well-oiled machine. On the off chance that the scrum ace's activity is done and everybody in the scrum group is playing out their job, at that point the improvement group can convey.

5. No single purpose of control that could come up short: Since a scrum ace doesn't control the group, the nonattendance of one doesn't leave the group in chaos. The scrum ace sets up a framework that everybody can follow in their nonattendance.

Why the product owner role works

Reasons

1. Time amplified for business quantifiable profit: The item proprietor isn't liable for conveying the work or keeping up the procedure however just for making need calls and keeping up the prerequisites excess. This permits a lot of core interest.

2. Devoted wellspring of necessities: There is nobody else in the association that should be counseled on a task's prerequisites. Senior partner necessities course through the item proprietor for a solitary purpose of contact.

3. One individual answerable for changes in necessities: As the business picture changes just a single individual needs to catch the new prerequisites and update them.

4. Accomplishes the best bargain: Even senior partners should confide in their item proprietor with an official choice. This adjusts the business and makes proper tradeoffs to benefit the item.

5. Adjusts the client and group, day by day: This job is the interface between the business and the group. Their essence at all the scrum gatherings implies that the group is continually following up on the most recent data.

REASONS WHY THE DEVELOPMENT TEAM ROLE WORKS Reasons

1. A gathering of committed specialists: Explicitly getting the group out as specialists, implies that scrum groups are collected to take care of issues without anyone else. This opens up different jobs to concentrate without anyone else specialized topics.

2. Adaptable to business needs: Scrum groups adjust to a given circumstance so as to get an item augmentation constructed. Any choices ought to be attached distinctly to a business prerequisite. This thus gives a business long and transient adaptability and lessens squandered exertion for focused exertion.

3. Lean and financially savvy: The little size joined with high level of ability implies that things complete to a high level of value with insignificant specialized correspondence.

4. Less administration required: Teams sort out themselves. This implies every other person can focus on their own job.

5. Profoundly adaptable when given the asset: Large groups can be isolated and composed through customary gatherings called scrum-of-scrums. The groups each have scrum experts to keep them composed. Proviso - when at least two groups deal with a similar code-base, the group should choose if this is attainable.

Scrum Master Faces: Some Common Problems to Expect

The Scrum Master has the essential job of encouraging this work technique and guaranteeing that there is no obstacle in the group's endeavors at accomplishing their dash target. Nonetheless, little glitches and unforeseen blunders consistently happen, and some are normal to such an extent that all scrum bosses ought to have some readied or imminent arrangements prepared for them. It isn't just efficient and proficient, yet in addition takes into account the honing of one's emergency the executives capacities over the long haul.

One of the most well-known issues that happen is that the item proprietor can't give the group the item build-up in time. Not knowing the needs of the item proprietor, it is hard for an improvement group to go forward in real life.

In such a situation, the scrum ace can look over among different alternatives, contingent on the definite conditions. Either the whole group could be permitted to enjoy a reprieve from dashing, particularly if the deferral should be by a day or two. Then again, an advancement group could likewise continue with its arranging gatherings without offering need to overabundance, particularly if the group has just finished some effective runs.

The group would then be able to make an unfinished version of needs in the event that they know about the general course the item is taking and present it to the Product Owner for endorsement or change. Additionally, the group could enjoy this reprieve as a chance to survey their work and assemble criticism so as to further improve the scrum procedure.

Another issue which is genuinely normal, particularly in MNC's the place a lot of work is directed abroad, is that severe time boxed dashes are not kept up. Notwithstanding, to guarantee that the scrum example is pursued, a severe approach ought to be pursued wherein such rupture of system is unsatisfactory. On the off chance that outrageous circumstances are confronted, the run consummation can work upon a model of motivations also. Likewise, in many situations, abroad units are generally ignorant of Scrum and how it functions. Along these lines, legitimate preparing, yet a compact, short one must be directed for generally the cruising will not be smooth.

Chapter 23: Scrum Team

Scrum is a framework that has to be adapted to the production environment in which it is being used. It is not a method that tells the development team what to do but rather lists what needs to be done. The Scrum framework is a flexible tool that encourages the Scrum team to prioritize and map out the product's roadmap as a collaborative effort.

If applied correctly, Scrum can help a development team produce high-quality products by maximizing their time and effort. This is done in a self-organizing way, whereby each team member takes on the responsibility for their role in the development of the project.

To ensure the success of a Scrum implementation, there are certain rules, processes, role assignments, and values that must be properly applied.

Scrum Team

There are three major roles in a small Scrum team, which is usually no bigger than 9 to 10 members. The team must be small enough to work in collaboration with each other and is usually located within the same space or at least have powerful online tools to keep the team members in constant communication with each other.

The main roles are:

Development Team

The development team consists of the developers that are a group of highly skilled individuals capable of self-organizing their workload and collaborating with their team members to make sure they are all working toward the same goal.

Characteristics of the Development Team

- Responsible and confident enough to optimize their workload as they are empowered by the organization to do so.

- They have cross-functional skills that ensure that they can work on all aspects of the product increments.

- Regardless of what their work is, all developers share the same title to ensure everyone is equal across the team.

- Accepts that accountability for the project goes to the team as a whole unit, regardless of their skills.

- Only the development team can create an increment, and all the team members have to agree for the increment to be 'Done'.

Product Owner

The Product Owner has the responsibility of ensuring that the Product Backlog reflects the needs and requirements of the business or the customer for the system in development. They have to ensure the value of the product that is delivered by the development team.

Characteristics of the Product Owner

- They are capable of creating a clearly defined Product Backlog.

- They are responsible for and capable of ensuring the Backlog Items are properly ordered and have a function or feature that is of value to the product.

- Must keep the Product Backlog clearly updated and visible for all to see at all times.

- They must ensure that the development team has a clear understanding of each item on the product board.

Scrum Master

The Scrum Master is the referee of the team and has to make sure that the team understands the rules, works according to the values, and ensures that everyone has the means and tools to achieve their goals.

The Scrum Master must make sure the product is being kept in line and must be the one to mediate any problems or iterations that do not stay on track. The Scrum Master is there to support and coach the team through the project.

The Scrum Master has to balance various interactions between the stakeholders and the development team. He is the one that will coach the team through various changes and interactions that add value to the product being developed.

The Scrum Master, in essence, serves three groups.

Scrum Master Interactions with the Product Owner

- Ensures that all the goals of the Product Backlog are clear and understood by the entire team.
- Helps the Product Owner constantly find techniques for effective management of the Product Backlog.
- Helps the Product Owner organize the Product Backlog to ensure it has maximum impact in order to create value.
- Helps the Product Owner facilitate requested events.

Scrum Master Interactions with the Development Team

- Ensures that all the goals of the Product are clearly understood.
- Helps the development team to self-organize.
- Helps to facilitate events that require immediate change as and when they arise.
- Ensures the Daily Scrum runs when planned and tries to find effective solutions for problems that may have arisen.

Scrum Master Interactions with the Stakeholders/Organization/Customers

- Coaches the organization as to the Scrum framework.

- Helps to plan the Scrum implementation with the help of the organization/stakeholders/customers.
- Collaborates with other Scrum Masters in the organization to ensure the effectiveness of Scrum throughout the organization.

Scrum Values

In order for Scrum to work for the organization, the Scrum team must be able to commit to learning to work by the five Scrum values. These values are what embody the pillars of Scrum which are transparency, inspection, and adaptation.

5 Values of Scrum

1. COMMITMENT

Each team member commits to doing their best to ensure they achieve their goals and by so doing, achieve the goals of Scrum.

2. COURAGE

Each team member must show they have the courage to soldier on through tough times/problems, and always do the right thing.

3. FOCUS

Each team member's focus should be on the goals of the Sprint in order to achieve the overall goals of the Scrum team.

4. OPENNESS

There must be open communication between the team members, management, and stakeholders. All problems or roadblocks must be reported and challenges brought to the necessary parties' attention.

5. RESPECT

Each team member must respect the other team members and what they have to offer the team.

Scrum Rules

In order to achieve the goals of Scrum, there are 12 basic rules that should be followed in order to ensure that development runs at its optimum, spares no wasted time, and delivers the expected product.

12 Basic Rules of Scrum

1. There is a 'Sprint Planning' meeting for every Sprint.
2. The 'Sprint Planning' meeting is time boxed, usually to 2 hours per meeting.
3. Every Sprint should take the same length of time.
4. There should be no breaks between sprints. When one finishes, the next one should start after the planned Sprint meeting.
5. Each Sprint should be designed with the intent to demonstrate the software at the end of the Sprint.
6. A Daily Scrum must be held every day for the duration of the project.
7. The Daily Scrum must be time boxed to 15 minutes or less.
8. After every Sprint, there is a Sprint review.
9. The Sprint Review should be time boxed to 2 hours.
10. There should be a Sprint Retrospective meeting after every Sprint Review. No new Sprint should start without the Sprint retrospective.
11. The Sprint Retrospective meeting should be time boxed to 2 hours.
12. The Scrum Master is responsible for making sure everyone follows the Scrum rules.

Scrum Events

Scrum works with prescribed events in order to cut down on those emergency meetings that are not planned into the already tight schedule of the day.

Each Scrum event is time boxed, which means that it is given a set time to completion or a maximum duration. Anything that is not done or declared within that time frame must be moved over or left off. Kind of like predefined sizes of packing boxes, if the item does not fit in the box, it must be put into the next box or determined whether it is needed at all.

Sprint

The Sprint is the main Scrum event and has strict rules that govern the planning, developing, and ending of a Sprint. There is also a recommended procedure for canceling a Sprint.

The Scrum framework works on the concept of breaking a project down into smaller, more manageable projects. The goal of the Sprint is to be able to release at least a workable demo or functional portion of the project. When a Sprint is completed it is marked as "Done" by the development team who all have to be in agreement that the Sprint is ready.

Each Sprint will consist of its own little project plan which consists of what is being developed, how it is going to be developed, and how much effort it is going to take to develop it.

Every Spirit must come with the flexibility to be able to change and adapt at any given time during the Sprint's life cycle.

Every Sprint can take no longer than 1 month (30 days) to complete. If the Sprint is going to take any longer, it needs to be broken down further.

For Every Sprint, There Must Be the Following Events:

- Sprint Planning

This is where all the planning of the Sprint is done. It is here that the Development team collaborates over what features are needed in the Sprint.

Sprint planning has a time box that is set to a maximum of 8 hours. The meeting is held by the Scrum Master who oversees the entire proceedings.

The Product Owner ensures that the team clearly understands the goal of the Sprint and fits the required functionality.

During the meeting, the team discusses topics such as:

- What items from the Product Backlog can the team put in the Sprint?
- How will the team proceed to get the work done in order to complete the Sprint?
- The goal of the Sprint.

- Daily Scrum

This is a time boxed daily event of up to 15 minutes that all team members are expected to attend. It is here that work for the day is planned out and discussed to ensure every team member is still set on the correct path.

It is here that the team collaborates on problems that may have arisen the previous day. All members leave the meeting with a clear view of how close they are to completing the project or Sprint.

These daily meetings have been shown to increase the probability of both the Sprint and overall project getting completed on time and conforming to a high standard.

- Sprint Development

This is where all the actual development work gets done by a team of highly skilled individuals. Each team member works toward a common goal of completing the project on time and meeting all the project requirements.

- Sprint Review

At the end of each Sprint, the team along with the stakeholders have a Sprint review where the product is inspected. This is where the team gets to show the stakeholders the outcome of the Sprint Development and ensure they know what features went into the Sprint.

It is at this review that the team discusses how they will optimize the next Sprint and goes over what could be done in the next Sprint to optimize the value of the next Sprint.

The product is usually reviewed in this meeting in order for the team to get valuable feedback from the stakeholders and to get to schedule any changes or fixes to the Sprint that may be needed. In some cases, they view whether or not the Sprint is needed at all, especially if something has changed in the project since the last Sprint Review.

- Sprint Retrospective

This is where the Sprint team gets together for a maximum of a 2-hour meeting in order to go over what they can do to improve upon the next Sprint. This meeting takes place after the Sprint Review and before the next Sprint starts.

Each Sprint is inspected with regard to the people developing the Sprint to discuss how well they handled the work and any pitfalls that could be avoided in the next Sprint.

The team discusses any extra tools that may be needed, processes that could be improved upon, or teamwork that needs to be addressed.

The meeting is overseen by the Scrum Master to make sure the meeting is a productive one that does not run over the allotted time box.

Scrum Artifacts

A Scrum Artifact is an item that is designed to add value to the project and that maintains a history or clearly defined information for all to see in order to gauge the project status.

Scrum Artifacts include:

Product Backlog

The Product Backlog is the wish list or requirement list that makes up the entire product or system that needs to be designed, developed, and implemented by a skilled team of Scrum Developers.

The Product Backlog is the sole responsibility of the Product Owner to maintain and ensure that any fixes, patches, new features, and so forth are listed as and when they are asked for.

The Product Backlog gets added to on the fly and can be ordered, prioritized, and then re-ordered and re-prioritized. The Product Owner must work on the assumption that the list is never fully complete.

The Product Backlog list is also maintained well after the initial projects as there are always calls for bug fixes, updates, upgrades, etc.

Sprint Backlog

The Sprint Backlog is a mini Product Backlog and contains only the items that are required to make up the Sprint. It identifies all the work that the Scrum Development team has listed as necessary to complete a part of the project.

The Sprint Backlog is updated and tracked on a daily basis to determine the progress of the Sprint and ensure that is it going to meet the required completion target date.

The Sprint Backlog is developed and maintained by the Scrum Development team and overseen by the Scrum Master.

Artifact Transparency

It is the duty of both the Scrum Master and Product Owner to ensure that the Scrum Artifacts are available for all to see in order to monitor the project's progress. Transparency is one of the pillars of Scrum and is one of the main reasons it is so efficient.

The Scrum Master must, therefore, make sure that the information about the Artifacts is updated every day and positioned such that is visible.

Scaling Scrum

Scrum was originally intended for a single Scrum team working incrementally on a larger project.

But as industry standards change and more organizations are adopting the Scrum framework, there arose a demand for more than one Scrum team to work on even larger and more complex projects.

As most processes and systems today are scalable, Scrum found a way to make the Framework scalable. It is based on the principle that if Scrum can be scaled for a small team, it should be able to be scaled to adapt to larger projects requiring multiple teams.

Scaling Scrum can occur at one of three levels namely: Programs, Portfolios, and Projects. The problem that Scrum encountered with Scaling to multiple teams was in how they collaborated and the organization of that collaboration.

This is where the Scrum of Scrums meetings come in. Instead of the entire project team meeting each day, representatives of each small Scrum team meet. In this meeting, they will discuss similar topics to what is discussed at a Daily Scrum meeting, only at a more complex level.

Because it is not always possible to house team members in the same location, be it nationally or globally, the Scrum of Scrum meetings allows for video conferencing, so each team member has the chance to meet face to face. This meeting in itself can pose a challenge for the Scrum Masters to coordinate due to different time zones, cultures, etc.

Scaling gets a little more complex depending on the project and may even need the Scrum of Scrums of Scrums meeting where representatives of each team get together to discuss and coordinate sections of projects that directly relate to teaching others.

Scrum Estimation

Estimation is the process whereby the entire Scrum team works out an estimated total time for various tasks and sprints.

After the prioritization of the Product Backlog items are done and the Product Owner has approved the prioritization and ensured that all the User Stories are clear and concise, they are ready for estimation.

User Story Points are used to estimate the size of the Product Sprint.

The effort that is needed for the increment is determined by past experience.

Estimation Techniques

Each User Story is estimated as to the degree of difficulty it presents. In order to determine the difficulty level, there are several types of scales that are used in Scrum.

- Numeric Scale which is number 1 through to 10.
- Fibonacci Sequence runs from 1, 2, 3, 5, 8, 13, 21, and so on.
- T-shirt sizes that are scaled as XS, S, M, L, XL, XXL, XXXL.
- Dog breeds that go from a Chihuahua to a Great Dane.

The entire Scrum team chooses the scale that works best for them and is to be used for the duration of the project.

Chapter 24. Empirical Process Control

Scrum Pillars of Improvement

The three pillars that uphold the scrum framework are transparency, inspection, and adaptation.

Transparency

The success of any project is achieved by getting all parties engaged, working together, and committed to the project's goals and objectives. For this to happen, each member needs to feel wanted and that they are an important asset in the project by having access to all the information that pertains to the project. Therefore, all parties must present the facts as they are and be transparent in their relationships with others which cultivates trust and collaboration.

Scrum encourages healthy communication through Scrum ceremonies within the team and using demos across teams. Sharing information across teams helps engage others in resolving issues or offering alternative methods to tackle particular tasks. It makes sense to share information with other teams in the project or department because you will be working towards the general good.

Transparency also makes it easier to resolve problems. Needless to say, it is very difficult to identify an issue if not all the cards are on the table. However, with transparency in an organization it is easy to follow the course of activities and identify a mishap. If issues are resolved this way without assigning blame, the organization gains a competitive advantage because it is able to address issues very fast, preventing more complications and possible damage.

Inspection

In Scrum, inspection does not refer to the assessment done by an inspector but the evaluation that is done by everyone on the team. Team members are obliged to inspect the processes, practices, products, people issues, and the improvements being made.

The Scrum users should be allowed to inspect the progress of the development process as well as the deliverables. This way, they can identify any undesirable aspects. However, the inspection should not be done so frequently such that it will interfere with the project development process. It is advisable that such inspections be done by individuals who are skilled. If not done well, a wrong product could be developed which will be rejected by customers. Always inspect the product being developed.

Being critical is not being judgmental, fault finding, negative or looking for someone on whom to place blame. Inspection is only done with the intention of improvement. Scrum's projects are only required to improve with time to deal with the issues that a team could come up with and increase productivity by making incremental changes.

Inspection is done during the daily scrum and the retrospectives and requires transparency within the team and across the organization. Without full knowledge, the inspection would prove difficult.

Inspection does not only benefit the development team, but the product team as well. After a careful inspection of what has been produced so far, the product team may decide to start rolling out the project into the hands of the consumers and get useful feedback. The feedback allows them to make changes to ensure that what is being produced is right and that it will meet needs in the market.

The most important thing to remember when doing a Scrum inspection is doing it in a non-blaming and non-judgmental way. The key is not in finding out whose is at fault; but it is in finding out what has happened, what can be done about it, what the team can learn from it, and how to make improvements in the future.

During the inspection process, the inspector may find that some aspects of project development are not in line with what was agreed. This can result in a product which is unacceptable. This calls for the process to be adjusted so that it can be in line with what was agreed. Such adjustment should be made immediately so that further deviations can be prevented. If adaptation is delayed the deviation may go too far, and it may become hard to correct it.

Adaptation

Unless the team has all the tools they will need to make changes to what they have done, inspection is pointless. It is not enough to identify and point at issues and mistakes correctly, there needs to be a capacity to make changes. Scrum has a 'fail fast, fail often' policy that teams use to address and uncover issues very fast. It allows the team to see the incredible contribution it is making and only work towards enhancing that.

Therefore, as the project progresses, a Scrum team increases its pace while an ordinary team will slow down and lose interest. Adaptation for the team, just like inspection, means that the team looks at its progress so far and identifies places that would require improvement as a team and how to pursue this success going forward.

Another reason for adaptation is the fact that many factors shift during the development process. There could arise a crisis, new priorities, upsizing or downsizing, leadership change, market disruptions, and world events that will shake up the course of the project. A traditional team would have a difficult time restructuring the already planned work and adapting to the constantly changing realities. The team will have to renegotiate budgets, change requests, make new contracts, and other activities that derail progress. However, teams using the Scrum framework can adjust to changes easily and hence deliver relevant valuable products.

It is critical to take note of the fact that the three pillars are not just useful for addressing problems, they are also used to measure successes and help the teams capitalize on their strengths. The pillars also help teams identify their strengths and take advantage of their competitive advantage.

Chapter 25: Events

Scrum projects are carried out through a series of events, which are geared towards producing all of the project deliverables. Additionally, there are other Scrum Events which serve to manage timelines and quality of the deliverables, as well as conduct self-appraisals of the overall Scrum (and Sprint) processes that were followed, and adopt measures to streamline them where necessary.

The Scrum Agile Framework uses artifacts to be able to offer information that is accurate about the product; what occurs while it is under development, the tasks currently being planned, and also the activities currently done. You will find numerous artifacts which could be feasible in a task, though the primary are: The product Backlog which is list of all the specifications, features, functions, and repairs that would must be produced on the item for any later releases. As the product is consumed, feedback is provided and also the backlog changes and gets bigger.

It is actually easy for the Backlog to change totally based on technology, business needs, and market conditions. It is ever evolving; so as long as the item exists, so also will the item Backlog. Usually the things in the item Backlog possess a description, order, estimate, and value given to them. It is not a completed list, and continually changes based on what the item requires at the moment.

It is a listing which is customized throughout the process; anytime new work appears; the Scrum team provides it with the Sprint Backlog. Usually things on the Sprint Backlog are deemed not needed, therefore it's likely that various regions of the program may be taken out of the list. Just the Scrum Team can in fact modify the Sprint Backlog during a Sprint. It is created specifically for everyone on the team also allows them to stay on course and focused.

They normally use this info after the task is done. And this info is likewise used-to assist the team to determine the number of Product Backlog objects are selected during Sprint Planning.

The Sprint's objective is delivering Increments which clearly show the products likely functionality when launched, and also an Increment of product functionality is presented with each Sprint. And also, as the Scrum Team usually spends more hours working in concert, the definition of Increment should grow to incorporate stronger criteria for increased benefits.

It is common practice for everyone and any items to get an Increment for any work carried out on them. The primary take-away from this is that the Product Backlog and also the Sprint Backlog are being used to describe work that has to be completed, work that will bring value to the venture.

Here are the scrum events:

The Sprint

Within the Scrum Framework, all project activities designed to deliver items in the Scrum Product Backlog are performed via an event known as the Sprint (or "Iteration"). Sprints are usually confined to durations of between 1 and 4 weeks.

The objective of the sprint is to create the ideal conditions so that the project team "sprints" to finish all of the deliverables that are on the Sprint Backlog.

Sprint Planning

Team members are allowed to freely express their views on whether the commitments can be met, or if they see potential hurdles in delivery. Once the team has agreed upon what is to be included in the current Sprint, they commence discussing HOW to deliver on the WHAT.

The HOW session takes all of the WHAT deliverables and breaks them down into specific tasks, estimates timelines for them, and assigns responsibilities for each task to individuals (or groups) on the project team.

The Scrum Team meets at the start of every Sprint, and also it's below exactly where they determine and commit to some Sprint Goal. The Product owner provides the item Backlog, clearly shows the tasks, as well as asks the team to buy the tasks they wish to focus on. The Scrum Team also figures out the demands which is utilized to help stated purpose and can be utilized within the Sprint. Additionally, the Scrum Team is going to identify the single jobs it'll take for each particular requirement.

Daily Scrum

A short, fifteen-minute conference which is held every single day in a Sprint and also with the Scrum Master. During this particular conference, the Scrum Team members coordinate on the priorities. They discuss what's most crucial to get accomplished throughout the day, what they finished in the past, and in case there can be some hurdles they may encounter when practicing the present day's work. Doing this aids the streamlining of everything, and also prevents some problems showing up unexpectedly. The Scrum Master facilitates the Daily Scrum Meetings and participation of all team members is mandatory. These meetings are "stand up" sessions, and should be no more than 15-minutes in duration. If there are significant items flagged during the session, they should not be ignored due to lack of time. "Off line" meetings could be scheduled to deal with such items separately.

Sprint Review

Since each Sprint is meant to culminate with completion of certain deliverables, this implies that the Sprint Review will be held once those deliverables have, in fact, been completed.

Sprint Retrospectives are sort of similar to a Sprint Review, this is a conference which happens after every project or Sprint. Nevertheless, it's not led by the item owner, but by the Scrum Team themselves together with the Product owner. They explain what went well, what changes which are possible that they can make, and also how they can create all those improvements. Additionally, they discuss the way to make the team work more effective in case there are issues taking place. It is essential to speak up about problems, otherwise, it can create problems later on which could stop the project from continuing.

Sprint Cycle

Creating a team of individuals to achieve a thing as advanced as the Scrum procedure can be a tough task. It is required that you make sure that everybody is working towards the same goal, and also involves a certain procedure known as the Group Development Process. This procedure is a five step system which ensures the Scrum team is as effective as they can be.

The first four stages are Forming, Norming, Storming, as well as Performing. These stages are needed for the Scrum Team to develop and applying this method will help them to assess difficulties, find solutions, plan work, tackle problems, as well as provide the very best outcomes possible.

It is interesting to be aware that, especially in Agile application development, teams will display a behavior known as swarming. This is when the team comes together to focus and collaborate on solving a singular issue. This action is adapted from whenever a swarm of bugs is centered on the same event, like a swarm of wasps attacking someone because said person determined it will be a good idea to hit the wasp's nest with a baseball bat.

Using the Group Development Process strategy results in maturity along with a very effective Scrum Team. It is important to remember that at times a procedure done this way can take time. Many businesses are definitely more concerned with quick results and jumping into things instantly, without worrying about just how vital team development is. Using a technique this way is going to lead to good results.

Forming scrum teams

For a Scrum project to run successfully, the Scrum Master should identify the right team members. A Scrum team should be made up of several members with each member possessing some expertise in a particular field. The members of the development team are expected to be independent, customer-focused, self-motivated, collaborative and responsible. The team should be capable of creating an environment which accommodates group decision-making and independent thinking so that they can reap the maximum benefits from the structure.

The Scrum Master facilitates the formation of new teams.

The following are the steps necessary to form a new Scrum team:

Initial Meting

In this step, the assembled team has to discuss the roadmap, development vision and high-level features. Initially, they have to work independently on their work and act like a group of people instead of a team. At this stage, there is no clear alignment and trust, so the team members must avoid conflict and focus on agile planning and information collection.

The Scrum Master has to work to promote positive behaviors of the team. Teaching and directive style of leadership is used at this stage. The activities given below are done:

- Orienting all members of the Development Team through a kick-off workshop.
- Creating a conducive working environment capable of aiding collaboration.
- Engaging with customers, businesses and stakeholders.
- Encouraging and guiding the team on how to handle challenging topics.

Storming

The members begin to air their opinions and challenge any situations they feel to be wrong or unfair to them. Arguments and personality clashes raise tensions in relationships. It is hard to make decisions at this stage due to the high level of uncertainty. The Scrum Master jumps in to help the team members resolve their conflicts and disagreements. The style of leadership changes to provision of guidance through coaching and mentoring. In the storming stage, the Scrum Master has the following roles:

- Facilitating workshops during which conflicts will be identified and resolved.
- Showing the value in diversity and differences and empathizing tolerance.
- Promoting values and principles of Agile.

Planning the Sprint

Any work that is going to be generated during the Sprint should first be discussed during the Sprint Planning portion of Sprint. This plan should be created in a collaborative fashion and include the entirety of the Scrum team. Sprint Planning should be kept to less than eight hours each month, with shorter Sprints having shorter planning periods as well.

When it comes to determining exactly how the work in question is going to be completed, the development team determines this aspect of the process after the Sprint Goal has been created and the next round of backlog items has been chosen. The development team has complete control when it comes to determining how best to add the chosen functionality to the next increment. This work will naturally require varying levels of effort and work from smaller groups within the development team of various sizes.

Any backlog items that are chosen should all work to deliver on a single element of the products function, which is often reflected in the goal for the specific Sprint as well. It can also be any other type of coherence that serves to keep the development team working together towards a common goal as opposed to splintering into numerous smaller, more personal, goals.

While the development team is in the midst of a Sprint, it should also keep the Sprint Goal and what is required to see it completed successfully in mind. If during the Sprint, the work takes an unexpected turn it is then the responsibility of the development team to speak to the product owner to ensure that the Sprint can proceed successfully.

Daily Scrums are vital when it comes to ensuring open communication between the development team, often to the point that they remove the need for other meetings entirely, thus naturally increasing productivity as a result. They also make it possible for the entire team to be aware of any impediments to the Sprint as quickly as possible. Their daily nature also ensures the team has the ability to make decisions quickly while improving their knowledge at the same time. As such, it is a key component when it comes to the Sprint's ability to improve thanks to adaptation and inspection.

The Norming Stage

After reaching an agreement and a consensus, the team begins to show cooperativeness and cohesiveness. Each member understands his or her role, and the ground rules are laid. The team members begin to take responsibility and show togetherness towards a mutual success. Due to accountability, they start to understand the contributions of each member.

Now that the team is empowered, they begin to assume authority, and the leadership style is changed to emphasize facilitation and support to the team. The Scrum Master's tasks include:

- Organizing the customer workshops.
- Organizing the external activities so as to increase socialization.
- Developing a community of mentoring and practice.
- Focusing on incremental improvement and constant innovation.
- Preventing conflicts from occurring.
- Helping and facilitating the organization as a whole to support the team.

This stage is actually about cohesion within the team. It is essential for every part to accept each other's efforts and to undertake in community building while making an effort to resolve team issues. Team members should be prepared to alter their prior opinions and ideas when presented with information from various other team members by asking questions of one another. The team acknowledges that leadership is discussed and there's no demand for any cliques. Having all of the members get to find out about one another as well as discuss with one another is essential in strengthening trust, which then contributes to the improvement of the group as a whole.

It is also crucial that you have established rules for the way the team operates in every meeting. The workers have to talk about strategies, like place of the conference, how long the conference usually takes, and what time it begins. They have to discuss how the conference is going to flow and what you should do in case conflicts happen. Inclusion plays a crucial job within the Scrum Team. Every group member must feel that they belong, so they really participate in all of the activities. The primary objective is finding a set of rules that everybody is able to agree to and really follow. Doing this can assist the team to work as best as possible.

The team is going to feel a sense of companionship and relief whenever interpersonal conflicts are resolved. In this particular stage, imagination is high; there is a feeling of sharing and openness of info, both on a private and job level. Everyone feels great about being a part of a team which gets things done. The one downside at this point is the fact that the users resist change of every type and fear scandals that could lead to the future breakup of the team. They might determine the sole method to stay away from said breakup is by resisting forming it in the first place.

The Performing Stage

Once the roles have been established the team is capable of focusing on a similar goal, which will in turn lead to success. A skilled and motivated team working in a self-organized way can address issues quickly. The team is now empowered fully and capable of providing solutions to any problem on their own.

The following are the roles of the Scrum Master during this stage:

- Encouraging a high level of autonomy.

- Supporting the team members to grow in alignment with the project goals.
- Facilitating disengagement activities and development review.

Adjourning Stage

This stage was not initially a part of the task and was inserted in later years. But because it had been put in at a later period does not indicate it's any less critical! At this stage in time, the team has almost certainly fulfilled the task vision. While the complex side of things is finished, the team has to determine points on an individual level. They have to focus on just how they worked together as a group and see if there can be some improvements which may be made.

The team also recognizes achievements and participation. They could also use this as a chance to say private goodbyes. The team worked closely with each other on a rigorous project. It is essential to wrap things up on an individual level, or else there may be a sensation of incompleteness. And what if the team gets back together on any future jobs? It is crucial they go over the procedure and methodologies that succeeded and also aspects that failed.

The team is able to go through and decide in case there is anything that could be salvaged with a small amount of change. Information gathered during this particular time could even be utilized for performance evaluations. Thus, it is crucial that the team takes this stage seriously. At times it can be hard to stay within the stages. There may be a person that's particularly stubborn, or perhaps some folks simply do not particularly work effectively with others.

There are a few distinct measures that a team is able to take to make sure they build correctly through the various stages. The team has to ensure they change up the duty of team facilitator. Each person must have an opportunity to be in charge as well, as doing this creates a sensation of equality and inclusion. The mission and purpose of the group has to be clear to other members involved. And the quest really should be looked over often.

Individuals are likely to respond much better and are even more accepting of other's in the case that they feel they have had the opportunity to be heard. Each session must end with criticism that is constructive rather than destructive. It is essential to lift one another up and be useful towards one another rather than putting one another down. And it is also essential to keep in mind that the constructive criticism needs to be about the group approach and be nothing personal. Everyone should contribute as well as perform the work.

The above steps should produce a working Scrum team. Keep in mind that the teams may have to revert to the earlier stages of the model in the case of unexpected market conditions or the addition of a new team member.

Chapter 26: Artifacts

Scrum artifacts - results/products of our management activities - are designed to increase transparency of information related to the delivery of the project, and provide opportunities for inspection and adaptation.

There are six artifacts in Scrum:

1. Product Backlog: An ordered list of everything (aka stories) that might be needed in the final product
2. Sprint Backlog: Selected items (stories) from the Product Backlog to be delivered through a Sprint, along with the Sprint Goal and plans for delivering the items and realizing the Sprint Goal
3. Increment: The set of all the Product Backlog items completed up to the end of a certain Sprint
4. Definition of "Done": The shared understanding of what it means for a piece of work to be considered complete
5. Monitoring Progress towards a Goal: The performance measurement and forecast for the whole project
6. Monitoring Sprint Progress: The performance measurement and forecasts for a single Sprint

Items 5 and 6 might look more like activities, but they are considered artifacts in the Scrum Guide, and therefore we will explain them as so. You can imagine their output (tracking information, burn-down charts, etc.) as the real artifacts and these two items as ongoing activities (like Product Backlog grooming) or part of the Scrum events (part of Sprint Review and Daily Scrum).

Artifact 1: Product Backlog

The Product Backlog is an ordered list of everything that might be needed in the final product of the project, in other words parts of the expected final product (a wishlist). All items are described in simple business language (non-technical) and all of them are presentable to every stakeholder. Every requirement and every change in the project will be reflected in the Product Backlog.

The Product Backlog is dynamically changing and improving; it is never complete. We do not wait until the Product Backlog is complete to start delivering the items; the first Sprint can be started as soon as the Product Backlog is showing the near future.

The Product Owner sets a number of factors to determine the value of each item for the business; return on investment is usually one of the factors. All these factors will be summarized into one value (importance) and this is shown with each item.

The Product Backlog items will then be ordered based on their value, in a way that the higher an item is, the sooner it will be delivered by the Development Team. As the items located at top of the Product Backlog will be delivered sooner, they will also be more detailed and clear compared to the lower items.

The next figure shows a sample set of Product Backlog items presented in a number of cards.

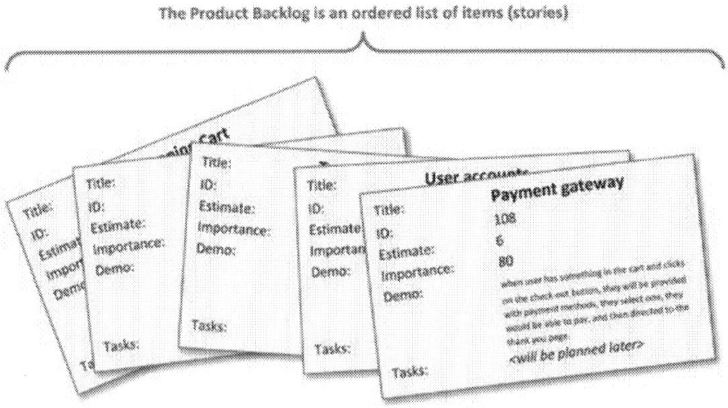

Each Product Backlog item also has a work estimate. These estimates are solely done by the Development Team, and are used in comparison to the capacity of the Development Team in a single Sprint, to determine the number of items that will be selected for that certain Sprint. Many additional information might be added to each item to help the Scrum Team take control.

This figure shows the type of information available for a single Product Backlog item in a typical Scrum tool. This is also a good example of a Scrum tool.

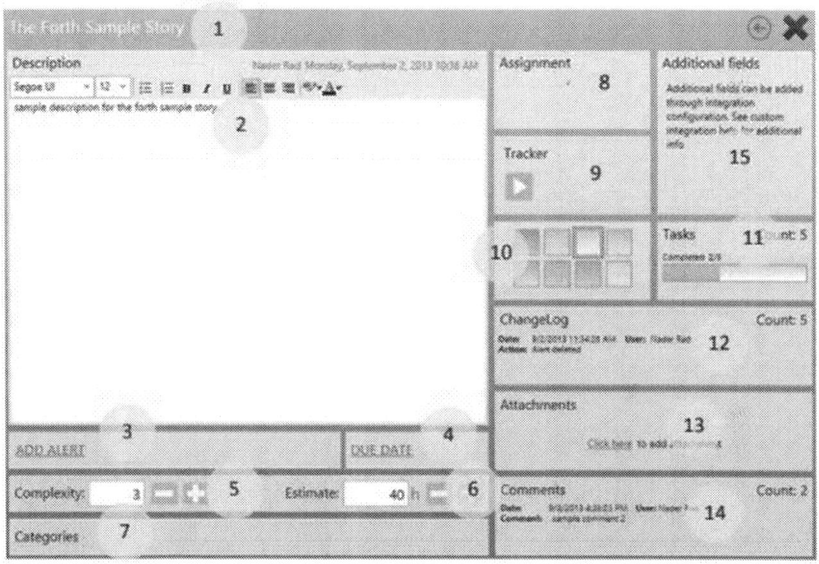

A sample screenshot from desktop Scrum tool, Eylean

Take your time to study this diagram as it contains a lot of information. These are the different parts of this dialog box:

1. *Story Name* – "The Fourth Sample Story" in this figure.
2. *Story Description* – Quality criteria, explanation of the scope, etc. It is useful to store all the relevant information here, so that the whole Scrum Team can have access to it.

3. *Alerts* – Optional custom alerts can be set here.
4. *Due Date* – You can also add optional custom due dates and use them to track stories. For example, you have decided in the middle of the Sprint (part of the detailed planning) to finish a certain story in a particular date, and you set that date here.
5. *Complexity* – It is a field used to defining the nature of the story and can be used for Sprint Planning. Usually the more complex a story is, the more uncertain its estimate would be.
6. *Estimate* – This is the estimated volume of the story determined by the Development Team.
7. *Categories* – When there are lots of stories in the backlog, it is a good idea to categorize them for ease of access and maintenance. This can act as a normal WBS (work breakdown structure) in traditional projects where deliverables are grouped together.
8. *Assignments* – The story can be assigned to any person in the team. However, the whole Scrum Team would remain accountable for it.
9. *Tracker* – You can record time spend on each story for further analysis, refining estimates, billing, etc.
10. *Colors* – You can set different colors to each story to differentiate them visually in the Scrum board. This is a way of grouping/categorizing items.
11. *Tasks* – You can breakdown the story into tasks (detailed planning) and track them separately. A simple progress would be calculated for each story based on the number of completed tasks. Tasks are created by the Development Team.
12. *Change Log* – The history of the changes made in this story (such as creation of tasks) would be stored to be used later.
13. *Attachments* – You can attach relevant documents and use the software as a document management tool too.
14. *Comments* – Each member of the Scrum Team can leave comments and collaborate with others. This field is very helpful and we always ask team members to use it.
15. *Additional fields* – If all of the above fields are not enough for you, you can define your own custom fields

and use them for other planning and control needs. One important use of Scrum tools is collaboration. Collaboration features are more important when the Scrum Team is not co-located and traditional ways of collaboration are not possible.

The following figure shows a sample Product Backlog created in an online Scrum tool. The Product Owner has identified the stories, but the estimates are not done yet (question marks on the right side of the rows).

Current status of the sample:

- Identified stories yes
- Estimates no
- Sprint plan no
- Tasks no
- Completed tasks and stories no

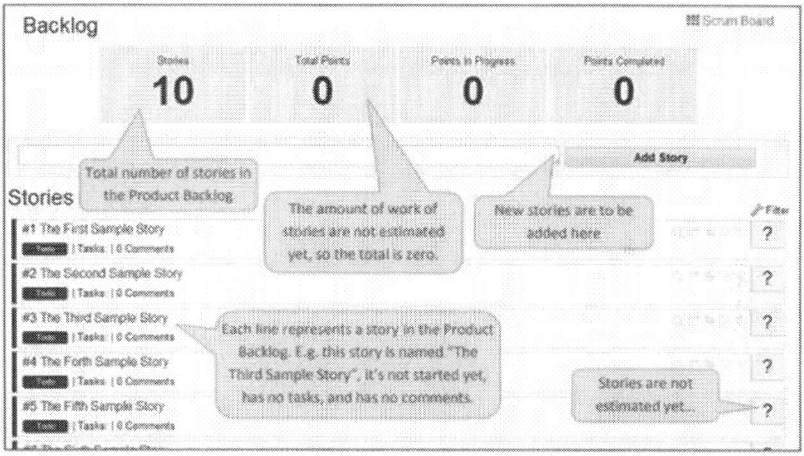

A sample screenshot from online Scrum tool, ScrumDo

The Scrum Team should add details, estimates, and order to the Product Backlog items all the way through the project, which is called Product Backlog grooming. It should not consume more than 10% of the time of the Development Team.

The Product Backlog is created more based on discussion rather than documentation. The Product Backlog items (aka stories) should be easy to understand for non-technical stakeholders.

The following figure shows the sample Scrum tool after the addition of the estimates.

Current status of the sample:

1. Identified stories / yes
2. Estimates / yes
3. Sprint plan / no
4. Tasks / no
5. Completed tasks and stories / no

A sample screenshot from online Scrum tool, ScrumDo.

The total amount of work in this sample is shown to be 234 points. It is common to break the large stories (such as the tenth story in the sample which is estimated 100 points) into two or more stories later.

Sometimes multiple Scrum Teams work on the same project. The Product Backlog is a representation of the scope of the final product and therefore, there should be only one Product Backlog, no matter how many Scrum Teams are working on the project.

Artifact 2: Sprint Backlog

The Sprint Backlog is created during the Sprint Planning event which is the first event in a sprint. During the Sprint Planning event, the Scrum Team collaborates on creating the Sprint Backlog, which consists of the following:

- A number of items selected from the top of the Product Backlog, based on their estimated work and the estimated capacity of the Development Team
- The Sprint Goal, which will help describe the real meaning of the items and direct the efforts of the Development Team
- A detailed plan for delivery of the items and realization of the Sprint Goal during the Sprint

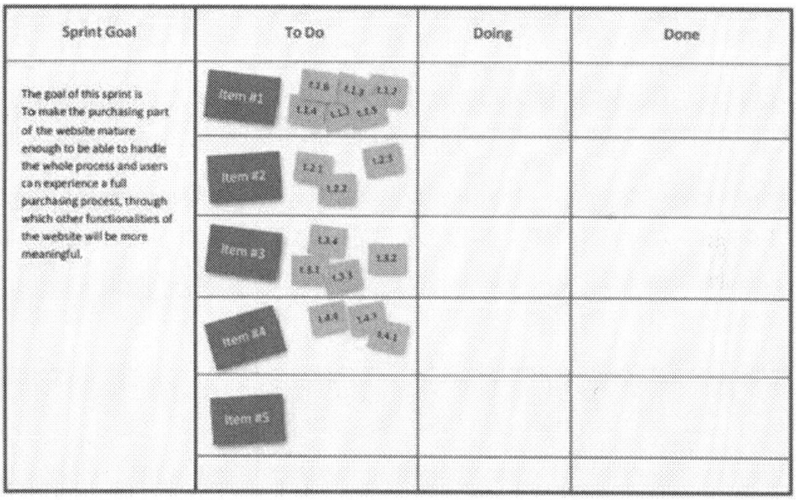

The Sprint Backlog is frozen after the Sprint Planning and the Development Team will focus on delivering an Increment of "Done" based on this plan. The statement "the Sprint Backlog is frozen" means that items (stories) in the Sprint Backlog cannot be added or removed during the Sprint. However, it might be necessary to re-negotiate, justify, or clear some of the items during the Sprint, which should be done in the presence of the Product Owner. The detailed plan which is normally not complete at the end of the Sprint Planning will become more complete as the Sprint continues.

The following figure shows the sample project in Sprint Planning time: a new Sprint, called "The First Sprint" is defined with start and end dates, and Scrum Team are now ready to select items from the top of the Product Backlog to be assigned to this Sprint.

Current status of the sample:

- Identified stories / yes
- Estimates / yes
- Sprint plan / on-going
- Tasks / no
- Completed tasks and stories / no

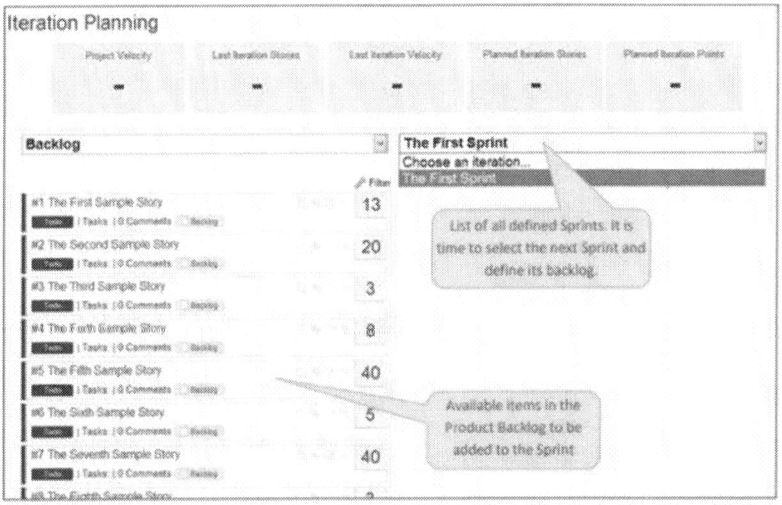

A sample screenshot from online Scrum tool, ScrumDo

Suppose that the estimated capacity of the Sprints is 50 points. In this case, all we can choose for the Sprint is shown in the next figure.

Current status of the sample:

- Identified stories / yes
- Estimates / yes
- Sprint plan / almost finished
- Tasks / no
- Completed tasks and stories / no

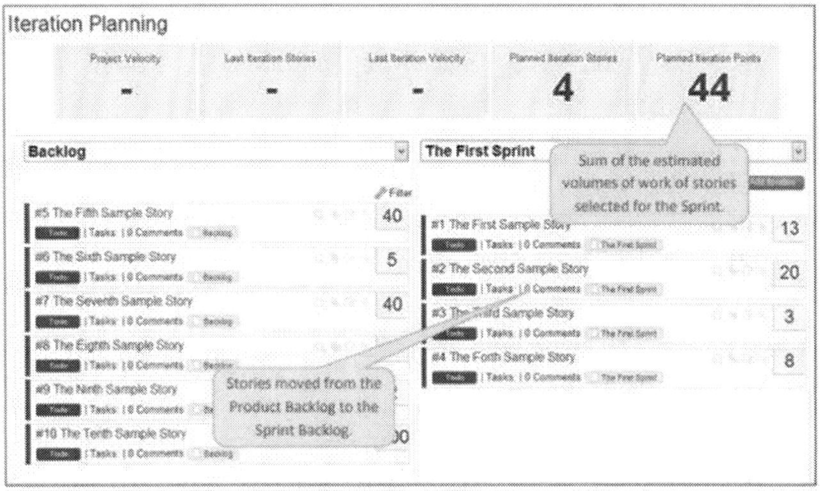

A sample screenshot from online Scrum tool, ScrumDo

Now we have four items with an estimate of 44 points. We cannot add the next Product Backlog item, because it has 40 points and we only have about 6 points free in our Sprint capacity. It is common for the Product Owner in such cases to reorder the backlog; for example to bring The Sixth Sample Story above The Fifth Sample Story, and so we can add it to the Sprint Backlog (next figure).

Current status of the sample:

- Identified stories / yes
- Estimates / yes
- Sprint plan / yes

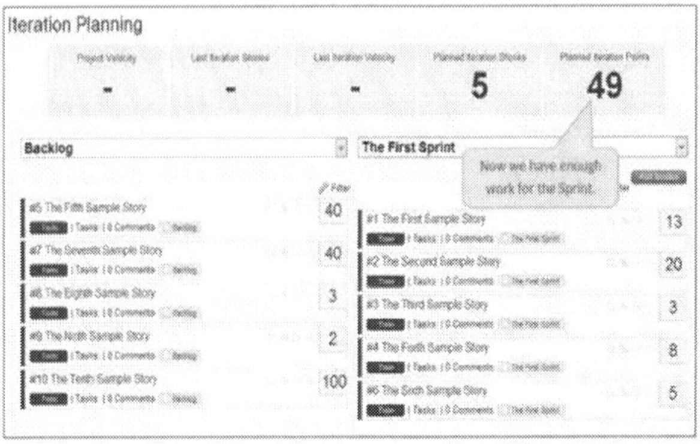

A sample screenshot from online Scrum tool, ScrumDo.

- Tasks / no
- Completed tasks and stories / no

The next figure shows the Sprint items, along with a summary, and a burn-down chart.

Current status of the sample:

- Identified stories / yes
- Estimates / yes
- Sprint plan / yes
- Tasks / no
- Completed tasks and stories / no

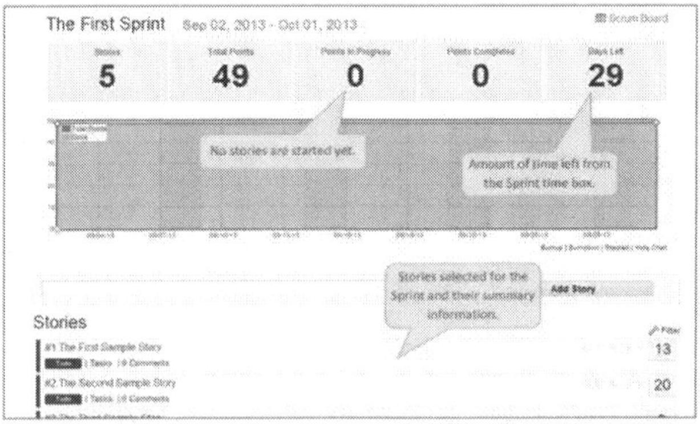

A sample screenshot from online Scrum tool, ScrumDo.

This screen acts like a dashboard and we can use it to plan and track the items. In the next figure for example, some of the items from the top of the list are broken down into tasks. Most Scrum tools are equipped with collaborative features which are especially useful for remote teams (comments for example).

Current status of the sample:

- Identified stories / yes
- Estimates / yes
- Sprint plan / yes
- Tasks / yes (only for some stories)
- Completed tasks and stories / no

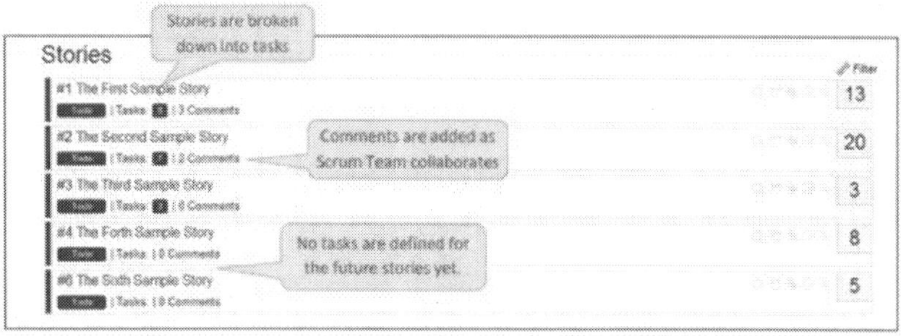

A sample screenshot from online Scrum tool, ScrumDo.

As we go through the Sprint, some tasks and items get Done and more items are detailed.

Current status of the sample:

- Identified stories / yes
- Estimates / yes
- Sprint plan / yes
- Tasks / yes
- Completed tasks and stories / yes (some of them)

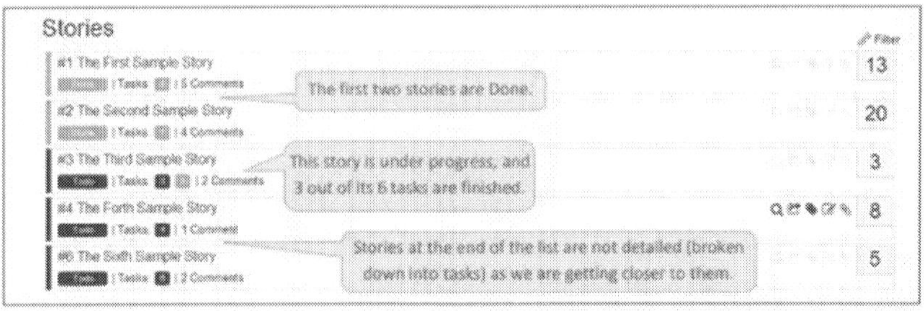

A sample screenshot from online Scrum tool, ScrumDo

The Scrum tools usually update the burn-down chart as we progress through the Sprint.

Use of Kanban in Scrum projects

It's common to visualize the Sprint items in a Kanban style board and most Scrum tools support such a view; the next figure shows a sample.

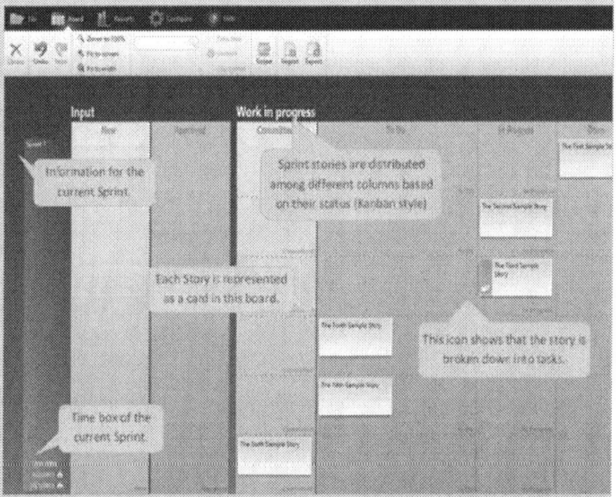

The columns of the Kanban board are customizable and we can add as many steps as needed, such as designing, developing, testing, and integrating. Each card would be moved from left to right to visually indicate its current state. We can also incorporate the good practice of Kanban, limiting work in progress, by limiting the number of allowed cards in each column. By accepting this limitation, we accept to focus on a few number of stories at each point in time and get them done instead of starting new stories.

The minimum columns in a Kanban board are:

- To Do – Things waiting to be started
- Doing – Things we are doing right now (usually limited in number)
- Done – Things that are completed

Artifact 3: Increment

An Increment is a sum of all completed Product Backlog items at the end of a Sprint. Each Increment must be "Done", and must be releasable. The Product Owner may or may not release a certain Increment, but it should be releasable (shippable).

The next figure shows how the number of stories in the Product Backlog decreases Sprint by Sprint, as the number of features in the Increments increases.

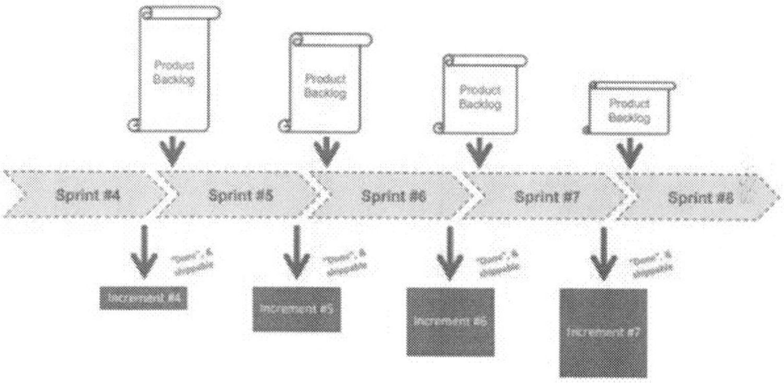

Note that the Increment concept is cumulative: each Increment also contains the features of the previous ones.

Artifact 4: Definition of "Done"

There should be a shared understanding of what it means for a piece of work to be "Done". This definition of "Done" must be discussed and agreed upon by the Scrum Team at the beginning of the project so that future Increments would be releasable.

When multiple Scrum Teams are working on a single project, it might not be possible to use the same definition of "Done" for all teams, because they might be working on items of different natures. In such a case, each Scrum Team will define its own definition of "Done" and delivers its items based on that definition. However, the integration of those definitions of "Done" should be capable of creating a potentially releasable Increment in the project level.

Artifact 5: Monitoring Progress toward a Goal

Up to now, we have use the burn-down chart to visualize the progress of development during a Sprint. You can also use a burn-down chart to visualize the progress of the whole project and this is called the project burn-down chart.

The Product Owner is responsible to monitor the progress of the whole project toward its goal. This should be done at least once per Sprint Review. The Product Owner determines the amount of remaining work and compares it to the remaining work of the previous Sprints, and forecasts the completion date of the project. All stakeholders should have access to this information.

The project burn-down chart shows the amount of remaining work, instead of the amount of completed work; therefore, the line for actual performance goes downward as we proceed, and the faster it goes down, the happier we will be!

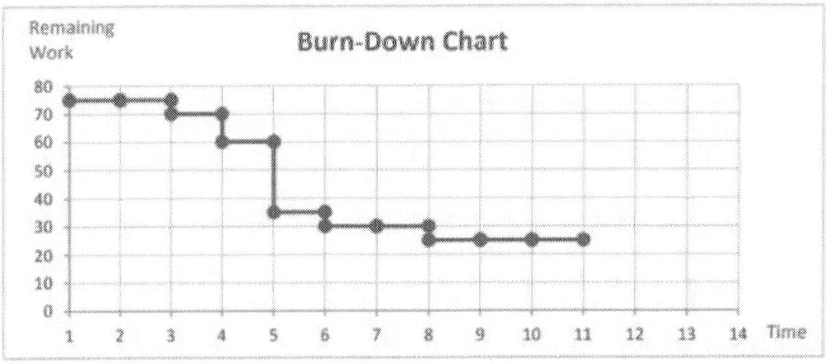

The vertical axis shows the amount of work (which is a sum of all the estimates for each item in the Product Backlog), and the horizontal axis shows the amount of time passed from the beginning of the project or the number of Sprints passed.

We usually add another line to present the uniform distribution of the volume of the work across the initially estimated number of sprints. This line acts as our planned progress, and will be used to compare to our actual values.

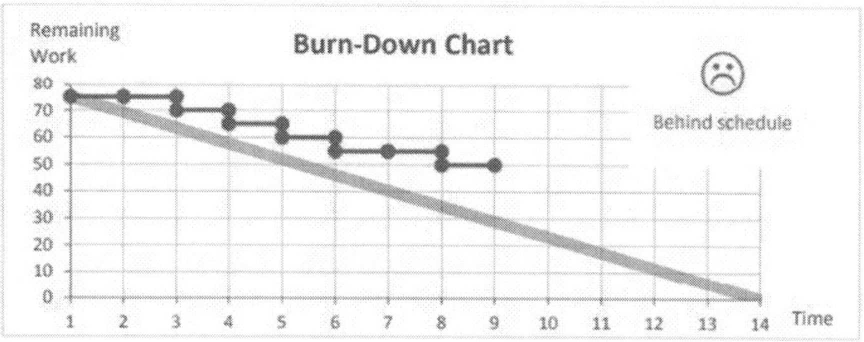

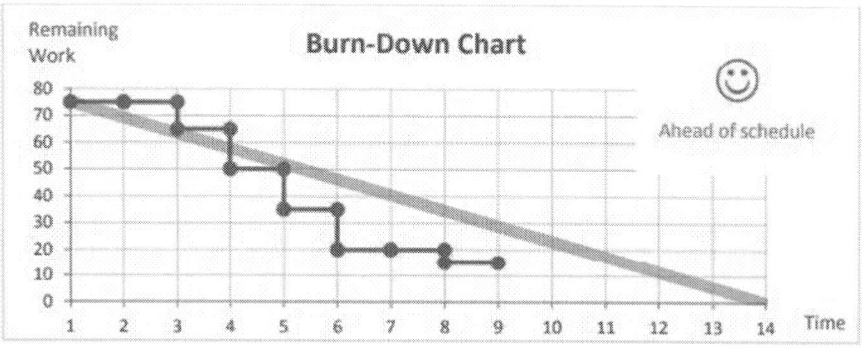

Artifact 6: Monitoring Sprint Progress

Besides the monitoring done for the whole project, we should also monitor the progress of each single Sprint throughout its life. This is the responsibility of the Development Team and should be done at least once per Daily Scrum.

This information is used to calculate the likelihood of achieving the Sprint Goal and completing all items of the Sprint Backlog.

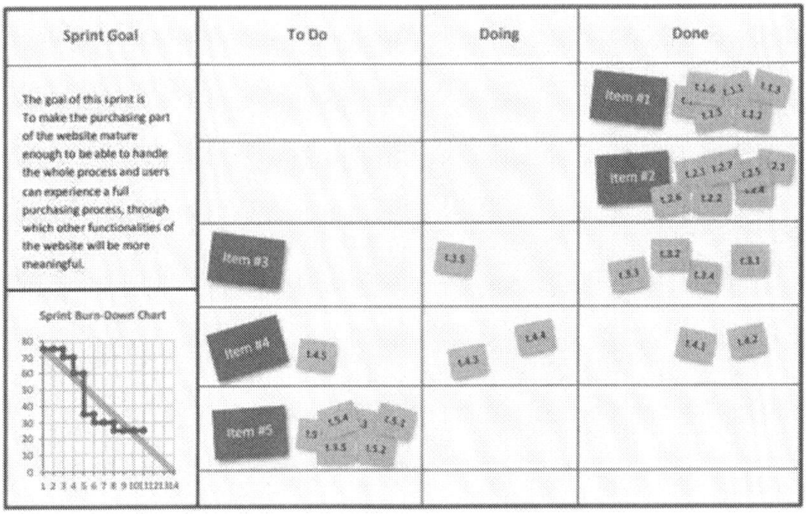

The Sprint progress information can be represented by a burn-down chart, and this chart can be a part of the Sprint board, where everyone can see.

Chapter 27: Manage Projects with Scrum

When a company wants to have a new product or create a new system, they usually hire someone that can make the process faster and efficient. If they choose to assign that role to someone from their internal system, most often that role is given to the head of the department. Contrarily for the companies that are into the product market, they often assign this job to their product managers. In Scrum, this person is called the Scrum Master. To make the best possible formulation of the project and perform the most effective execution, the Product owner (usually CEO) helps IT and engineering departments in terms of staffing and support. When it comes to Scrum management, the first step is to have a project manager or Scrum master that will closely work with the product owner. The scrum master has the role of coach and he or she forms the teams. During the whole process, Scrum master provides guidance and individual coaching to the team and helps in optimizing the productivity of the development team in general. Collaboration between the Product Owner and Scrum Master is significant for maximizing ROI and for controlling the deliverables at the same time.

When it comes to deliverables, the Product Owner has control on the macro level while the Scrum master uses this to help the development team to self-organize on a micro-level. Just like in earlier Scrum implementations, the Product Owner is the person that needs to develop a plan, or rather a roadmap that everyone else will follow. This plan doesn't need to have all the details just the most important elements. All other details depend on functionality and forecast of goal descriptions and its release. Although this first version of the plan should be followed, it changes throughout the project and most often these changes are made daily.

The role of the Product Owner is also to exert risk reduction and control on an empirical basis and as a response to the reality of the project. This empirical system is based on the premise that the Product owner won't try to fit that reality into his or her initial plan, on the contrary, the Product Owner is supposed to be able to perceive the reality of the project and make decisions according to that perception. Like every project in Scrum, iterations are the main way of running the development process. Increments need to be delivered by the end of each sprint, and the Product owner is responsible for managing the business conditions for the project, technology that needs to be used and results that he or she needs from the development team. This information needs to be provided by the Product Owner in detail and at the end of every iteration. The plans that the Product owner delivers for the sprint represents empirical evidence of what development team has achieved and what needs to be done yet.

Mechanisms of control using frequent inspection and techniques for adaptation are also uncommon for many IT projects. However, Scrum gives tips and detailed information about the empirical management of the project. The fact that it is an agile process enables the management to achieve maximized value for the project that needs to be delivered. This means that project managers become Scrum masters and their role to predict and assign tasks while writing reports and making forecasts is no longer useful. In Scrum, project managers have a new and different role in coaching and guidance. Management influence has some pressure points that need to be considered. These pressure points are mostly used to measure if there was an increase in productivity in ROI. These measurements don't include aspects such as written code lines or points of functionality. Scrum uses practices that help management to stay on top to observe and measure the effort of the development team and guide them in the right direction. The key role of Scrum master is to make sure that the team will be able to respond to any complex situation and make the most valuable system possible.

Project management in Scrum has to establish what the vision of the project is and to set a time frame and release strategy that will follow that vision. In Scrum, iterations last for thirty days each and at the end of each iteration Product Owner has to receive and rate the results. The product owner sets the alterations and adjustments that need to be done following the rating. This aspect depends also on the business environment so the Product Owner has to determine empirically what will be the next steps for everyone. Since assumptions that the projects are unable to predict are detailed and underlying, Scrum has iterations instead. These iterations represent Scrum's way of managing the working results. It makes the management team be constantly present and to search for ways to make the most valuable result while maximizing the productivity of the development team.

Having a basis in planning, inspection, and empirical responsiveness is not a common practice in all IT projects. Still, during the last decade, this kind of work preparation was well accepted and a wide number of product companies use it. Many tips and details can be found on introducing planning practice in agile processes. This kind of tips can be very useful for traditional companies, and they can be found in Scrum guides in most IT shops.

One of the practices is based on formalizing the role of the "user" and renaming it into the Product Owner role. The product owner in this practice has responsibility for the ROI of the project. This practice succeeded to resolve the problem that many projects had. This problem is the involvement of the user in the automation of the projects. One of the tips that are best recommended for the initiation of any project is the workshops. Workshops should be three days long and they should start with building functionality of the team and the product. Through these workshops, every member of the team should be familiarized with the Scrum management, roles that exist in that management and new roles that are assigned to all team members. Scrum is supposed to be used within the business unit. This means that people who will use the final product should be those who have an influence on the project in all its stages. They should run the project and make decisions in terms of backlog definition and progress ratings. With Scrum, these users are given a chance to lay out the project and its requirements.

Scrum influences team proactively. If the management is good enough Scrum can be an intelligent way to get the best possible results while keeping the whole team satisfied. Scrum Master and Product owner don't need written reports so they can study them. They need to be in the place where the work happens and to inspect activities of the project and tasks that are done. Scrum abandoned the rote application of project management, which is why such expectations are nonexistent in agile practices in general.

There are many benefits of Scrum implementation. One of them is that the user (customer), or in Scrum-the Product owner has control over the project development. Another benefit is that the Product Owner is the one who makes requirements and changes during the progress of the project. Scrum is beneficial because it ensures that prioritized functionalities are the ones that are built first. Scrum is focused on functionalities that are prioritized and it emphasizes only those which Product Owner wants to get. This is significant in terms of time frame, budget, and maintenance of the whole project. Additionally, new working functionalities emerge during every sprint, which allows the Product Owner to decide if he or she wants to release some of the already finished features at the preferred time. This kind of system is beneficial for budget management because the project doesn't need to get funds for more than a sprint (thirty days) in advance. With Scrum implementation financial return from the investment is maximized, and it also allows Scrum to identify things that can be done to increase productivity daily.

Nobody should underestimate the implementation of the Scrum methodology whether it refers to its difficulty or its organizational structure. Many decades and an enormous amount of money was spent on traditional project management and its teaching. Whole institutions were developed with the purpose of training and certifying an individual to become professional project managers. In IT sectors, almost every member has either been employed from this kind of management, or they learned from them. Most of IT employees worked on projects where they were subjected to traditional management. This kind of work is reflected in personal IT practices and expectations. Developers that undergo this kind of project work have a certain attitude about project values and interaction with the users. Furthermore, in this type of management, users work with the IT department in a way that they pass the projects "over the wall". Many years will pass until the project failure guilt is entirely deflected from this kind of system.

However, Scrum doesn't use this kind of approach. Contrarily, it is straightforward and simple if you wish to resuscitate a single project for example. And the best thing is that the results are better on so many levels. Developers use the process' agility, and organizational structure gets the success that they aspired to. Implementing Scrum into wide organizations is, however, way much harder. It requires careful evaluation, thoughtful implementation, and planning, and almost as a rule, the whole organizational structure needs to change if the company wishes to stick with the Scrum. All these steps return the company's efforts fast which is also one of the greatest threads of Scrum as an agile management process.

Development that is driven by value

The product owner won't start funding the system development project if he or she doesn't have a vision of value that the project and its product will bring to the overall business and its unit. Project plans are made to calculate the cost of the development process and they are the Product owner's estimation of the price, functionality that he or she wants to achieve with the project, what is the desired quality of the product and what are the implementation days for it. Still, these planning activities are considered to be just mechanisms because usually, the Product Owner has to be present during the whole development process constraining costs, justifying missed implementation dates or ensuring that functionalities build during the development phase are by the plan. During this kind of chaos, the value that the project needs to deliver can be slightly forgotten.

On the other hand, in Scrum, the Product Owner is refocused from this kind of mess to the value that the development system needs to deliver. This value is often expressed with a formula in which value is based on the Product Owner's choice in terms of quality, costs, time frame and overall functionality of the project.

Projects that are driven by value have variables that are determined by the Product Owner during all stages of the system development. These kinds of projects leave the Product Owner to authorize development rates for every sprint and make changes following the progress. Changes usually refer to variables that influence dates for delivery and already delivered values. For example, in the case of deregulation, a project that has already started can change significantly. This means that the Product Owner might want to maximize the value of the project and to increase the cost for its maximization.

When the sprint ends, the functionality of the working system delivered by the team are reviewed with the Product Owner. During the review, the Product owner can decide to change and reprioritize requirements for the next sprint. He or she can ask the team to implement the increment they demonstrated at the end of the sprint, or increase future sprint's cost and request additional work on the backlog of the product. Product Owner can make adjustments and decrease or increase the quality of the project by changing the number of functionalities that the team has to deliver during the further sprints. He or she can also stop funding more sprints because the value that they have received isn't adequate for the number of resources that the Project Owner provided for the project.

Well understood management roles are one of the key aspects of successful implementation of the Scrum methodology. This is one of the most critical points for every project that uses any agile process in general, not just Scrum. Without proper management and its guidance, project teams can be formed without some set of skills that are absolutely necessary for the process. Or the project itself can be set on the wrong premises. Management roles in Scrum exist to prevent dysfunctional organization structure and to increase the value and quality of deliverables that the development team needs to build. These roles outline responsibilities for each team member and assign them with activities that need to be done through the project.

Product functionalities that are potentially shippable and their increment

Many people had questions about Scrum methodology and how it can support software system development that is FDA approved, mission-critical, etc. This doubts referred not only to Scrum but to all agile methods used in software development processes. One of the reasons that these doubts have arisen was the fact that one of the most popular agile methods described software construction as a single-use which meant that only organization that develops it can use it. And this development for any software system is mostly used by the organization's internal IT department, or independent information technology organization contracted by the company.

In Scrum, development teams are required to build a product that has enhanced functionality in every sprint. Enhancements have to be shippable in case the Product Owner decides to release or implement that functionality. To be sure that deliverables have working functionalities that are potentially shippable, the team must test every line of the code and make sure that the code works. This code becomes the basis of the functionality and it has to be documented in the user's manual or Help files.

If product enhancement developed for the sprint has some exact use, the organization has to define requirements that are additional for the product and creates standards and conventions that need to be followed. A good example of this is the fact that every product developed to be used in circumstances that can be critical for life has to be approved by the FDA (the Federal Drug Administration). This refers to all products that are connected to health care and its settings if the product is manufactured or used in the United States of America. FDA needs to have some information to provide their approval. Firstly, they need to check if the product has specific functionality operations and if it is traceable. And every time the product gets an increment, these requirements have to be fulfilled for each enhancement separately and be available for FDA approval if needed. Similar requirements are needed for the products that are modeled mathematically and have performances that are not just shown through statistical measurements. These models have rigors that are considered to be and additional feature for every sprint during their development phase, therefore, their increment also has to be potentially shippable.

If the Product Owner wants to implement enhanced functionality, the next step is to establish Sprint activities for the product release. These iterations need to finish increments that are selected and finalize them into a fully shippable deliverable. If product enhancements are approved by the Product Owner as the ones that fit the desired value, further sprints are shorter. We can use the FDA again as an example. If a project has a product that is FDA approved, every enhancement that is developed further for that same product should have deliverables that will be made by the same standards for approval. If these deliverables haven't been made properly, they need to be adjusted to the point where the FDA can approve them so they can be included in the sprints for the product release.

If a project tends to develop a unique product for non-single use, it means that the system development process can be scalable and it will ensure that the team builds enhancements that work and shape them into potentially shippable deliverables. If the product doesn't already have standards, practices or conventions for these increments, they need to consider developing them as a part of the requirements. Increment standards are usually staged as a priority for any enhancement work and they need to be set in the initial phase of the sprint. That is how they ensure that the increment that is developed is potentially shippable and following the needed regulations. These iterative processes in which agile methods are used to develop increments are also known as "sashimi". "Sashimi" is defined as a slice of deliverable that contains all the characteristics of the final product of the project. The term "sashimi" originated from the word sushi. This metaphor is used because just like one slice of sushi is similar to all other slices, the "slice" of the product has all properties of the final product too.

Chapter 28: Project Preparation

Project planning is not a top-down activity. It is not about the Product owner or the Scrum Master handing out responsibilities or supervising the work after coming up with the development plan on their own. Rather, the entire team does project planning. For example, the section of the team that is handling a particular task is the one that provides an estimate of how much time it will take to complete it. They also determine the features to be executed in each sprint. Therefore, project planning in Scrum is a collaborative exercise.

This list is not exhaustive. The best practices will be a lot clearer to you once you're aligned with the vision of Scrum and its benefits. You'll find that a lot of these points become obvious once you start thinking the right way!

Treating the Product Roadmap Correctly

A product roadmap is an elite planned document that describes the reasons why the product is being developed. It is also described as a visual summary that maps out the product vision and the strategy to be taken over time.

The roadmap is an important component of the production process for many reasons. It enables concerned parties to come to an understanding of why and how to prioritize certain aspects of the product development process. It enables the manager to understand and better organize the product's strategic vision.

The roadmap is an important tool that aids product managers to communicate more persuasively their strategic vision to all parties including the developers, the organization executives, customers, and other relevant parties. Lastly, the roadmap becomes the all-important guidepost throughout the development process, allowing everyone handling the product to check in regularly to ensure that the products being created still serve the needs and purpose they were intended to.

Some of the things you will want to avoid when creating or using a product roadmap include:

Mistaking the roadmap to be a list of features

Just like listing several features does not make a product; it does not create a roadmap either. Therefore, when creating one, dwell on themes and not features. A theme is an assurance that you will resolve a customer's problem. It requires you to conduct extensive research to identify the business values, the levels of effort, and the need for urgency in certain areas of your plan so that you can correctly know what to prioritize when creating the roadmap. Themes are also important because they shift your attention from the competition and the individual needs of the stakeholders to focusing more on the value you intend to bring to your customers.

A product roadmap is not a release plan

The product roadmap ideally provides direction for the next two, three years while a release plan focuses only on the next two or three sprints.

A product roadmap should not contain any dates

Since a product roadmap does not dwell on releases, it should not contain any dates. Changes and distractions come up every time, and the Scrum model encourages the team to take in all changes in the making of the product. Therefore, if you insert dates in the roadmap and the project timelines are changed as you change strategies, the stakeholders will not be interested in the narrative, they will consider the project a failure. This is also quite damaging to a team's reputation. However, if you cannot avoid dates, make the scope as broad as can be so that the time therein accommodates changes and allows you to deliver before or at the time promised.

The tool is overrated

The product roadmap tool is overrated. You do not need it to come up with a roadmap. Index cards and a whiteboard are fine, and so are Google Docs, Excel, and Keynote. Choose what best suits you. Only the content matters, the presentation is not as important.

Requirements

A requirement is simply a function, feature, or service that a user desires. Requirements present themselves as constraints, functions, business rules, and other elements that must be available to meet the needs of the users.

For example, if a customer wanted a custom-made car, the requirements of coming up with this would be based on the features of the car such as a comfortable seating position, a propulsion system, a steering capability, etc. The solutions to these requirements would be bucket seats, an engine and a steering wheel, in that order.

When stating requirements, ensure that they do not point to a particular solution for as long as you can because tying the project down to one thing limits its flexibility. A solution developed too early easily becomes an impediment to creativity, time, and the budget.

Requirements fall into three categories:

Functional Requirements

Functional requirements are those that express the feature or function and provide a description of what is required. For example, the requirements 'find a venue for the meetings' and 'visit the customer's site' do not indicate how the solution will be achieved. However, 'rent a conference hall' and 'drive to the customer's site' are possible solutions. However, these solutions do not negate the possibilities of taking alternatives. You could walk, fly, or take a train to see the customer. You could also choose to construct a conference hall. Therefore, stating the requirements without providing a definite solution provides room for innovation and flexibility as the project progresses.

Non-Functional Requirements

Non-functional requirements indicate how well or to what extent the solution needs to reach. These requirements primarily describe the attributes of the solution such as its reliability, availability, security, maintainability, and other adjectives that have to do with responsiveness and performance. For example, availability for 24 hours each day or a 2-second response time.

User Story

When a requirement is expressed in the voice of the end-user, it is called a user story. These requirements are also called features, epics, and themes.

User stories are becoming more popular in Scrum and other Agile methodologies for many reasons. They help to unleash the true motive behind the requirement. They express the requirement in a meaningful user-friendly language. They focus on priority requirements without having to delve into minor issues earlier on. They express the need from the viewpoint of the people that the solution is expected to influence.

Steps of Requirement Handling

An honest gathering of the requirements is the foundation of the successful execution of a project. The following steps are critical in ensuring that all the deliverables of the project will meet the expectations the customers have.

Identify all the stakeholders of the project

The first step towards developing the requirements is identifying the key stakeholders of the project and the effect they have on the outcome. Identifying these stakeholders is easy, beginning from the primary to the secondary and to the tertiary level stakeholders.

You will need to brainstorm with the team members, the sponsors, and the functional group leaders. Involving these people is meant to help you avoid leaving out any relevant stakeholders and avoiding gaps in the requirement handling process.

Provide the stakeholders with the right questions

Now that you have identified the rightful key stakeholders, it is now time to ask them the questions that will allow you to understand their most basic expectations from the project. Knowing the right questions to ask is an art that you will need to learn, but you will get better at it with time. The questions also help the stakeholders to refine their expectations because many of them may not even understand what they are looking for, but asking them the right questions gets them to the core of the matter. It may take several attempts to get to the right answers.

Identify the best requirement handling techniques

Techniques like groups, surveys, brainstorming, reverse engineering, prototyping, one-on-one interviews, and direct observation are used as avenues for gathering requirements, each offering unique benefits, which are also dependent on the nature of the project. You will need to choose a suitable technique for the specific project by weighing out the cons and pros of each.

Put it down on paper

Since Scrum has a free flexible model, it is easy for people to overlook the need for appropriate documentation. In the management of projects and requirements gathering to be specific, details of all errors, results, changes, and conversations held must be written down. Without proper documentation, it can be difficult to resolve issues that come up during the course of the project. Documentation also reduces the uncertainty that many have regarding the success of the project.

Perform a proper analysis of the results

Since you have succeeded in gathering and documenting the requirements, you will also need to analyze the results to confirm the accuracy, completeness, and truthful nature of them. Ensure that you prioritize requirements that fall into the operational, technical, functional, and implementation categories. In addition, you should arrange the requirements in order of their significance.

Confirm the results

Just before you hop behind the project's steering wheel, take a moment to verify the exceptions made, the obstacles encountered, the findings, feasibility, and other significant matters before going on with the project. This you can do with the help of key stakeholders. Confirming the results helps to avoid misunderstandings and uncertainties once the project is on the road. It also ensures that all parties concerned agree.

Sign Off

Once the results are out and verified by the stakeholders, it is now time to seek sponsors and to have the stakeholders sign off on the project. The signing off is a physical confirmation and seal to show that all parties are fully aware of the requirements and have accepted to the gathering process used, the terms, and the findings made before commencing the project.

The basic process of recognizing the stakeholders, asking them the right questions and working with them to recognize the requirements before proceeding to document, analyze, verify and sign off, are the critical steps that take place at the beginning of project management. These steps also help the stakeholders to keep track of all activities with the hope that the outcome will meet the needs as intended.

Product Backlog

Although the team cannot do things outside the scope of the product backlog, the absence of a product backlog does not mean that the team will not deliver. Therefore, the backlog is only an option that the team has for delivering the required result, rather than a commitment.

Adding or taking out an item from the backlog should be very fast and cheap because the order of items on the backlog changes with time, as the team develops a better understanding of the process and the expected solution. This ability to reorder the list, adding new items, removing some backlog items, and the ability to refine continuously the product backlog as the project proceeds is what gives it its dynamism.

Best Practices for the Backlog

- Always have a clear vision of the product you seek to develop as you manage and maneuver the Product Backlog. Any change that you make must agree with the product vision.
- The order that the items in the Product Backlog take will depend on the urgency, dependencies, risk, value, and the amount of experience or learning to take out of doing them.
- Ensure that the Product Backlog can easily be understood and available to all members of the team. This sounds matter-of-fact but you will find that in many projects, the Product
- Make the Product Backlog a responsibility that requires the input of all the Team Members. While it is the Product owner's responsibility to order and maintain the Backlog, the entire team is responsible for what goes into it.
- Ensure that the Product Backlog remains manageable. It is tempting to want to resolve all user issues and to avoid disappointing the stakeholders by continuously adding items or stories to your Product Backlog. However, having to update the Backlog several times can consume quite an amount of time. It is also not fair to say yes knowing that you surely will not live up to what you have promised.
- Let the stakeholders in on the Product Backlog. Always make the Backlog visible and avoid hiding it in some complicated program or tool. If the Shareholders have access to it, they can continuously monitor the project's status and provide useful feedback. In the end, this communication builds trust that proves valuable especially when you have to make difficult decisions.

- Ensure that all the tools you adopt support your use of a Product Backlog. If using a tool brings about too many unnecessary constraints, try another, or better yet, avoid the tools completely. Most times, teams are overwhelmed by the amount of work using a certain tool creates. Therefore, if you realize that a tool is causing too much work, avoid using it.
- When you need to increase the transparency, reorder or adjust the balance of the Product Backlog, employ the Backlog Prioritization Quadrant technique.
- Ensure that at all times there are at least two sprints of the Backlog items that are ready for the undertaking. For a sprint to be ready, it has to be clear about its agenda, practicable, and testable.

Estimating Backlog Using Fibonacci

All items on the Product Backlog depend on the team's and the product owner's estimation to plan their release dates and to prioritize them. This means that the project requires an honest estimate of how difficult the tasks are and how long it may take before they are completed. Ideally, the product owner should not attend the meetings where the team is making estimations for the project to avoid applying pressure to the team knowingly or otherwise.

The Scrum Framework does not provide any recommendations or tools to be used when estimating the time, it will take to deliver on certain takes. In fact, in the Scrum Framework, estimation is not even done in terms of time. Scrum uses a more complex metric to quantify the time and effort to be used. Common quantification methods are by using t-shirt sizes like XS, S, M, L, XL, a numeric sizing method that is 1 to 10, or by the famous Fibonacci sequence of 1,2,3,5,8,13,21,34. It does not matter what scale you employ because the important thing is that the entire team and stakeholders understand what the readings of the scale mean.

The Fibonacci system, in particular, is a sequence of numbers that might appear incongruous at first glance, but it has a very scientific significance based on the laws of distribution and physics. In this system, a number is the sum of the former two. Here is an illustration: 1,2,3,5,8,13,21,34,5,89,144,233,377,610,987, ...

When using these numbers to show the immensities and sizes of items on the Product Backlog, embrace simplicity to avoid confusion. For example, you could use only the numbers between 1 and 21, and reserve large numbers like 987 for ludicrous requests, like when a stakeholder asks you to fly them to Mars in a cardboard box, for example.

The key to using this system successfully is to embrace relativity. For example, if a Backlog item is a report and although you have done plenty of them by now, this one shows some complexity especially because of the underlying data. Rate this report as a 3.

If the Backlog has another report, compare it to the first. How does it measure? Is it smaller or larger? If it is bigger, a 5 or 8 would do, and if smaller, a 2 is excellent. Do this for all entries and you will end up ranking the items correctly.

To ensure that the Fibonacci scale works for you perfectly, perhaps you could start by picking what you consider the smallest and easiest task on the Backlog. Assign this item 1 then determine which is the toughest or largest task and assign to it number 21. Now, you have established markers, you have sized the Backlog using Fibonacci numbers, and you can begin working on them from the top.

As you get further along the Backlog, it is likely that some items will begin to get fuzzy and start seeming as low priority tasks. In fact, it is never assured that you will get to the bottom of the list. When this happens, do not feel the need to resize the Backlog again because the list is already in priority order. Only continue to work beginning from the top.

Teamwork is Important

As you size the items on the Backlog, do it as a team. Working as a team also provides an opportunity for new team members to learn from seasoned team members. Characters who are stronger and more vocal are also denied the chance of becoming too overbearing and exerting their influence on the project and its outcome.

Once you are done sizing the Backlog, present the list to the product owner so that they can see the proportional size of the features they have requested and possibly make changes to their priorities if need be. If the product owner asks for a change in priorities, only move the items' position in the Backlog.

Chapter 29: Planning a Sprint

Putting together a group of people to accomplish something as sophisticated as the Scrum process can be a difficult task. It is necessary to ensure that everyone is working towards a common goal, and requires a specific process called the Group Development Process. This process is a 5 step program that ensures the Scrum team is as successful as possible. The first 4 stages (Forming, Storming, Norming, and Performing) were developed by Bruce Tuckman in 1965. Tuckman said that these stages are necessary for the Scrum Team to grow and that using this process helps them to face challenges, tackle problems, plan work, find solutions, and deliver the best results possible. Tuckman later added in the final 5th stage (Adjourning) in the year 1977. It's interesting to note that, specifically in Agile software development, teams will exhibit a behavior called "swarming". This is a performance shown as the team comes together, collaborates, and focuses on solving a singular problem. This behavior is adapted from when a swarm of insects is focused on a common event, such as a swarm of wasps attacking a person because said person decided it would be wise to hit the wasp's nest with a baseball bat.

Using the Group Development Process method leads to maturity and a highly efficient Scrum Team. It's necessary to remember that sometimes a process like this can take time. Most companies are more concerned with immediate results and jumping into tasks right away, without thinking about how important team building is. Using a method like this will lead to positive impacts and the Scrum Team's success.

1. *Forming Stage* - It is very important to get the Scrum Team off to a successful start. This stage is used for the team members to get to know one another and find out different things they have in common. They use it to connect in a way that will allow them to work

together seamlessly. If this step is skipped, the team might find it difficult to move through the later steps of the process. One way for the team to connect with each other is by doing fun ice breakers. Team members can share personal information; movies they like, their favorite music, or their favorite foods. There might be another team member who likes the same things, which will help them to connect to each other. Also during this stage, the team members are relying on a group leader for guidance and direction. The members are looking for acceptance from the group and want to feel like it's a "safe space". They're looking to keep things simple and wanting to avoid controversy, which means typical serious topics and feelings are avoided. Orientation also plays a big part in this stage. Team members try to become more oriented to not just each other, but the tasks as well. Usually, discussions are revolved around figuring out the scope of each task, how to approach it, and similar concerns. In order for the team members to grow from this task to the next, they must step out of their comfort box, and risk the possibility of conflict.

2. *Storming Stage* - Storming is an apt name for this stage. This one is the most likely to have arising conflicts and competition. The "fear of failure" or "fear of exposure" might come into play and increase the desire for structural clarification and commitment. Members will question who is going to be in charge, who is responsible for what, what the rules are, the reward system, and what the criteria for evaluations are. There might even be behavioral changes in attitudes based on issues of competition. Team members might ally with other team members, especially ones that they are already familiar with. It is even possible that cliques might form, which some of the team members would be against. Some members might feel more comfortable speaking up, while others would feel it was better to remain silent. It could end up with the Scrum Team feeling splintered and not as if they are a team. It's important to figure out different working styles and other

obstacles that are standing in the way of the group completing their goal. The best way to solve conflicts is through a collaborative and problem solving based approach. It's the only way for team members to unify and work together. The only reason for skipping a step like this is if the Scrum Team is already established and has been working together for a while. It's possible they already know each other's working style and are already banded together as a team. If this step is needed, then the only way for the Scrum team to move to the next one is by adopting a problem solving mentality. And the most important trait for each member to have is the ability to listen.

3. *Norming Stage* - This stage is all about cohesion within the group. It's important for each member to acknowledge each other's contributions, community building, and attempt to solve the group issues. Team members must be willing to change their previous ideas and opinions when presented with facts from other team members. This should go along with asking questions of each other. The team acknowledges that leadership is shared, and there is no need for any cliques. Having all the members get to know each other and identify with each other is important in strengthening trust. Which then contributes to the development of the group as a unit. It's also important to have established rules for how the team operates in each meeting. The team members need to discuss logistics, such as location of the meeting, how long the meeting will take, and what time it starts. They need to talk about how the meeting will flow, and what to do if conflicts happen. Inclusion plays an important role within the Scrum Team. Every group member needs to feel like they belong, so that they actually participate in all the activities. The main goal is to find a set of rules that everyone can agree to, and then actually follow. Doing this will help the team to operate as the best they can be. The group will feel a sense of camaraderie and almost a feeling of relief when the interpersonal conflicts are resolved. In this specific stage, creativity is high; there's a sense of

openness and sharing of information, both on a personal and task level. Everyone feels good about being part of a group that gets things done. The only drawback at this stage is that the members resist change of any kind, and the ones that fear the inevitable future breakup of the group. They may decide the only way to avoid said breakup is by resist forming it in the first place.

4. *Performing Stage* - This stage is not reached by all groups. If they have reached it, the group has formed a tight knit team that trusts each other and is ready to perform tasks efficiently and effectively. Team members are able to work independently, in subgroups, or as the group as a whole with equal productiveness. Everyone's roles are able to change and adjust depending on the needs of the group and individuals. This is the stage where the group is the most productive. Each individual member has become self-assuring and feel as if it's unnecessary to seek group approval. Team members are both task-oriented and people-oriented. There is a certain feel of unity and. Group morale is high, group loyalty is strong, and everyone knows who they are as a group. Products that the Scrum Team works on can change over time, so there is a strong feel of support for experimentation in solving issues. The team is capable of working together well enough to adapt and accept that change. Everyone knows that the overall goal is productivity reached through problem-solving and hard work. Performance is also best if the team follows the rules set in the Norming Stage because it's used to solve personal conflicts. If such a situation occurs, the team would need to review the rules and enforce what the team originally decided on.
5. *Adjourning Stage* - This stage wasn't originally a part of the process and was added in later years. But just because it was added at a later time, doesn't mean it is any less important! At this point in time, the team has most likely fulfilled the project vision. While the technical sides of things are done, the team needs to check in with things on a more personal level. They

need to reflect on how they worked together as a team and see if there are any improvements that could be made. The team also recognizes participation and achievements. They can also use this as an opportunity to say personal goodbyes. The team worked closely with one another on an intense project. It's important to wrap things up on a personal level, otherwise there could be a feeling of incompleteness. And what if the team gets back together in any future projects? It's important that they discuss the process and methodologies that succeeded and the ones that failed. The team can go through and decided if there was anything that could be salvaged with a little bit of change. Information gathered during this time might even be used for performance evaluations. So, it's important that the team takes this stage seriously.

Sometimes it can be difficult to follow the stages. There could be a person that is especially stubborn, or maybe some people just don't particularly work well with others. In order for the group to reach its best potential, they must be flexible enough to accept when they need help. There are a few different steps that a group can take to ensure they develop properly through the different stages:

1. The group needs to make sure they change up the responsibility of group facilitator. Each person should have a chance to be "in charge" and doing so creates a feeling of inclusion and equality.
2. The purpose and mission of the group needs to be clear to all members involved. And the mission should be looked over often, just in case anything has changed or any member has forgotten what it originally was supposed to be. It's entirely possible the mission changes, depending on what the customer's feedback is after a Sprint. Keeping the mission statement updated will help everyone to stay on task.
3. Rules are very important and need to be established and monitored throughout the entire process. Having the rules helps everyone know where things stand and what to do if a rule is broken or in question.

4. The group should remember that conflict can be a positive thing and is completely normal. The conflict could even be necessary for the group's development. One member might disagree with another on how to complete a task. Because of the two members disagreeing, they might actually invent a third way to complete said task that is much more efficient.
5. The group should remember to listen to each other. Having one person to speak over everyone isn't productive and can cause the group to be upset or resent each other. If everyone remembers to listen, then everyone feels as if they are heard by the other members. People tend to respond better and are more accepting of other's if they feel as if they've had the chance to be heard.
6. Each session should end with constructive criticism instead of harsh "advice". It's important to lift each other up and be helpful towards each other, instead of putting each other down. And it's also important to remember that the constructive criticism should be about the group process and nothing personal.
7. Everyone should contribute and do the work. Having one person do all the work makes said person feel resentful toward the whole group. And if only one person is doing the work, then it's entirely possible that the product won't be finished on time and any deadlines will be behind schedule. The same thing goes for one person sitting out while the rest of the group does all the work. That one person will get credit for work they haven't done, and it's not fair to the rest of the team.

Scaling Scrum

Scrum was first introduced as a method used mainly for smaller projects. Many believed that's all it was good for but didn't really know if it was possible to scale Scrum because it's never been done before. So how can Scrum even be scalable? It actually is possible, through something called Scrum of Scrum Meetings.

Scrum Teams ideally have between 6 and 10 members. However, if there is a need for more than 10 people, then multiple teams are formed. This is fantastic for larger projects and requires open communication and synchronization between each team. Each team picks a representative, who then meets with all the other representatives. They update each other about progress, different challenges being faced, and coordinate activities. How often Scrum of Scrum Meetings take place is determined by the size of the project, how complex the project is, inter-team dependency, and the recommendations of the Scrum Guidance Body.

So how do the meetings work? It's recommended that the teams have face to face communication between them. However, this isn't very often possible, since many companies have various teams working in different time zones and locations. If this happens, then social media and video conference calls can be used. These meetings, called the Convene Scrum of Scrums Process are run by the Chief Scrum Master and helping the Chief are representatives from various teams, who are usually the Scrum Master of their individual teams. For the especially large projects, involving many different teams, having numerous meetings may be necessary. And because it can be difficult to have everyone together at the same time, it is vital that all important matters be discussed whenever the meetings take place. However, before the meetings even take place, the Chief Scrum Master announces the agenda, which the individual teams can then look at and think about any other items that need to be discussed. And any issues, changes, or even risks that have the possibility of affecting the many teams should be brought up and talked about during the meeting. Even challenges facing the individual teams should also be brought up, because there's always the possibility of it affecting multiple teams.

The individual representative from each team should update the other teams. When doing so, it's best to follow these 4 guidelines: What work has my team done since the last meeting? What will my team be working on until the next meeting? Is there anything that remains unfinished that the other teams were expecting to be done? And Will what we're doing affect the other teams?

The most important rule about Scrum of Scrum Meetings is ensuring that there is excellent coordination across the different Scrum Teams. There are many instances of tasks that involve inter-team dependencies; meaning one team's task may depend on another team's delivery of another task. So, it is vital that each team is open in their communication and everyone works together. Doing this ensures the best possible results without any issues along the way.

Chapter 30: Execute a Sprint

Given that a sprint makes up one part of the entire Scrum project, the Development Team needs to have a clear understanding of how to plan each sprint effectively.

By managing to plan each sprint effectively, the Scrum team can handle the project's requirements and deliver the project's output according to the deadline. Consequently, the team needs to gain a keen understanding of the following meetings:

1. The Sprint Planning Meeting
2. The Sprint Review Meeting
3. The Sprint Retrospect Meeting

These three different meetings, which happen at various stages of the project, enable the Scrum team to produce the outputs that are required as a part of the project. As such, the Scrum team needs to take advantage of each meeting in order to plan work effectively for the following sprint.

So, let's drill down into what each of the above-mentioned meetings entails.

The Sprint Planning Meeting

The first Sprint Planning Meeting takes place right after the Development Team has been assembled and the Product Backlog has been built.

At the first Sprint Planning Meeting, the Development Team will determine which tasks ought to be the first in the queue. What this implies is that the Development Team needs to figure out which user stories and which tasks require immediate attention.

This is where it gets tricky.

The Development Team may decide to tackle the most important tasks first. As such, the most important tasks may be due to the fact that these are tasks which serve as the foundation for the rest of the tasks in the Product Backlog.

In other cases, the Development Team may choose to get through the easiest, or the hardest, tasks first and then focus on the remaining tasks which may demand more, or less, attention. Under these circumstances, the Development Team has the option to decide what they will work on based on the number of sprints they have available and the amount of work to be completed.

It should be noted that the number of sprints does not depend on the Development Team. While there might be cases in which the Scrum team decides how long a project will take, most of the time, the project doesn't have much of a choice. For example, they may only have four weeks to complete a given project time and/or budgetary constraints. In such cases, the Development Team needs to make the number of sprints available work with the number of tasks to be completed.

After the initial Sprint Planning Meeting, the Development Team will get to work on the first sprint until its completion. Subsequently, Sprint Planning Meetings will depend on the output of the previous sprint and the feedback received from the customer.

In addition, there may be change requests from the customer. So, these elements need to be taken into account when engaging upon the next sprint's Sprint Planning Meeting.

Regarding change management, it's crucial to note that changes should not be introduced mid-sprint. When changes are introduced mid-sprint, the Development Team's rhythm may be upset and lead the team to lose focus. Moreover, the time taken to plan the sprint may end up being useless if the Scrum Master and/or the Product Owner agree to change setting at mid-sprint.

If things change so drastically, especially due to unforeseen conditions, it might be best to cancel the sprint and start over. Now, canceling a sprint is not the most advisable thing to do, the Scrum Master and the Product Owner may consider doing so in order to avoid useless work and get the project back on track.

One other thing: the Sprint Planning Meeting must be attended by the entire Development Team and the Scrum Master. They will sit down and go over what must be done in the upcoming sprint. This meeting can be held at any time, though it would probably be best to hold it on a Monday morning right at the outset of the new sprint. That way, the Development Team and the Scrum Master will have the rest of the week ahead of them to begin the new sprint.

The Product Owner may choose to attend the Sprint Planning Meeting though it is not necessary. The Product Owner may choose to attend especially when there have been change requests on the part of the customer. Otherwise, the Product Owner may choose to forego the Sprint Planning Meeting, though the Product Owner may request to meet with the Scrum team with the intent of gathering information to update the customer.

The Sprint Review Meeting

At the end of the sprint, the sprint's outcomes are presented to the customer at the Sprint Review Meeting.

The purpose of this meeting is in line with one of the principles of Agile which is to deliver value to the customer even at early stages in the development of the project. As such, the Sprint Review Meeting is intended to present the project team's advances in order for the customer to see how the project is coming along.

The Sprint Review Meeting can be as simple, or as elaborate, as the project team sees fit. For instance, it might be a formal event in which an early prototype might be unveiled. In other cases, the Sprint Review Meeting may be a test run of the product. In such cases, the customer has the opportunity to test out the product and provide their feedback. However, when the team chooses to hold the Sprint Review Meeting, the main objective is to demonstrate that the project has progressively achieved its objectives.

At the Sprint Review Meeting, the entire Scrum team should be present in addition to the customer and all project stakeholders. This implies that the Sprint Review Meeting aims to achieve cohesion among all of the actors involved in the project.

Now, the feedback provided by the customer at the Sprint Review Meeting is of the utmost importance.

In some cases, the customer might be thrilled and not provide any significant feedback. In such cases, the customer's blessing serves as a means of motivating the team to move forward and provide guidance for the upcoming sprint.

In other cases, the customer may provide feedback on the features and elements that make up the final product. This feedback may be related to simple aspects such as layout, color, and other visual aspects of the product, while feedback may also refer to more profound aspects such as the solution it actually provides to the end user.

Also, the Sprint Review Meeting provides an opportunity for the customer to present change requests. These change requests may not be related to the actual work of the Scrum team, that is, the customer requesting changes based on ineffectiveness on the part of the Scrum team. Rather, it could be that the customer has realized they want additional features or functionalities. Furthermore, the customer may choose to change their mind on specific features thus requesting changes.

If, and when, the customer chooses to make a change request, the Product Owner is the one who needs to translate this change request into the type of language which the Development Team can understand and turn into actions that reflect the change request on the part of the customer.

The Sprint Retrospect Meeting

At the end of the sprint, the final phase that takes place is the Sprint Retrospect Meeting. This meeting is intended to give the Scrum team the opportunity to debrief and reflect on the past sprint's successes and shortcomings. As a result, the Scrum team will be able to analyze what they feel needs to be improved while making sure that the good trends continue.

This meeting also provides the opportunity for team members to address issues and challenges which they have been facing throughout the sprint and the project. For example, there might be a gap in the technical knowledge of the team. As such, the team may choose to bring in an expert who can support them such as an Agile Coach.

In this specific example, an Agile Coach is an expert in Agile and Scrum methodology. This Coach will help guide the Scrum team in learning the finer points of the Scrum methodology while ensuring its correct application throughout the various tasks and sprints.

Furthermore, the Scrum team may find it important to address issues that may potentially come up and deal with them in a proactive manner. Consequently, the Scrum team may choose to find the necessary elements that will enable them to deal with such issues before they become a problem.

The Sprint Retrospect Meeting may also serve as a springboard into the Sprint Planning Meeting. The reason for this is that customer feedback is also discussed at the Sprint Retrospect Meeting. Thus, the Scrum team has the opportunity to discuss the customer's feedback and incorporate it into the upcoming sprint. This would provide a logical segue into the next sprint.

By the same token, the Sprint Retrospect Meeting can also deal with change requests from the customer as a result of their feedback following the Sprint Review Meeting. Also, the customer may have made a change request at some point during the sprint. Since the Scrum team does not incorporate changes mid-sprint, the Product Owner may choose the

Sprint Retrospect Meeting as the opportunity to bring up the matter and then transition into the Sprint Planning Meeting so that the matter can be discussed and then integrated into the Sprint Backlog in the next sprint.

Finally, it's worth mentioning that the Sprint Retrospect Meeting doesn't have to be a boring affair. This can be done in a setting in which the team can relax and enjoy some time together as a team. It could be on a weekend or during a team dinner. The important thing is to have enough time to relax and discuss matters openly and honestly.

As long as the team is able to deal with things openly and maturely, there will always be positive outcomes at the Sprint Retrospect Meeting. Hopefully, both the positives and the negatives will lead to a good Sprint Planning Meeting and a subsequent successful sprint.

Chapter 31: Keeping. Track of a Project

The next step you'll need to work on is being able to determine who in your company should be responsible for the various aspects of your project. Just like the company itself, every task needs someone presiding over it to ensure that it's getting done to a satisfactory result. Problems that may start out in the functional portion of your business can grow and travel through the ranks until they're all the way up on the CEO's desk, which is something you want to keep from happening.

Project deliverables, accountabilities, and various responsibilities should be divided amongst the various ranking members all the way from Executive Managers down to Yellow Belts. Remember, these are the tiers that flow from top to bottom:

- *Executive Leadership* – These are your top brass. These are the people who sit on the board, who rank around and with the Chief Executive Officer and more like them. These are the leaders who can authorize process changes for the people who work underneath them, and who can authorize the use and change of company materials and resources.
- *Champions or Quality Leaders* – Champions and Quality Leaders are the ones who are largely in charge of the implementation of this methodology. These are the people who hold sway with a large portion of those who work the pedals and gears that drive your business forward. These people can and should be chosen by upper management *carefully*, as these are the people who will be mentoring the Black Belts to ensure they're getting the best out of your team.
- *Master Black Belts* – The Champions and Quality Leaders will choose the Master Black Belts to help

them to reach all the Black Belts in terms of mentorship and support. The Master Black Belt should be a stable resource for those in the organization who need guidance or assistance in implementation and utilization of Six Sigma.

- *Black Belts* – The Black Belts should be considered the Movers and Shakers of your Six Sigma methodology implementation and utilization. Their primary task is to ensure that each of the projects currently in motion are being conducted in accordance with the rules and guidelines of Six Sigma, as well as administering any projects that pertain specifically to the implementation of Six Sigma. The Black Belts should often be left to work on their own, as they will largely be autonomous and self-sufficient. Master Black Belts simply stay alert in case Black Belts need and subsequently call on them for assistance and guidance.
- *Green Belts* – Each tier from Black Belt upward is entirely focused on the implementation and instruction of Six Sigma, while the Green Belts will be working on certain project goals and other projects that were in motion before the implementation of Six Sigma began, thus keeping all wheels in the machine turning and all projects in forward motion.
- *Yellow Belts* – Yellow Belts are the people with little to no experience with or understanding of the methodology and its use. These are the employees that will continue their daily operations as normal, making only the changes that have been ordered by those above. These employees will be learning about the methodology while instructed to carry out daily duties to help the company to progress.

Everyone on the totem pole must be responsible for some aspect of the projects, as this is an overhaul that affects the entire company, from the ground up.

You want management personnel to have a say in the changes that get made because they are the ones overseeing their staff on these implementations. You want non-management personnel to have a say because they will largely be the ones who are responsible for implementing the changes and getting them cemented in place. Everyone on the ladder will have an important part to play.

Just like the business itself, Six Sigma requires team effort and it requires that you be coordinated, dedicated, and educated on the methodology to pull it all off.

Choosing a Solution, Implementing, and Following Up

Picking the solution to the problems you've identified is something that has been mentioned a few times already in this text. Many people are confident in their ability to look at a problem in front of them, assess the data associated with that problem, determine the change that needs to occur, determine the thing that will affect that change, and set it in motion.

This is the act of identifying and choosing a solution you feel will work in your business. There are, however, a couple of other steps that sometimes are forgotten, particularly by those who reside in the upper management portion of the business.

Implementing the Solution You've Chosen

Now that you've found the solution and you're reasonably confident that it will make the desired changes to your business, you need to implement it. This means identifying the pieces of it that can be taken on and carried out by the people in your team. Assigning a piece of the solution to each person or department across the board will help to shoulder the load and make the changes easier on everyone. If the whole team moves as one, there is less hectic motion and chaos.

You and the appropriate members of your team will need to formulate the steps and procedures that need to be completed in order to result in the successful implementation of this solution you've chosen. Ensure that all of the people on your staff understand the problem, the solution, why the solution will work, how the solution will work, and what their roles in all of that are.

The next step is crucial because, if it fails, you need to start over and find a new solution.

Follow Up to determine if Your Solution is Viable

Giving everyone a job to do for a solution that is not viable will, in the very best of cases, result in no movement on the problems at all. In the very worst, you're back to square one with more problems than when you started. You want to make sure that everyone on the team is carrying out their duties with minimal difficulty and with maximum yield.

Be sure that your team is aware they can comfortably bring any difficulties or shortcomings of the project to your attention so reassessments can be done and changes can be made to the solution that's been implemented.

Proper and regular reassessment of the comings and goings of your business gives you a clear and accurate picture of what your business is doing, how your business is doing, and whether or not your business is successful!

Six Sigma is a methodology that is hands-on and which requires that time and effort be put in by all who contribute to the team. However, if you are determined to provide the best possible product and experience for your team and for your customers, this is the methodology with which to reduce your overhead, maximize your profits, minimize your workload, and grow your business.

Conclusion

Well, if you have made it to this point, it is because you are serious about Scrum.

As we have discussed earlier, Scrum is a rather simple methodology to implement but it takes time to master it. Not only does Scrum require a fair amount of work in developing working proficiency, but it is certainly worth it.

I would greatly encourage you to put in the time and effort into mastering your project management skills. As such, Scrum can help you get the right skills and the right people you need in order to make the most out of your endeavors. Best of all, Scrum is the type of methodology you can implement virtually anywhere at any time.

At this point, it is time for you to get your feet wet in the Scrum world. As you gain experience, you will be able to improve your knowledge and understanding with each iteration of the process. In addition, the lessons learned that you are able to collect will help you to build a working doctrine in your particular field.

So, what's the next step?

If your organization is considering the implementation of Scrum as a project management methodology or just a regular business practice, then, by all means, share this information with your colleagues and business associates.

You can begin by discussing how Scrum can benefit your organization. Granted, it should be said that Scrum may not be ideal for everyone. There might be a valid reason why Scrum may be ideal for your organization. Notwithstanding, you can get together with your colleagues and figure out how Scrum can help you improve your overall business processes.

Best of all, you can begin to implement the use of Scrum in an incremental fashion. That means that it does not have to be an overnight process. By incrementally implementing

Scrum, you can find your bearings slowly. As you build up your experience and understanding of Scrum and Agile, you will be able to put it to work for you and your organization.

Ultimately, your efforts will lead you to learn more about you and your organization. You will learn how you can improve your organization's overall processes and business practices.

If you have found this book to be interesting and informative, please share it with your colleagues and business associates. Also, don't forget to leave a comment. I am sure that other like-minded individuals will find your comments to be useful. There are others out there who may have heard of Scrum but are not sure what it is. So, your input will certainly be appreciated by many folks who are wondering if Scrum is right for them and their organization.

I hope that this book has met your expectations. It was written with great care and patience. Should you have any questions or any comments, I would be glad to hear about it. If anything, engaging in a useful discussion will help us all learn more about Scrum and how it can be refined and improved over time.

Thanks again for reading.

Part 3: Kanban

If you're looking to find a way to get maximum work efficiency, you're going to find a tool that can help you do exactly that through this book. This book will guide you on how to use Kanban and other work visualization tools in order to help you and your team boost your productivity.

It's a struggle to stay focused especially if the workload accumulates quicker than you can finish whatever you are currently handling. Not only that, it can become even more stressful when someone cannot finish the task they are working on because their skills do not match what they're doing, or they're unmotivated.

Sometimes, it's the skills mismatch that causes the loss of motivation. When these things happen, expectations coming from the higher-ups and customers or clients are not met. Everyone becomes unhappy and the company loses resources. This is a far too common scenario.

I remember working with colleagues on several projects at once, thinking that multitasking helps finish the tasks at a faster pace. However, it became too stressful and somewhere in the middle of working those projects, the progress slowed down significantly, and the quality of the output did not meet the demands of the clients. It cost us precious time, money, and potential clients since we were not able to accommodate new projects since we were still working on some projects.

There were also cases in which I worked on team projects, where each of the members is assigned specific tasks, and that the progress and results of each task are dependent on each other. Working on team projects required each and everyone in the team to have a full grasp of the progress of every aspect of the project. It was difficult especially since it's not easy to point out problems in the project due to everyone being busy on their specific tasks. It led to problems occurring during the project duration and it was too late to do something about the problems.

That's why I developed this book. I want you to know that there are tools out there that you can use.

With this book, you will be given techniques on effective visualization of the work. Not only that, but this book will also provide ideas on how to achieve the ideal output and work efficiency you're aiming for.

What Is Work Visualization?

Work visualization is simply the practice in which all aspects of work and workflow information is presented in visual form, hence the name. It involves presenting this information to all team members, managers, and stakeholders so that they can consume and process information quickly, and use it to be reminded of what needs to be done, who needs to do it, and where the team is in terms of progress.

Work visualization practice is a relatively modern practice. Traditionally, information about project status and direction cannot be easily accessed. People had their reports, project plans, and PowerPoint slides in their own desks and file cabinets. You had to request data from individual members manually, which takes time. In addition, some of the information is bound to be outdated. With work visualization, a more transparent manner of working is made possible.

Work visualization helps everyone in the company to see, know, and learn together. It is a simple and creative way of solving problems that can be used at every level of the organization. It enables everyone to see the differences between what was planned and what happened. Everyone can then help in finding root causes and developing countermeasures. It encourages people to work together on the problems and develop accountability towards achieving objectives without being overburdened.

Kanban is a work visualization technique that is aligned with Lean Thinking and Agile principles. Lean thinking, after all, is all about elimination of wastes, and Kanban is one tool that will highlight all the processes that produce waste. Agile methodologies, which Kanban falls under, focuses on maintaining quality and standards and controlling the total costs involved in the production of a particular product while meeting the demands of the customers. It goes with the idea that the demands coming from the customers should be met effectively at a rapid pace. And in this book, you'll learn about how to use these tools for your business.

Kanban in Action

Kanban is a scheduling system being used in just-in-time manufacturing and lean manufacturing in Japan. It works by enabling you to spot areas having problems through performance indicators such as cycle time and lead time. This approach is so effective that several companies from all over the world such as Spotify, Auto Trader (UK), Pixar, Zara, and DJ Orthopedics have been known to use it.

Mattias Jansson, working as an operations engineer at Spotify shared that the main problem in their operations was scalability. The operations team just cannot keep up with the needs and demands of the company. By implementing Kanban as the workflow management tool, lead times became shorter, many internal tasks are completed, and the departments the teams work with became happier with the performance.

Auto Trader, a company based in Manchester, UK decided to use Kanban to their advantage when they realized that many of the issues they've been facing are brought by various teams (e.g. Sysadmins, Release Team, Service Desk) working against each other. Prior to using Kanban, the email system the company was using had been contributing to the lack of teamwork, and to make up for the inefficiencies and difficulties in prioritizing, employees had to work a grueling 70 hours a week.

Ed Catmull, the president of Pixar, has recognized the need for Kanban in film production. A finished movie is basically an organized sequence of events. To complete the projects, each team transfers the idea to the preceding team, until the idea is pushed deeper into the chain. Through using Kanban boards, everyone working on a project has an idea of what the others are working on and everyone has an idea as to how their work can affect the works of the other members.

Kanban systems are applied to the store level at Zara. The store managers are given the responsibility to determine what, when, and how much of a product will be produced. Data on what the loyal customers demand are the basis of the orders they send to the headquarters twice a week.

Hospitals can also benefit from the use of Kanban. Seattle Children's Hospital, for example, has been experiencing shortages in various items such as surgical dressings, clamps, catheters, and specialized tubing. This led to the nurses having to stockpile the goods at random locations in the hospital to make sure that they have the necessary items whenever the situation called for it. Unfortunately, this non-standardized way of inventory storing led to work delays, which reduced the time that can be allotted to treat patients. When Kanban was implemented, a designated storage area was established, and information is collected, and this database is maintained so that supplies are available when needed and the amount of expired goods is minimized. When they do expire, they are disposed of quickly. As a result, medical practitioners are given more time to deal and treat their patients.

Sustainability is one of the hallmarks of Kanban and Lean thinking, and one of the companies who have been integrating this principle into their manufacturing process is Nike.

Kimberley-Clark Corporation, makers of Kleenex, worked with Unipart on enhanced staff development and engagement, which lead to a reduction of staff absenteeism and better staff morale.

John Deere, 2003 world's biggest agricultural machinery manufacturer, spent $100 million in transforming its Iowa, U.S. operation to lean manufacturing which led to employees being able to identify and eliminate non-value-added activities wherever possible.

Companies working following the agile approach have a large network of suppliers and related companies that aid them in delivering products of high quality, which also gives them the advantages of being able to increase production as the consumer demand increases while also being able to redesign the products with issues from consumers.

By implementing Agile, 3M gained the ability to create self-organized teams which are also reactive to customer requirements and also were able to push forward priorities that they seem fit.

ANZ, a banking company based in Australia, now has the capability of releasing new functions on their banking application as needed and has enjoyed massive recognition as a result.

Google, by applying customer feedback to their improvements based on Agile, allows users to participate in Beta testing, which help identify bugs, major issues, and reports needed to apply to further update their products.

Spotify applied an agile environment by organizing its employees into squads. As the agile scrum method emphasizes on dividing work into chunks, Spotify used that principle by assigning each squad different tasks at hand. Results from that make Spotify one of the leading music streaming services globally.

Applying these techniques to your business will help you achieve success. There's nothing to lose and everything to gain when you gain an understanding of these techniques.

Many companies that have started implementing these techniques and reaped success afterward.

Chapter 32.
The Kanban Method

There are a lot of different processes that are used when it comes to working with a manufacturing company or with software development. One of the methods and techniques that are becoming very popular to use is Kanban. This is a process for software development that helps to provide more efficiency compared to some of the other methods. Although producing software is a creative activity and it involves some different processes compared to producing a lot of cars, the mechanisms that are needed for managing both of them can still be applied. When we talk about a process for software development, we can think of it like a pipeline that has some requests that enter in one end, and then these are turned into improved software that will come out on the other end. Inside this pipeline, the business is going to have some process in place that can help get all of this done. The process can range from an informal ad hoc process to one that is very formal and comes in a ton of phases. We are going to look at the simpler process. There will be three main steps that come with looking through Kanban and the pipeline that comes with it including analyzing the requirements, developing the code, and testing out how it all works. Each company can choose exactly how they want to do all of this and the number of steps that you need to take to get it all done.

The Origins of Kanban

Kanban is basically a scheduling system that was developed and used for just in time manufacturing and for lean manufacturing. This system was developed by an industrial engineer from Toyota as a way to improve the efficiency of the manufacturing team. Kanban is just one of the methods that can be used to help achieve JIT. The system will take its name due to the cards that are used in order to track production that occurs within the factory.

Kanban was developed to be used in the manufacturing world, but it has also become an effective tool that can help support the efficiency of many different types of industries and it can help to promote improvement wherever it is needed. The problem areas for the team are going to be highlighted with the help of measuring out the cycle time and the lead time of the full process. One of the benefits that you will see with the Kanban system is that it can help the team establish an upper limit to the amount of WIP or work in progress so that they don't take on too much and create a bottleneck in the system. In addition, one of the goals of the Kanban system is to make sure that there is never an excess amount of inventory that builds up in any part of the production phase. Limits on the number of items that can be waiting at supply points can be established and then they can be reduced as different inefficiencies are identified and the team is able to remove them. If the limit is exceeded, this is going to point out that there is some kind of inefficiency that your team needs to focus on removing.

The Principles of Kanban

Kanban is going to be based on three main principles that can make it easier to handle. The three basic principles that come with working in Kanban include:

- Visualize what you need to work on today or the workflow: When you are able to see all of the items in context with the others, it can really inform you of what has been done, what is being worked on, and what still needs to be accomplished.
- Limit the amount of work that is in progress (WIP): This can make it easier for the workflow to be balanced. This ensures that your team isn't going to start and commit to too much work right from the beginning.
- Enhance flow: When an item or a task gets finished, the highest thing from the backlog is going to be pulled into play and used.

The process of Kanban is going to promote a continuous collaboration. In addition, it asks for an active and ongoing learning and improving system because it will define the best workflow for the team to get things done in the most efficient manner possible.

The Core Properties of Kanban

There are five core properties that come up when you are using the process of Kanban. Knowing what these are, and how they work together, can make a big difference when it comes to how successful your project can be. The five core properties that need to be present in order to see success with Kanban will include:

Visualize your workflow

The team needs to have a good idea of what it takes to get an item from a request from the project owner to completion with a finished project. The goal of using Kanban is to make a change that is positive to ensure optimization of the workflow throughout the whole system. After understanding how this kind of workflow functions in the business right now, you can then aspire to make improvements and adjustments to have it work better. If you try to make changes ahead of time, it can make things difficult. The best way for a team to visualize their workflow is to use card walls and add in different cards and columns in there. Each column that is on the wall will represent steps that occur in your workflow. Sometimes it can even be beneficial to visualize the work that is coming in and will need to be handled. The team will have to work together to determine which categories they would like to add to the Kanban board. You can then use different colored Post-It notes to help you address these and give them the categories that seem to work the best.

Limit the WIP

Another thing that you need to work on here is learning how to limit the amount of work in progress. This one implies that the pull system has been implemented on parts or on all of the workflow. The elements that need to be done right away, or are seen as the most important, are going to be the things the team is working on right away. The new work is going to be pulled into the following step as soon as there is some capacity with your WIP limit, but not before. These constrain are going to help you figure out where some of the problem areas are in the flow, so you have a better chance of resolving them. Learning how to limit the amount of WIP that you have at a single time can make the team more efficient at getting the work done.

Manage flow

The main reason that a lot of companies are going to implement the Kanban system is because they want to be able to create some positive change in the system. Before you are able to get that change, you must know what change is necessary. You can figure this out by looking at the way that value is able to flow through the whole system, take an analysis of the areas that are causing problems, then implementing the changes. As you go through and repeat this cycle, you will be able to see what effects the changes had on your system because you will need to know this before moving on. The process has to keep going on, it is one that will never be done, but it ensures that the system works and that your team is being as efficient as possible.

Make the policies for the process explicit

Before the team can do any of its work, the process needs to have a chance to be defined, published, and socialized. Without a good understanding of how the process works and how the work needs to be done, any discussion of the problems that come up will be emotional, subjective, and anecdotal. When all members of the team start to understand what you are doing with this process and what the overall goals are, then it is easier to make smart decisions about any change that can move you to a more positive direction. One place where this can be important is when you come up with the definition of done. How is the team going to know when they are done with a step, or when they finish one project and it is time to move on to another one? In fact, it is possible to have this done definition for each step of the workflow so that there are requirements before an item can be pulled forward. Some tools, like LeanKit, can let you do this automatically on your electronic board, but you can easily adjust this on a manual board or any other tool you choose to use.

Use models and the scientific method

And finally, Kanban is going to encourage small continuous, evolutionary, and incremental changes that can stay around. In many cases, Kanban is going to suggest that the team uses the scientific approach in order to meet these goals. There are different options that you can choose to make this happen including the Theory of Constraints, the System of Profound Knowledge, and the Lean Economic Model.

Getting Started with Kanban

While we will go into more details about this part as we progress through this guidebook, starting Kanban is not meant to be a difficult process. It is set up as a way to help you develop a product more efficiently than you were able to do in the past. With the help of diagrams and other tools, Kanban can make it easier to help you get your work done, and for everyone on the team to know what works needs to be done. Some of the steps that you can take to get started with the Kanban system include:

1. Map the value stream or your development process: In this, you can ask where do feature ideas come from and who is responsible for these? What are the steps that an idea has to go through to get from an idea to a finished product in the hands of the user?
2. Define the start and then the endpoints for your Kanban system: These should be the place where political control is determined. Don't worry too much during this stage about having a narrow focus because it won't take long before people outside of the span are going to ask to join in as well.
3. Agree: This is the point where everyone needs to agree on the steps that need to be taken and what is going to happen during the process. Some of the things that your team should agree upon before starting will include the following:

a. The initial limits for WIP and any policies that can be in place in order to change those limits or break them temporarily.

b. The process for prioritizing or selecting the features that needs to be done.

c. The policies for the way you will classify your services. This could be things like fixed delivery date, expedite, or standard. Determine if you need to provide estimates. And when the team has to choose the work they will do, how will they make this selection.

d. How often reviews should be done to ensure the system is still working.

4. Draw up the Kanban board: This can be as simple or as complicated as you would like. All that you really need here is a whiteboard with a marker or some post-it notes. Do not spend too much of your time trying to make this board look perfect. It is going to evolve and change often so keep it simple and allow it to have room to change.

5. Empirically adjust: As more of the project gets done and more requirements come in, there will need to be some adjustments made to the system. Make any of these adjustments to the board as needed.

The idea of Kanban is pretty simple to work with, and it allows a team to visually see what has been done, what is being done right now, and what needs to be done in the future. It is a visual representation, which happens to work the best for most people who are working on a project. They can just glance up and see how the process towards completion is going and feel motivated as things move from Work in Progress over to finished or completed. It is a great way to make a team more efficient and will ensure they get the work done in no time.

Chapter 33.
Kanban Use

Managing your people is not an easy task and issues in the business make things a lot worse. You'll need the right tools to deal with various issues. Implementing Kanban, Lean Thinking, Agile, and Scrum to your business will aid you in those endeavors.

Using the Kanban method

Kanban is a method used for workflow management which is designed to help you to visualize the work you have and maximize the efficiency of the work you are doing all the while being agile in doing the work. A Kanban board can have as many columns depending on the process of work you are planning to do. The simplest form contains three columns - Requested, In Progress, Done.

Key Performance Indicators aid you by providing criteria that determine whether the performances in the business are going well or not. Unfortunately, some companies do not apply these indicators in the business, and some are not able to monitor these indicators. Either way, it causes these companies a lot of money, resources, and time.

By placing your projects in a Kanban board and setting up a limit in the "In Progress" column, you will be able to multitask projects. As long as you set up a limit in the "In Progress" column, which is based on the amount of work your team can handle at the moment, it is likely that the work will be done at the projected deadline you set. Additionally, Kanban's flexibility allows you to still point out problems that need to be addressed despite you are handling several projects at one time.

Identifying problems in your business can be easier through setting up your projects in a Kanban board. In a manufacturing setup, you will be able to see the bigger picture and identify the issues, be it knowing what causes the delay in the production of the item you sell or learn whether the overall process of producing your product is efficient. In an office setup, you will know as to what causes your team to not meet their deadlines, or you will be able to create a better-standardized process of dealing with projects since you have learned the one before does not work efficiently.

Seeing the bigger picture lets you see what goes well and what needs improvement or change. Using the Kanban method in your business helps your teamwork out efficiently and maximize the output of your work. With that, you will be assured that everything goes well for your business.

Kanban is a simple software, which is not just about working with a whiteboard and listing out the tasks for a team using different cards.

The current trends show that Kanban is being used in different industries and areas and is gaining immense popularity. Small agencies, start-ups, and even traditional organizations have begun to use Kanban systems.

Kanban in Software and IT

Kanban is not a project management or software development tool, and this has been made evident right from the start. Kanban does not talk about how software must be built or provide a list of methods to use to manage a project. It does not talk about how a process should be planned or how software should be implemented.

Therefore, Kanban, unlike Scrum, is a system that helps an organization and teams within that organization improve their work. Microsoft used Kanban in 2004 for its software development operations, and since then it has been used in different software teams across the organization.

The beauty of the system is that it can be applied to multiple methodologies and processes. If an organization is already using Agile methods like XP, Scrum and others or traditional methods like iterative or Waterfall, Kanban can be applied to those methods to improve processes, improve quality of work and reduce cycle time. This will help an organization continue to deliver products and services of excellent quality.

Kanban in Software or Product Development

Many tech product development and application software development teams have used Kanban to implement Agile and Lean principles. The Kanban method gives the teams a great set of practices and principles that will help them visualize their work and deliver products and services at high speed.

These teams will also be able to get constant feedback from customers to help them improve their processes. The teams are also able to market their products to their customers with greater speed.

The Kanban system has undergone an evolution over the last five years in many industries, especially the IT industry. Kanban is considered to be one of the best methods that can be used by teams to manage and improve the services in a gradual manner.

The Kanban method also provides teams with essential techniques and principles that improve Service Level Agreements (SLA), minimize the risk during the process, reduce the cost of delay and deliver products at the right time.

Kanban helps delivery teams and customers collaborate effectively using concepts like Class of Services, 2-phase commit and deferred commitment to ensure that the right processes are worked on at the right times.

Businesses have begun to use Kanban after the advent of Portfolio Kanban. Enterprise Services Planning and Upstream Kanban are used to improve market performance and achieve great agility.

Kanban and Enterprise Agility

The Kanban method helps an organization improve the delivery of products and services gradually. This is done by removing any bottlenecks or impediments in the system thereby improving the workflow and reducing the time taken to complete a task. This system helps teams deliver continuously and obtain feedback from the customers within a short time span. This feedback allows the team to improve the product or service and helps the team become responsive.

The Kanban system enables the principles of any Agile Manifesto and helps teams deliver products and services that are needed by customers. The Kanban system works with Agile methodologies and techniques to improve processes for better performance of the organization.

Kanban is a natural fit for most non-IT business processes since its roots lie in manufacturing. If an organization wants to become Lean and Agile and deliver products of high quality, it must make use of the Kanban system.

Large and medium organizations have been using 6-Sigma and Lean initiatives to improve their production workflow for several years. However, Kanban systems enable every business, regardless of size or type, to improve every business function like Marketing, HR, Procurement, Sales, etc.

Kanban is being applied in multiple project management contexts including engineering and construction projects. Multiple organizations like recruitment organizations, staffing companies, insurance companies, advertising agencies, and many other companies are using Kanban systems to eliminate waste and streamline their processes thereby improving quality and throughput.

Chapter 34.
Kanban Advantages And Disadvantages

Advantages

Kanban has many advantages that will help when it comes to project management. Here are some of those advantages:

- You'll get flexibility

An advantage many are thrilled to gain when using Kanban is flexibility. A lot of projects can be too rigid to deal with because you're not sure if the tasks you're assigned can work when different circumstances come about or if the time frame is possible within the current scenario. But with Kanban, you'll be able to make adjustments on the go and still get things done.

This is especially true when the situation calls for swift changes and tiny adjustments. After all, you can't expect a customer to have the same attitude toward a certain product that you and your team do. You also can't assume that your inventory will never fluctuate.

That's why with Kanban, you'll be ready to make adjustments when the situation calls for it. Need to adjust the time needed for a certain task to get done? Go for it. Have a workflow that might not work for the upcoming inventory resupply? Done.

The flexibility you gain with Kanban will help you respond to the ever-changing atmosphere of your projects. So, even if one little factor shakes things up, you can still get things done without losing the overall objective.

- You'll have improved visibility

When it comes to the Kanban method, visualization is vital. That's why one advantage you'll gain is improved visibility.

While average project management systems let you have minor visuals, such as sticky notes, Kanban goes beyond that and makes the visuals essential.

So, your visibility on the overall structure of the project, along with the backlogs, the processes, and other data, will no doubt show you that you now have a better picture on where the project is finally heading to.

- You'll be able to improve workflow efficiency

Another great advantage of using Kanban is improving workflow efficiency. When you've visualized your workflow and gained better visibility, you'll get more things done. This means that the hassles, bumps, and other hiccups you had to experience with your project can all be scraped to the side because you'll have a better idea on what needs to be done to get your project completed on time. In short, you can get done with what you set out to do and be finished without breaking a sweat.

This will also help you honor the fifth principle of Kanban, recognizing improvement opportunities with models, because you'll be able to identify some of the areas in the project workflow that need to be addressed. And when you do that, you will significantly improve the efficiency of the workflow.

- You'll be able to achieve ongoing delivery

A great advantage you'll get with Kanban is being able to maintain ongoing delivery. This means being able to get all the things you've assigned in a project done in small portions to achieve steady output. It will also gain magnificent trust from your customers, clients, or superiors because it will show that what they expect from you will be done without any worry of delay.

- You'll have better focus

Focus is always important to have when you're doing important tasks, but sometimes it's hard to really concentrate on that when doing projects these days. You already have the tasks in mind, but when you're in the middle of it all, you'll find yourself and the rest of your team switching back and forth between tasks and not get anything done at all. That's why using Kanban will give you the benefit of having better focus.

How you ask? With your process policies and WIP limits implemented, you and the rest of your team will be able to set forth what is most important and get those tasks finished before moving onto the other tasks. This will also help you develop your focus on doing singular processes, so when all is said and done you can see that you've finally finished what you set out to do.

- You'll achieve increased productivity

Another great advantage you'll get with using Kanban is increased productivity. This means you'll finish the work you've started because why go through a project that just keeps going on and on without an end to it? The Kanban system will show you that you can gain the closure to the project you manage by being able to set the measure to which you'll start until you finish.

You'll also be able to learn the ways of measuring how long it will take to get tasks done and how to measure how many tasks can be done within a certain time. This data will help you understand how fast and effective everything needs to be to get your project finished on time.

- Wasted work and time will be reduced

With Kanban, you gain the advantage of reducing wasted work and time. This is quite beneficial because it means the worries of overproducing, waiting, over processing, and other forms of wastes in production terms will all be scrapped from the workflow. Instead, you'll be left with what is essential and be able to improve on what has been given to you.

This advantage has been a long-running tradition for Kanban because it was the main element that helped Toyota improve their manufacturing process. Creator Ohno himself identified different types of wastes in the processing line that he advised to be taken out as he was developing Kanban in the 1940s.

- Predictability chances are raised

When you're managing projects, it pays to know whether or not the chances of succeeding are high enough. Will you be able to make the delivery on time? Is the inventory ready for another re-supply? The advantage of using Kanban is that the chances of predicting correctly are raised quite considerably. What this means is there's certainty to be had in the process, which is rare when compared to most project management methods.

This also gives you the opportunity to make use of historical data, where you can see what worked and what didn't work in the past. By analyzing this, you will be able to make better decisions and set up the important tasks and processes to achieve the goal that you've set for your project. This means the fear that forecasts may be inaccurate will be reduced significantly.

Further, Kanban provides a way for the customer, client, or superior to predict that the completion time for a project is always guaranteed when you are managing it. And when this happens, it'll help build the trust and faith that they have toward letting you have control over future projects.

- Team capacity is strengthened

Traditionally, when teams are tasked to do projects, they do the planning right away. But the planning ends up being more like stacking the tasks and getting them done in no particular order. However, the problem with this is that the team may face difficulties trying to get things done because they'll go beyond the capacity that they are capable of in a given time.

That's why when Kanban is used, it shifts a team's mindset to where they're able to add more ordered tasks to the workflow, but only when they're able to do it. Plus, with the WIP limits set, the team will know that they have limits, and when they've reached them, they'll be able to keep themselves from adding more until they've completed what they've already set out to do in the first place.

- You will improve collaboration within your team

Project management doesn't mean you have to do it all alone: You also have the rest of your team to help you out on what will work best. Traditional methods usually don't put much work in on collaborating because, as long as the tasks and objectives are assigned, there's nothing much else to communicate about. But with Kanban, the advantage of improved collaboration is a guaranteed.

This means no one is left behind anymore in the team. Everyone has a role and every member, including you, can contribute. That means the processes, solutions, tasks, and opinions can all be shared. It can also establish a way for the team to brainstorm their way to victory.

Disadvantages

While Kanban is promising with all the advantages you've just learned about, there are some disadvantages you must know as well. These include:

- Variability still exists

Kanban doesn't take the variability out of the picture completely. This means that the flow and the way your system is working with the project may cause confusion, mixed signals, and low-quality results. So, if a customer's needs don't match what you already set to do or unexpected factors come in, the objective you're aiming for may end up becoming different from what you originally thought in the first place.

- Issues may arise with sudden changes

Another disadvantage when using Kanban is that issues may happen with sudden changes in supply and demand. This is because Kanban is best used with projects that have singular goals that are stable and repetitive. While flexibility is also an advantage, there may be times when unexpected and fluctuating changes will bring about consequences that the Kanban system isn't built for.

- Quality mishaps may occur

Because variability still exists, quality can be affected too. Yes, Kanban is the system that will help you manage your inventory and get things accomplished, but quality isn't factored in for this one. What if one product needs a little redesign? What if a few items on the shelves have to be looked at one more time before they're sent out for delivery? These little factors aren't standard for Kanban, so expect quality mishaps.

- Production flow processes might get mixed up in other areas

Another disadvantage when using Kanban is the various production flow processes in a company will have mixed results. While Kanban is well-suited for singular teams, having multiple teams with different tasks, product types, and goals won't exactly work very well. This can result in the company getting more downs than ups when trying to manage their productions.

- Not having traditional time tracking habits may cause confusion

A misconception you'll learn about below is that Kanban doesn't allow you to track time on the tasks you'll be doing. In reality, you do track time, but just not traditionally. This can lead to confusion because most of the time, project management always involved tracking time. That's why it'll be a disadvantage to use Kanban if you're used to the ordinary way of tracking time.

Chapter 35. Kanban Implementation

Your organization can understand lean management easily because it is such a simple method for improving business activity. To illustrate the simplicity of a lean methodology, you cannot get a better example than the Kanban process. It is a tool that controls the flow of information and materials. Despite its simplicity, many organizations are still confused by the concept. Maybe it is because it is so simple. Implementing Kanban should be easy, but it is often implemented below its true potential. This then leads to the process being abandoned. This is why implementing it effectively is so critical.

Below are rules, guidelines, and considerations necessary to a successful Kanban system implementation. Before you begin the process of implementation, consider the following:

A Kanban process can be:

- A device to communicate from the operation last conducted to the usage point. Or, from the supplier to the customer.
- P.O.'s provided to your suppliers.
- Orders for work to your areas of manufacture.
- A tool for visual communication.
- A method for reducing paperwork.

A Kanban system should not be used for:

- Batch or lot or single item production. Something you only create a few times a year should not be managed with a Kanban process.
- Stock designed or used for safety purposes.

- Inventory held by a supplier. For example, consignment or dropshipping is not appropriate for a Kanban system. This situation is not considered a "win-win" lean situation.
- A tool to plan long-term. Traditional management methodologies are best for situations like introducing new products, changes to a customer's usage, and changes in engineering.

To start, within your company, select one area to implement a Kanban system. Begin implementation with less than eight items in this area. Alert your business regarding the implementation and answer questions they raise about how the methodology works. Once the initial implementation is successful and smooth in the one area of your organization, consider adding more areas or items to the process.

Guidelines for Successful Implementation

1. Prior to implementing a Kanban process:
2. A reduction is arranged. If this is ignored than the typical process, a "batch production," continues because the sizes of orders are still large.
3. Production and requirements are uniform or level. Kanban can work for complex situations, but when it is early in the implementation phase, it is best, to begin with, requirements that are more uniform.
4. Suppliers outside your organization need to be certified. The history of the supplier's outside quality is the reasons for not requiring the inspection of their deliveries. This way "on hold" or "rejected" deliveries do not prevent the workflow.
5. Choose a bright color for any Kanban related container, cart, or tote and paint them all. A vibrant green is a good choice if you are stuck on what to choose. This allows all members of your organization to recognize a Kanban tool, especially during the implementation phase. It is also an easy way to keep

track of all the materials necessary for your new system, ensuring all items stay in their correct place.

6. "Supermarkets" are a good tool to use if you use it well:
7. A "supermarket" provides a temporary place for a supplier to house items that are between the customer and the user.
8. This is best employed when several customers are internal and rely on a supplier that is external. Another reason to employ a "supermarket" is when several customers are internal, and a supplier is also internal.
9. This method provides a barrier between the many customers and the supplier, so the supplier does not receive several signals from all the requests.
10. The "supermarket" sends the only signal to the supplier that is at the highest priority

The Rules for Implementing a Kanban Process in Your Organization

1. Your customers, suppliers, stakeholders, and entire organization need to be involved in your implementation. Do not even try to launch a Kanban process without their knowledge. Anyone that adds value to the chain of production needs to be included. After all, these are the people that support and report your company as a revolutionary. They must be a part of the revolution, too.
2. The source is the origination point for quality. Customers should never receive a defective product or poor information. Immediate correction is required. Otherwise, you risk losing your customer's pipeline.
3. Support equipment must be reliable. Choose an area to implement a Kanban system where there is TPM or Total Productive Maintenance.

4. Lead times and setup should be short. Requirements for delivery should occur evenly every month. This means a Kanban system should be focused on parts and products that are consistent. Reduce setup and efforts to minimize the lead-time for raw materials for items that differ each month according to the requirements of the customer.

5. Programs to reduce setup at the supplier level, whether external or internal, should be developed. If they do not have their own program in place, you should assist them with one. Lead times and the capacity to manufacture should not be influenced by the time required to set up. That is the only time when a Kanban process should be implemented.

6. Customers should receive the supplier's materials directly. Non-certified suppliers, or those that still require inspection upon delivery, require the usage point to do the inspection. If this is not possible, then a certified supplier should replace the option in use.

7. Trial and error are necessary to find how it will work best for your company. This is because nothing is fixed. When there are changes to the level of sales or containers or cards are reduced because activities are continuously improved, you need to be ready to make changes to your system. This is especially important during the implementation stage of the Kanban system.

How to Implement a Kanban Process Effectively

Once you identify the area and actions you want to address with a Kanban process to begin, you will want to follow the steps outlined below:

1. Create a visual of what you want to accomplish. Assemble a series of photographs that show off how it should look along with a label that is clear and definitive. Make it so simple that even someone not working in your organization can understand it.

2. Theorize the consumption of the product on a daily basis. Use your own observations, data, or ask your employees about how much consumption possibly occurs. Accuracy is not essential at this point. Keep this step simple.

3. Determine how or what you will use to send a signal. Consider things like cards, containers, spaces, color, and if you will use a digital or manual system. If you are completely new to using a Kanban system, consider keeping it simple and doing it by hand to try it out. Do not get caught up in the fancy, expensive software system unless you are ready to expand your Kanban process to other areas or more items.

4. If the materials are heavy, do not use bins. Instead, use carts that roll. Choose a bright color, like a vibrant green as suggested. If your colors are vibrant green, choose something different. This process requires you to make choices based on your common sense. Decide what you think is best and try it out. You can always alter your choice if you find it is not the best fit.

5. The quantity of Kanban cards or bins must be calculated. This is done through a mathematical equation:

Kanban # = Daily Qty X Lead Time in Days X (1 + ss) / Qty Inside the Container

- Kanban # - The number of cards or containers
- Daily Qty – The number of pieces utilized each day on average
- Lead Time in Days – Estimate how many days a depleted material is replenished. Always estimate more days than you think necessary to be safe.
- (1 + ss) – Stock for safety is "ss." Typically this is either 10% or 15%. In the equation, ss will appear as 0.1 or 0.15.

- Qty Inside the Container - Choose a number that will provide you with between 1 to 5 days of consumption. Sometimes the number in a box from the supplier will make sense to your production line while other times it will not. Use common sense to set an original estimate and adjust as you implement the process.

To provide you with an example situation, imagine the following:

- Kanban # - Unknown
- Daily Qty - 60
- Lead Time in Days - 5
- (1 + ss) - 10%
- Qty Inside the Container - 15 items

The equation will appear as such:

Kanban # = 60 X 5 X (1 + 0.1) / 15

The answer then reveals:

Kanban # = 22

This is the number of cards or carts you will use in your Kanban.

Assign roles to team members. Make sure each role understands what is expected of them. For example, a user must understand and agree to your estimations. They must also place the signal in the designated location and participate in the process. There is also a role for the person responsible for moving signals, cards, and restarting the process. The people in the warehouse also play a critical role that you assign. They are the ones refilling containers or carts with the appropriate materials.

This means that they need to know what to do when they get the signal. Finally, you need to assign the facilitator role to the Kanban process. You typically fill this role; however, you can hire an outside contractor or professional to fill this role or assign someone from your team. This role is present during the entire process and can assist in training and problem solving with the rest of the team. To successfully implement Kanban to your project, this role must be filled with an active participant for a minimum of 1 month.

Basically, engaging your people and providing the tools of the Kanban system is the best way to implement a Kanban process successfully. It can resolve production problems or illustrate deficiencies in your line. It can save you time and money. But if you do not roll it out well, you can end up making stakeholders and clients unhappy, disgruntled your employees, slow production time, and cost your company money. This is why, despite the simplicity of the Kanban methodology, it is important that you take your time and launch it well. Having employees and stakeholders focused on the goal, while your line is producing quality work steadily at a fast pace, and waste is reduced is all worth it!

Chapter 36.
Project Management And Kanban Systems

Project management refers to running an enterprise or checking off tasks from a checklist. The basic idea behind project management is to carry out tasks smoothly in order to complete them on time. The concept remains universal, regardless of the scale of the project.

It is a great idea to use a Kanban system in project management. Those who do will associate project management with visual management. It is obvious that nobody will have an idea of the progress of a project if there is no visual representation of the progress. And thus, it becomes more important to have cues in place that can help to understand where a certain project is headed. It is important to organize in order to achieve goals.

Software projects are usually defined as complex ones where projects can be imposing. The project manager will have a tough ask and is required to fulfill a multifaceted role. He must manage teams, take care of the budget, plans, and also assess the risks involved. The customers and stakeholders have to be kept in good books and sub-contractors have to be dealt with.

In order to take care of these diverse tasks, most companies go for project management implementation. Despite a good plan in place, it is still possible for the project to fail. As per studies, despite best efforts, only about half the projects that are undertaken are completed on time and within the set budget. It is believed that this trend is only growing worse with time, where managers are unable to complete tasks.

But with the implementation of Kanban systems, not only will it be easier to finish projects on time, but it will also save money while doing so. Here is a look at the concepts of Agile and SCRUM.

With process centric PMMs there is always more emphasis on being able to deliver specific requirements than delivering quality and value. With the use of SCRUM, a concept that emerged in the 1990s, people turned to Agile. The focus started becoming too much on teamwork and project management took a back seat. At least that was the case in theory. SCRUM as a concept usually works with a set of predefined roles and events and makes use of specific vocabulary.

But SCRUM is not regarded as the solution to project-based problems. There are certain aspects that can influence the success or failure of SCRUM, and they are as follows.

- The maturity of the company and the understanding of agility
- The overall maturity of the team and the level of competency
- Allotting members to different projects
- Owning a project effectively
- The level of transparency that exists and visualization

These are the main requisites that must be met for SCRUM, but hardly ever are. The system can be transparent, but not everyone is a fan of it. Some might feel like everyone is exposed to everything and there are open discussions and debates on the same.

SCRUM can be tough to use in organizations that promote intense command and control. It can pose a challenge to scale down SCRUM and bring it down to a certain level and how risks and interfaces should be managed between different teams working on the same product. SCRUM can work well on smaller projects, as it does not do well with larger programs.

To narrow it down, traditional methods have not been successful in giving us the desired results, nor has SCRUM. They leave behind a few challenges.

Kanban for Project Managers

The Kanban system can provide a solution to prior problems. One reason why people adopt it is because the system keeps up with an organization's current titles, roles, and hierarchies. Kanban can be referred to as a mindset over a method.

Kanban helps to begin work on the important bits first. This means there is more time to tackle whatever is important and then move on to other aspects. As we read, there are a few basic principles associated with Kanban that make it a great system to adopt. These are aspects, such as visualization of work, managing the flow, improving the collaboration, implementing feedback loops, amongst others.

There are a few parallels with SCRUM, such as the visualization and feedback, but the approach is not the same. Kanban allows you to work on different issues on the same board, and your focus will be on finishing tasks, namely the philosophy of stop starting and start finishing.

This philosophy is quite important because a lot of projects are not completed owing to glitches that can occur in the final stages.

Kanban helps you remain organized and systematic, and does away with task lists, email lists, to-do lists, and others.

Kanban can be implemented to fulfill all types of work, including technical work, repetitive work, working on deadlines, and unexpected work.

The main idea is to limit WIP to control it. It is important to visualize subcontractor work and meet deadlines. This can give you a bird's eye view of the project and bring value across the board.

A Kanban system also helps to shed light on previously invisible work. This helps to put finishing touches on all aspects of a project.

It is possible to incorporate the Kanban system in all types of organizations, and here are some of the things required.

- A whiteboard, some sticky notes, and magnets
- Work out expectations with the steering committee
- Explain to your team how simple project reporting will be and give them control
- Explain to them about certain metrics and trends and variances that might occur
- Explain how visualization can show them the real status of a project at a certain point in time
- Show your team how to work on Kanban using boards
- Tell them the importance of stop starting and start finishing
- Show them the importance of predictability and stability

Is Kanban the Ultimate Solution?

No, Kanban cannot be viewed as an ultimate solution to problems. The best solution to bad project management is to lend more control and shift power into the hands of the project manager. Through the use of Kanban systems, a manager can control the outcome in a better way. This is especially relevant for companies that deal in complex projects that can find it a little tough to understand proper functioning of the project. The project manager will have to take care of many aspects associated with the project, including solving dilemmas and different complex situations that might arise. With the use of Kanban, all this can be resolved to a large extent.

How Kanban Works

- Kanban helps to assign work and can be equally shared amongst members of the team. All members are required to manage their share of the work based on their preferences and priorities they set

- All member's progress can be viewed easily to understand where the problem lies and work on it to solve it
- If there are visual reminders of progress, then it is easy to know whether more members need to be added to the team to share the load, and it also becomes easier to know if any of the existing members need help or guidance
- Both individual and teams can be identified and measured using the same metrics on a Kanban board. It is ideal to make use of digital scales, as they can give you an accurate reading and also cut down on your input
- All members in the team will have access to whatever is going on in the organization and know exactly what another person is up to

Some project managers make the mistake of micromanaging people. This means that they tend to over guide their employees owing to the power and control that they are given. This can lead to a lack of responsibility among employees. Employees might start feeling like they do not have to work hard and end up not contributing towards the end goal. All teams involved should make sure that they are well organized. They must plan their work out and understand what they have to do to reach the end goal. If the boss ends up micromanaging every step of the way, then employees will not be able to work properly and will end up wasting their time and his.

What You can Gain by Using Online Project Management Tools

If a project manager has access to online management tools, it will be easy for him to understand which team member is available and who is not. He can be up to date with the progress of the project. The tools can help to save the manager's time. He will know exactly how much time is being taken to complete the project. He can add comments, reviews, and analyze the project more easily. Online Kanban tools will help the manager reduce time spent on carrying out meetings and communications. These tools are especially useful for companies who work on large projects, as it can save them time and unify the different departments that are scattered all over.

Why is Kanban so Effective?

Kanban systems are so effective owing to their simplicity. Team members and managers can easily list the tasks in the backlog or on the to-do list part of the board and choose the tasks that need attention immediately. They do not have to think about missing out on important tasks owing to excess workload.

If they are able to control the project, they will be satisfied with what they are doing. If a card is moved from the to-do list to the done list on the board, then it will feel good. This will motivate them to go after the other tasks and keep their teams motivated as well.

What Makes Kanban Versatile?

Kanban tools can be quite versatile. They can be used across different departments and in different ways, as it is a very simple tool to use. There are only limited departments where Kanban cannot be adopted. It can easily fit into most departments. Kanban is mostly used in processes that can help to envision and make tiresome days less hectic and more organized. Managers and members who are part of the team will be able to plan their schedule in a better and more efficient way and understand if they have everything under control. If the project manager is under stress, all he has to do is look at the board and it will calm him down.

How Visual Thinking Helps

As you know, it is much easier for a person to get a message if he has access to a picture compared to just words. Just by visualizing the flow of work, a person will be able to know exactly where a project stand. He will have access to the tasks that have been fulfilled and what needs to be done. As per studies, most people will automatically start visualizing tasks even if there are no visual cues. They will think visually and establish a structure that is well organized. More and more businesses have now started to realize the value of using visual boards and are adopting Kanban systems. Regardless of their size and structure, they are taking Kanban systems on and using them to enhance their overall working. Looking at smaller teams and how they work will tell you how Kanban can be implemented. The team will start performing better and the organization will start looking for more ways to incorporate visual cues to finish the project on time. When knowledge about Kanban and its use goes around the organization, people will find it easier to implement it. They will be able to successfully incorporate it in their business.

If a team is looking to enhance its productivity, then here are some of the steps to follow.

- It is essential to not engage in multitasking, as it will prove to be a burden. Sometimes multitasking might be necessary but not always. There might be times when engaging in it might be useful, but if it is done regularly, then it will slow you down
- It is important to take breaks in between as it can help to reenergize and feel better. You will be able to work more freely and with a lot more enthusiasm
- The best thing to do is finish the toughest task first. It is important to go after tough tasks so that they can be done first, and you have enough time on your hands for other work
- Make sure you are not using your phone when working. Put it on silent mode
- Limit the number of meetings. Only call them if it is important
- Make sure you prioritize your tasks to ensure that the most important ones are tackled first

Kanban boards were first introduced to work in manufacturing forms but will fit right into corporate offices. In fact, it will do best in project management. It can be used as a supplementary tool for others. They can be used to evaluate on-going projects and plan future ventures. By using Kanban boards, a company can increase its team's efficiency, maximize time available, and manage projects in a better way.

Consistent Improvement

One big advantage associated with using Kanban boards is that they can help to instill continuous improvement. It is one where agile method can be beneficial in improving current conditions in the workplace. Project managers and people who are working on the team will be able to review their progress consistently and be able to organize the work efficiently. They will also be prepared to respond to any changes. Project managers can use the boards to not only simplify the projects but also address issues that are currently a part of the system. These issues might be posing a hindrance and stalling work. It is thus important to address the following aspects.

- Allocating resources
- Managing the workflow
- Identifying inefficiencies

By using online Kanban tools, it is possible to focus on functionality and versatility to supplement an existing project's tools. Kanban can help a team spend less time understanding a new system and focus more on going after its goals.

Allocating Resources

Project managers make use of online Kanban tools to allocate resources and assign work to others. By allocating resources efficiently, project managers will be able to avoid any delays that might occur and deliver results on time. These resources can refer to on site members and off-site members and third-party services. Here are the stages involved in resource allocation.

- Creation of work items

- Assigning work to teammates
- Collaborating with teams to prioritize work

Once a project has started, it is important to assess the progress on a regular basis to introduce any improvements. Kanban boards can help with this process such that every time a new project enters workflow, the right type of resource can be implemented in the best way.

Workflow Management

Kanban boards will help project managers and their team to have a visual understanding of workflow. This workflow is nothing but a sequential flow of work or tasks. It refers to the order in which the task will move. There might be multiple tasks that are going on at once and should move in an orderly manner for the end goal to be achieved.

Using a visual representation of the different steps can serve as an indicator of how work is flowing. It will give us an understanding of the different elements involved and how they are working to help attain the end result. It can promote collaborations between different team members and departments. It will also help to find newer and better ways to solve any issues that might arise.

Waste Reduction

Organizations that use lean usually tend to reduce costs by means of waste reduction. This waste is mostly from processes that are not efficient or a result of different opinions.

Waste can be in the following types:

Defects

Defects refer to things that are not working properly as stated in business requirements.

Overproduction

Overproduction refers to producing too much product and can result in throwing it away.

Idle Members
Idle members refer to members whose work is delayed due to dependent tasks.

Kanban boards can be useful for project managers to find any issues or troublesome areas that might end up creating problems. Say for example cards are building up and creating a bottleneck. Team members will be given the task of getting rid of some of the load. This is especially important if the cards are causing a block or imposing impediments and preventing progress. These should be identified and rectified at the earliest so that they do not affect the final result. Once they have been addressed, people can go back to their old tasks.

Kanban Boards for Software Development

Software projects are usually complex in nature, and this can get to clients. It is especially annoying for those who are looking to finish fast. Kanban boards can provide visual relief and offer transparency to team members and stakeholders to follow. Since Kanban boards are flexible in nature, they are quite popular among software developers who engage in repeated work techniques. These repeated work techniques could make it easier by putting focus on certain aspects that can help to move the project forward. These are better known as minimum marketable features. When performed correctly, these satisfy a shareholder's expectations without delving into too much risk. If a person goes beyond repeated processes, it can lead to backtracking. Some reasons include changes in technology, changes in objectives or goals, changes in the reach of the project, changes in its budget, or shifting focus from the project, amongst others. As we know, project management should be flexible enough to adjust to changes. Working on iterated processes can help to reduce waste and remain more productive. There are high chances of avoiding issues that can crop up and ensure timely delivery of a project.

Chapter 37.
Kanban For Lean Manufacturing

As one who is familiar with both Kanban and Lean manufacturing might gather, the two make quite a natural pairing that work hand-in-hand very well. When a manufacturer is looking to trim down the waste on their production line and they're looking to use a methodical approach to weed all of that out, this means they're "going Lean," or "running Lean."

Now, because Kanban is a systematic approach to the replacement of materials as is needed by the production areas of the business, it's clear why the two are such an ideal pair. One who wants to cut down on the defects per million and who is also looking to keep inventory waste from plaguing their business, these are the two most prominent methodologies that can provide a working solution.

Managing Inventory in a Kanban Environment

Running Kanban in your manufacturing environment means that you're trying to keep your inventory right in a very delicately balanced range. You want to have as little inventory as possible on hand, while still being able to produce the needed number of products and while functioning at full capacity.

When looking at this system, you can see how it worked as an ideal means for grocers and supermarkets to keep an ideal stock without losing profits on old or expired merchandise. This simple system led to the creation of an efficient system for Toyota, which is known as Toyota's 6 Principles of an Efficient System.

1. Those who are "downstream," (customers, line operators, and anyone who deals with or comes into contact with the materials or their suppliers) will

remove materials in the exact amounts that are specified by the Kanban system.

2. Those who are "upstream," (managers, materials handlers, or suppliers) will deliver materials in the exact amounts that are specified by the Kanban system.
3. Neither movement nor production should occur without an assigned Kanban task.
4. Each movement and production task should be part of a Kanban card or list.
5. Those who are downstream should not ever be receiving defective or incorrect materials from those who are further upstream. Customers should not get incomplete or defective products, and line operators should not be receiving inadequate materials, etc.
6. As the number of Kanban processes increases, a measure decrease in the levels of inventory occurs while the identification and resolution of problems occurs concurrently.

When one is looking to apply this methodology to one's inventory, this is when the bin system comes into play. The production areas should be given two bins from which to pull their materials, and cards can be used as an effective means of identifying the contents of each bin.

The employee should pull the needed materials from the first bin to begin with. Once they've emptied that bin, it's sent away, and they begin to work out of the second bin. That first bin being empty serves as a signal to those upstream that more inventory will be needed before that second bin is emptied.

It's best for a company to have a firm grasp on the timeline at work with this system. Those upstream should know exactly how long it takes for the production area to utilize one bin of materials, as well as the lead time involved for procuring more materials. This allows those upstream to plan accordingly and to ensure that the production areas are never waiting on materials.

There are various things which work consistently in every context and every team. This is one of the reasons why Kanban is widely applied today. Kanban will allow you to do things that work all the time regardless of what you are working on, where you are doing it from, and how you are doing it. As long as you do it in the correct way, there is no scenario where Kanban will disappoint you.

Implementing Lean software development using Kanban will help your team to achieve better results. First, let's look at some of the myths that exist about Kanban.

IT projects are complex, and if you are an IT project manager, you must learn to play a multifaceted and complex role. You'll need to manage teams, plan contracts as well as other risks which may affect you. You need to ensure that your managers and stakeholders are satisfied.

To organize these diverse tasks, many companies have moved on to implement a PM method (PMM) of that type. Many are disciples of IPMA, PMI, PRINCE2, and others. However, you may be tempted to ask why do so many projects keep failing? According to the "Pulse of the Profession" report released by PMI, only about half of the projects started are completed within time and budget.

Kanban with Lean

There are various things which work consistently in every context and every team. This is one of the reasons why Kanban is widely applied today. Kanban will allow you to do things that work all the time regardless of what you are working on, where you are doing it from, and how you are doing it. As long as you do it in the correct way, there is no scenario where Kanban will disappoint you.

Implementing Lean software development using Kanban will help your team to achieve better results. First, let's look at some of the myths that exist about Kanban.

IT projects are complex, and if you are an IT project manager, you must learn to play a multifaceted and complex role. You'll need to manage teams, plan contracts as well as other risks which may affect you. You need to ensure that your managers and stakeholders are satisfied.

To organize these diverse tasks, many companies have moved on to implement a PM method (PMM) of that type. Many are disciples of IPMA, PMI, PRINCE2, and others. However, you may be tempted to ask why do so many projects keep failing? According to the "Pulse of the Profession" report released by PMI, only about half of the projects started are completed within time and budget.

Agility causes many people to switch to Scrum

Nowadays, the weight of fulfilling requirements is more than delivering quality and value. Following the emergence of Scrum in the 1990s, the pendulum switched towards the agile direction. The concentration was to become team centric. To some levels, Scrum seems to work in theory because of a defined set of events, roles, and artifacts.

However, Scrum has not been the answer to all project problems. Aspects which may influence the success or failure of scum projects consist of:

- Team maturity and competencies.
- Quality product ownership
- Company maturity and level of agile understanding
- Acceptance of visualization and transparency
- Assigning of team members to multiple projects.

The truth is that the requirements for a great Scrum aren't always fulfilled. Agile teams tend to work in non-agile organizations, and the teams don't need to understand the DNA of Scrum and what it means in relation to team behavior. The product owner role in Scrum is usually not filled effectively, and not everyone can know what everybody else is up to.

Additionally, Scrum is very hard to use in organizations that have a strong control-and–command culture. It is again a big task to scale Scrum to the program and portfolio level. How are you going to deal with risks, interfaces, dependencies, etc. between numerous Scrum teams that are working on a single product? Although Scrum is better on a single product, it is not the best on a portfolio or program level.

How Kanban Improves the Lives of Project Managers

Kanban tries to provide what Scrum and other traditional waterfall methods don't. One reason is that Kanban respects the current roles of an organization, etc., and it begins the journey of improvement from that point. Kanban is more of a mindset than a method.

With Kanban, you'll always work on the most significant tasks first as quickly as you can. This behavior emerges from the six main Kanban practices as detailed previously. Kanban will allow you to handle different kinds of work in a single board and concentrate on the flow and task completion. This is basically what is needed in projects because it prevents tasks from staying at 90, 95, and 98 percent complete for ages. Above all, you eliminate your project activity lists, plans, and Excel sheets.

Kanban will Capture and Measure All Types of Work

While you might find it hard to plan all your projects in sprints, Kanban will let you capture and measure all kinds of work. Typically, this consists of:

- Work that has deadlines
- Unexpected work
- Repetitive PM work
- Technical work

Although it is sensible to reduce work in progress (WIP) on work within your control, it doesn't always translate to an outsourced or subcontractor's work. However, it is good to visualize your subcontractor deadlines and do a follow-up. Hence, you will receive a holistic view of your project as it is visualized on the Kanban board. It will also generate value to visualize and measure the work which was initially invisible.

It is, however, possible to work all this way in all kinds of work organizations, as long as you are allowed to do so.

Can Kanban solve all your project problems?

No, Kanban is not going to provide solutions to all your project issues. But the solution to poor project performance has always been to focus more on bureaucracy, processes, and control mechanisms, and that has made it harder to use. Additionally, organizations that take part in complex projects find it hard to understand their role in the project ecosystem.

There shall always be a decision, dilemma, and complexity which no method can fix. But Kanban will make your life easier and lead to a higher success rate on your projects.

Chapter 38. Apply A Kanban Process To Software Development

Software development has been using different project management philosophies for decades, but that raises the question why you would prefer a Kanban system to other methodologies, such as SCRUM or sources, similar to a Gantt chart? To begin with, you must look at the differences between the most important methods.

Kanban versus other methods

SCRUM is still a popular project management process that is currently used in software development. Although it is another successful, flexible project management approach, there is a big difference between the Kanban process and SCRUM.

For example:

- A Kanban system does not contain time periods such as SCRUM required.
- A Kanban system has fewer tasks, and these are larger than SCRUM tasks.
- A Kanban system does not assess the process often or not at all, such as in a SCRUM environment.
- A Kanban system only takes the average lead time of a project into account instead of basing the project time on "team speed", as in a SCRUM setting.

For practitioners who are used to the SCRUM environment, they think that a project consists of the speed of the team, the increased dimension and scrum meetings, the idea of removing them outrageously. These activities are the primary methods for controlling development in a SCRUM system! The real problem with this concept is the illusion of control.

Managers constantly strive for this control, but the reality is that they will never get it. The supervision and influence of a manager only works if the team wants to work. If they jointly decide not to insist on the completion of a project, it doesn't matter what the manager does; the object will fail.

Imagine a different scenario: one in which people have fun at work and work efficiently. Managers then do not have to control the environment. Control in this setting would actually disrupt the situation and increase costs. In a SCRUM institution, control measures entail costs because constant discussions, meetings and time are needed when changing sprints. Most sprints require a day to complete and a day to start. Those extra days can be considered as "missed" opportunities. If you look at it as a percentage, a 2-week sprint requires 20% of the time spent preparing and packing. That is a lot of time! In some SCRUM environments, 40% of the time can be spent on supporting the methodology and not on completing the mission.

The Kanban system; however, focuses on tasks. This differs greatly from a SCRUM process. SCRUM practitioners want a successful sprint. Kanban practitioners want completed tasks. Tasks in a Kanban system are approached from start to finish, not tied to a sprint time frame. The completed work is presented, and the project is deployed based on when it is ready. Tasks do not have an estimated time set for completion by the team. The reason is that there is no need for this time estimate, and an estimate is often wrong anyway. If a manager believes and supports his team, why would an estimate be necessary? Wouldn't the team want to produce as well as possible in the fastest possible time? Instead, the manager focuses his own attention on developing a pool of prioritized tasks. The team's focus is on completing as many tasks as possible from the pool. It's that simple. Control measures are not required. Managers add items to the pool and reorganize the priorities of tasks if necessary. That is how a Kanban practitioner carries out a software project.

Example kanban lists for software development

Sample lists or columns on a Kanban software development board include:

1. OBJECTIVES. Handy but optional. Important goals can be placed here. This is more for a regular reminder of the team than for a usable list.
2. story. Tasks on the deck are placed on this list. The card at the top has the highest priority. The team then takes the top card and moves it to the following column, usually referred to as 'developing'.
3. ELABORATE AND ACCEPT. Other descriptions can be used for this column before continuing to the "ready" list. Every team and every workflow differ from each other. Anything that is uncertain about the team's approach, such as an approach to an incomplete code or designs that have not been determined, can be assigned to this list. The team must then discuss and decide how to handle it before it is moved to the following list.
4. Develop further. Until the task is completed, the card remains on the 'develop' list. It doesn't matter what needs to be completed for the card or task, but if something needs to be done before the task is completed, it will be placed on this list.
5. DONE. Once a card is on this list, it indicates that the task has been completed. It tells the team that nothing else is needed for this task.

This proposed layout means that each list or column can contain a high-priority task. Every task on the board must be completed as quickly as possible. Sometimes a column is created for only items with a high priority. This can be in the 'goals' column or another column with the label 'speed up'. This tells the team that all items on the list must first be completed. This means that everything on this list is only of the utmost importance. All other items must be placed on the 'story' list until the 'speed up' items are completed.

Other interesting functions on a Kanban board are the numbers under each list or column. These numbers determine the number of cards or tasks that are allowed for each list. This is also called "work in progress" or "WIPs". These numbers are not scientifically determined but are rather chosen by the manager based on their discretion. The number is usually related to the number of developers assigned to the list. It represents the capacity of the team to work. For example, if there are eight developers, "develop" can get a number four. Two places results in bored team members and they will talk to each other too much. By placing eight, each person must work on their task but remain on the list for too long. This means that the focus on the Kanban process has been forgotten; the time spent on a task that needs to be completed from the start until the finish is not shortened.

The benefits of a Kanban system for the Software Development Team

There are several reasons why a Kanban process is beneficial for your software development team. To start, several tasks can be completed at the same time, shortening the time needed to complete each of them. The actions taken are only necessary, so there is no link framework or the tracking of different articles. Planning is not necessary. Tasks are developed when the project starts, not before. Then, "showstoppers" or problems in the process are identified and solutions are found as a team to advance the process.

For example, if a task requires the help of another department, but the other department is working on a different set of tasks, the production of the project must stop. But an efficient Kanban team recognizes the need for teamwork and will work together to solve the problems so that all departments can continue to function efficiently. Finally, it is possible to calculate the lead time of average tasks. Cards can be tracked based on their start date, all movements on the board and when they are complete. Even waiting times between each step can be averaged. This information can be valuable for a manager's calculations for planning purposes.

The rules of Kanban

There are only 3 primary requirements in a Kanban setting, even for software development:

1. Production is visual:

a. Tasks or cards are created to divide work. The cards are then added to the board.

b. The board contains lists that are presented as separate columns. Cards are located in a column in order of priority.

2. Every part of the production works to minimize WIP, or 'work in progress', which refers to the maximum amount of work completed at the same time.

3. Shortening the amount of time spent on the process is the goal of working consistently on developing the system and determining the average time for a task to be completed. This time is determined by measuring the time for each step in the production cycle.

These are the only three requirements of a Kanban system! SCRUM contains nine primary requirements. XP required 13. The traditional RUP process has more than 120! This alone illustrates Kanban's big difference and advantage in software development.

Chapter 39.
KANBAN BOARDS: Dos And Don'ts

When you're setting up the Kanban board, it's important to know some of the do's and don'ts. Whether you're going for the digital or physical form, the principles of making the board apply to both.

- Begin with a simple form and adapt it to changes as you go along

When you're making the board, go with a simple form first. So, start with the three principle areas and work your way up from there. Then, as you learn to work with the board, you can start adding other sections that work well with the project. What matters most is starting with the tasks you've put on your cards so that your project is getting somewhere.

Once you're getting into the flow, you can then adapt to the changes that occur during the project. When working with a team, let them know why you'll start the project this way and adjust it so that when they see the changes, they'll be ready to tackle the tasks ahead with a strong and steady workflow.

- Come up with unique policies

While you are encouraged to set up policies right from the get-go when setting up the board, it's also good to add additional policies that are unique to the project you're managing. There might be a time that the policies you need are only relevant for the current project but set them in place anyway. It'll help in the long run.

It can also help customizing the WIP limits you'll set. For example, you can set a limit of five task cards present in the "Doing" part of the board. When two or three task cards are cleared, you can add two or three more task cards from "To

Do" section. This will show that the project is flowing smoothly as more tasks are getting done.

- Encourage feedback and inquiries

When you're using the Kanban board, it's good to have feedback and inquiries on the tasks and processes laid out in front of you. This can help you make the board livelier because it'll help you dig further into what the project is all about.

One way to go about this is to take a step back and see how the processes are doing. Is communication with the ongoing tasks clear across your team? Do you need to change the WIP limits? Is it better to have the "Done" part of your board have more task cards than the other sections? Having all these considerations will give you more insight on what needs to be done to make the Kanban board better than ever.

- Don't overcomplicate the board

When you're making your Kanban board, it's best to not complicate it. While you are free to add some sections that may help based on the project you're working on, putting too much on the board can hamper your progress with the project.

Whether you're on your own or with a team, it'll be overwhelming when you see that just a few days ago, the board just had a simple set of tasks and now it has so many tasks that you're not even sure if what you've added is still relevant to the project.

So, when adding things to the board, be vigilant and ask how relevant the tasks are to the project. Once you're clear on it, add it. Otherwise, leave it be and concentrate on what is already right in front of you.

- Don't oversimplify the board either

On the flip side, it's best not to oversimplify the Kanban board. Why? While simplicity can keep things from being overwhelming, it might make things stale and boring. It might also make you and your team frustrated because the act of doing the tasks and signaling that you're done them without much of a challenge seems like no great achievement.

So, it's a good idea to add a little spice to the board and keep things fresh. For example, you can add some new tasks that will level up the challenge when you or a team member finishes one of the ongoing tasks. Another example is giving a thorough and encouraging update on why one task can contribute significantly to the project more than others.

- Be picky on the metrics and data that matter

When setting up your Kanban board, it's important to be fastidious on the metrics and data that will matter most to your project. Why? Because this can provide a lot of information that may come in handy for future tasks. If you simply get metrics for the sake of it, that'll only be wasting your time. That's why it's important to stick with the essentials and go with the ones that will really matter for your project long-term.

- Keep a good and tight security on the board

It's a good idea to keep rigid security on your Kanban board. For physical boards, always have a storage area where it can be put in when you or your trusted teammates are not around. You'll never know if something will happen to it or someone might add something irrelevant by mistake, ruining the momentum of the project.

Digital boards are stored mostly in cloud-based storage, but it's still important to be safe with them. That means having a password set so that no one will be able to put irrelevant data on the board or steal data off the board.

- Come up with ways to keep the board maintained with either form

The Kanban board holds the visualized workflow of your project, so it's important that you keep it maintained. Depending on the form, there are ways you can do this. For the physical board, you can try keeping tabs on some of the task cards that may need an update. You can also change the materials slowly so that they'll be more durable in the long run. For the digital board, it will be easier because you'll only need to tweak a few settings and have a set routine to do other tasks that will help you out, like collecting data for forecasting future projects.

- Know the ways to distribute board information when needed

When you already have a Kanban board, you'll want to distribute the information on it when there's a need. What if you need copies of it to send to your team members in faraway places? How about when you're on vacation and need the board in a form that fits your devices? Be familiar with the ways in which you can distribute the board, and you're good to go.

- Always have a backup version

When you're setting up the Kanban board, it's always best to have a backup version. Things can be unpredictable, so you should never depend on good fortune. Before you think to yourself that nothing is going to happen to your Kanban board, you'd better think again and back it up straight away.

The physical board can be backed up by creating a second version of it and storing it somewhere safe. You can also manually mimic the main board you have. It can be a bit tedious, but in the long run, it'll serve you well when the main board gets lost or damaged.

The digital board will be a cinch because you can store it in other digital storages. You might even consider getting your own private server and uploading it there without anyone being able to access it unless you grant them permission.

- Don't have multiple boards right away

When you're making a Kanban board, it's a good idea to have just one board when you're starting so that it's unified and is a signal that there is nothing else hidden. This is because if you have multiple Kanban boards right from the start, it can be confusing to know which is which and what needs to be done when.

This may also cause you and your team to be uncertain about whether or not you'll even be able to complete the project because what you thought to be the most important task is actually not important at all. So, to make matters simple, just keep one board for now.

- Slowly add more boards when needed

On the flip side, when you and your team are getting used to the flow of the Kanban board, you can slowly add more boards. A good way to know if you're ready for this is if the team is expanding and you need more organization to manage the project. In this case, you can make another board that is specific to one team and still keep the main one. Remember to stick with the principles and you'll eventually be able to have multiple boards as long as they remain controlled.

- Use the features that are relevant for the board

Whether you're using a physical or digital board, it's good to use the features relevant to either form. For the physical board, though it doesn't have as many features as the digital board, you can still use the traditional ways that many companies have used to keep track of the data needed. For the digital board, you can check on the many features included and classify which ones have the most impact on your project. Once you have what you need, you can disregard the other features and move along with the completion of your project.

The Kanban board might seem like an unnecessary concept, but overall, you'll find it's an important part of the Kanban system that you'll need to integrate when you adapt the method for your projects.

Chapter 40.
Kanban Cards

Kanban cards have gone through a massive change, from their time in manufacturing to now when they are used in the Agile Software industry and personal work.

In any Kanban card manifestation, the Kanban card and board are important visual tools created to reduce waste and improve the productivity level.

You are going to learn everything about Kanban cards. You'll be introduced to the history of Kanban cards, its use, link to Lean management principles, and much more.

Kanban Cards. What are they?

The term Kanban is from the Japanese language. It can be split into two. "Kan" stands for "Visual" while "Ban" stands for "card". This means 'card you can see' when translated roughly.

Things that Make Kanban and Kanban Cards Best

When you look at the concept created by Taichii Ohno, the founder of Kanban, it tends to consider emotional and psychological features associated to change. This was one of the reasons why Ohno came up with a well-defined set of guidelines to provide action and explain the process required to make sure a system is efficient.

Proven to deliver results, these ideas can be implemented via the 6 general Kanban practices and 4 basic principles which we've referred to previously.

To succeed, all members of a team must agree upon the system. The tasks accomplished by everybody should follow the defined standards and the rules before he or she can pass them on to another person or team.

Ensuring that you keep the Kanban information updated and easy to access for every member of the team is important. This is why digital and online Kanban boards are very useful. It is easy to access them anytime, in any place and instantly stay updated without the need to depend on manual updates and physical cards.

The Design of the Kanban Card

There are two forms of the Kanban card: the physical cards and digital cards that have been created and are used online.

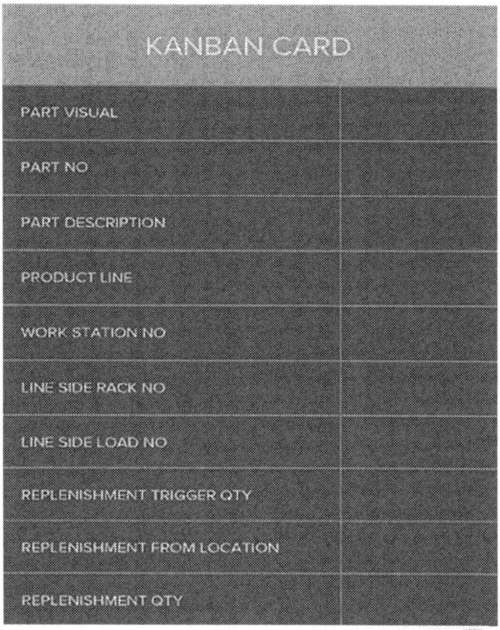

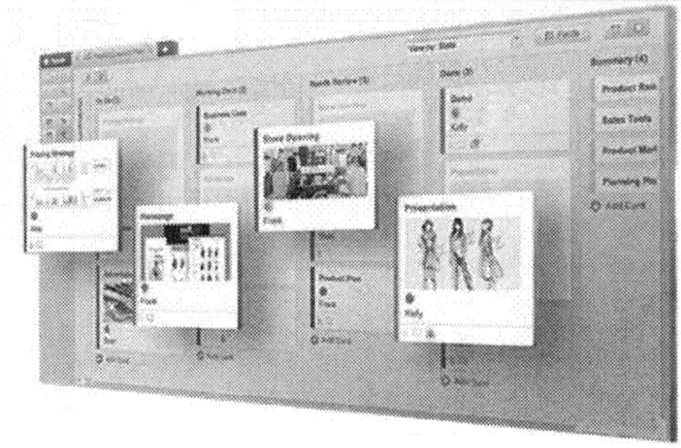

The steps will always be the same whether you choose to implement a physical or digital Kanban card. The information and details contained within them is after all, the most important thing. However, the most important thing to remember is the steps and how you can apply them in your process. Often, this will include certain aspects that you'll perform (i.e an action as opposed to an analysis or thought process). There is no need to lose everything you're currently working and start something from scratch. Kanban calls for a slow form of improvement. This implies that the risk score is low in overlaying a specific part of your project to be part of the development. The steps outlined below can help you start:

Step 1: Visualize your work

You'll need to list out each and every step from scratch and create a column for each process. The following thing is to write the tasks on a different card. Once you have finished, you can color various parts of the work to increase visualization and visibility should you so choose.

Step 2: Limit work in progress (WIP)

If you have the work potential of a hundred percent, which many are often tempted to designate at the start, you have very little room for error in a pull system. Irrespective of the type of project the team is doing, there is the maximum limit that a work can remain efficient if it is put in a process for one time. Figuring out the efficiency of work with regards to the potential amount of work your team can carry is crucial.

It is better to underestimate and increase via experience as opposed to overestimating and having to change your limits to account for work spillage.

Limits are usually applied to the work that is almost done. The main function of the WIP limits is to smoot the workflow and eliminate waste.

Step 3: Adapt, monitor, and improve

Improvements depend upon objective measurements. Therefore, you need to look and apply the correct metrics to enhance your process and optimize their flow and efficiency. If you apply the above steps, you'll need to select and determine the place that your teams should be, and what can work well for your specific workgroup.

The number of Kanban cards you require

This has always been a key question in Kanban system design. Many people find it difficult to choose the number of cards that they need to use. In the "push" systems, where ideas and material are transferred so that it adheres to a time-based schedule, work can be forced downstream continuously. "Push" can still lead to congestion. This increases exponentially as other items continue to join the queue. Kanban is a "pull" system that eliminates underproduction and overproduction, maintain inventory, and activate cooperation as we've previously mentioned and described. There are certain formulas used in production that you can use to decide the number of Kanban cards required. This formula is from the MBA Course on Production & Operation Management at RAI University.

$$y = \frac{DT(1+x)}{C}$$

Y = Number of cards
D = Demand per unit of time
T = Lead time
C = Container capacity
X = Buffer, or safety factor

Members in a workgroup need to choose the number of Kanban cards that should correctly control a process. The level of complexity, the team members, and the category of the project can affect the numbers. Since Kanban requires one to learn what works best, determining the number of cards is an evolutionary process.

Don't be afraid of getting it wrong the first time. As always, underestimate your numbers and then build up instead of going the other way.

Types of Kanban Card Holders and Boards

If you use physical cards to monitor the Kanban process, then you must display the cards for your team to determine the status of the process. The cardholders found on Kanban boards should allow easy navigation of the cards. There are different ways that you can use to show the Kanban inventory cards and monitor the inventory. Below are some of those options:

Kanban Bin Systems: To track the inventory, it has a 2-3 bin holder systems. The production line or in a new supply setting is where the items are replenished. The first bin allows a worker to select tasks. The whole bin or Kanban card will then be returned once the bin is empty. While the order for the first bin is handled, the worker can select other items on the second bin. The location of the supplier is where the third bin inventory is kept.

Kanban Racks and Card Holders: Cardholders and racks are placed on the wall to illustrate the flow of communication within the project. The capacity or demand is shown in the signal cards. The work items are represented by magnets, plastic chips, or sticky notes which can be seen on the board. Each piece shows items that are in process as they move around the board.

Kanban boards: A simple whiteboard can function very well as a Kanban board. The workflow's three main areas are shown on these boards. That is "to-do", "in progress" and "done". The boards depict the visual status of a project and are the easiest to implement for a small to medium sized team without the complexity or cost of an online system.

Chapter 41.
Kanban For Agile Project Management

To be able to define the relationship between Kanban and Agile project management, we must first speak a little about the latter. Agile is a set of principles and ideals designed to help managers adhere to a goal. Agile promotes continuous iteration of development and testing via something that is known as the Software Development Lifecycle (SDLC). It heavily relies on constant feedback to provide a good product.

The Agile approach understands that developing products can be a daunting volatile task and provides a framework to self-organize teams and allow them to respond to change. It is currently used by almost all companies planning and delivering products which have made it an essential approach to use if you plan to stay afloat in today's competitive world.

Kanban is itself one of Agile's two most popular methodologies along with Scrum. Scrum is a project management methodology created to structure projects beginning with the ideation of a product. The product's requirements are translated into features and put in a backlog. A time frame that is usually called an iteration or sprint is set. The product features and specifications are split into these sprints so they can be focused on.

The goal Scrum aims to fulfill is the creation of learning loops to gather and integrate feedback. Scrum users take on specific roles and hold regular meetings to keep things moving forward.

Kanban And Scrum's Main Differences

Even though Scrum and Kanban seem to tackle similar principles and goals like helping you build better products and services smoothly, they do have some philosophical and practical differences.

Scheduling
Scrum is entirely reliant on time frames. Since the team decides on a prioritized list of things to take on during a sprint, anything outside of that scope will be relegated to the following iteration. The idea is that after each sprint, the team will discuss ways of optimizing their processes and become more accurate when estimating and planning future sprints as they have already assessed their capabilities and blockers. Kanban, on the other hand, does not focus on sprints. However, it is iterative by nature since continuous improvement is something to be expected. Limitations found in the workflow are considered early in the Kanban process.

Roles
At least three roles need to be assigned for Scrum to work appropriately: product owner, Scrum Master, and team members. Each one of these roles has its own set of responsibilities, which should ultimately result in an efficient workflow. No such roles are predefined under the Kanban framework. It does make sense to have some type of hierarchy within a team using Kanban, but these roles should theoretically be defined when the need arises.

The Board
Even though very similar, a Kanban board and a Scrum board are different. A Scrum board is labeled after the different periods that make up a sprint. After a sprint's retrospective meeting, the board should be cleared to be available for the following sprint. On the other hand, the Kanban board is labeled after different workflow states while also acknowledging the number of stories allowed at each column during the same time. It is intended to enable the team to enforce and determine their limitations in advance. There is no real need to reset a Kanban board since it has a limited number of stories that can be placed under one column at a time and it does not work on sprints. Work here will continue to flow as long as there is any.

How Kanban And Scrum Overlap

Both methodologies allow teams to break down a large number of complex tasks and complete them efficiently. They place the utmost value in continuous improvement and optimization of the work and processes. Both also rely on almost exclusive visual elements to define a workflow that keeps all team members in the loop of what is and what will be.

Kanban and Scrum are valuable each in their own ways. This might be making you feel like you need to choose one of them. However, your decision doesn't need to be so black and white. Many teams are using a hybrid of both frameworks. The best thing to do is to become familiar with both and experiment using elements from both in your working environment. Working with your own structure is one of Kanban's main principles.

Kanban And Scrum Hybrids

If you plan to use both, some writers have suggested that you start working with Scrum as the structure that holds a team together until you reach a point where the time-boxed meetings mandated by Scrum are not necessary. This goal can only be achieved through testing and optimizing.

Other variations of the Kanban/Scrum hybrid are based on moving past removing fixed time frames. You can also use Scrum's approach as a way of actually executing tasks while at the same using Kanban as a lens through which you engage and improve your work. This model suggests having sprints if crucial, and it also suggests implementing specialized teams and functions.

Several organizations use Kanban for teams whose tasks are more responsive (like support teams), and Scrum for groups that get to plan for the future due to the nature of their work (like software development teams). It all depends on the context.

Where to Go from Here

It can become a pretty difficult task to create a global definition for Agile methodologies when one of its primary features is that you can adapt it to each working environment. What's important to keep an eye on is not a textbook definition to start with it. What matters is that you use structure and discipline as a cornerstone on which you can build your processes around.

New teams will benefit from Scrum as it offers them more structure. Organizations who require Scrum's learning and framework along with the continuous flow provided by Kanban will benefit from a Scrum/Kanban hybrid.

The terminology might vary between them, but they heavily focus on reviewing and improving the workflow, just as all Agile methodologies. You need to understand the main concepts behind both, define, implement, and continuously reflect and improve.

Kanban Visualization, Clarity and Its Benefits

Project managers are usually as busy as could be, they have to keep track of team performance as well as the quality they are putting out. You might already be using visual aids like Gantt charts or Excel spreadsheets, but larger projects specifically require different approaches. They might be too complex to fit in a single document, which in turn does not help with an overall workflow visualization. Visual project management tools like Kanban are here to do just that: facilitate your work.

Project management comes down to making ideas a reality. Doing that will be even more complicated if you do not count with the right information to make accurate decisions; it is essential to have that information displayed memorably. Additionally, if team members can't access the same information and understand it, they can't cooperate efficiently and collaborate.

A visual management tool helps you avoid that as it relies on fundamental concepts of perception to ease data consumption and processing in the brain. Kanban helps you:

Save Time
You are probably spending most of your time on communicational activities like messaging, joining meetings, and reporting. You might be spending even more time on them than you feel comfortable with.

These types of activities usually slow you down and rob you of the time and energy that should be spent on actual work that gets things done.

With a Kanban board your team has the chance to share all information concerning a project in one single place, which makes it easier for them to access it, helping you move past those long hours of attending unnecessary meetings, back and forth conversations, and responding emails.

Increase Problem Solving Speed
Every team leader's goal is to solve issues as fast as possible and then move on. Being able to identify bottlenecks as soon as they appear on your workflow is going to help you do that.

With a clear Kanban workflow, you will be able to figure out if a task is not moving as fast as it should be. This allows you to find timely solutions for bottlenecks, issues, and blockers as soon as possible.

Improve Efficiency
For any business, efficiency is equivalent to the best use possible of resources. Kanban helps improve productivity through WIP limits as they help you reduce waste of resources.

It also helps workers focus on single tasks rather than jump from one to the other, avoiding multitasking, and enabling them to complete tasks sooner. In the same way, your organization will be benefited with the quality they manage to put into their work.

Increase Accountability
Kanban promotes accountability across businesses; it enables workers to make their own decisions and act as driving forces on the outcome of a process. Team members feel more motivated to add more value when they see themselves as leaders.

The visual layout of a Kanban board allows each team member to define and pull their work according to their circumstances, making them more accountable for their progress and resulting in more engaged individuals with higher productivity.

Improve Team Performance
Since Kanban encourages you to improve your workflow continually, it encourages team members to share feedback on time. The visual representation of your progress helps teams learn from each other daily.

Your team's performance will improve over time, leading to better products and even happier customers.

Successfully implementing Kanban goes far beyond having a board and adding columns to it. It comes down to how transparent and easy to understand it is, so that team members find it helpful and add more value. Adopt a Kanban board to make it happen.

Chapter 42.
Kanban Basic Principles

Visualize What You Do Today (Workflow)

Having a mental picture of what you are doing today enables a team member to have a clear representation of what to expect. You understand the processes involved as the project moves from the first request to its completion. Since you know what will happen as the task moves from one column to the folloing, you use visualization to seek ways of improving the system. The imagery can assist you in identifying potential problems that may cause the workflow to slow down or have a break down in progress.

You can create a Kanban board to assist you in forming a picture of the workflow where the cards and the columns provide you with relevant information. For instance, if a person has five projects, he or she can start by developing a Kanban board on a wall or whiteboard. He or she draws a board with four columns labeled as 'backlog', 'to do', 'in progress,' and 'completed,' respectively.

The person then writes on sticky notes vital details regarding the projects, with each ticket or card representing a specific work item. He or she places them on the board according to the flow of the ongoing work. He or she moves them in line with the corresponding status. When a team member accepts a task, the associated Kanban card systematically moves from the 'backlog' column to the 'to do' lane.

Once he or she begins working on the project, he or she consequently moves the matching Kanban card to the 'in progress' column. When the individual finishes the work, he or she also pulls the relevant Kanban card to the column titled 'completed.' It creates a visual representation of how the tasks regarding the five projects are continuing. It also indicates how the individual can expect future similar projects to proceed. The visualization also enables the person and his or her team members to identify which areas they need to improve to enhance workflow.

You can choose to use a Kanban system with a workflow that you feel best suits your job requirements. The Kanban method is flexible and allows room for change, which enables you to format or adjust the board to adapt to the needs of the work. Thus, you can use a workflow that incorporates personal preferences, such as Kanban card details. Understanding the flexibility and workflow helps you to apply the Kanban system in visualization effectively.

Limit the Amount of Work in Progress (WIP)

Limiting the quantity of work in progress enables a team to balance the number of projects to which they commit at a given time. The primary aim of the Kanban method is to enhance efficiency by reducing, as much as possible, the time it takes a team member to start and complete a task. Carrying out several projects at the same time leads to the team members losing focus. They divide their attention in an attempt to accomplish the various functions. However, this effort to finish the work quickly ultimately leads to distraction, time-wasting, and inefficiency in performance and production.

This principle works similarly to how inventory supply at stores operates. The owner only pulls inventory from the storage to the shelf once the customers purchase and empty the shelves. Likewise, the system limits the amount of work that a team can work on at a given time using a reasonable pace and with efficiency. A person can pull a work item from one column to the following only after the other task is over. The individual in charge of that task moves the corresponding Kanban card to the relevant column, which creates room for another project.

For example, if a system has a work in progress limit of three, it means that a maximum of three tasks can exist simultaneously on the 'in progress' column. The team must work and complete the three tasks first before being able to add new work items to the lane. This restriction allows the team members to focus entirely on those three items, which helps them to complete the task quickly. It also allows them to solve any issues that may arise relating to those three work items in an efficient manner.

Limiting the work in progress is the core principle of the Kanban system. If a system that you use does not contain a limit in work in progress, then you are not using Kanban. The amount of limitation is what enables the Kanban method to create and improve efficiency in the workflow while producing quality results. You can apply this principle when you implement it in sections or to the entire workflow system. It will assist you in identifying problem areas in the flow and maintaining an orderly organization of projects. It will also ensure that you achieve consistent levels of quality and efficiency.

Pulling Work from Column to Column

Kanban is a system that uses visualization to indicate the flow of work as team members act on particular assignments. The workflow comes in when a person moves the cards on the Kanban board in line with the equal status of production. When you transfer the tickets in an organized and systematic way, it helps the system to function efficiently. It increases the speed of the movements as well as enabling smooth flow in the entire system. The Kanban method aims to achieve a fluid and fast-flowing system, which, in turn, enhances performance and productivity.

This principle of Kanban refers to the management of the work as opposed to the people. It allows a person to understand the processes involved in accomplishing a work item. As a result, he or she can comprehend the system and quickly identify any problems that take place in the workflow. A person who swiftly recognizes and solves an issue helps to improve the efficiency of the Kanban system. A smooth workflow ensures consistent products as well as providing services of value to clients of interest.

A person pulls work from column to column according to the order of the Kanban cards. For instance, he or she places four cards in the 'backlog' column, and each card contains user stories from one to four. The individual puts the cards in a descending order where the Kanban card at the top will be the first to move while the fourth one at the bottom will be last. He or she then moves them in order of urgency to the 'to do' column, from which the team members will commit to a project when ready. Following the limits of the work in progress of a particular system, the person pulls the first card to the 'in progress' column.

If the work in progress limit is two, then he or she pulls two cards from the 'to do' lane and sticks them in the 'in progress' column. The team members commit to the tasks in the 'in progress' column and work on them until completion. Finally, once the work is over, the person pulls the Kanban card of the corresponding task to the 'completed' column. Afterward, he or she moves to take up another Kanban card for a new job. The person takes it from the 'to do' column and pulls it to the 'in progress' lane. This cycle repeats the workflow until completion.

Each cycle represents the workflow process from start to finish. The shorter the sequence is, the smoother the workflow is, and the more efficient the Kanban system is. Therefore, this principle seeks to shorten the production cycle by managing the workflow and eliminating delays by promptly solving issues.

Kanban employs all three principles to ensure maximum productivity in minimum time. A person should comprehend them and know to apply them accordingly. It is essential to understand these principles and the Kanban system operation. They help an individual and company to achieve tremendous and consistent success.

Chapter 43.
Kanban Boards For Project Management

The Kanban board allows teams to visualize the work and the workflow. Teams can use this board to optimize the workflow. If you want to use a physical Kanban board, you can use a whiteboard and sticky notes. These notes will communicate the progress, issues, and status of every task. You can also use online Kanban boards, but these are only a refinement of the physical Kanban board.

The Kanban technique only emerged in the 1940s when Toyota re-imagined its approach toward engineering and manufacturing. The line workers used actual Kanban cards to let their suppliers know there was a demand for some parts in the assembly line. This made it easier for teams to communicate with each other about what work needed to be completed and by when. This process also helped with maximizing value and reducing waste.

This new version of Kanban came into existence in 2005. The core principles of Kanban, covered in the first book, are the same in most industries, including human resource management and software development. The following are the principles of Kanban:

- Visualize your work.
- Limit the work in the process.
- Focus on the workflow.
- Practice continuous improvement.

Visualize the Work and Workflow

When it comes to manufacturing, the complete workflow is always visible. One can view the workflow through the production line. In work that requires some knowledge, the process is opaque. This means that you will need to map the process on the Kanban board and use cards to represent the work. This provides visibility into the workflow and also gives people a chance to look at the different aspects of work.

Since most teams have their own process to complete their tasks, Kanban boards will give teams the freedom to map their workflow. You will need to lay the simple processes out on the board in the form of vertical lanes. If you have complex processes, you can use horizontal and vertical lanes. When you map the process that is unique to your team, you will make your process transparent. This will help the entire team understand what the status of the process is.

There are multiple sample boards available on the internet that you can use to see how Kanban works. Every lane is a step in the process, and Kanban cards are placed against each lane to indicate the status of the process. When you customize the board to reflect your team's process, you can use to board to give your team information about what the status of the workflow is.

You should know that the card color could determine the type of work or its priority. Any visual indicators like avatars or user icons can be placed on the card to indicate whom the work is assigned to. You can also use these icons to indicate the class of service, the source of demand, and any other detail that is relevant to the work your team is doing. You can always decide what your board should look like and how each card should represent the work you are doing. There are many benefits to visualizing your workflow and your work. You can start with understanding how your brain processes information. The human brain can understand any visual information sixty thousand times faster than it can understand text. Since you can create a picture of your work using a Kanban board, the visual display makes it easier and faster for team members to understand the progress and status. You can display these visual details in one place, which minimizes the time the team takes to track the progress. This will also reduce the number of status meetings that you will need to have. The stakeholders and team members can use the Kanban board and cards to communicate high-value information in a simple and transparent way.

Optimize the Flow of Your Work

The above benefit is only one of the many benefits of using the Kanban system and Kanban board. Through Kanban, teams can get rid of visual to-do lists. They can effectively optimize their workflow and their tools that will improve collaboration. This is because teams can limit the work in progress, be transparent about their work, and gather the necessary metrics to improve and measure productivity and efficiency. The objective of the Kanban system is to limit the quantity of work that is under process so that the work that flows into the system can be managed easily. In simple words, systems can handle only some amount of traffic, so it is important to ensure that the traffic moves smoothly through the various steps of the process. When the system is overloaded with work, things will certainly slow down, and the flow will turn into a jam. It is easy to spot the work that is stuck on a Kanban board, since any backlog will affect the work that is in the lanes. This will give the team clarity about what work needs to be completed immediately to remove any backlog. You can use more than one work-in-progress limit on a Kanban board. This limit is more of a constraint that is applied to some parts of the workflow or to the whole process. When you use these limits, you can improve how the workflows through the steps that you have defined on the board. This will help to improve the efficiency of your team. When your Kanban system is correctly implemented, it will become the center for continuous improvement. A team can always measure its effectiveness by tracking its lead times, throughput, quality, and more. Analysis and experiments can help the team and the organization change the system. This will help the team improve its efficiency and effectiveness.

Choosing a Kanban Board for Your Team

Some teams always want to use a physical Kanban board. This board is either drawn on a wall or a whiteboard, and the team can use sticky notes and Kanban cards to view the workflow. This is something that will work with every team that is located in the want building. This is because every member of the team can interact with the Kanban board and does not have to rely on their colleagues or the management to give them an update. There are some teams that prefer to use low-tech applications and therefore choose to use the Kanban board. The metrics can always be measured through some manual calculations. Physical boards are a great way to start with Kanban for teams that are located in the same area or building. That being said, Kanban works best for teams whose work does not intersect. Teams that are distributed will need to use a virtual Kanban board. The same goes for small teams that trade work between each other and for enterprise organizations that want to expand. A virtual Kanban system will provide the following:

- Real-time accessibility for stakeholders and remote workers
- Additional collaboration features
- A detailed trail that allows stakeholders and remote workers to view the history of a card
- Ability to integrate with different systems to remove duplicate data
- Sophisticated metrics and reporting that will take less time to generate when compared to physical Kanban boards

An enterprise team should always look at virtual Kanban if they want to improve security features and enhance scalability for any pilot project. You never have to switch tools when you need to expand. This will help to improve productivity and reduce the cost that the team will incur.

Regardless of whether your team chooses to use a physical or virtual Kanban board, the board by itself will make your work transparent. This will help you define the status of the project or work at a glance and will also help to optimize the workflow to improve efficiency.

Chapter 44.
Kanban Certifications

When you're beginning with Kanban and wondering how you can get certified, it can be daunting to know how to get started. Don't worry, listed below are the recognized Kanban certifications worldwide. While the teaching methods are different, the main goal still remains the same.

Team Kanban Practitioner

The Team Kanban Practitioner (TKP) certification gives you the skills to help your team achieve higher levels of efficiency and collaboration. Suggested for managers, this certification is open to everyone at any experience level. This is also a great to get started with option because there are no prerequisites needed, so even if you haven't got the other certifications, you can sign up to get your TKP certification right away.

The TKP certification has four objectives for those who will sign up for this:

- Improving communication within the team they're managing and encouraging a stronger sense of collaboration.
- Being able to organize the team's workload for further progress toward project completion.
- Having the skills to manage risks and unexpected circumstances.
- Gaining better visibility on goals and objectives.

In many ways, the TKP certification is the way to go if you're eager to get your team up and running through the Kanban method with a strong start.

Kanban Coaching Professional

If you're the type who likes teaching others and want to pass on what you know about Kanban, then the Kanban Coaching Professional (KCP) certification is for you.

Considered as the highest position a Kanban coach can achieve, the KCP certification is a total evaluation of a professional's overall history in Kanban coaching. For you to get this certification, you'll need to be someone who is already a trainer, consultant, manager, or practitioner dealing with the Kanban method. This can be a challenge to obtain, but if you're eager to teach others the greatness of Kanban, you'll want to get this one.

There are also valuable points to consider when you pursue this certification, such as:

- Gaining access to forums that are only available for KCP certified individuals.
- Being able to get updates and other forms of knowledge that will provide you with new techniques associated with Kanban that you never see in the areas open to non-KCP certified individuals.
- Having the opportunity to contact coaches and clients about methods in Kanban that will help you further boost your skills.

Kanban Management Professional

The Kanban Management Professional (KMP) certification is very popular and well-known worldwide. When pursuing this one, you'll gain an understanding of making decisions that help you improve workflow in projects and skills that will assist you in giving a company the highly sought-after customer satisfaction most companies are in need of.

This certification also includes specialized training for the Kanban method that provides many benefits. Also, just like the other certifications, KMP certification has these valuable pointers:

- You're able to gain better skills in managing inventory with a better understanding on what to do when the supplies are running low.
- You'll have a better grasp on how the WIP limits can be implemented so that you'll be able to manage teams better with the tasks they've been assigned.
- You'll be able to move from one process to another without losing pace or focus. This will give you the ability to manage a project when its broken down into different parts.

Accredited Kanban Trainer

For the trainer who wants to teach Kanban, this one's for you. The Accredited Kanban Trainer (AKT) certification gives you the skills that are necessary when you're seeking to offer training classes that deal with the Kanban method. It also gives you the opportunity to be a trainer in organizations that deal primarily with Kanban and with clients who pay for private classes.

The certification is also valuable thanks to these benefits:

- Having more opportunities for job positions that let you be the trainer and project manager in high-value companies.
- Being able to get a team up and running with confidence and power.
- Getting the skills to handle all types of Kanban methods and knowing which of them to implement on different projects.

Another great thing about this certification is that it gives you access to other resources that most certified individuals can't get, making it very attractive if you're the kind of person who likes having high-level knowledge on any subject matter.

Boosting Your Skills with Certifications

Once you obtain the certifications, they won't be much of use if you're not going to take advantage of the skills, you'll gain from them. But how will you do that? Here are a few ways:

1. Take advantage of what the certification classes will offer you

When boosting your skills, it's a good idea to take advantage of what the certifications hold for you. They all vary in accordance to what they're designed for, so keep that in mind. This means if the certification grants you skills in managing a team, then take advantage of that. But if you're the type of person that takes on projects alone, you should go for certifications that are designed for managers.

2. Apply and practice what you have learned in the projects you're managing

When you've gained a certification, you should apply what you've learned to the projects you're currently managing. This will strengthen your skills because you're now able to practice what your classes have taught you, and practicing theoretical knowledge is always the way to go when you want to improve your skills.

3. Be creative on how you can apply your skills with areas you feel need Kanban

Another way you can strengthen your skills is being able to come up with ways to apply those skills in areas you feel need Kanban. This can bring a lot of value to your life, because even the most unlikely of areas can be successful with Kanban. It can boost your skills because applying your knowledge tests just how much you understand of the Kanban methodology.

4. See how you can combine it with other project management methods

When you have a certification and are eager to improve your skills, why don't you try combining it with other systems? Kanban can be combined with Scrum, and with the skills you've learned while getting certified, you'll have a better idea of how to do that. This can better your understanding of the method because it will help you see how well Kanban can be adapted to other method's features.

Once The Certification Is Achieved, What Are The Advantages?

Kanban certifications may not look like much on the surface but will bring about many opportunities for you. Here are reasons why:

1. It'll open up job opportunities

With a Kanban certification, you'll be able to find many opportunities for jobs in various sectors. There might be a company that needs a Kanban expert in their department. There's bound to be a small business that wants someone with the knowledge of Kanban methodology. There may even be a well-known company abroad that'll let you test your Kanban skills to improve their company's workflow. However, you go about it, one thing's for sure: The opportunities are there.

2. It'll get you high gear in your career

Another benefit for getting certified is your career advancement will get a very significant boost. How so? If the company you're working for honors the Kanban method as an essential part of its workflow, you'll be able to make use of the skills you'll learn through certification and show your bosses that the projects they assign you and your team can be done effectively and efficiently.

3. You'll be able to get advanced levels

The Kanban certification will also help open up the path toward learning about the advanced levels of Kanban training. You can think of the certifications you'll learn about below as level 1 while the advanced levels are levels 2, 3, and above. And with the advanced level of skills you learn, it'll help you boost your skills to the max.

4. You'll have more knowledge on how Kanban can be applied to other areas

When you become certified, you'll have way more knowledge about Kanban. As you'll learn from the places that can give you certification in the Notes section, there are private forums where other certified professionals gather to share their tips and tricks on how to make the most out of Kanban.

5. You can teach Kanban to others

Two of the certifications you'll learn more about below let you learn Kanban and teach it to others. One of them gives you a chance to be a teacher while the other gives you the opportunity to be a trainer. This is a benefit because being able to share your knowledge of Kanban will no doubt boost the morale of the students you'll teach. It'll also help you keep the Kanban method alive with others.

Chapter 45. Abc Classification

On this guidebook, we have spent some time talking about inventory and how it works in the Kanban system. With many traditional forms of business, having a lot of inventory stored up to meet demand was a part of the game. This is how many businesses would make sure that they had enough products for their customers. It could make the process faster, but often it ended up adding more risk to the process because they could easily be off with their predictions and then they end up with a ton of inventory that they paid for, and they pay for storing, that the customer doesn't want.

With Kanban, inventory is not used as much. The idea is that the inventory is not an asset, it is a risk and a waste because of the costs that come with it. This method can sometimes run into trouble if the lead times are too long, but that is something that has to be worked out when it comes to using this method. With the right suppliers, the right plan, and everyone using the visualization, it won't take long to get the product to the customer on time without all the wastes.

One method that can be used to help manage the way that the business is run, to determine if there needs to be any kind of inventory and more is the ABC classification. This kind of classification is going to be a type of ranking system that can identify, and group items based on how useful they can be for achieving your goals in the business.

This kind of system is going to take the different aspects of the business and group them into three categories. These three main categories are going to include:

A: Extremely Important

B: Moderately Important

C: Relatively Important

The ideas that come with ABC classification are going to be associated pretty closely with the 80/20 rule. The 80/20 rule is going to be a metric used in business that says 80 percent of the outcomes for the business are determined by 20 percent of the inputs. The goal of using the ABC classification is to provide ways for a business to figure out what makes up that valuable 20 percent so that they can then control the segment as closely as possible and maximize it as much as possible. Once all of the segments have been identified by the business, each one is going to be handled in a different way. The most attention is going to be given to A, less attention will be handed to B, and then the least amount of attention is given to C. ABC classification is often something that is going to be associated with controlling inventory, but it is also used to help rank the different customer segments, but segments of the business can cause the most risk financially, which employees are seen as the most valuable, and where it is likely that a bottleneck will become a problem.

Defining the ABC's

The first thing that you need to do in order to get started with an ABC analysis is to separate out your products or customers into each of the different categories. Remember that we have A, which includes the items that are the most valuable to the business and therefore need the most attention, then we have Class B and Class C. Let's take a look at how we should separate out each of these in the ABC analysis.

Class A Inventory

The items that fit into the class A are going to be about twenty percent of the inventory at most. But they are so important because they account for at least 80 percent of the profits that the business is able to make. Some of the characteristics of this classification include:

1. Items in this part are going to cost the most to use. This could be because the unit is higher in cost or the volume usage is high on an item that has a low unit cost.

2. These items can present a bigger risk. Because these are necessary items with a higher expense, these items need to have a lot of human capital invested in them. Most inventory managers need to spend the majority of their time and attention on replenishing these items. Without the right stock levels of these, there can be a lot of consequences.

3. These items are going to be replenished using a sawtooth curve. Because the costs that come with these items are higher, there are fewer on hand, even though the orders are placed on a regular basis. This means that a low lead time and standard costs are important on these

4. The lead time on these should be somewhere between three to ten days. These are going to comprise the majority of the on-hand value for a company.

Class B Inventory

After you have figured out the most important items to put into Class A, it is time to work with the Class B items. These are going to account for somewhere between 15 to 30 percent of the items for the business. These are going to have a lower impact on inventory spending, around 15 percent for the year, but are still things that need a little bit of attention as well. Some of the characteristics of Class B include:

1. These types of items are going to require some standard costs that need to be paid at predictable intervals. These items are going to be needed for production on a regular basis and they will be on a routine for ordering but won't be needed as much as class A items.

2. These items are going to be important enough that the team should manage them, but they don't need the high level of control that the class A items do.

3. These items should be on hand but keeping them at moderate quantities should be fine. Keeping as low of an inventory as possible is the goal and you should limit the number of transactions wherever you can.

4. The typical target lead time for these items will be between 5 to 15 days. The items that fit into this category will contribute somewhere between 15 to 25 percent of the inventory value.

Class C Inventory

Finally, we are going to move on to the items that fit into class C. These are the majority of the inventory stock, with at least 50 percent of the items fitting into this category. Even though there is so much in here, these items are only going to account for five percent of the amount that the company is going to spend. Some of the characteristics of products that would fit into this category include:

1. These items aren't going to cost a lot, but their consumption is very high. This could be things like stampings, literature, springs, and such. However, there are times when a class C item is going to be more expensive, such as a sub-assembly that may be $700, but the team only uses a few times a year.

2. The replenishment of these items should be as automated as possible. These shouldn't require any attention from the team because they are then neglecting the more critical items in the other categories. Because there are so many items in this category, going through and actually working with them, rather than automating it can waste a lot of time.

3. Procurement managers need to focus on reducing how many transactions are needed to acquire these types of items. The tedious task that comes with this kind of work, such as making the order and inspecting it before moving to the right

department, can cost a lot more than the direct acquisition of those items.

4. While these items are only going to take up 5 percent of the spending budget, they are going to represent 20 percent of the on-hand inventory dollars because it is easy for companies to overstock these items to avoid shutdowns that come when they run out.

ABC classification can be useful when it comes to handling your business. It ensures that you are going to be able to provide the customer with the products they are looking for, without a huge lead time in the process. You can decide which products are the most important, based on how much they make you, and then work your way on down the line until you reach the products that don't make up a lot of your profits but are still important.

The Steps to ABC classification

While the concept that comes with ABC classification is pretty simple, going through an inventory that is large or complex can seem really overwhelming and tedious. The payoff of this can be really great, even though doing the classification the first time is going to take some work. After you have committed yourself and the team to do an ABC analysis of the inventory, the following will be the steps that you must use to get it done.

Separate the items that are purchased from the ones that are manufactured

There should be two item lists here. One of them will be for the items that the company purchases and the other are for the items that the company manufactures. This helps you to get a good look at the highest, middle, and low costs in each category. Because the annual cost of all those manufactured items often ends up being higher than the purchased parts, often these are the items that are going to take over the limited class A spots. These can push out some of the purchased items that should be done in Class A into the lower categories. One thing to consider is to count maintenance, repair, and operating items on your list. The expense of these supplies can be easy to forget, but they do add up and you do want to have a good look at the value of your inventory. Remember, anything that contributes in some way to the value stream, it then deserves a bit of your attention.

Collect the annual usage data and the standard cost data for all part numbers you purchased

Now you will need to go through and create a spreadsheet that has three columns. The first column needs to have the part number of each item in your inventory. The second column should have the unit cost for every item. And then the third column is where you need to write out the annual demand that the customer has for each item.

Calculate out the annual amount you spend on all the parts

With that spreadsheet that we talked about before, you need to create another column to calculate the annual amount that you spend. To figure out this number, you just need to take the standard unit cost for the parts and multiply it by the annual demand to get this number. Now, take advantage of the sort function of the spreadsheet so that you can sort out the rows based on the annual spend. Do this in the descending order so that those who have the highest spend each year have their values at the top. When you have it all sorted out this way, you can use a non-sorted cell in order to figure out the total amount that you spend for all of the parts.

Add in another column that shows the cumulative running total

Now we want to calculate out the cumulative annual spend. This is simply going to be a running total of the annual spend on each item that will accumulate to equal the total annual spend of all the items. For each of the rows, you want the cumulative running total to be equal to the sum of the annual spend of itself, plus the annual spend of all items before it when you sort this out by descending order.

Identifying items that go to Class A

The first thing that we need to do here is to figure out which items should be considered Class A items. To find that, you first need to find the point that will act as a threshold for 80 percent of the total annual spend. To do this, use the following formula:

Target total annual spend threshold = total annual spends for all purchased items X .80

You can then round this to the nearest ones, tens, or hundreds place (depending on how large the number is to start with), in order to get a good estimate of your threshold for the items that fit in there. Now, take a look back at the cumulative annual spends that we worked on and compare them to this target. Find the first row that is greater than this target and let this be the first estimate of your cut-off for determining if an item should be Class A or not. Now you can move on to comparing the annual spend of the items on the threshold between Class B and Class A. If you see that there are two items that are pretty similar on either side of the threshold, this means that you need to either raise or lower that number. You want to make sure there is some type of meaningful gap between where an A item ends and where the B items start. You don't want the threshold to deviate too much, but a little bit is not a bad thing. Once this point is established, you can add in another column to that spreadsheet that will house the ABC classifications for each part as you go through. In this column, you can enter A for each item that, based on the analysis that you just did, qualifies as an A item.

Identifying items that go to Class B

The following category we are going to work on is the items that fit into Class B. These are the items that will take up about 15 percent of the amount that you spend each year. To find the threshold that will separate out the items in Class B from the items in Class C, you need to figure out the value of 95 percent of the annual spend. This 95 percent is used because it shows you the amount that both Class B and Class A contribute to the total. But since we already went through and know what the A amount is, we can use this number to help us find the best cutoff between the C and B inventories. This estimated cutoff can sometimes include the items that you designated to Class A, depending on if and how you went through and adjusted the threshold manually in the past step. Make some adjustments manually so that the cutoff point is meaningful, just like we did with the Class A items. Then you can designate the right non-A items below the identified threshold as B items.

Identifying items that go to Class C

All the remaining items, the ones that didn't fit in with the requirements that we put in for Class B or Class A can go into Class C. There are going to be way more items that fit into Class C than the other two combined, and Class A should be the smallest.

Repeat this with all the manufactured items

Now that we know the steps that are needed for doing an ABC analysis, you can repeat the steps for all of the manufactured items in the company as well. Remember that it isn't that unusual for the manufactured items to have a high total annual spend as well. This methodology is still one that is sound and can work, regardless of the amount the annual spend comes out to. It is also the main reason why we went through and separated out the purchased parts from the ones that were manufactured in step 1. The extremely high cost that comes from manufactured items is often the result of a duplicated demand. When one part is used in a way of fabricating another, then those parts will then be used in an assembly before it becomes part of the finished product. This means that the parts that become a part of the finished product can be counted a few times in the demand column, so sometimes it is hard to figure all of this out.

Chapter 46.
Personal Project Management Using Kanban

The Kanban system has been greatly modified for modern use today through different mobile apps and computer software. This has, in turn, made the system much more relatable and easier to use for project management of non-technical projects. These are some of the applications that will be explained below.

Apart from turning powerful ideas into working plans, project management apps put lists tasks and files together for your team to collaborate. They give clear details about the available solutions. Each project has tasks, which are then divided into micro-tasks, and then the tasks are carried out using the different management system to enable you to achieve the goal. Mostly, where the project is on an ongoing basis for example, "make more motorcycle spare parts," these sub-tasks are necessary as the whole project and the system is what makes everything success. For example, 60 years ago, Toyota came up with the "Kanban" system, which ensures every part, is made carefully at every stage and at the required time. Such systems help in producing the best product and at the right time as the workers can be able to see the progress at every stage and rectify a problem if any. This system assists the teams to manage editorial workflows, simplify purchase processes and other necessary things.

For the successful completion of any job, there must be processes and steps being followed. Taking a factory example, a motorcycle is made from spare parts which were also raw materials assembled at a point. Consumer goods like juice have to move down the supply chain, from the factory to a stockroom and eventually to the store shelves. The beauty of Kanban is that all these processes clearly fit into the system.

Kanban employs the use of visual cards which detail the different tasks to be done in list format on a board. To better understand how workflow can be managed with Kanban, it is important to understand the meaning of the various terms used. Here are the Kanban basics.

➢ *Kanban card-* Kanban card stores any item that is related to your board and list as a task to be completed or a specific part to be made and lives in a list on board. The traditional project management tools call it a "to-do" or "task."

➢ *Kanban List-* A list comprises of cards and multiple lists make up a board. Each card represents a task to be done in the project. Ideally, a list is a to-do list.

➢ *Kanban board-* this is a board that puts projects or workflows in the same interface and in an interchangeable way and guards their states against invalid changes. This is called "project" or "workplace" in an A traditional project management tool.

Today, the Kanban system is one of the most used and most effective project management systems. Each project is defined on a board. When managing a project, there are two major ways in which you can list your tasks. One way is to use the board to track the progress for some specific tasks. This particular use involves moving cards from one list to another as the task moves along. These lists can be named as to be done, in progress and done or completed. Another alternative is to use a Kanban board as a to-do list for your tasks. This involves listing the specific tasks to be done under the lists.

Examples of Online Kanban Systems

To be you started, below is a list of the best Kanban board apps, which you can incorporate into your project management:

i. Trello. This is one of the most widely used apps. It is preferred for being simple, complete with different features and has a power-up option, which allows you to link your board to other apps such as Slack and your Google Calendar. Most of the references in the book are drawn from Trello operations.

ii. Lean Kit. If your tasks are larger in size, this is your go-to. You can customize the sizes of your columns for effective management of your board.

iii. MeisterTask. This app allows you to prioritize tasks and also links to your email, which is very helpful communication-wise in the long run.

iv. PivotalTracker. This app uses the icebox system where you can add tasks that are yet to be done. It also enables you to see lists that can be completed together.

v. Blossom. This is great for more visual planning. It is also known for giving great detailed reports on projects.

vi. KanbanFlow. Its most unique feature is the Pomodoro timer. This is used to help everyone in the team space out their work to avoid burnout.

vii. Kanbnery. This app holds various templates that you can use to design your board and further customize for the project you are working on.

As we have established throughout the book, Kanban has great potential when it comes to ease of use in project management. Taking that most people work online today, and especially when working remotely, use of online Kanban systems is at an all-time high. However, to successfully manage your projects and tasks, it is important that your board has some key features, which make your work much easier. Most apps such as Trello have these features. When selecting a system, you ought to look out for various features namely:

Movement of Cards between Lists and Boards. As mentioned above, a project on Kanban is represented on a board, which is made up of lists. Each list is, in turn, made up of cards, which basically highlight the different tasks to be performed. Taking that specific tasks are listed on cards; it is important to have the ability to move a card from one list to another or even from one board to another. This is a feature that is present in most online Kanban systems.

Ability to Invite People to your Board. When working with teams, sharing a board is a necessity. This is because it allows for instantaneous updates of tasks and this is accessible to all team members at all time and real-time. Once you create your board, you can go ahead to add colleagues, friends, clients and so on by simply sending them a direct invite from your board. This is done by sending a direct email invite from the board. Moreover, you can go even further and add specific people to a specific card or task such that they track the progress of the specific item. People can leave comments on specific tasks, whether it is a progress report of how far they have gone with the implementation or key things that other team members should note from the execution of that particular task.

It is important to note that once you add someone to a board, they have the ability to alter the board, move cards and even edit deadlines. Therefore, you must ensure that you only add relevant parties to a card. Also, note that you will keep getting notifications every time someone changes something on the cards. Depending on personal preferences, this can be quite helpful or annoying. Therefore, you can always unsubscribe from emails to avoid a cluttered inbox.

Use of Labels and Tags. Most apps allow you to add tags or labels to the board. These are helpful in the organization of cards on a list. It is possible to customize your labels, and this perfectly allows for a smoother workflow.

Cards and Checklists. As mentioned, a card highlights a specific task to be completed. However, the task has other key actionable items. This is where the use of a checklist becomes imperative. A checklist consists of different things to be done and it helps to break down a task even further. Moreover, you can assign an item on the checklist to someone by tagging them with @Username. Finally, remember to have your teammates tick tasks as completed once they are done. This makes it easier for others to follow the progress at a glance.

Discussions and Adding Notes. As mentioned above, most online Kanban systems give you the option to add comments, notes, and links on a card. This is very important for tracking back information. Projects that involve teams need swift and effective communication at all times. This ensures that everyone is kept informed on the progress and therefore, work moves on swiftly. You can also tag a team member in a comment and respond directly using the @ function. Each card has its own discussion space making it easier to find conversations. Unlike offline Kanban boards where it is harder to list everything on a post-it, online systems enable you to write down everything you think about or encounter in the process and have it permanently saved on the cards for future reference.

You can also add key details on the card under the description part. This could be a high-level description of the project or links.

Setting Deadlines. One key feature is the ability to add dates to your cards. This could be a start date or a due date for a particular task. You can also incorporate different add-on features that enable you to time and schedule your work. A repeater, for example, schedules a particular task for each day of a week as you wish over a period of time without you having to manually input all that data.

Conclusion of Kanban

Kanban systems were built in the 1940s by Taiichi Ohno for Toyota. The technique was then adopted by several organizations more prominently in 2004 by David Anderson for IT companies to enhance their overall functioning.

Using Kanban systems can help an organization identify different tasks that have to be finished to complete a project. The Kanban board will be used to mention the different processes and mention the stage at which it is. It will help teams to find any obstacles or bottlenecks and ways to solve them to forward the project to the future stage.

Kanban is an interesting system to be used for project management. From its humble beginnings as the system that would bring Toyota back into the game to its current form, it has brought a whole new way of managing projects for companies and offices.

Sure, it may have its ups and downs, its benefits and risks, and its oddities, but it cannot be denied that the results it brings can really make a difference. When you add the factor of scaling, ABC classification, other project management methods, and certification, it shows you that Kanban can be used in more ways than one.

It has also brought a whole new notion to what it really means to manage projects. After all, being able to visualize your workflow, set your limits, define policies, and manage tasks to achieve a fully completed project is truly a marvelous feat. To top it all off, Kanban can even be used on your own if you choose. It's a matter of taking the core principles and adapting them to any situation.

Further, there's the fact that Kanban has not only been used in physical form successfully but has also found success in digital form. It's been so successful in digital form that software development companies have made tools that streamline the Kanban method in a way that lets everyone have their own Kanban board with just a few clicks.

With that, this is your chance to take the first step to visualize what your workflow is and manage your projects the way they were meant to be.

Your succeeding step is to observe and plan your transformation. Stop wondering how you can become more lean, agile, and efficient. You just read all about it! Now is the time for action. Now is the time to prepare your Kanban board and visual system to make your life easier and your team happier. Now is the time to lower costs and increase production using a simple and effective method.

While you are planning, get the buy-in from your team, company, stakeholders, and even your customers. Sell them on the benefits of adopting a Kanban system, and stay close to the process, refining as needed, so it is the most efficient system for your business. Remember, the goal of this is to assist your team members in working alongside one another efficiently while also benefiting your company. Keeping your eye on this goal during each decision you make will help with all the changes and challenges.

Through Kanban systems, an organization can identify the different processes that must be completed to achieve the final goal. The board lists out these processes and segregates them into the different stages they are in. This also allows the team or the members to identify potential bottlenecks and also find ways to resolve them.

Over the course of the book, you will gather information on how Kanban can be used by different departments to improve quality and also deliver products on time. Kanban systems can also be used to derive estimates for delivery of products through some statistical tools.

To conclude, the Kanban system is an effective tool, which helps to maintain transparency, thereby giving the organization an understanding of how work is progressing between different departments.

A Kanban methodology applies to a variety of situations, despite rumors it is "outdated." As it is with new technology, do not jump onto the glossy "bandwagon." You have read the options and reviews. Determine the unique needs of your organization and create a way to make this basic system work for you. Do not forget, before you roll out your Kanban board; compare them against the checklist to make sure they are "good!" It is a great practice to do each and every time, or at least until you have a firm grasp on the process. The more and more you use boards, lists, and cards, the better your team will get at running an effective Kanban project and process. As they continue to feel empowered and successful, imagine the positive atmosphere and engaged work environment you will have! Success will come to you in a variety of forms thanks to you implementing this methodology in your company. Congratulations on taking this step towards a more productive future for your company!

Chapter 47.
Kaizen

Kaizen is a way by which an organization's activities are grouped together using the principles of economy, order, discipline, and common sense. In many businesses that have lean production or manufacturing processes, Kaizen is an indispensable part and substantial contributor.

Kaizen pertains to undertakings that seek to improve business processes or functions on a continuing basis and involves everyone in an organization from the chief executive officer all the way down to the lowest ranking employee or volunteer. In Japan, it's normal to call any technique that improves the way businesses are run as "Kaizen."

Kaizen and Your Personal and Professional Success

Success is all about being able to accomplish goals both big and small. However, some goals are just too big to go at one swing, which can be quite overwhelming. They can be so daunting that merely taking the first step towards accomplishing them can be so intimidating that the temptation to procrastinate or completely ditch such a goal can become so strong. Very big goals, which include very rapid and radical personal and professional changes, may initially sound good but when you really think about it, can, make people even more resistant to necessary changes.

If you insist on having very big and lofty goals, your chances of experiencing successful and continuous self-improvement are much lower and become discouraged from continuing.

Also, you'll need significantly more resources to succeed with very large goals. And finally, life can throw so many curveballs that can make it harder and harder to successfully accomplish very large goals, let alone accomplish several on a continuing basis.

It's for these reasons why Kaizen involves making small and continuous improvements to your life's most important areas, from personal to professional. With smaller but continuous improvement goals, your chances of success are much, much higher.

Even better, such small changes accumulate and compound over time resulting in more meaningful improvements, much like how compounding interest works.

The History of Kaizen

The story that is Kaizen began when Toyota Motors in Japan started to apply the concept of "quality circles" in its car-production processes, which as partly influenced by teachings of management gurus who have visited Japan after the Second World War.

A quality circle refers to a group of employees or workers with similar or identical duties and responsibilities that regularly convene to identify, evaluate, and address work-related challenges.

This concept garnered a lot of buzz in the Japanese business sector during the 1950s and to this day, the concept of the quality circles or Kaizen groups continues to be practiced in Japan.

The Kaizen business philosophy and practice was popularized the world over thanks largely to Masaaki Imai's works. He was a prominent management consultant and organizational theorist in Japan and was popularly known by his works on quality management, which prominently included the Kaizen practice.

He started to introduce the Kaizen way of business productivity to companies in the west by putting up the Kaizen Institute Consulting Group or KICG. Today, KICG's teams have conducted Kaizen courses and implemented Kaizen methodologies to practically all types of businesses the world over.

And because the Kaizen philosophy's been successfully applied to all kinds of businesses, there's no doubt that we can apply it to our own personal and professional lives as well.

Kaizen Blitz or Event

Kaizen blitzes or events refer to the activities that aim to solve or address specific productivity problems or challenges by employing the Kaizen philosophy. Kaizen events are development projects that are so focused that they can come up with breakthrough improvements within a very brief period of time. And by "brief" I mean an average of two to ten days.

For Kaizen events to be able to accomplish such meaningful results in short periods of time, they need three things: a very clear and concise goal, readily available resources, and fast results. When these three things are present, Kaizen events can produce meaningful, clear, motivating, and satisfying results.

On a personal note, Kaizen events will refer to our personal endeavors or activities that have very clear goals, which are supported with the necessary tools and resources and can provide meaningful results that will allow us to accumulate many smaller improvements or "victories" en route to bigger personal successes.

Chapter 48.
The Kaizen Principles

To effectively implement Kaizen in our lives, we'll need to learn its foundational principles, which will guide us when we embark on continuous improvement endeavors. These principles are:

Continuous Improvement: Companies that implement Kaizen in their business communicate to the world that as an organization, they don't rest on their laurels, i.e., they will not succumb to the temptation of believing that they've already a "good enough" level of service or product and in the process, become complacent. Kaizen-adopting companies are always looking for ways to improve - even in the smallest ways.

On a personal level, be it with our relationships, personal growth, or professional endeavors, we can apply the same principle to experience massive success in life. If we'll be honest with ourselves, we know that all of us aren't perfect and as such, there'll always room for improvement, however, small such improvements may be. Heck, even people like Bill Gates, Elon Musk, and Oprah Winfrey continue to work on themselves despite their already very lofty statuses in life because they know deep within that they can't rest on their laurels if they want to continue being very successful in what they believe they're called to do in life.

Getting Rid Of Antiquated Practices: One of the biggest reasons why many people and organizations become complacent and aren't able to continue improving is because they hold on to practices and traditions that are antiquated, i.e., outdated and are no longer relevant or working as effectively as expected.

One such company was Netscape. If you're not familiar with Netscape, it's because it's already dead! And why did it die a rather quick death after achieving the pinnacle of success as the world's primary web browser development company? It became complacent and hung on to antiquated practices that no longer served their markets as efficiently as its primary competitor back then, which was Microsoft. And guess who's still around the block and still making hay because the sun continues to shine on them?

That's right - Microsoft! And the reason why they're still very much alive and kicking is because they continue to seek ways to improve and, in the process, continue to stay very relevant to their customers.

On a personal level, we also need to get rid of antiquated practices or beliefs, the latter is what leading self-help guru Vishien Lakhiani of Mindvalley calls "brules" or b$llsh! % rules. These practices or beliefs, while they may have served us very well in the past, are no longer applicable or relevant today to the point that they aren't just not serving their purpose but they're hindering us from fulfilling ours. One brule or antiquated practice is using a pager.

What's the point of using it when the technology supporting it no longer exists? Many people stopped using it simply because the death of its supporting technology forced them to stop but if such technology was still alive, chances are that some people would continue using it despite the availability of more efficient devices.

Proactivity: The term "proactive" was popularized by the late, great self-help guru Stephen Covey in his groundbreaking bestselling self-help book "The 7 Habits of Highly Effective People." In it, he defined the word proactive as having the initiative to do things without being told or being compelled to by exigencies. He also defined the word as having the attitude of accountability, i.e., taking responsibility for one's actions, the results of such actions, and his or her situation. Instead of saying "It's not my fault that I'm poor - I was born into a very poor family!" we can say, "I may have been poor, but if I die poor, it's on me."

Why is being proactive a crucial principle in the Kaizen philosophy? It's because if every person in an organization deflects his or her responsibilities at work, how will the organization move and get things done? If people need to always make excuses for procrastinating or failing to fulfill their responsibilities, organizations will just be throwing precious resources away and end up not being able to accomplish the things they need to.

And because continuous improvements often involve things that are not yet urgent or don't appear to be important as of that moment, it takes proactivity to consistently go after them. And if people don't take responsibility for them in the organization, no one will do their part.

For the same reasons, we need to develop a proactive attitude if we're to successfully and consistently apply the philosophy of Kaizen in our lives and eventually, experience massive success in both our personal and professional lives. We can't afford to wait for some exigency to compel us to "level up" because by then, incremental changes may no longer suffice and only radical, one-time-big-time changes may work, which are much harder to accomplish.

Never Take New Methods for Granted: If one of the principles of Kaizen is ditching antiquated practices and beliefs, it doesn't imply that the latest ones will automatically work or be much better than the old ones. Remember, antiquated doesn't necessarily mean "old" - it implies something's no longer relevant, applicable, or effective based on current circumstances. But old practices and beliefs can continue to be relevant and effective, such as the age-old practice of honoring our parents or not stealing. Even if more and more people are treating their parents like crap, it doesn't mean we should readily adapt such a new and "modern" belief and practice it because simply put, it's just not relevant, effective or right.

A very practical example of this principle was my recent purchase of an app called Recastly. It was an app that was promoted as a revolutionary new way of creating marketing videos that can really help draw in more leads for your online marketing efforts. It was an app that automatically generates sub-titles for your videos, which is a very helpful feature when it comes to online marketing videos.

But while it was new and revolutionary, I found it to be a waste of both my time and money because it hardly ever worked for the 4 months that I used it and worse, customer support replies after an average of about 3 weeks per message.

At the end of the day, I compelled them to refund me and I had to go back to old school style of generating subtitles for marketing videos. The new failed to trump the old and the old still crushes the new, in that instance.

Correct the Wrongs: Continuous improvements will involve errors along the way. In fact, it's often through errors that we'll know what things we'll need to improve on. That's why Kaizen-companies take process or transactional errors or glitches seriously - they provide insights for further improvements.

It's no different with our personal and professional lives. Things can - and will - go wrong along the way. The key to handling them well is perspective: will we look at errors, mistakes and failures as such or as opportunities for continuous improvement? Our perspective can make a huge difference. If we look at "wrongs" as failures, chances are we may become more discouraged than encouraged and when that happens, we may not take any action to correct them as soon as possible.

But if we look at them in the same way we do free lunches, i.e., opportunities to seize, then we will be encouraged and be stoked to work on them as soon as we can so we can continue making improvements that will further build up on our personal and professional successes.

Empower Others to Speak: Kaizen-practicing companies are able to successfully improve their business processes and bottom lines consistently because they have access to goldmines of ideas for continuous improvement. And how are they able to access such goldmines? By empowering everybody in their organization to speak up and provide potentially important information that can help the organization continue making improvements to their processes or fix long-standing challenges.

It doesn't mean everybody's opinions will be acted upon. It just means these organizations acknowledge everybody's potential to provide information or suggestions that can enable the organization to solve existing challenges or continue to make improvements.

We can do the same in our personal lives even if we don't have a company or employees under us. We can empower the people closest to us to speak up when needed so we can continue making incremental changes or improvements in various areas of our lives that can add up to our personal and professional successes.

They can include our parents, our siblings, our closest friends, our work colleagues - especially those we think are always trying to get on our nerves. While it can be quite irritating to hear from such work colleagues or from people who seem to be very critical to us, they can be goldmines for self-improvement information because they don't have any desire to kiss our butts and get into our good graces. As such, we can be assured that at the very least, they're not pulling any punches that can help us become much better people.

More than just being goldmines for information on the things where we can make improvements, we can also empower others to speak up in terms of ideas on how to implement improvements or changes that we've already identified as important. We can think of this as crowdsourcing of implementation ideas. People who aren't directly involved have a higher chance of providing objective ideas and perspectives on how to best implement important changes or improvements in our lives.

Ask Why Five Times: Prior to finalizing any important decisions, we must ensure that such decisions can really address the root issue or challenge we're facing that needs to be addressed through improvements. Often times, we don't get to the root causes because we stop asking prematurely. To ensure a very high degree of success in terms of fleshing out root issues or challenges, asking "why" (five times) can become a very good way to learn. Often times, the real root causes of issues and challenges are uncovered after asking "why?" at least three to five times. And nothing else can optimize our chances of making meaningful incremental changes than knowing the areas of our lives that really need to be addressed and nothing else can derail our self-improvement efforts by barking at the wrong tree due to inability to address the root causes of issues and problems.

Economy: Being able to consistently make incremental changes or improvements in our lives require that we have enough resources for them. That's why it's important that the incremental improvements we make in our lives are economical, i.e., cost-efficient. What good will it do if our personal finances suffer in the name of self-improvement? And when you look at how Kaizen's applied by businesses, cost-cutting or saving more money is often at the heart of such improvements.

Cutting down on unnecessary expenses is almost always a continuing self-improvement effort because many of the things we need to do in life require having enough funds. Whether it's to get into excellent health and fitness or being able to leave our children a good inheritance, money's needed. And the more money we're able to save, the more resources we can have for continuing self-improvement whether it's in our personal lives (relationships, personal growth, etc.) or our professional lives (business, work, investments, etc.).

Never Stop: As I write this, a thought just popped into my head: the theme song of any Kaizen practitioner, whether an individual or a company, should be Bon Jovi's hit song Sleep When I'm Dead. This is because that's what Kaizen's all about - continuous improvements, however small, for as long as we're alive. Nobody's perfect and as such, there'll always be room for improvement. And if we never stop improving, opportunities for greater personal and professional success won't be far behind.

Chapter 49. Advantages Of Kaizen Implementation

Effective Management-Employee Communication

This is both a requirement and a benefit of applying kaizen. You need effective communication to instill your goals and strategies to your employees. You also need that in collecting information about problems and in getting feedback for the changes you introduce.

Teaching your goals and strategies right from the start helps ensure that you and your employees stay on the same page as you expand your business. This also gives your employees insights on the possible career growth they can have with your startup. Having such insights let them consider if they're going to stay with you for a long time.

Eliminating the blame game and encouraging them to inform you about problems speed up crisis management. These actions, along with allowing them to give feedback, boost their confidence and make them feel less stressed at work.

According to the Canadian Centre for Occupational Health and Safety, work-related stress causes short-term effects like headaches, chest pains and muscle tensions. It can badly affect sleep as well. This further causes employees to make poor judgment and neglect their duties at work. Such effects mean losses on your part. Imagine paying for their time, but not getting the work you required them to do.

In contrast, having a great workplace environment makes employees want to work better and stay longer. This can also be beneficial in your branding efforts later on.

Furthermore, effective communication is needed in reviewing your kaizen efforts. This turns into advantage as you or your employees can alert about the possibility of getting sidetracked. The sooner you realize it, the sooner you can work your way back to accomplishing your goals.

Elimination of the Seven Types of Waste

A complex manufacturing procedure and product surplus make it look like your business is doing well. Does your revenue increase though? Are you able to achieve your long-term goals as well?

What seem like signs of business doing well are actually forms of waste. As they're kinds of waste, it's only right to eliminate them. To eliminate them, you should be able to identify them first. According to Ohno (1988), there are seven types of waste in the business process. You can remember them as TIM WOOD.

1. Transport

From the delivery of raw materials to the shipment of finished products, several movements are involved. In the case of manufacturing food products, the steps include cleaning produce, processing, packing, labeling and warehousing. The plant should be organized with the first station being the cleaning area. Then to it should be the processing area, followed by the packing and labeling stations.

Organizing that way is a no-brainer. However, one of the common mistakes of inexperienced manufacturers is that they organize with maximizing space in mind. They try to fill as much space as possible. Others focus on keeping manual labor in one part, while the steps involving machines are on another area.

A problematic workplace setup creates the transport waste. This type of waste refers to the unnecessary movement of products. Aside from wasting time, the unnecessary movement puts your products at risk of mishandling. They may get misplaced as well. The complex setup may also cause collisions between workers.

2. Inventory

Raw materials, work in progress and finished products signify costs until they're delivered to the consumers. After all, you're paying for the supply of raw materials, the electricity for powering up machines, the delivery of your products to consumers and the labor needed to carry out the steps in your business process.

If you store excessive raw materials, unfinished products, and finished ones, you're bound to deal with the second type of waste: inventory. The surplus is deemed as a waste because warehousing alone costs money but doesn't give you anything in return. Perhaps, you can say it gives you assurance that you can use the extras in case there's a disruption in your production. But there's also the possibility that, when a finished product is discovered to be defective, that means you're less likely to sell your surplus unless you lower the costs.

Moreover, if there are no disruptions in your production processes and the demand for your products remains the same, the surplus will stay in your warehouse for a long time. Some manufacturers end up offering the extras as bundles just to clear their warehouses. The "buy 1, take 1" marketing strategy seems like a good one until you realize how you have to reduce the price to get rid of surplus.

3. Motion

The third type of waste happens when the equipment and workers are inefficient in what they're supposed to do. It's somewhat related to the transport waste. Their main difference though is that transport waste is about damages from moving products, while motion waste is about the damages from the workers and equipment that directly make the products.

Wear-and-tear damage in equipment is a classic example of motion waste. Equipment breakdowns are another example. You can also consider overworked and injured workers.

4. Waiting

Also known as delays and idle time, the fourth type is all about wasted time in the production process. Waiting can happen when you're understaffed or when work is poorly distributed.

Excessive delays in the production are bound to adversely affect your delivery of goods. Consequently, they can result to complaints and cancellation of orders.

5. Overproduction

Dubbed as the worst type of waste (Perrin, 2015), overproduction can trigger and worsen the other six. As its name suggests, this refers to the excessive production of goods when there is low or even no demand at all.

Overproduction is the number one cause of inventory problem. If you don't address the overproduction problem, you're going to worsen your inventory waste. Disposing the surplus means additional work later on.

Instead of delivering newly finished products to retailers or to the consumers, you may also end up storing them for the meantime and shipping the surplus from the past production. This becomes a form of transport waste.

As a remedy to the surplus, you may lower production in the upcoming few days or weeks. This means some of your employees will free up some of the work time you're paying them for.

Overproduction can trigger quality control problems as well. This is especially true if you're in the food manufacturing industry. When you're storing the excess, you need to be more mindful of expiry dates. Otherwise, they may end up rotting in your warehouse.

6. Over Processing

Front and back cameras are one of the advantageous features of smartphones. One in front and another one at the back are enough. Why add more? Shouldn't phone manufacturers just improve the quality and features of dual cams instead?

Such is just an example of over processing. Adding the extra camera means costs and another step in the production process. Perhaps, the only advantage of having such is that when one camera breaks, you can still have a couple left. You won't feel the need to fix the broken cam. But, as it is a feature you paid for, will you just leave it like that?

Over processing refers to the addition of unnecessary steps in your production. This waste also covers the use of raw materials that are more expensive and of higher quality than what you required for your production. If you're ordering the materials from overseas despite having local suppliers, you'll also deal with over processing, transport, and waiting waste.

7. Defect

Out of all the types of waste, defects are the easiest to understand. Defective products mean you can't recoup your expenses for their production. You wasted time, raw materials, electricity, and your workers' efforts. Depending on the severity of the defects, the goods could be considered literal waste as well.

It's only right to issue recall for defective goods. If you refuse to do so, you risk good reputation. Moreover, you lose loyal customers in the process. But just like Toyota's journey, it's still possible to bounce back and become better than before.

Getting rid of the seven types of waste helps you maximize your resources. Consider the reduced operational costs. You can use the capital you saved for paying loans or for investing on necessary equipment. When it comes to labor, you can use the waiting time for training in a more advanced work.

Eliminating waste is one of the objectives of lean manufacturing. Lean is basically a methodology. It involves streamlining your processes.

By knowing the seven types of waste, identifying areas you need to improve on becomes more manageable. The term lean kaizen denotes an approach of ensuring continuous improvement and eliminating waste.

The production is the most crucial step in a business process. In the case of providing software, the development phase is the most important part. If you're offering services, training and customer service are the most essential. In these steps, you can actually find the abovementioned types of waste. For service providers though, the defect refers to unsatisfactory work while overproduction may be equated to extensive service hours without extra charge.

Some types of waste can also be found in other business functions. You can relate them even in the administrative work that doesn't have direct involvement with products and customers. Delays and inefficient employees (motion waste) are the two common types of waste in non-production steps in your business process. Below are some examples:

- Keeping several boxes of printing paper for administrative work is an example of inventory waste.
- Erroneous data in reports is a form of defect.
- Buying, using and maintaining the most expensive computers when there are affordable and equally efficient options form part of over processing waste.
- Printing more flyers than necessary is an example of overproduction.

Safer Work Environment

With effective communication, your employees can inform you about health risks in the workplace. You can address them right away to avoid accidents. While it's true that your insurance may cover hospitalization costs of an injured employee, nothing can protect your startup from the backlash from the other employees. If news of the accident becomes public, you'll earn bad reputation as well. The results are worse when there's death involved.

Instead of the repercussions of workplace accidents though, you should ensure safer workplace because it's only ethical. Your workforce is a valuable resource. As a resource, you should give them an environment that helps them maximize their performance and protects them. Value them and make them feel valued.

Better Customer Experience

As an entrepreneur, you shouldn't think you're only offering products or services. You should keep in mind that you're providing customer experience.

Many products these days are more of luxuries, not necessities. Smart TV is one of the notable examples. It's mainly for entertainment. You can use it for video conferences, too. However, a smartphone or high-tech laptop can be enough for such task.

Yet, people still buy smart TVs because it allows them to watch live broadcasts of games. The bigger screen and better video quality make them feel like they're part of the audience.

Some smart TV ads show a family watching together or one adult relaxing on the couch. They're basically selling the experience you can have when you use the product.

Luxury bags are worth noting as well. Some ladies just want them because the brands make them feel like they're members of the elite. The bags can also give them the notion of elegance.

How about your offer? What kind of experience do you wish your customer will have when using your product or getting your service?

Lean kaizen helps you improve the customer experience you can provide. The continuously improving product is the biggest reason. Having confident and efficient employees, especially those who directly deal with customers, is another factor.

Chapter 50.
Some Methodologies Applicable To Kaizen

The Five S's of Kaizen

5S is the foundation of Japanese Kaizen philosophy. Though entrepreneurs and business leaders from the West have lent it their own twist, at its heart, the Japanese model of Kaizen philosophy is primarily driven by the 5S.

The Kaizen 5S model emphasizes on having visual order, neatness, organization, and standardization. Some results one can expect from the 5S model include greater overall efficiency, enhanced profitability, better safety norms, and more professional service standards. These are all things a startup strives to accomplish in the long run.

As a startup, your enterprise can experience several benefits of implementing the 5S program. On the face, it appears as though only manufacturing businesses can benefit from Kaizen. However, this is only a misconception. It can be applied to just about any sector—from professional services to healthcare. Every area or department within a startup or organization can benefit from the 5S model.

Here are the Kaizen 5s:

1. Sort

This is known as *seiri* in Japanese and sorting involves eliminating all unnecessary and defunct items from your workplace. These items are believed to hinder productivity, space, time and energy. Therefore, anything that doesn't serve a purpose in the functioning of your startup is best eliminated to make way for newer, fresher and more productive items that serve a clear purpose. Decluttering is a big component of Kaizen. If you keep items you don't need, you'll spend plenty of time and energy looking for items that are required, thus losing precious resources in the bargain.

Seiri involves sorting out. As per *seiri*, employees should always sort and organize things. Label, classify or categorize items as, "necessary" "critical" "most important" "urgent" "not urgent" "most important" "not needed now" "useless" and more. The categories can be classified as, "urgent but not important," "urgent and important," "neither urgent nor important," and "important but not urgent." This way you know what tasks or files a high priority is and what can be tackled later. Throw away everything that is useless or doesn't fit into your scheme of things. You may be carrying things from an old business to the startup. It may no longer serve a purpose to what you are currently doing. Ditch things that are no longer, valid, applicable or relevant to the current startup

2. Set in Order

This is also known as *seiton*. It speaks about creating a particular order and location for every item. Everything should be in its place if you want to be able to save time, money and energy in looking for it. Kaizen is about orderliness. Having a set order and system in place for things allows the Japanese to be more efficient. It leaves more time and energy to focus on procedural systems. *Seiton* is about organizing. According to research, employees waste more than half of their precious time looking for important documents. When every item is kept has its own place right from the onset, it is easier to find it when it is urgently needed.

Why is *seiton* important? It ensures systematic arrangement for effective, productive and efficient retrieval. You must be able to find where everything is kept, which means everything should be in its place for facilitating east retrieval. The place for every item should be clearly marked and labeled. There has to be a demarcation of space of each item right when the business is launching. When *seiton* becomes a habit, it ensures a smooth and unhindered workflow. Ensure that equipment which is frequently used is easily accessible.

Similarly, employees shouldn't have to struggle too hard to access the material. This saves their time and effort, which can be productively channelized towards other systems and processes.

3. Shine

Shine or *seiso* is about cleanliness. Keeping your work area clean reflects a healthy, positive and productive state of mind that leads you to be even more efficient and productive. Will an ill-kept and dirty space inspire you to do good work or be productive? Little chances! *Seiso* involves organizing the workplace. A shining and clean workplace breeds good vibes that encourage positivity and productivity.

As a startup, you need to ensure that rules for cleanliness, neatness, and hygiene are set at the onset. Keep all documents in efficiently labeled files and dedicated folders. All bills should go in one file, while all invoices should go into another. Keep all checks in one file, while receipts can go into another. Simply following these small practices can help you streamline the process to make it more efficient. Try to come up with new ways to keep your space clean, shinning and organized. Use space optimally for storage. Ensure that there are enough efficiently designed and optimized storage options such as cabinets and drawers for storing your stuff.

Shining or *seiso* is an important aspect of Kaizen. Cleaning the workplace along with maintaining all the equipment regularly should be a part of your cleanliness and maintenance policy. Keep your space clean, organized and tidy. After each cleaning session, follow up on it to ensure the cleanliness is maintained. According to the Japanese philosophy, a shining workplace leads to higher efficiency and gains.

4. Standardization

Standardization or *seiketsu* is adopting best practices within the workplace by fixing a standard norm for systems and procedures. Each organization should have a set of standard rules and policies to drive its systems to ensure quality and optimize productivity. Work practices within the startup should be consistent, uniform and standardized to ensure greater discipline and efficiency. All workstations should be uniform. Employees should be able to walk into their workstation every morning and view the same equipment or tools, which are kept in the same location or spot every day. Everyone should be aware of their responsibilities and commit to following the standardized code of conduct set for all employees.

5. Sustain

Sustain or *shitsuke* is continuously improving and never slipping back into old ways. It is related to self-discipline. All employees need to respect an organization's rules, policies, and regulations. For instance, not walking into the office wearing casuals (if there is a dress code) on a weekday or entering office without an identity card.

Most startups make the mistake of taking things lightly in the beginning, focusing on luring employees with the fun, light work atmosphere, and play syndrome. However, self-discipline is important for the long-term sustenance of a business. You may find a relaxed policy effective in the beginning. Once the business decides to scale up though or grow by leaps and bounds, it will be tough to keep up with a set of employees who aren't disciplined. They can end up lowering the organization's overall productivity, efficiency, morale, and atmosphere.

Once all the earlier 4S's have been set, you have to ensure that your organization doesn't slip back to its old ways by following *shitsuke* to the fullest. When you follow the earlier attributes, it becomes a way of life. Keep your vision focused on this new way of doing business, while not allowing yourself or your startup employees to slip back to their old ways. Remember, continuous and not momentary improvement is the key. Adopting continuous improvement leads to lesser wastage of time, higher productivity, better quality and rapid lead times.

There are several benefits of incorporating a culture of 5S's within the organization including higher productivity, reduced clinical defects, quicker, and more efficient products/service and a safer work environment.

While the first 3 S's are relatively simple, several startups face problems in the 4 and 5 S. However, it isn't something that is tough to accomplish. It can be achieved with consistent training, practice, and implementation.

The Six Sigma Methodology and its Steps

Some business owners or executives can feel like they need to break down all the processes of their company in order to make way for a new process with fewer defects in it. This is rarely, if ever, the case. Many processes can be augmented with the implementation of the DMAIC method to help bring all the processes into current and workable methods.

At this point, you are familiar with DMAIC (Define, Measure, Analyze, Improve, and Control). This is an integral part of utilizing Six Sigma in your business once it's already running. It allows you to make the changes you need to make without putting a stop to the production that's currently at work in your business. This methodology, when applied to your business, must be addressed and applied in its individual parts as though they were steps.

- *Define* - This step is crucial, as this is the starting point from which you can outline the goals you wish to achieve as a team and as a business. This is where you write down the needs you have for improvement, this is where you document the things that you think your team should be able to attain and deliver. If you are unable to identify the goals for your team, then your team has no clear direction, which can cause massive failure down the line.
- *Measure* - Make an accurate assessment of how your company is currently doing and make a note of how well you would like them to be doing!
- *Analyze* - This step demands that you make an assessment of the current processes so you can see what the correlation and relationship is between

parameters and performance. This makes certain that you are monitoring the right things and getting a clear picture of your success as a business.

- *Improve* – Based on your findings and your actions up to this point in the process, you will feel that the most organic and logical following step in the process is to make the improvements that you've identified as necessary and possible. These improvements should all optimize operations, reduce or eliminate loss, and maximize efficiency.
- *Control* – This is the stage that allows you to sort pull back from things and simply monitor the processes operating on the parameters that you've set for them. At this stage, minor tweaks and occasional stabilization should be all you need to keep things going at a good clip. In some cases, you will find that you need to reevaluate the goals and processes so the business can continue its upward progress. In all other cases, the business should seem largely autonomous in bringing about positive results and products for your business.

You might find that this incredibly simple process is far more effective than you initially thought. This is not a miracle process, but you would be amazed at what an honest look at your business's operations and loss will do for increasing and improving production!

Chapter 51.
Tools Choice: Tools Applicable To Kaizen

The purpose of a Kaizen project is to ensure best practices are incorporated into day-to-day processes, thereby making them more efficient.

It is important to note that although Kaizen Events are usually 3 to7 days long, a lot of time must be invested to plan all back-end activities prior to running actual events.

Kaizen project managers must consider this time while planning Gantts and budgets for their Kaizen campaigns.

SIPOC Diagram

SIPOC is an abbreviation for Suppliers- Inputs- Process- Outputs- Customers. A SIPOC diagram identifies the suppliers, inputs, process steps, outputs and customers associated with a process.

SIPOC diagram:

Suppliers This column mentions-Who provides the inputs?	**Inputs** This column list of inputs provided by suppliers	**Process** This column describes- What are the various steps of a process?	**Outputs** This column mentions the various outputs from the process	**Customers** This column lists- Who receives the outputs?

'Suppliers' are anyone or any source which provides 'Inputs' for the work to happen. Suppliers may be external or internal to the organization. Like Suppliers, 'Customers' may be internal or external to the organization.

The SIPOC diagram is usually created during the 'Plan' stage of the Kaizen project and represents a general view of a process. SIPOC assures that all criteria and functions regardless of being major or minor, are identified and considered at the start of the project; hence SIPOC diagram assumes great significance within the PDCA cycle.

The benefits of SIPOC diagram are numerous. SIPOC diagrams help Kaizen teams, Process owners and their Sponsor, agree on project boundaries and scope.

SIPOC diagrams also help Kaizen project managers create realistic project plans and construct accurate budget proposals. For best results from Kaizen campaigns, SIPOC diagram must be customized for every process prevalent in the company. Outlining SIPOC diagram at the outset of the project have known to reduce Kaizen campaign costs by as much as 10%.

Brainstorming

Brainstorming is an interactive team technique of collecting suggestions, opinions, recommendations to solve a problem or find solutions to sort out an issue or problem. Groups of 10-12 people are optimal for effective brainstorming sessions.

Ideas must be written down than said aloud. They should be written clearly, so the meaning is clear to everyone in the group. In addition, the idea(s) should be put up in a place where everyone can see them.

Brainstorming sessions begin by forming sub-groups who list out different ideas around solving a problem. All ideas are recorded as received or as they come in without making judgments about their practicability or viability. Ideas may be collected from individuals or sub-groups; however, it is of paramount importance to differ judgments until all possible ideas are collected and recorded.

Another point to note is that the brainstorming group must comprise a mix of process experts and novice to bring fresh air into the discussion i.e. to think outside the box yet offer usable solutions.

Several factors can contribute towards success or failure of a Brainstorming session, such as, blocking, collaborative fixation, apprehensions, free riding, personality traits, social matching etc.

Tip: Encourage anyone who has a contribution to make speaks whenever he or she wants.

Tip: Ideas must not receive any criticism, judgment or discussion at the time of collation.

Visual Management

It is said "A picture is worth a thousand words". An example of explicit Visual Management (also called Visual Control) is flow of people at an airport. Isn't this view familiar?

Almost everyone at an airport follows instructions provided by signage to reach their destination- boarding gate, food court, restrooms, baggage, customs, immigration, transit etc.

Airport Operations & People Flow by Visual Management

Similarly, a gadget placed near boarding pass kiosk/ counter shows maximum size of overhead baggage permitted, hence prevents over-size cabin bags from getting on the aircraft.

Visual Management begins by making the work visible. Visibility provides transparency of work as well as ease of understanding tasks to be done.

Let us take another example- Hearing siren or watching a flashing red light of an ambulance or a police car quickly informs everyone around to stay clear and give them priority on the road.

Same is with traffic or stop lights. Red for 'stop', orange for 'caution' and green for 'go' is a universal sign language.

Using the traffic light color code in Kaizen Gantt Chart or a RACI Matrix simplifies the project management process itself, because of instant understanding of the project status. This is more helpful in multi-locational and multi-cultural organizations.

Another application of Visual Management to Kaizen are 'Kaizen Activity Boards' that depict task status as- Doing, Done, To Do, New Ideas, On Hold etc.

Traditionally, Kaizen Activity Boards used hand-written sticky notes. However, they can be digital too.

5Ws 1H

5W + 1H Kaizen Tool

What?	Who?	When?
What to do? What must be done? What is being done? What else can be done? What else must be done? What else should have been done? What must not be done?	Who does it? Who must do it? Who else can do it? Who is doing it?	When to do it? When is, it done? When should it be done? When else can it be done? When should it not be done?
Where?	**Why?**	**How?**
Where to do it? Where is, it being done? Where should it be done? Where else can it be done? Where else should it be done?	Why do it? Why do they do it? Why do it at all? Why do it this way? Why not do it this way? Why are they doing it? Why shouldn't it be done?	How to do it? How has it been done? How is it being done? How can/should it be done? How can this be used else where? How can it be done differently?

The 5Ws 1H technique helps in information gathering. According to the principle of 5Ws 1H, an investigation is thorough if it answers the following questions-

1. *Who* did that?
2. *What* happened?
3. *When* did it happen?
4. *Where* did it happen?
5. *Why* did it happen?
6. *How* did it happen?

These questions are not crisp 'yes' or 'no' types. Rather each question must receive a detailed factual answer possibly with figures and graphics, which would help with the investigation to solve the problem or at least help find potential solution (to the problem).

Gemba Walks

Gemba in Japanese means workplace, precisely Gemba means work site- the place where actual work happens. For example, 'production or assembly lines' in a manufacturing company or a 'store front' in a service-based company.

Every activity that happens in a manufacturing or service company has its respective Gemba. For instance, a loading process within a manufacturing company has- warehouse, loading bay, sampling booths, quarantine area as Gemba.

Gemba Walk technique involves department heads, supervisor, C-suite executive going to the site where work gets done to observe and identify opportunities for improvement. Informal talks with employees during Gemba Walk also improves employee motivation and work output. Employees feel 'appreciated and engaged' in achieving organizational excellence goals.

The concept underlying Gemba Walk is that employees closest to the task have the best grip on the process- its benefits, challenges, limitations, ideas for improvement. Such frontline employees usually have practical, easy and cost-effective solutions for improvements that add up to a significant benefit over time.

Another advantage of Gemba Walk is the top management executive or supervisor shows his/her dedication to the spirit of implementing a culture of Kaizen or consistent improvement at workplace. This boosts success of Kaizen campaigns.

The executive facetime with employees during Gemba Walks sends a message that top management 'care' to know employee ideas, suggestions and feedback.

FMEA

FMEA stands for Failure Mode Effects Analysis. FMEA is an approach used to identify possible failures of a design, process, product or service based on experience with similar products and processes. It is widely used in development research and manufacturing industries during various phases of the product lifecycle. Effects analysis refers to studying the consequences of the failures on different system levels.

Failure modes are the ways by which the element might fail. Failures are defined as defects or errors particularly those that affect the end-users (customers). Failures can be actual or potential.

Effects analysis is the way to study the consequences of each failure mode. It gives an indication of the 'risks' involved if appropriate steps are not taken to mitigate, prevent or control failures.

Failures must be prioritized based on the seriousness of the consequences, frequency of occurrence and the easiness of detection. Thereby, FMEA purports the reduction or elimination of failures especially the highest priority failures.

FMEA documents the present information and actions regarding the risks and probability of failures. Ideally, FMEA is utilized at the design phase to prevent the occurrence of failures at the latter stages of production. Later, FMEA is utilized for control before the manufacturing process starts and during the process.

Auditing

Auditing refers to a systematic and independent examination of books, accounts, documents, records, vouchers, facility, product, data, within an organization to assess how far the information records are accurate, conform to standards and/ or comply with regulations.

Several types of audits happen within manufacturing and service organizations- quality audit, vendor audit, regulator audit, client audit, financial audit, operations audit, energy audit etc. Additionally, audits may be external and internal audits, which is self-assessment, usually done prior to an external audit or before initiating a Kaizen program.

Pareto Chart

You made a bucket list of problems and underlying processes to be sorted out ... now where do you start? Which of the different causes do you tackle first?

A simple tool for assessing the relative importance of several different causes is the Pareto Chart.

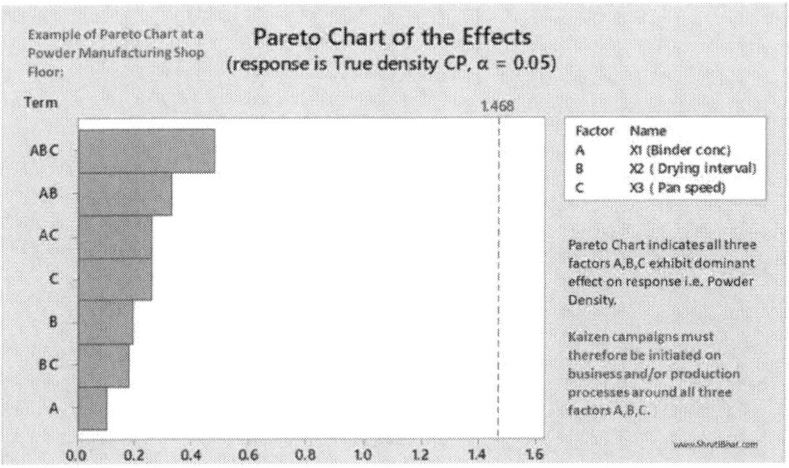

This chart is designed to present the causes in order from most important to least important. Pareto contended that 80% of problems were the result of 20% of causes. Pareto

Chart shows that a problem usually stems from a few major causes.

Pareto Charts are used to assess the relative importance of different causes of the problems. Also, to rank causes from most occurrences to least occurrences.

Control Chart

Control Charts are made up of a horizontal line that represents the norm of the process. There is also a line above and below, to represent upper and lower control boundaries. Various samples are gathered over a time period and added to the chart. There is a quality problem, or one that should be investigated, when there are measurements that extend above or below the norm line.

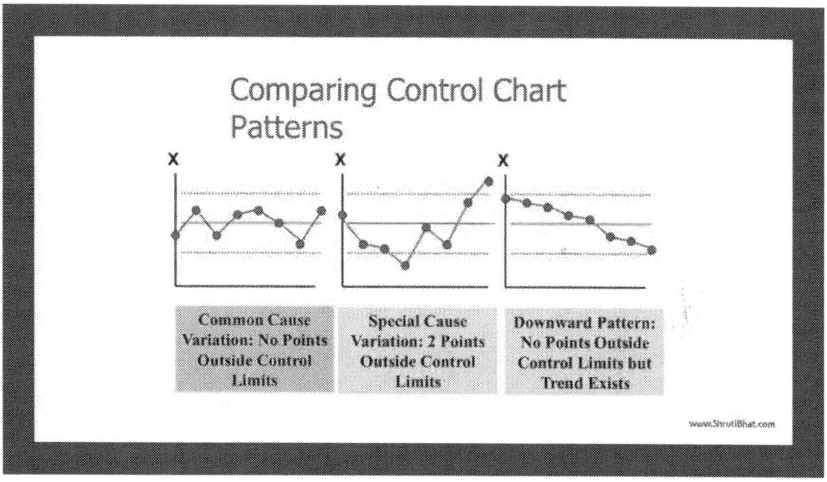

Different types of Control Charts such as Xbar Chart, Xbar- R Chart, Xbar- S chart, P-Chart etc. are How do we choose & use the correct tool?

Conclusions of Kaizen

Inefficiency affects organizations of every type and size. Even in the most positive economic climate, companies benefit from decreasing defects and avoiding wastes. When times are tougher, enhancing efficiency can often mean the difference between keeping the business's doors open and a fold up.

Initiating Kaizen-based continual business process improvement campaigns keep companies on a growth curve.

Kaizen or 'Make Better' requires a mindset shift from an 'okay process' to 'continually better process'. The improvement is done not as a chunk, but as incremental changes accumulated overtime. The changes are rapidly implemented hence Kaizen is also called 'instant revolution'.

Kaizen may be applied to manufacturing as well as service-based organizations. Implementing Kaizen awards competitive edge & consistent growth to a business. Personal Kaizen further improves employee's quality of life both at personal and professional fronts.

Printed by Amazon Italia Logistica S.r.l.
Torrazza Piemonte (TO), Italy

16585625R00394